The Disputatious Caribbean

The Disputatious Caribbean

The West Indies in the Seventeenth Century

Sarah Barber

THE DISPUTATIOUS CARIBBEAN
Copyright © Sarah Barber, 2014.

Softcover reprint of the hardcover 1st edition 2014 978-1-137-47999-0

All rights reserved.

First published in 2014 by
PALGRAVE MACMILLAN®
in the United States—a division of St. Martin's Press LLC,
175 Fifth Avenue, New York, NY 10010.

Where this book is distributed in the UK, Europe and the rest of the world, this is by Palgrave Macmillan, a division of Macmillan Publishers Limited, registered in England, company number 785998, of Houndmills, Basingstoke, Hampshire RG21 6XS.

Palgrave Macmillan is the global academic imprint of the above companies and has companies and representatives throughout the world.

Palgrave® and Macmillan® are registered trademarks in the United States, the United Kingdom, Europe and other countries.

ISBN 978-1-349-50259-2   ISBN 978-1-137-48001-9 (eBook)
DOI 10.1057/9781137480019

Library of Congress Cataloging-in-Publication Data is available from the Library of Congress.

A catalogue record of the book is available from the British Library.

Design by Newgen Knowledge Works (P) Ltd., Chennai, India.

First edition: November 2014

10 9 8 7 6 5 4 3 2 1

Transferred to Digital Printing in 2015

Now that the times abound with HISTORY, the AIM is better when the mark is alive.

> Francis Bacon, *The Advancement of Learning*

Contents

List of Figures and Table — ix
Preface — xi
List of Abbreviations — xiii

Introduction: Disputation — 1
1 Place — 9
2 Resource — 45
3 Connection — 83
4 Body — 119
5 Will — 155
Conclusion: Design — 193

Notes — 197
Bibliographical Essay — 253
Index — 259

Figures and Table

Figures

0.1   T. Bowen, *West Indies from the best Authorities*, from Richard Blome, *A Description of the Island of Jamaica* (London, 1672)   2

0.2   Her[man] Moll, *A Map of the West-Indies or the Islands of America* (London, 1709)   4

1.1   H[erman] Moll, *A New Map of the North Parts of America Claimed by France* (London, 1720)   43

Table

2.1   Ships and their West Indian cargoes   80

Preface

To all those people who need to be dissuaded that research is not just a hobby and that research into Caribbean history must mean endless jollies to the beach and the rum shop, I cannot deny how much I have enjoyed researching and writing this book. But only one person got to experience some of what it might have been like to be a research assistant, and the frustrations, dangers, and adventures it entailed along with the joys; and so to Lee Partis, gratitude and respect for being there.

A large number of people were generous and helpful in facilitating access to source material. I'd like to thank Lancaster University and the British Academy for financial assistance. My grateful thanks to the staff of J. P. Knight, and particularly to Captain Perry, his crew, and his Suriname "ferry", and to all those in Britain, Ireland, America, and the Caribbean who have shown hospitality and welcome along the way. There are far too many institutions, heritage sites, and repositories to list them all, but I would particularly like to mention the archivists and keepers at South Carolina Department of Archives and History, Hamilton College, John Carter Brown Library, the National Museum of Bermuda, the Barbados Department of Archives, and the National Archives of Jamaica. I extend due acknowledgment to those individuals who were generous in allowing me access to materials held in private hands.

Among those whose contributions have been invaluable in helping me make sense of all that research material, I particularly note Susan Amussen, Sir Hilary Beckles, Trevor Burnard, Stephen Constantine, Harold Cook, Thomas Glave, Evan Haefeli, Allan Macinnes, Emily Mann, Ben Marsh, Philip Morgan, Diana Paton, Corinna Peniston-Bird (a special mention in dispatches for all that reading and discussion), Louis Roper, and Angus Winchester. Many students have given thought-provoking, interesting comments, and I would like to single out the late Martin Sutherland, and the students of my Special Subject.

Throughout I was made acutely aware that not only did disputatiousness reign in the seventeenth century, but it retains its power over histories and heritage and it also will no doubt continue to follow me. This book may be disputatious, but the portrayal and the consequences of contention fall on my head alone.

Sarah Barber
Lancaster 2014

Abbreviations

BDA	Barbados Department of Archives, St Michael, Barbados
BL	British Library, Euston Road, London
BLARS	Bedfordshire and Luton Archives and Records Service
BM	British Museum, Russell Street, London
Bodl.Oxf.	Bodleian Library, University of Oxford
BristolRO	Bristol Record Office
CCALSS	Cheshire and Chester Archives and Local Studies Service
CJ	*Journal of the House of Commons*
CKS	Centre for Kentish Studies
CUL	Cambridge University Library
CumbriaRO, Carlisle	Cumbria Record Office, Carlisle branch
DerbysRO	Derbyshire Record Office, Matlock
DevonRO	Devon Record Office
DHC	Dorset History Centre, Dorchester
DRO, Jm	Registry Office, Twickenham Park, Spanish Town, Jamaica
GA	Gloucestershire Archives, formerly Gloucestershire Record Office
HALS	Hertfordshire Archives and Local Studies, Hertford
HC, BLAC	Hamilton College, Beinecke Lesser Antilles Collection, Hamilton College, Clinton, New York
JBMHS	*Journal of the Barbados Museum and Historical Society*
JCB	John Carter Brown Library, Brown University, Providence, Rhode Island
JHI	*Journal of the History of Ideas*
LancsRO	Lancashire Record Office, Preston
LJ	*Journal of the House of Lords*
LMA	London Metropolitan Archives
LPL (FP)	Lambeth Palace Library, London (Fulham Papers)
NA	Nottinghamshire Archives

NAAB	National Archives of Antigua and Barbuda, St. John's, Antigua
NAJm	National Archives of Jamaica, Spanish Town
NAS	National Archives of Scotland, Edinburgh
NorthumbriaRO	Northumbria Record Office, Gosport, Newcastle-upon-Tyne
ROLLR	Record Office for Leicestershire, Leicester and Rutland
SCDAH	South Carolina Department of Archives and History, Columbia, SC.
SCLA	Shakespeare Centre Library and Archive, Stratford upon Avon
SHC	Somerset Heritage Centre, formerly Somerset Record Office, Taunton
SurreyHC	Surrey History Centre, Guildford
TCD	Trinity College Dublin
TNA	The National Archives, Kew (formerly the Public Records' Office)
TRHS	*Royal Historical Society Transactions*
UCL	University College, London
ULBC, ML	University of Leeds, Brotherton Collection, Marten Loder Manuscripts
UMJRL	University of Manchester, John Rylands Library
UN	University of Nottingham, Manuscripts and Special Collections
WMQ	*The William and Mary Quarterly*
WSHC	Wiltshire and Swindon History Centre, Chippenham
WSRO	West Sussex Record Office, Chichester
WYAS	West Yorkshire Archives Service, Bradford

Introduction: Disputation

"Disputation," an Anglophone construction from Latin, to mean controversy, active doubt, and confusion, is culturally and temporally particular. Britons debated relations between man and God, man and man, and formed and reformed links and hostilities across domestic boundaries. Then they sent their restlessness overseas. The long seventeenth century, presaged by the nationalistic adventurism of the late Elizabethan era, gave way in 1603 to the Union of the Crowns and the British imperial vision of James VI of Scotland and I of England and Ireland. From the safety of our twenty-first century remove, we are led to believe that when the last (Protestant) Stuart died in 1714, disputatiousness was being tamed by a profitable empire and a "balanced eighteenth-century constitution."[1] Our long seventeenth century ends around 1720, to denote a time at which metropolitan institutions were reining in colonial disputation.

In 1585 Sir Francis Drake undertook a West Indian voyage. He attacked Spanish settlements on first the south and then the north American continent, and collected, on his return, the distressed settlers at Raleigh's outpost at Roanoke, Virginia.[2] Thomas Chaloner lauded Raleigh and Drake during the British civil wars because "the fiery trialls which you are now in [shall] fit your hearts for high and Nobler ends," in a poem, "The Fruits of Self-experience" in *New Survey of the West-India's* by "The English-American," Thomas Gage.[3] Gage would reveal "who they be abide, Or what Religion, Language, or what Nation/ Possess each Coast." Now, civil dispute—"(Oh grief!)"—resolved, these Crusaders would make "tawnie *Indians* quake for fear, / Their direfull march to beat when they doe hear; / Your brave red-Crosses.../ The noble Badges of your famous Nation/...You shall again advance with reputation, / And on the bounds of utmost Western shore / Shall them transplant, and firmly fix their station."[4] Richard Blome dedicated his account of where in the Americas the "*English* [we]re Related" to Sir Thomas Lynch, Governor of Jamaica, and bounded an area north to south from Roanoke to the Guianas and east to west from the Miskito coast out into the Atlantic.[5] After a century of fixing, Herman Moll dedicated to William Paterson, failed Scottish projector of Darién, a rationalization of English American proprietorship, including "the Property of Carolina...but they did not take Possession of that Country till King Charles the II's time in 1663." This was the so-called Royal Colonial Boundary, the "Limit line" that ran from thirty-six degrees north "West in a direct-line to y^e South Sea"[6] (see figures 0.1 and 0.2).

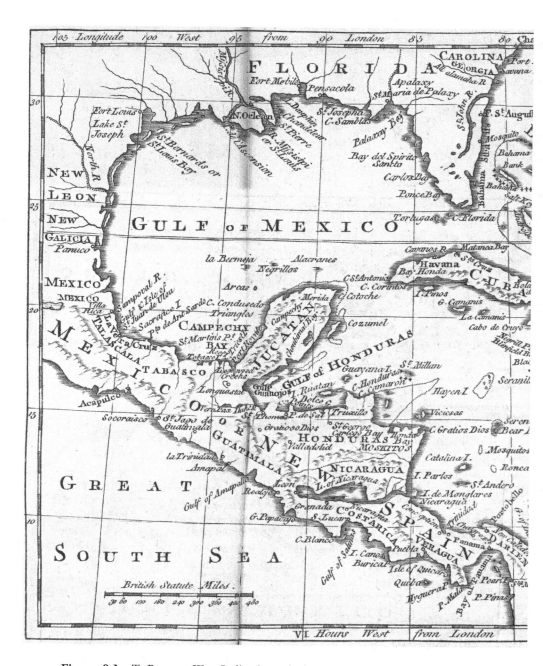

Figure 0.1 T. Bowen, *West Indies from the best Authorities*, from Richard Blome, *A Description of the Island of Jamaica* (London, 1672): an insert within a map of Jamaica commissioned by Sir Thomas Modyford. The former English islands off the coast of Nicaragua, St. Andrew and Providence, are marked St. Andero and Catolina I.

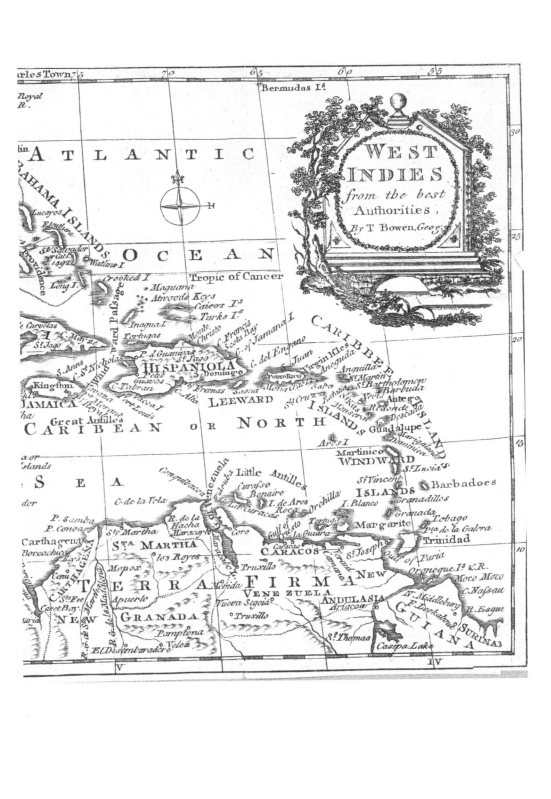

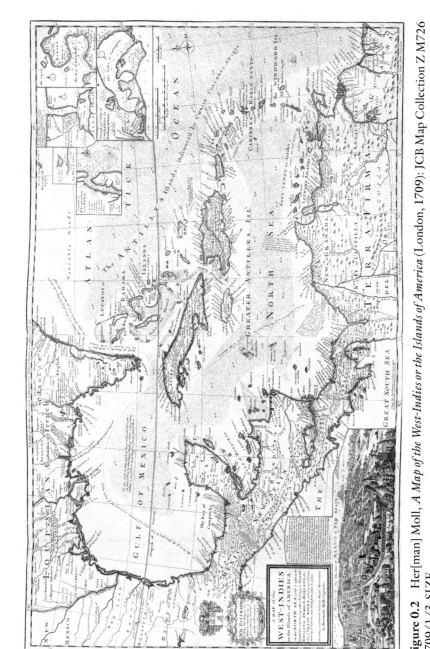

Figure 0.2 Her[man] Moll, *A Map of the West-Indies or the Islands of America* (London, 1709): JCB Map Collection Z M726 1709/1/3-SIZE.

The West Indies delineates a region, stretching from the eastern seaboard of central America on one side, to Bermuda on the other, in which the peoples of the Northeast Atlantic went island-hopping, adventuring, pioneering new frontiers, swashbuckling, and making trouble. It is more specifically defined by latitude: between thirty-six degrees north and the equator. It was the "toasted" earth of the "torrid zone," a term that has the advantage of operating in several European languages, but most of the places visited by Britons had been named by the Spanish.[7] Presettled peoples, in keeping with an area explored as a means to find a westward passage to Asia, were collectively called "Indians." In Arawakan Taíno, *Xaymaca*, "Land of wood and water," became Jamaica, but Kalinago groups had largely pushed out Arawak peoples from the Guianas.[8] The English took the word for "person," *karibna*, from the "antient Inhabitants, which came from Guiana...strong, and violent men, they being the most Warlike nation of the West Indies, but cruell and man=eaters," and claimed "The Caribee Ilands," eventually, but not definitively, defined by Charles I's letters patent to the Scot, James Hay, first Earl of Carlisle, the "Lord Proprietor of the Caribbees or Carliola."[9]

The "fruits of self-experience" are the accounts of diverse British and Irish people who wrote about themselves, American indigenes, and the Africans they transported. Of a region encompassing three million square miles, that on which Britons tried to settle but seldom made good (in this period at least) totaled about 5,000 square miles, that is, less than Connecticut or Yorkshire. One hundred and thirty years of vastly dispersed ventures of multiple ethnicities were described in vibrant and immediate Anglo-Saxon. The historian's sources are therefore constructed by those with access to writing, with past subaltern lives (only partially) reconstructed from material culture. Our disputatious individuals, in challenging environments, were contrary, often self-contradictory, their expression archaic, and what they had to say often coarse and difficult to hear. Their voices are unexpurgated, except when it becomes necessary to step in to render comprehensible passages with little or no punctuation or that retain obscure medieval sigla. Therefore, among the latter, the runic thorn (þ), which resulted in "the" or "that" being rendered "y^e" and "y^t"—but distinguishable from "y^r" for "your"—is retained, as are the superscripts that indicated letters omitted. It seems reasonably clear that "w^{c}h" and "w^{t}h" are "which" and "with," and that a superscript *r* denotes a vowel omitted, as in the standard legal documents that transferred "these p^{r}sents" to "heirs Execut^{rs} Administrat^{rs} and Assigns." However, marks and symbols that indicate contractions are increasingly hard to render and therefore the tilde (~) has been substituted by the omitted letter(s), as has the macron $\bar{p}$ that rendered "persecute" and "person," "psecute" and "pson"; "partake" and "parish," "ptake" and "pish."

From within a disputatious confusion of peoples, constantly redefining themselves, moving around, between and among disparate and diverse places, changing allegiances and describing all in their idiom, an author has to create structural sense for a modern audience. Further, this history carves out the far less well-known seventeenth century as a period worthy of study on its own terms, while also participating in a grander history of American colonialism and British empire. Existing orthodoxies break down, and new patterns emerge. Ironically, the best way to illustrate the author's difficulties is to think of compiling the index. White British people can, usually, be indexed by name, making the index a disproportionate list of the names of the elite. So if a reader is already familiar with, for example, the pirate-governor Sir Henry Morgan, he can be found in the index. But one would not necessarily know to search for a humble individual, and how important does a piece of information have to be or how many times must an individual be mentioned before he or she merits inclusion? Where contemporaries would refer to "Indians," the index can substitute "indigenes" and refer to Kalinago, Cherokee, or Kuna. Slaves direct from Africa can be listed as Coromanti, Kongo, and so on; less comfortably as Creole for those born in the West Indies, but on being renamed in America, they cannot take an individual place in the index, despite the importance of characters such as "George," a rebel leader in Antigua. If christened, black people (sometimes) acquired a recordable name, but Peter Perkins of Barbados makes it into the index for the importance of his experience, while Margaret Cary's baptism does not.

Imagine the disputatious Caribbean (re)rendered here as circles of narrative, which can be discreet, concentric, hierarchical, overlapping, or interlocking, so that despite the white, European, male, literate, elite preponderance of sources, autonomy and weight can, as far as possible, be given to each individual, irrespective of gender, color, or status. Narratives may operate in the public, political sphere; could be more personal; or, more private still, could be intimate.[10] Now the narrative of Governor Morgan is no more or less important to the political narrative of the West Indies than that of George the slave: they are both "grandy-men."[11] We are able to reconstruct narratives in which the garden is an important—and indexable—signifier of everyday identity whether it be the master's retreat, the employment of slaves such as "Golden-Gloves," or the provision-ground of maize and cassava cultivated in an "Indian-garden."

The chapters are titled in such a way as to describe their overarching theme, while minimizing (as far as possible) Eurocentricism. "Place," chapter one, allows the region as a whole to be defined and described, and political boundaries, markers, and allegiances to be discussed alongside domestic spatial identities and intimate perceptions of home. Here is fixity—territories, manors, settlements, buildings, roads, paths, and frontiers—and movement—water, migration, merchants, pirates, and runaways. But these topics are difficult to put into an index. "Barbados," or other specific territory, is referenced throughout, and not only as a place in chapter one. Similarly, if asked where one would look to find out about sugar, the simple answer is chapter two, which charts its rise from indigenous grass cultivated in Guiana to refined grocery in British larders. But the chapter is titled "Resource" and not "Resources" so as not to privilege the metropolitan narrative of trade, empire, and the monocultural dependency of The Plantations, but to explore a regional perspective of natural, intrinsic resource that touched all of its people. In one narrative circle, sugar is more important than tobacco, and far superior to potatoes: in the narrative of feeding oneself, priorities are different. Chapter three examines interpersonal relationship, but marriage and family tend to be defined by formalized religion and Eurocentric norms, friendship is only referenced among white society, and love is both elevated and debased depending to whom it refers. White, male political affinity, inheritance, network, patronage, faction, and party clouded the nature of "Connection," and men's relationships were reduced to "having connections." Here, due weight is given to those humble individuals who could maintain connection without instrumentalism. Chapter four inquires into many aspects of the Body, from the loftiest body-politic, to the most intimate corpus: did contemporaries regard the differences between African, American, and European bodies to be more than skin-deep, while each decision to brand black skin powerfully exposed the degradation of humanity, a world away from putting fire to hide or timber?[12] The theme of chapter five is agency, a term that has come into vogue with the rise of the social sciences: in the seventeenth century, it was more likely to be expressed as willfulness.[13] It is a descriptive, neutral term with which to discuss human deliberation: whether and how they could achieve means and ends. In its widest sense, this is the relationship between power and authority and expressions of "positive" and "negative" liberty.[14] This chapter, therefore, contains the heart of the debate over servitude and slavery, in that those subjugated were denied both means or ends. The chapter, however, examines smaller gestures and how we might read these as effective assertions of will.

The five chapters are in essence, geography, economics, society, cultural history, and intellectual history, with heads—Place, Resource, Connection, Body, Will—that aim to move beyond Euro-hegemonic structural concepts, to bring multidisciplinary fluidity to a vast but ill-delineated subject over a *longue durée*. Both the Caribbean region and its conceptualization are more defined by the watery spaces between, than the rigid categorizations imposed on land.[15] Specific aspects of the seventeenth-century Caribbean can be isolated, but the text benefits from being taken in its entirety. It builds into a whole, revisiting in other contexts, people, relations and ideas that have been referenced before. Sugar and its derivatives make it into the index: "slavery," "plantation," and "women" do not, though they are vital to the whole. The seventeenth-century Caribbean was unedifying and confusing, but 400 years later its legacy is still visible and often raw. Despite its chaotic, disputatious past, we must conclude that behind every human action no matter how grand or humble, lay conscious design, and in articulating multiple designs, the importance of the seventeenth-century Caribbean is reinstated.

CHAPTER 1

Place

In the seventeenth century the earth and its climates were conceived of as "limited by two *Parallels*, distant from the Equinoctial toward each Pole," with five zones of "a certain quantity of land"—two temperate, two frigid, "and one *Torrid*." Zones "distinguish[ed] the quality of the Air" in relation to heat and cold and the position of shadows.[1] Thomas Tryon's sojourn in the West Indies confirmed a jaundiced view of human nature because Britons seemed unable to temper their passions to the extremes of a place. There was "no Region so happy, no Elevation of the Pole so temperate, no Air so salubrious, as to keep People in Health whether they will or no, and those that obstinately violate Nature, and wilfully persue courses absolutely destructive, may justly be rank't amongst the number of *Self-Murtherers*."[2] The speed with which British settlers cleared the forest would, in a period of ecological awareness, be considered an obstinate violation of nature: contemporaries were more liable to note how much easier was their breathing. Wherever the land was not steep and mountainous, it was made suitable for cultivation and this entailed stripping it of its woodland. In the mid-seventeenth century, land was described as "fallen and unfallen," but the extent and rate of woodland clearance awaits a systematic study of the wording of hundreds of thousands of deeds, patents, and plat-books.[3] At the end of the century, however, woods were still privately managed, even in areas of relative population density: appraising land close to fortifications required public purchase, and privately owned woodland in St. James's, Barbados, was deemed to hamper the operation of Queen's Fort.[4]

Britons recognized a need to position themselves using "Globes, Maps, Platts; and Sea-drafts of New-discoveries," charts, and instruments, such as those sold by Joseph Moxon, at the Sign of the Atlas in London's Russell Street.[5] Every British man, at least, laid claim to his position, even if that were the freedom to be mobile across both land and sea, such that by the time John Locke codified a philosophy of propriety, a century of individual cases had cumulatively defined Britons' relationship to place.[6] West Indian magistracy relied on those who had a fixed interest in authority's handmaidens, stability and order. Correspondingly, there developed gradually a hierarchy in which a recognized interest in the land topped the hierarchy of place, followed by those who had a license to travel—merchants and mariners.

The Caribbean possessed two peculiarities that hampered Britons' attempt to view the new world as a replica of the old. The first was that it was not just themselves who inhabited or came to inhabit it. Some parts possessed pre-established indigenous communities, and some did not, which was further complicated by the fluidity (or absence) of settlement displayed by Americans already in situ. These were joined by gradually increasing the numbers of Africans transported to America, or being born in America, and with whom there developed a contested notion of place, along with significant numbers of other European migrants in both cooperation and conflict over place and possession. Second, the geographical form of such diverse lands, ecologies, and territories of the region lent itself to fluidity and flux, challenging the European fear of the disorder, instability, or unfixity of constant movement. That fear transferred to those who ran away from their ties—indenture, enslavement, obligation, debt—or, even worse, to those who exploited fluidity in the Caribbean to escape their place, such as pirates and mutineers.

The personnel and institutions of control were determined by the area of land under their purview, the close physical proximity of land within the archipelago, one with another, and the interconnectedness of the whole of the eastern seaboard. This made for uppity neighbors. Any administrator of the Leeward Islands was forced to be a "Continuall Vagabond goeing from one to the Other."[7] Daniel Parke regarded this as injurious, whereas his hated rival, Christopher Codrington, manipulated his authority as both territorial governor and individual planter, by stalling decision making with constant recourse to his private island of Barbuda.[8] Islands and forms of fastness territory enabled individuals to escape the government, like Robert Sanford who was accused of using the pretext of recovering runaway slaves in Surinam to muster the slaves, himself, some soldiers, and some indigenous people to flee to St. Vincent.[9] The relationship of land to water suited those who wished to elude a creditor. William Berkeley complained that Governor William Sayle of Bermuda had seized his person in order to prevent him from sailing in *The William*, but when Sayle was himself dismissed, Berkeley spent more than 13 years chasing around the West Indies, New England, and Virginia in a vain quest to extract compensation.[10] Gilbert Formby and Henry Ashton (both from Liverpool) were employed as ship's security but "run off" at Barbados and headed "(by Stelth)," for Virginia: "Security is not worth anny Thinge."[11] Lawrence Crabb, trying to keep his head above water in Antigua, was unable to turn a profit because—although this was not the sole reason—his creditors sailed away without paying.[12]

But if the territorial authority of a governor was dependent on the security of the people, an island territory required particular defensive requirements. Bermuda was such a "fforelorne Place," with its inhabitants "bred to Sea" that they would not put themselves under any form of authority; neither that used on land, nor on the ships of the Royal Navy.[13] The islands were a pressure-cooker enclosure of domestic populations, required to be kept entire and safe by sea. Island groups, like the Leewards, contained divided peoples and potentially divided allegiances, so with large Irish and Scottish populations and the presence of the French, sometimes on neighboring islands and sometimes cheek-by-jowl, the English feared being overawed, and were apt to "runne away [and] stragled to other places." Worse, English emigrés put their personal safety before that of the island territory and carried their arms away with them.[14] The private and personal endeavors of settlers of islands, such as Barbados, could be rendered useless when supplies were shipped in from elsewhere.[15] Councillor Colonel Richard Bayley of the Barbados militia was instructed in 1667 to ready the ports, particularly Speightstown in the northwest, close to his own interests, for defense of the island at sea. While the threat of enemy incursions was no doubt there, his care was to concentrate on victualing, such that the island was not depleted of resources, nor the ships used to carry away residents. In tiny Nevis, the domestic house of Elizabeth Barnes accommodated soldiers, weapons, and ammunition, for which she was paid a mighty 8,700 pounds of sugar.[16] The balance of internal and external defense was a delicate one.

Stone, in short supply throughout the region except for Barbados and Bermuda, was reserved for fortifications, as a first line of defense against people rather than the elements. The same conditions which made Bermuda such an attractive prospect for settlement, could work in its favor when plans were afoot to render its Atlantic isolation strategic. At the very end of the century, its former governor, Isaac Richier, suggested a role for it as an *entrepôt*: "Concerneing the Charge and materialls to ffortifye Bermuda[,] Stone and Lime are there (the best for such use and for houses) to be had without any other Charge then Mens Labour, there is Sufficient Stumps and Rootes of Trees upon the Kings Land to Burne the Lime; and the Stone is in most places, and to be raised with little trouble being soft and poarous, but most durable[. E]ver since the Island was Inhabited the people in generall was imployed in Building and repaireing of fforts and fortificacons."[17] Building and repairing fortifications was the major—sometimes the sole—consideration of governors, particularly in the latter half of the century when the West Indies became embroiled in inter-European wars. The public accounts for Montserrat in the 1670s show spending on little else except repairs to the "old fort" (Old Road Fort?), those at Plymouth—a fort with bastions—and Kinsale. Rough stone was brought by sloop from elsewhere to be worked by a team of masons, with additional work in timber, wattle, and daub.[18] Willoughby-Fort was Surinam's only non-timber building, a bastioned star construction at the mouth of the Surinam River, while its counterpart in Bridgetown was a basic square, crenellated design at the mouth of the Carlisle River; that is, as a last line of defense for the boats approaching the wharfs. The square James Fort at the north end of Carlisle Bay and the more sophisticated Needham's Fort on a spit of land to the south were reinforced by small gun platforms and batteries.[19]

It was important there be a physical authority in the territories, in the figure of a resident of as high a status as possible, which, in view of the number of different territories comprising the Caribbees, and the distance between authority in Whitehall and that on the ground, was rarely achieved.

Governors were responsible for the movement of others on and off their territories, and issued licenses to travel. In such a diverse, scattered territory, all supplies no matter how humble, all messages, and all labor forces were moved around by water, and thus in the issue of travel licenses it is hard to separate social control from the public coffers. Contested authority was the inevitable consequence of the clash between the liberty to travel and truck and the sanction, protection, and allowance offered by those who believed liberty should be bounded and circumscribed. Examples of cases raised against governors from the early 1640s included Captains Gell, who refused to transport a banished woman from Antigua back to Barbados, and Ackland, who, tired of his tickets for travel not being entered, resolved to carry goods off the island without a further license.[20] In the figures that are available to us, presumably typical, between 1672 and 1674 Montserratians paid twice as much for licenses as they did in fines for misdemeanors, and half as much as total import duties.[21]

The authority to travel traveled up the line. Sir William Stapleton, as governor of Nevis, expressed his indignance at receiving a copy of an Order in Council forbidding governors' return to England without leave. It was worse than death to him to desert one's post, he protested. Since he had failed to secure slaves in Tobago, privateers or mutineers, so in turn he would expect the greatest censure to fall on those in overall authority who tried to escape the fixity of their responsibilities.[22] During the Nine Years' War, Christopher Codrington was given the task of distributing the Crown's subjects around his territories. Ordered to combine to take Guadaloupe and Martinique, he had then to ration out from among "Our Forces" just sufficient to take and keep possession while not spreading his resources too thinly.[23]

Given a network of islands and their connection to mainland colonies such as Surinam, Carolina, and Darién, the interplay of territories in the hands of European enemies, or the presence on the seas of indigenes, care was taken to note the best routes to negotiate the region. The Bahama islands were strategically positioned at the mouth of the Gulf of Mexico, "commonly Called the Windward Passage from Jamaica." On the other hand, the island of Providence sat cradled in the central American isthmus, always prone to Spanish attack. In one such attack, in 1640, the flotilla was dissuaded from attacking the leeward harbor when forts, guns, and two ships were sighted, and struggled to sail around the windward side of the island and back to Brooke Fort where it could anchor overnight; the Spanish forces split, "being kept by the Current, as also some times by boisterous windes, and sometimes by flatt calmes from recovering up to their fellowes."[24] The Scots at Darién found their position difficult because "this Coast lyes toward the Entrance of a deep Bay," high mountains either side, and thus the "true Trade Wind" was masked, and "our Harbour of Caledonia was none of the most Commodious, for Ships could easilie get into it, but not so easilie get out again."[25] Europeans used the proximate but scattered multiethnic populations to undermine the authority of their rivals. The Spanish sought to use renegades in Providence, "seeing many English and Negroes had formerly so desp[er]ately adventured to flee from us to them in severall boats [and] kanooes, [and] y^t too, in so long a voyage wth many times stormy [and] tempestuous weather as there could bee little probability of their safe Arrivall."[26] Thus, the transient quality that became a feature of many populations was compounded when inability to protect a territory by sea prompted secondary migration, and rather than their position between trading posts being an advantage, those who felt unsafe in the Bahamas could move to Carolina, Virginia, and north.[27] At the turn of the century, Bahamas' Governor Elias Hackett and his family were dispatched in a sloop to a desert island, and by turns described the people he served as "almost all such who for several enormous crimes and villanies have either fled from, or been thrust out of all the other Colonies in America."[28]

Francis, Lord Willoughby of Parham, was notorious for not wanting his mainland patrimony mapped or delineated, since this would determine the limits of his jurisdiction.[29] No doubt, therefore, when his deputy, William Byam, described the Guianas as an island, he would have displeased his master, but it did effectively highlight how isolated were the pair from any concern by Whitehall, even while they were besieged by the Dutch, the French, and their allies. It also emphasized how placement was determined by discriminating between territory and the indigenous peoples who inhabited it.[30] The Kalinago were (at least in this instance) allies because they lived in fixed "stations." There was danger in movement, either by natives or by newcomers. Byam saw in Surinam's expanses of "low land," "full of woods," and "Bad Travelling...without Boats" the peril of "the vast distance of o^r settlements" and the jeopardy in which English authority was placed by a mainland colony that held out the freedom to roam.[31] On the other hand, Renatus Enys, reporting to London in 1663, ascribed the harmonious state of Surinam to insignificant indigenous numbers in sparse and therefore unthreatening settlement.[32] Two decades after attempts to people Surinam, another attempt was made on Carolina. Here again, a settlement with frontiers and boundaries between us and them—the latter could be indigenous, French, Spanish, or occasionally Scottish—altered the relationship between different levels of authority and that between Whitehall and Charles Town: internal dissention among the multiple proprietors, and between proprietors and settlers, placed authority at risk and was cited as reason for the Crown's purchase in 1729.[33] Ironically, such direct oversight would render the Carolinas better able to defend themselves, with a more self-sustaining economy. Ignoring all testimonials that Carolina was unhealthy, it was nevertheless considered better placed than Jamaica to act as the naval base for the whole region, producing plentiful and cheap naval stores and commodities. Meanwhile, the sluggish process of the purchase of Carolina earned revenue in itself, as proprietors, agents, lawyers, and witnesses were detained at Whitehall to attend meetings of the Carolina Board.[34] Vast numbers of legal cases over ownership and land were heard in London, requiring proprietors absent themselves for long periods, without necessarily weakening their identification with their tropical possessions.[35]

Sir Francis Bacon counseled the search for "pure soil; that is, where people are not displanted."[36] The British achieved this twice. When sailors under Sir George Somers were shipwrecked on the rocks of Bermuda in 1609, and those in the *Orange Blossom* made a landing on Barbados in 1625, these islands were not then inhabited, despite evidence of a past presence. Kalinago in St. Christopher's visually represented their world on the rocks, often in timeless images, but along with generic faces, animals and birds, are specific symbols of Europeans. Downstream, internal and outsider threats were visualized in the evil spirit of a monkey. Initial Anglo-indigene relations were cooperative (Sir Thomas Warner was alerted to imminent attack by an indigenous woman), but a combined Anglo-French force eventually attacked, throwing bodies into the Pelham River.[37] The aftermath of battle provided the English with an opportunity for traditional naming. This would be Bloody Point.[38] Service in defense of the (English) settlement offered the lord proprietor the excuse to reissue under his authority land that had already been settled, such as that of Warner's Suffolk neighbors, Samuel and John Jeaffreson.[39] The settlers on Old Providence, so provocatively close to the Main, renamed the site of the Spanish repulse of 1640:

> [T]he place where God had given us the victory wch was aforetime known by the name of Knaves Acre,... now upon this occasion was tearmed Bloody beach where after Sermon [and] praier ended we made a fier of the Gods and idolatrous monuments of o^r enemies in ye viewe [and] sight of o^r heathens, whom we did informe y^t the Gods whom ye enemies trusted in [and] called upon could neither save their worshipps from slaughter, nor themselves from ye fiers.[40]

There has been surprisingly little work on place names designated by Europeans.[41] The obsession with fixing and holding the land, giving each plantation the name of its owner, is more prosaic and less sentimental than other Europeans, but a boon to the historian.[42] One of the few to run counter to the trend, Christopher Codrington purchased the Antigua plantation of Governor Keynell and renamed it Betty's Hope, after his daughter. By the century's close a fashion, though not a widespread one, had developed in which marking the supposed end of toil betokened an established estate. Colonel Randal Russell of his lands in Nevis and Robert Cunyngham of his estate in Craig in Scotland chose to mark their travails in the West Indies in properties called "Russell's Rest" and "Cunyngham's Rest," respectively. While on the part of Robert Cunyngham he was naming his estates in Scotland, his sentiment remained with his house and plantation in Cayon, St. Christopher's, and he made particular investments in creating a garden, which is where he stipulated he should be buried. Cunyngham was a patriotic Scotsman, whose trade passed through London, Philadelphia, and Cork, but he thought of himself as "of Cayon." In fact, he died in Edinburgh, and it is unlikely that his body was "repatriated."[43]

Britons set up dichotomies of description. They traveled across the ocean and around the region, but they identified themselves with situation and settlement: the place names of the former hugely outnumbered by the latter. From humble beginnings grew the particularly English (and later, British) characteristic of plantations. Initially, any person who located themselves by turning the earth was a planter, such that in 1640 Governor Henry Ashton defined territorial authority with the phrase "put a spade into the Ground."[44] By the 1740s the Caribbean had become known for systemic monoculture, chattel slavery, and the vast, unbridgeable chasm between a white elite and black slaves termed "Plantation Society."[45] The pattern of this change has determined our view of the footfall of Europeans (and Africans) in the region, for as Vere Langford Oliver announced in *Caribbeana*, men "entered upon...Plantation[s] as a waste Place, and with very great Charge and Trouble brought...[them] to...perfection."[46] After the civil wars, the Crown, in the form of Charles II, began a process of tidying up possession in the Caribbees, which had struggled under heavy taxation and the insecurity in which many had "lost their Grants, Warrants and Evidences for their lands—and other have not apparent Titles" and Sir Nathaniel Johnson was considered a person in whom to invest authority in Jamaica because of his "usefull [and] wholesome Laws...for obliging every owner of Lands to cultivate [and] improve them, whereas before they mostly lay wast, [and] were own'd by such as were not in a Capacity to make use of them."[47] The planters generated their own interest in the new world, contributing capital, debt, obligation, time, presence, their own labor, and others' employment, out of which emerged a sentiment of place, but in Britain, new world land was predicated on an investment which had to show a return, to the detriment of any sentimental connection. The British began with a presence in the Caribbean which reflected the relationship between land, fixity, and interest, and as the seventeenth century progressed, estates were engrossed, switched to monoculture and slave labor, which overshadowed and superseded planters' initial physical investment in the land. The return was ultimately increasing proprietorial absenteeism, and a detached sense of profit and the leisure it purchased, best enjoyed in Britain.

The fundamental units of division expressed the relationship between Britons and the land. In Bermuda, the Company of Adventurers ordered the islands to be laid out in "tribes and shares," set out in 1617 by the surveyor to Governor Tucker, Richard Norwood. Numbers of shares were allocated by status and investment; then by lot—with some dispute as to whether Tucker and Norwood used their access to knowledge to over-reward themselves—and a further area reserved for public land out of which communal expenses would be met.[48] Land allocations—calling them tribes and naming the tribes after predominant shareholders—seemed to tie it to individuals, although the term carried heavy Old Testament connotations. Bermuda was further unusual in that some form of physical premises designed for worship predated the subdivision of land.

Elsewhere (except perhaps, for Bahamas, where tribes may have operated), land division followed the basic unit of boundary and administration, the (English) parish, preceding any establishment of formalized religion, and irrespective of the religious professions of settlers.[49] It was a civil unit of administration, dressed in the language of faith, to devolve day-to-day decisions to "local" parish worthies, thereby creating new levels of deference to constables, churchwardens, and vestrymen, defining community, but varying across the region in how far it created or reflected it. This foundational assertion of community formed the basis for the work of territorial division, physical construction of community space, and structures of authority and management. Land was parceled up, and allocated to settlers, adventurers, company shareholders, or soldiers, depending on the method of foundation, in a process in which surveying, measuring, clearing, establishing, and peopling went hand in hand. Deeds operated a form of words that was already familiar, but which became entrenched in the West Indies: land was "given granted bargained sold enfieffed and confirmed," its position identified by its "lying and being in the parish of" whatever, "bounding and [a]butting" on other allocations, landmarks, or geographical features.[50]

Whether tribe or parish, no matter how early in the settlement process, no matter how varied the demographics of the territories, or how value free the decision to subdivide the land, there was invariably a process at work whereby the civil authorities distinguished themselves from the ecclesiastical, the two operated in tension, and a means to resolve the tensions became recourse to the Church of England, which itself came with its own history of civil-ecclesiastical synergy and of establishment and dissent. In the early years of a settlement, reference back to its particular suitedness to the English provided some order and purpose to Canaan, while at the same time, the West Indies played out the disputes that developed over financial support to maintain an infrastructure for an institution dependent on the Anglican communion, the authority of the Bishop of London, the payment of the tenth, glebe-land, ministers' houses, and churches.

In Antigua, the procedure of establishing parish boundaries had to wait nearly 50 years of settlement. Parish boundaries were set by island representatives—and therefore an Act had to be passed—and only in 1681 did the Governor and Council, in the presence of the Assembly, formally divide the island into parishes, "To the Intent that P[ar]ish Curches [sic] might be built att the charge of each P[ar]ish, and that provision be made for the maintenance of a Minister in each P[ar]ish as alsoe the poore in each p[ar]ish with other Necessary p[ar]ish charges in manner as itt is used in England" such that the Assembly drew up an Act that "all the ffreeholders may be Convened together by order from The Governor and out of Them to Choose twelve able and Sufficient knoweing ffreeholders for Each P[ar]ish Concernes (vizt) the building of Churches maintainance of Ministers poore and other Parochiall charges who may be Enabled To Assess and Tax all the ffreeholders in their Respective P[ar]ishes for the Carying on of the p^{r}misses." Five parishes were then suggested. That of St. Paul in the far southwest was formed by "the Denissons of ffalmouth Randevous Bay and part of Willoby Bay That wch belongs to Capt Lees Company," that is, by conjoining certain estate boundaries and geographical features.[51] In St. Philip's, in 1713, the vestry "agreed to erect a fine building for ye worship of God in ye center of ye Parish" and had given a contract to carpenter George Pullen to finish it, at a cost of £1,100. We know of this, however, because Antigua was rocked by politico-religious dissention, and rivals (accused of being Catholics) had built a chapel, citing the inconvenient location of a church and chapel of ease only a mile from the most extreme point of a parish nine miles long and six wide, which many parishioners could not reach, especially for the four months of the year when the creeks flooded.[52] The new St. Philip's was constructed in wood, though "we us'd to worship before in a thatch'd hovel."[53]

Churches in Barbados were generally of stone: that in St. John's was repaired at least three times during the seventeenth century. Samuel Copen provided an image of St. Michael's Bridgetown in 1695: a simple rectangular stone building, steep tiled roof, and two tall Romanesque arches at the east end, which may have been windows.[54] There were synagogues in Barbados from the mid-1650s, at Bridgetown and Speightstown, and though there is no agreement whether the founders came from Curaçao, Pernambuco, or Amsterdam, they formed the community known as "the scattered of Israel."[55] Andrew, son of Richard Norwood, made a plan of the Bridgetown synagogue in 1664, showing a boundary, a building, and perhaps a smaller burial ground for Jews of ignoble lives. The fact that there was a burial ground attached to the synagogue was considered unusual among Jewish communities.[56] If it had not much changed between its first construction and around 1740, the synagogue in Bridgetown had a square central tower fronted by five Romanesque arches, a big window in each.[57]

Bermuda set the general standard for levels of building. There had to be some advantage in being an isolated, unpeopled, and rocky outcrop, and so lucrative and common were the Bermudan vessels transporting stone that when they flew the cross of St. George it was known as the "Sawed Stone Jack."[58] Daniel Tucker installed his wife, himself, and a "lieutenant of the castle" in two or three palmetto-leaf "cottages"—Tucker's Town—on the "surplus" land which was still unallocated by Norwood's survey, from which small wooden structures went to create a town of St. George's. Later buildings used masonry.[59] Generally speaking, enclosures or gatherings of settlements which might earn the epithet of "town" were points of disembarkation, further developing into facilities for re-embarkation: first Holetown, then Speightstown, Oistin's Town, and Indian Bridge in Barbados, for example. The late-century map published by Philip Lea, maker and seller of "Globes, sphers, maps, mathematical projections, books and instruments" at the sign of "the Atlas and Hercules in Cheapside," reveals that despite the expansion of Bridgetown, all four towns sprang from a basic "T" structure, in which buildings were constructed in ribbon formation along the coast from either side of a landing point, and back along a route connecting the coast to the interior.[60] The development of Antigua was delayed not only by the particularly fraught internal politics of the Leeward Islands, but also by the French threat. The process of reconstruction began in 1668 with a plan to build six towns, repealed after fewer than ten years to concentrate on defensive structures in their stead. Attention focused on securing the plots in St. John's in the northwest and Falmouth in the southeast, such that artisans could build with confidence.[61] When the Lords Proprietors planned Charles Town, towns and cities aimed at trade and industry seemed an alternative to plantation rusticity, building a self-sustaining community of indentured carpenters, joiners, brick-makers, and bricklayers, whose labor would build houses, which would then attract rent-free tenancies, and trades and shipbuilding would develop, such that founding the colony and making "y^t Colonie ffamous" would be simultaneous.[62]

The fullest treatments of urban communities have, ironically, been due to their vulnerability. Bridgetown was ravaged by fire in 1659, 1668, and 1673. A colorful picture of the infamous pirate town of Port Royal survives because we can cross-reference deeds with artifacts, swallowed by the sea after the earthquake of 1692: a material culture preserved in brine and mud. One of the best descriptions of its position and countenance was provided by the campaign against its rebuilding; only around 25 acres were left above—but only two to three feet above—water, and this would necessitate dwellings and storehouses being crammed so close together that again it would be at risk of fire and flood.[63] In the case of both, these survivals can be cross-referenced against extant deeds, wills, and inventories.[64] The Spanish capital of Jamaica, St. Iago de la Vega (Spanish Town), differed from those started by the English, in that it was inland and constructed around what appeared to them to be a scattered pattern of closed compounds.[65] In the case of both Barbados, from *circa* 1640, and Jamaica, from around 1660, the survival of deeds and indentures will allow for a nuanced and sophisticated study of the urbanization of the West Indies, once it is available in a searchable, multivalent form.

There was therefore a constant conversation between the availability of indigenous materials and their appropriateness to climate, defense, and the exigencies of West Indian conditions. The vast majority of buildings for the first two-thirds of the century were constructed in indigenous materials, but of limited lifespan, except for posts increasingly made from lignum vitae timber, or one of the other hardwoods collectively known as "ironwood." Even in Bermuda, where the abundance of limestone made for more permanent structures from an early date, the roofs were constructed from palmetto thatch, said to be more responsive than stone to swings of temperature: "without which Tree we could not live comfortably in this place."[66] The dominant vernacular style in Bermuda dates from the eighteenth century, with a huge chimney at the gable end, made from thin blocks of stone. The flammable thatch of the previous century dictated that earlier chimneys were separated from the gable, such as that in the building known as the Old Rectory in St. George's.[67] In 1682 the residents of Charlestown, Nevis, asked that no fireplace be built unless the chimney was in stone or brick.[68]

Barbados had a supply of coral limestone, producing buildings of a feint pinkish hue, and in 1682 Sir Richard Dutton revealed, in a response to interrogatories, that all houses had been built originally from wood, since decayed or destroyed by fire; but by his time stone was general, "after the English fashion for commodiousness and decency as well as strength."[69] Certainly, in the previous decade, the vestry of St. John's parish, planning to repair its church and construct a house for the minister, Commissary Benjamin Cryer, provided a detailed plan for a three-storey stone house, with three gables, which, if completed, may have looked like a (marginally) smaller version of the Berringer/Yeamans plantation house.[70] Cryer's house would have five bed chambers on the first floor:

> The body of the House porch [and] staire must be of stone walls Two foote thick and Eighteen foot high and the shades of the same thicknesse Tenn ffoote high with shadeing and Gable ends./ All ye Ground ffloores to be paved belonging to the House with paveing bricks laid in Mortar all ye roofe to be covered with plaine tyles pinned and laid in Mortar./
> The Walls to be all plaistered within, pointed without and ye Corners ffree stone./
> The partitions to be on both sides lathed and plaistered./
> The second ffloore to be laid with boards plained and Joynted./
> The third or Garrett story to be laid with boards plained and Joynted./
> In One of ye shades is to be a Chimney and Oven.[71]

All of Cryer's windows would contain glass. On the death of her husband in Antigua, Sarah Crabb took the opportunity to order five pounds' worth of diamond panes for lead glazing.[72] Thus by the start of the eighteenth century, a sturdy building had become key to establishing one's authority and credentials in a colony.

The requirements of a plantation to produce exotic commodity, especially sugar, also speeded the transition to stone and brick. A boiling house and distillery could be 33 yards in length, with a double roof, in a hardwood, with pan tiles over the coppers such that the fires under them did not set the whole ablaze. Less durable roofs could be used elsewhere. By building lofts over the roof, the sugar coppers and drip houses could be hung from the stanchions.[73] The roof was a tricky aspect: it needed to be solid and pinned in order to withstand the heat of the fires and strong winds, and yet its strength and fixity trapped the infernal heat within. Seventeenth-century windmills tended to be of the posted, wooden kind, often partially erected and then carried onto site: many stuck with cheaper cattle mills. One of the reasons that Barbados gathered pace as a sugar producer was its supply of indigenous stone and clay. Other locations, trying to develop monoculture toward the end of the century, found startup costs disproportionate to the returns: often stone had to be imported, as did lime and mortar, hardwood timber for construction and general timber for furnaces. Finally, much greater numbers of slaves had to be imported in order to build and maintain the plant. On St. Christopher's, even a figure as important as the Attorney

General, John Spooner, was using as a boiling house that which the French had built as a church.[74]

In the colonization of space, geographers identified as key to "imperial imposition" the creation of "official" buildings.[75] Accompanying the publication of Norwood's survey within John Smith's *Generall Historie of Virginia* were engravings of fortifications and of Bermuda's fine, Italianate state house, with its unusual flat limestone roof which proved a liability. Raised in 1620–1621, to the specifications of Nathaniel Butler, he demanded it compare with buildings he had "seene in other countries in parallel."[76] It "merged defensive architecture (a block house lies behind the facade, with walls of two feet thick, bonded with turtle oil and lime) with the splendour of a public hall."[77] Similar instructions sent by the Company directors of Providence Island, before one or other of Robert Hunt or Nathaniel Butler were dispatched to be governor, included building a government house.[78] Both Bermuda and Providence were instigated by a British-based company, which may explain why an iconic, central public building was an early consideration. While geographers noted public buildings to be a key aspect of colonial imposition, elsewhere in the Caribbean, these were few and far between.

We might expect an early-settled, developed location such as Barbados to have core buildings to centralize and demarcate its administration. In fact, it was not until 1675 that a rent for such buildings was arranged with Colonel John Stanfast for the house on the 270-acre Fontabelle estate in St. Michael's, north along the coast from Bridgetown, and subsidiary to his main estate at Stanfast Hill, St. James, at nearly twice the extent.[79] Stanfast's death coincided with the arrival as governor of Sir Richard Dutton, so the Council and Assembly negotiated a rent of £87 10s a quarter with his widow, Elizabeth.[80] Dutton paid £300 to stop the house from falling down, to be reimbursed from the public treasury, with further repairs in 1686: neither rent nor rates were paid regularly.[81] But this degree of formalization allowed space to develop ceremonial functions: Council and Assembly had a regular meeting place; public servants could be summoned to attend at Fontabelle; there could be rituals, such as the payment of gifts (usually money) to departing governors, and receptions for the new arrivals.[82] The accession of James VII and II was publically proclaimed in Cheapside, following a march from Fontabelle into town, at which we also learn that the streets of Bridgetown lacked conduits which would otherwise have run with wine as the procession passed.[83] During James's reign, there was public green space in front of the government house, where Sir Timothy Thornhill and John Harwood exchanged caustic and violent words about their families' loyalties during the civil wars.[84] Governor Francis Russell kept a well-provisioned sentry of English Life Guards and had the house (re?)glazed, which served to cocoon inside a strange household of dysfunctional servant families who embezzled his goods and money and ate him out of house and home.[85] His unfortunate tenure in office and untimely end thereby afford the historian detailed inventories of the domestic interior of government house, with its best bedroom, but not that in which the governor lay, which had two closet rooms, broken open by the servants on his departure, and further bedrooms designated for named occupants. The house possessed a gallery, off which were further bedrooms, and there was a parlor and kitchen.[86] The arrangement with Fontabelle House lasted around 20 years. During the administration of Sir Bevill Granville, the Council rented Pilgrim House, raised on a hill to the east of town, with 22 acres of land. This became the official Government House, despite attempts by Governor Crowe to persuade Queen Anne to obtain something better.[87]

The need was acute in areas of disputed control, so in St. Christopher's it became necessary to build a house for the governor of the English quarters, who was obliged to reside in it, and £1,000's worth of timber was supplied from Antigua to repair and rebuild English planters' homes.[88] The large Irish population on Montserrat might render it internally unstable so Governor Roger Osborne came under suspicion when he seized the "Stately built stone-house" of his brother-in-law, Samuel Waad, who had acquired an estate of greater value than that of the governor. The house was probably subsequently (re)named States Castle, though the island map of 1673 shows a block-castellated building, situated half way up a hill to the windward of Plymouth Town.[89] In Montserrat in the 1670s, the only dedicated civic building discussed was a clapboard court house, and, depicted, a multistorey customs' house in Plymouth. The Assembly and Council of War were accommodated at the house of the Dutch/German merchant, Tielman van Vleck.[90] Much-disturbed Antigua began the process of providing spaces for the administration of justice in 1681, when in June a committee of both houses began to "Treate with John Lucas about Purchasing his house and Lands in St Johns Towne for Publique use as a Court house Roomes for ye Councill and Assembly att Generall meetings hee being willing to Expose The same to sale," though once inspected, the house was deemed unsuitable.[91] His Excellency, Valentine Russell, issued an angry, but possibly exaggerated outburst, that "for want of a place to doe Justice in," the judges complained "of holding the Sessions in The Streete," and incapable of enlarging the prison in St. John's, the Provost Marshall was ordered to keep prisoners at his house.[92] In the early eighteenth century, the island was still using public houses for court proceedings: trade and politics discussed in the downstairs' rooms; depositions and hearings held upstairs. Jonathan Hill ran such an establishment in St. John's, and Jeffrey Duncombe in Parham.[93] At the same time that Crowe was attempting to upgrade his official accommodation, Governor Daniel Parke was complaining that the plantation he was renting in St. Christopher's, as well as the timber house being built for him there, had blown down and washed into the sea: further, the furniture in his Antigua residence had been ruined.[94] Parke might argue that he was too good for the Leewards, having been overlooked as governor of Virginia, but as late as 1700 the burgesses of the Old Dominion did not have the wherewithal to build a government house there either.

The processes of colonization and new settlement gave added frisson to British debates about public and private space. Bodies such as law courts, vestries, or assemblies represented and were made up from the people of the colony; individuals such as a Lord Proprietor, governor, and often an Anglican (as opposed to other sects') minister were deemed both imposed and transitory. Between the two were councils, chosen from local representatives, but usually nominated. If a building symbolized community authority, it also came to identify settlers with their new place, rather than their old. Bermuda's State House fulfilled that function; on top of a hill but in the center of St. George's, it represented the ocean isolation that gave Bermudans nearly a century of self-containment. In places in which there was a separate "ruler's" residence, this served rather to emphasize the isolation of the individual and his authority, with consequent lack of acceptance. Mediating were those houses in which the public bodies met, and the individual ruler lived—spaces in which representative symbolism and aloof power collided.

There was puritan criticism within Bermuda of Governor Tucker, that he "obiected to the publick eye," and puffed up with self-worth, engaged artisans to find fresh water, clear land and build "a large, handsome, and well contriued house (yet by farr the best in the Islands)" at public expense.[95] His late-century counterpart, Richard Coney, presided over the death of the Bermuda Company, pleading one aspect of decay was his great personal expense to maintain a house and slaves while both collapsed from being left stand in water.[96] The greatest cultural capital acquired by a private residence detached from public accountability was the Surinam estate of Francis Willoughby of Parham: Willoughby-Fort defended what its proprietor called Willoughbyland, but his private residence was Parham Plantation, Parham House, or Parham Hill. The governor's faction was the Parhamites.[97] According to Aphra Behn's admittedly fictional and retrospective account, Parham House was "as much exempt from the Law as *White-hall;* and that they ought no more to touch the Servants of the Lord—(who there represented the King's Person) than they cou'd those about the King himself; and that *Parham* was a Sanctuary; and though his Lord were absent in Person, his Power was still in Being there."[98] In 1664 John Allin plotted an assassination attempt, ordering a hut to be constructed near Parham House where he "lurked" to observe the governor walking unattended: in the end, he waited till the Governor and Council gathered for a religious service in Parham's "upper dining Room" and then made his essay.[99] Among many charges of extortion issued against Sir Richard Dutton of Barbados was his innovation to make the gentry pay their own expenses when summoned to attend the Grand Sessions, while during his absences in England, he let out government house. The latter, he argued, was in order for it to be kept in good order during his absence and any monies he took from the public purse for the house (£2,500 it was claimed) were for its repair.[100]

Any, humble or exalted, who wished to turn an allocation into a prospect handed their fate to another. The role of surveyor, as a technician in whose hands lay individuals' hopes of freehold autonomy, acquired worthiness, hubris for himself, and jealousy from employers and clients. Richard Norwood's survey and maps of Bermuda set the standard, of both specific and general education in the region, and his treatises on geometry, navigation, and architecture ran to several editions. This did not save him from attack. He was accused of corruption, furthering his own and his master's interests by conducting the survey that directed the initial allocation of shares. He fell foul of the sectarian battle raging in Bermuda in the 1640s.[101] His work on trigonometry and navigation using the stars led him to confide that "it was a very hard matter (if not a thing impossible) to be a noted man in Judicial Astrology, and yet a good Christian." Accusations that working with triangles constituted witchcraft pushed him into hiding his work on Boaz Island.[102] The physicality of identifying plots varied little whether it was for the high and mighty or the humble, and reflected that of original English foundations of measurement while differing in scale and markers.[103] The systematic collection of deeds and titles to land usually arose out of dispute. The impressive deed books of Barbados were designed to cement the titles granted under the patent of the earl of Carlisle.[104] In 1671 the Council of Jamaica was forced to complain of "the many Abuses, & Law suites that...are likely every day to arrise from the Ignorance, and Multiplicity of Surveyors" and appointed named surveyors to several districts, who were "strictly required, not to take more then three half^d P acre of the Planters, paying the Charges of the hands."[105] The colony's governor added that the surveyor should not be a patented place for life, because Jamaica's surveyor "would live where he pleased"—that was, remotely—and "not where he was told," and was a cocktail of lazy, incompetent, and contrary. His successor spotted the oxymoron: that there was "nothing so disorderly as the method."[106] In St. George's, Jamaica, surveyor Mordecai Rogers referred to himself as a "Geodiagraph," one who rendered in line the mathematical surveying and measurement of land.[107] For a gentleman to feel in control, treatises in mathematics and surveying, theodolite, chain, and scales were more necessary than armor.[108] Henry Ashton of Antigua advised the earl of Carlisle, about to take up his patrimony in the Caribbees, that he would "want if yo^w bring not wth yo^w...An Artiste or two of reasonable practize in the Mathematiques, at least in those p[ar]tes thereof that concerne Architecture, ffortificacon, [and] survey," in short supply among the professionals who had already made their way to the colonies.[109]

A role predicated on precision and integrity progressively acquired inaccuracy and influence in the measurement of deliberated allotments, as the interchangeable "plot," "plat," and "plan" already referred to both imposed measurement and human stratagems. English land, plowed in strips of one furrow long—a furlong—was translated into "longlots," now usually on land initially incapable of being plowed. A hundred-acre longlot would measure one chain's length along the waterside and ten chains' inland: in areas in which more land was available or it was paramount that expanses were settled quickly, such as Carolina, a 400-acre longlot could be five times the length to the breadth.[110] The earliest plots in Barbados, along the leeward coast from Holetown, south to Black Rock, were measured a mile and a quarter away from the coast, and, if a tenth of the length lay along the seaside, computed 100 acres. The main north–south highway was marked along their eastern edge; the northerly end-point thus became a place name, Mile and a Quarter. Few survived, but there is a colored representation of "Fort Plantation," 300 acres allocated to Captain Thomas Middleton, stretching back from St. James' Church, Holetown.[111] It denoted the church, the saltpetre and powder houses close to the shore, fallen land, pasture, the main house, areas of rented land, and land in dispute due to encroachment (seemingly unresolved).[112] The legacy of longlots can be seen in the town plan of Charleston, Carolina, and the footpaths of Nevis. In Bermuda, the thin sliver of rock surrounded by ocean dictated that longlots here lay in stripes from shore to shore. The house known as Verdmont, built on Gilbert Hill, in Smith's Tribe, within 75 acres of land, enjoys a view to the sea both front and back.[113]

William Harding, an illiterate blacksmith; carpenter, John Smyth; and Thomas Brough, all defined themselves as "of Barbados." Brough witnessed a deed by which Harding sold a ten-acre plot that he had purchased from Smyth, to John Bradley: "bounding upon the land of Henry Whittaker on the south, and upon the land of Robert Shelley on the north, being to the foot of John Martin's, and butting to the first rising of the rock from the seaside," which probably is Black Rock. At a value of 1,700 pounds of cotton wool, Bradley purchased land, the sparsest of tools—a mortar and a tray—a table, and the first bedstead noted on the island.[114] Thomas Brough, meanwhile, was living in a thatched wooden storehouse on the leeward coast, partitioned to allow for living at one end and goods brought in from the country at the other. He had a lodger, who had traveled from Amsterdam, named Jacob the White. White purchased his section of the storehouse in order to extend it by eight feet to create more of a dwelling, and the pair intended to develop the business, with White seeking to take on the additional labor which could mean they could expand out of storing others' produce to grow, dig, and dress their own potatoes.[115]

John Hapcott, who surveyed 45 acres of Barbados land to be allocated to Captain David Bix, deemed it, to his knowledge, "free from any former lawful grant, [although others pretended an interest]...the line being marked according to the usual manner, the corner trees being marked with a x + D all but one that is over against that which was Nicholas Butler's house and that is marked with a X, there being twelve corner trees belonging thereunto."[116] Bix was a neighbor of both "Edward Sutton the Negro," and (probably the same person) Black Nedd, with land near Great Pond.[117] At the end of the decade, during which Barbados had supposedly undergone the "sugar revolution," plans were still modest. All we know of the otherwise unimpressive figure of Sir Poynings More of Loseley, Surrey, was that he spent prodigiously, but was moderate and noncommittal in his parliamentarian, Presbyterian politics, and he died early in 1649. From a family of planners, he never traveled to the West Indies, which makes all the more astonishing a document—which must postdate the civil wars but predate the Commonwealth—"The Price charge and ordering of an 150 Acres of ground for a Plantation in ye Barbadoes."[118] Of 150 acres of unfelled land ("bought for 450^{li} sterling"), it was imperative that 40 be cleared immediately for provision crops, reserving an allowance for transporting tools and 20 English artisans; the ground was to be cleared by 40 African slaves. Sir Poynings would need to spend more than £2,600 and wait three years before he saw any profit and there was further discouragement: while Barbados was already overcrowded, at least 200 acres was necessary if a planter intended to settle with family, servants, and stock.

In islands, available land was clearly limited, but larger and mainland colonies which might offer expansive, more rapid, and dense development were still dogged by caution. Despite brave projections of towns, "cities," artisans, and numberless settlers, arrivals were discouraged by the prospect of migrating to country more uncertain, dangerous, and slow to see a profit. They still quoted, but did not follow, Bacon's advice to settle in uninhabited regions. Albemarle, north Carolina, was allocated according to the custom of Virginia, which was 50 pole by the river side and one mile into the woods for every 100 acres. John Whitty had been a merchant captain during the civil wars in England, patrolling for royalist vessels along the Northumberland coast, and after the war, in 1656, he shipped them—some as prisoners—to Virginia, and settled himself. Within ten years he had amassed an estate of 1,500 acres and then issued proposals for migratory settlement into Carolina. Despite detailed planning, however, his aims remained modest.[119] In Albemarle, "To reduce Planters into Townes, is here almost impossible; when the Countrey is Peopled and Comerce increases, it may more easily be effected, By appoynting Ports and Marketts, whether not only Merchants, but all Tradesmen, and Artificers will resort for habitation, and in short time lay the foundations to superstructures of Townes and Cities."[120] From the outset, settlers in Carolina assumed a waterside longlot of one-by-one-hundred chains: ten acres was a sufficiency to plant and keep clean, while a density of 200 men in a mile and a quarter square would provide a quality of life more pleasant than most towns.[121] Thirty years later, when surveyors were mapping 500 acres for Carolina Proprietors Carteret, Colleton, and Ashley Cooper, the principle remained the same: "a pine," "an oake the corner as likewise Mr Mavericks," "a baytree," "an oake on the other side of the marsh," "a poplar the corner," "an oake stump," "landing place," "a dogwood the Corner," "an ash In the Swamp."[122] Greater sophistication had to wait for the turn of the eighteenth century, when the Surveyor General of Carolina, Landgrave Edmund Bellinger, created a "Platt or Modell of Charles Towne," the so-called Grand Model; each allotment distinguished in colored ink, and grantees issued with "certificates of measurement."[123] In the seventeenth century, schemes barely approached their ambitions.[124]

An accretion of mundane elements established sentimental intimacy with place. The individuals, all men, with no reference to family, were rooted in the soil because of, rather than in spite of, the absence of clear and sophisticated plans. Haphazardness created dispute, in which the authority of the magistrate came under challenge, with inevitable spats between neighbors, but the sense of having been marooned with basic resources and expected to forge a living molded the spade in the soil into a powerful symbol of identity. Returning to Messrs White and Brough, the simple process of storing goods brought to them from the island's hinterland to be warehoused and their plan to grow potatoes was evidence of a domestic market in simple starchy produce and self-sufficiency. Though Thomas Brough was a merchant, he had a connection to this place: Barbados was where he built a life, not removed a profit. Barbados was probably where he died.[125] This could extend to even the humblest of residents. On the estate of Ensign George Buckley in 1640 was a servant known only as "Daniel the Irishman."[126] Daniel joined the ranks of the "redlegs" on the east of the island, but when he died at the end of 1692, longevity and residence had so rooted him within St. John's that his community still knew him as "Irish Daniel." The same could be said of "one Rahanan Irish" or "David a Welchm^n, serv^t to Stubs ye Quaker."[127]

This form of being "of the country" was particular to the Caribbean. In the East Indies and Africa it referred to indigenous people.[128] Richard Jobson, journeying up the River Gambia, described renegade ("vagrant") Portuguese living with Mandinka women, trading in country goods, and coveting "the country people, who are sold vnto them when they commit offences."[129] In New England, the phrase distinguished urban from rural settlers.[130] Official papers seldom used the phrase with reference to the torrid zone and when it was, it served to emphasize the division between residents and those whose interests, mediated by the oceans, acquired political capital through their connection with the mother country, because they managed Britain's forces, administration, or economy. Thus Lord Ashley was assured that "all ye people in ye Countrey have an esteeme to his Lordpp...and that his care of us all this distance will not Impaire in the Conservac[i]on of our Civill rights."[131] When John Thurston asked several merchants to speculate on possible defense spending, they spoke disparagingly of "the country" to mean "them," the others, the people of Jamaica, who allowed "no more than £1250 a year (*their money*) for support of the Whole Charge of the fortifications there."[132] Rootedness proved a difficult sentiment for the English government. It expected some level of commitment to new place; suspicious, for example, of the motivations of those in Jamaica who were "a sorte, that designe nothing but their returne into England."[133] But they did not want too great a commitment, as ties to the new could distance one from the old.

When the British mapped themselves, they created icons out of the edifices of settlement. Buildings were invariably white, with red, pitched roofs. While the original French church in Bassetterre, St. Christopher's, was said to have been roofed with red slate, few of the early buildings in the torrid zone were constructed in a material which might be whitewashed. Even if, at the point at which the anonymous surveyor created the plat of Thomas Middleton's 400 acres, he had been possessed of a gabled plantation house, it is barely credible that his tenant, Patrick Rogers, on ten acres, was living in a whitewashed stone dwelling with red tiled roof.[134] Buildings are depicted to emphasize their position within green background terrain. This was the pattern in Surinam, where buildings varied only in dimensions, and in Tourarica were terraced.[135] Marked are "the planters names as they are Settled in their Plantations in the Severall parts of the Cuntry"; mostly individuals, but this could refer to collectives, such as "Jews," "Scotsmen," or the "town" of Tourarica.[136] Three different writing styles are employed. In large serif print are names of main rivers and settlements as anglicized local terms. A smaller serif hand was used for geographical features—Red Banke, Tygers Hole, Armadille Hill, Funck Tree—or European settlements—Scotsmen, "L^t: Gen: Byam," Pilgrim—but also Onaracabe close to the Jewish settlements, or the large gabled building called Supamica, and smaller ones like Carehebo. Two, on a creek of the river Commerwijne, Wepo and Tubenho, were half-built; some, like Yambo and Pramarico, were inhabited by indigenous people, as an italicized script added the word "Indians." Thus indigenous people are described as planters living in settlements, presented on a par with—though in reality, some distance from—the incomers, as William Byam had suggested.[137]

A plantation of 40 acres here would include a single-storey, partitioned wooden building, with thatched roof of steep gabled pitch, presumably not to ape the contemporaneous style of northern Europe but to be robust enough to withstand, and provide a run-off for, the rains. Heavily wooded terrain limited the size of plantation allocations—remarkable that a man of the status of Sir Robert Harley would hold just 40 acres, more evidence of realistic ambition—and it was calculated that it would take four slaves a year to "fall Cleare and plant" predominantly subsistence crops—"Indian provisions"—such as six acres of plantains, eight each of yams and cassava, four acres of both potatoes and sugar, and ten acres of maize. They were also to build a thatched house, with thatched door and partitions, of sixty feet long, twenty feet deep, and seven feet high. It should be "well pallasado,d" and the building be "substantiall," but it is difficult to know how robust such a form could be.[138] There has been some work on impermanent, and some work on vernacular architecture, but the latter is less aware of historical origin or change, and describes a wider American region than the conditions peculiar to the Caribbean.[139] This has contributed to the downplaying of seventeenth-century contributions to the shaping of the Americas. One is apt to view, and to debate whether to preserve, that which remains to be seen, relatively intact and above ground: that is, the major (stone) plantation house and the church. But early colonists needed to establish dwellings quickly and cheaply, fashioned from the materials to hand, and thus while buildings would tend to be based on what was found among indigenous peoples, combined with the traditions of incomers, the dominant structure in the early seventeenth century was a single storey, wooden, long rectangle; partitioned; often without a hallway but connected one to another through each room. Britons held true to the tradition of splitting timber, and producing "feathered" or "shingled" timber facades, undeterred by the flimsy result. By the turn of the century, as plantation houses were increasingly built in stone, they tended to retain a long, thin rectangular form, or possessed a stone pavilion core and separate boarded and shingled rooms adjacent.[140]

The distinction between vernacular and impermanent housing grew wider as the seventeenth century progressed reflecting the social gulf between first, proprietors and servants, and then land owners and slaves. In the later-century, slaves were increasingly employed in building, but presumably with little control over building for themselves, any agency they may have possessed predicated on, and nullified by, their slave status. It may be too strong to say of the seventeenth century that "[s]laveholders adapted old building types and developed new ones with the purpose of employing architecture to subjugate and control their human chattel," but the provision of housing by a master nevertheless imposed control and hierarchy.[141] The paucity and poverty of buildings provided for both servants and then slaves was such that they seldom registered on inventories, and were certainly not sturdy enough to be long-lasting, or provide an evidential trace.[142] Seventeenth-century maps are, more often than not, silent about the contribution of black workers. Plats of the Creighton Hall Estate, St. Thomas in the East, Jamaica, show a series of grounds, surveyed between 1665 and 1683, most punctuated by a dwelling house, works' buildings, rivers, roads, and boundaries, but without indicating anything other than proprietorship over land.[143] Plans of the same estate from the early nineteenth century detailed closely the houses of the slave workforce: Higman suggests it only became expedient to do so "with the approach of emancipation and the planters' desire to retain resident labour forces."[144]

It has been suggested that slavery necessitated a different relationship between "an area that has physical dimensions" (space) and an area which is "perceived and experienced" (place).[145] Plantations designated areas for slave-houses and slave burial grounds, while Oldmixon maintained that some plantations built a separate "Indian house."[146] In feudal terms, the Lowthers described theirs as "cottages."[147] An early-eighteenth-century survey which does indicate slave-dwellings is that of Codrington in Antigua. The main dwelling house was (unusually) square, surrounded by a wall, with turret rooms at each corner for particular services: the house complex also contained a formal garden with cisterns, another plot, and a yard with kitchen, blacksmith's, room for the servants, stables, and a hothouse for isolating and treating sickly slaves. On an estate of say, 500 acres, the central area of domicile embraced about 30, traversed by footpaths; the mills, boiling houses, still-houses, and curing houses clustered close to the house. In two separate areas there were 35 slave-houses to the west and a further 14 at the southeast, collected in an area between still-house and pond, about half by three-quarters of a mile. The slave-house nearest to the central complex was that close to the stable—66 feet (one chain)—and the nearest to the mansion house, 150 yards; the furthest away 350 yards.[148] Smaller neighboring estates, about half the size, such as the Garden Plantation, contained plant, the smaller house of an overseer, and—in this case seemingly surrounded by some form of boundary—31 small red squares to mark individual buildings. The Codringtons' slave-houses tended to be positioned randomly, whereas it was more usual for them to be laid out in parallel rows—"contiguous huts like an *African* town"—such as practiced by Codrington's neighbor, Tuit; or Robert Cunyngham, who began to lay out the houses on the Morning Star estate in November 1731.[149] From London, Oldmixon decided "the planter's house [must look] like the sovereign's" "in the midst" of an "African city."[150]

Unlike an English estate, therefore, where the great house was increasingly distanced from tenants' cottages in the village, the West Indian estate was deemed to replicate medieval lordship in which the gulf between possession and possessed was emphasized by proximity. For the first time since the twelfth century, lordly patrimony was being established on new ground.[151] Managing the built environment was a basic lordly responsibility, and thus it was designed and placed. If a slave was manumitted, however, how far did patriarchal direction and paternalist oversight give way to individual autonomy? John Hallett's will freed a boy, Virgil, "and if he pleaseth" he could "live in my ffamily where he shall be Maintained," without saying whether this transformation of patriarchy into paternalism tied Virgil to place in England or Barbados.[152] Can the dependence, fear, compliance, rage, or frustration engendered by slavery ever generate the same sense of home as that appropriated by Europeans? In the will of Rowland Hilton of St. Philip's, Barbados, most slaves were to remain on such plantations as Hilton should "Appoint." Does that give the families security of place, fix their enslavement, make them personal or real estate, or all of the above? Four were freed and could "remaine in yᵉ houses where they now Life [*sic*] & upon their Freedome to have foure Acres of Land Lying Altogather" where *they* should appoint along with wood and cane from the plantations from which to build their own houses.[153]

In 1733, on Cunyngham's estate in Cayon, St. Christopher's, there lived a Moko man, together with an Igbo woman, and their "Moko" daughter, who appear to have been enslaved together in Africa at the end of the seventeenth century.[154] They remained as a unit and went on to have another two children together. The full age range was 35–12.[155] The man had another son, around 1723, with a Mina woman. The eldest daughter had at least two sons, aged ten and six in 1733.[156] The grandfather was a carpenter: we know that in November 1731 he was employed in Basseterre erecting a wooden storehouse, bought as a frame from Boston, Massachusetts, and that the food for the ten men employed in this task cost their master one shilling. The 12-year-old boy worked as a shepherd, and the daughter in the garden, so while the storehouse was being built, she was employed in preparing 700 holes for coffee plants, and planting orange trees, globe-artichokes, a sapodilla, and what may have been a Mammee apple.[157]

All the members of this family were slaves, so in terms of the agency which might connote any sense of place, even a commitment to home, the information must be read in the light of a status dictated to them. Their master's careful note of their place, and in the case of Creoles, date of birth, demonstrates both Cunyngham's awareness of individual human agency and the extent to which his negated theirs. The three who arrived from Africa were not denied the agency of naming, but that by which posterity knows them was allocated.[158] Of the younger children, albeit their names were European in style, we do not know whether they were bestowed by their parents or by their master (more likely the latter).[159] But we know more about the day-to-day, sentimental spatial interactions and agency of these particular black people, than about most of the named white settlers or travelers within the region. The information is given, rather than self-created, but we can discern human agency in creating sentimental attachments to place. In its territorial manifestation, all our knowledge is filtered through the lens of slavery, but at a personal level, even if intimacy cannot be reconstructed, we know of a legacy from a particular part of Africa, a passage across the Atlantic, and an interaction with employment and mundane existence in the West Indies.

Robert Cunyngham's household space was defined by his "white and black family" noting the "country" of the latter, by which was meant where a slave had been born.[160] There were therefore those born in Africa, distinguished with a degree of sophistication; one born "at sea"; and those born in the West Indies, "Creol," by which was probably meant born in St. Christopher's, as one was noted from Barbados.[161] Slaves were distinguished and identified in a number of ways: by their relationship within a West Indian family, or by their employment, but in a situation in which several would be designated by the same familiar name, by a point of origin: Igbo Betty as opposed to Browne's Betty, who was rented from a neighboring estate. The origin of 248 of the 280 slaves at Cunyngham's is known. 112—nearly half—were born in the West Indies: 22 men, 38 women, 27 boys, and 25 girls.[162] The figures continue to bear out the impression that peoples from the Akan ethnic designation comprised a significant proportion of the trade in slaves, tentatively suggesting that St. Christopher's in this period was heavily reliant on first-generation immigrants from Africa.[163] Smaller numbers, by no means predominantly men, were drawn from Papel, Mandinka, and Bambara (Guinea-Mali); Igbo (Niger Delta); and Kongo (Congo/Angola). While the black experience of the Caribbean, enslaved or freed, African or Creole, was socially largely removed from that of any white settler, commentators in the Leeward Islands could posit a shared space, rooted in the identity of acclimatization. By 1733 there were (white) "Children in the Country, and such of our Women that never were in a Northern Climate" as well as (black) slaves that had "no more Notion of *Hail,* Ice or Snow, than one who has always liv'd in *Great Britain*...has of our White-Poll Mountain Pigeon, or of our Custard, Sour-Sap, or Mammee-apple."[164] The boundaries of the estate contained both mutual reliance and cooperation, and hierarchies of control.

In the seventeenth century, it seems internal estate boundaries were rare. By the early eighteenth century, there was a mixture: on the Antigua Codrington estates Betty's Hope was undivided, whereas Garden's slaves were enclosed. In view of his impending absence from his Nevis estates to run the Leewards' federation, Sir William Stapleton was keen to build walls, top them with prickly pears, and what Stapleton referred to as "the Cashee or ffrench fense to be planted, on the winward and Leewar[d] Sides of all the cross paths." Slaves inside the house, except for those with construction skills, were to be moved into the fields. Provision was made to protect both place and people from the damage that might be rent by bad weather and by people, both inside and out.[165] It is difficult to distinguish between the two. The seventeenth-century lives of white and black were more assimilated, within carefully delineated physical limits such as the estate, such that degrees of physical separation were blurred.

A similar case could be made for death. Notices of death are separated by the chasm between survivals of named, dated, and written historical records which are almost exclusively of the white population, and the material, anthropological, and archaeological remains of slaves, identifying "material 'Africanisms'", the most active practitioner in the West Indies being Jerome Handler, beginning with the slave burial ground at Newton's, Barbados.[166] The now geographically significant site was a plantation of approximately 500 acres in Christchurch founded by Samuel Newton.[167] The enslaved population utilized a sloping pasture of about one acre, which combining shallow soil and rocky outcrops made it permanently unsuitable for sugar cultivation, and thus remained undisturbed. Handler focused on two burials which suggested men claiming or imputed to have spiritual powers: one malignant, one authoritative. The latter was "No.72," a man of around 50, placed "gently" in a supine position; probably Creole, found with grave goods, and said to have been buried in the late 1600s/early 1700s.[168] Handler was able to say of Barbados burials with grave goods that they reflected African practice. The goods themselves, however, evinced both local availability—rum, cassava bread, sugar, tobacco, beads made from either local flora or English glass— and African importation: the pipes in this case were not modeled from local clay, and the cowry shells must have been carried to Barbados, but maybe locally acquired.[169] A contemporaneous site in Montserrat, however, yielded no evidence of grave goods.[170] The burial remains of people of African heritage thus become their own landscape: be it their domicile and labor within the plantation complex, houses, and burial site; alterations in the landscape made by burial mounds; the origin of objects found in proximity; and the placement of the body within the earth. They become the material object, their teeth and bones examined for the ritual origin of physical changes to the body, such as the filing of teeth, or mineral traces within the bones that provide clues to lifestyle and personal history.[171] Heritage work undertaken on the mainland of the United States suggests that burial was segregated by color.[172] All such burial sites posit the notion of continuous tradition, stretching to emancipation. But the seventeenth-century Caribbean is problematic: even if color and status delineated social divisions within a household, it was difficult to say how far segregation and separation was spatial. As slaves began to be adopted into Christianity, burials by color, status or belief may not have determined place. Whether one was thought possessed of a soul, a spirit, or a ghost, one's body returned to the earth.

The vestrymen of St. John's, Barbados gave thought to the delineation of space during the summer of 1679 when they pondered their failure to manage the 60 acres previously purchased from Philip Reenes. Six acres had been used jointly as a churchyard and by the clerk. Now, "for ye burying of Corps, a piece of Ground Invironing the Church be Inclosed on ye West and South of ye Church," and though the vestrymen claimed they were enacting the "pious intentions" of the original purchase, the allocation of space was determined by practical and prosaic civic concerns rather than by theological issues. The churchyard—the church in the center—was to be two acres in total, with a piece of 140 square feet to the west—designated for carriages and horses—enclosed by an extra-thick hedge on the Cliff-side, to prevent accidents while coachmen waited for parishioners to emerge from the services. On the outside of the churchyard enclosure would be a parish stocks, "with Tenn Holes at ye Least."[173] The Anglican burial ground was a place rather than a communion, serving the inclusive neighborhood. Everyone in Bridgetown would recognize "Little short Daniel y^t liv'd at Mrs Owens"—known by the community, assimilated into it, if not embraced by it.[174] It did not matter if the body being interred was anonymous (often children); were Dutch sailors; from the almshouse, pest or poor house, or jail. Bodies rested in the same ground, whether they had died from old age, disease, accident—several people were killed by cannon—or were executed. Several were marked "RC": "Edward an Irishman from Coll: Hallett" was unlikely to have been a regular congregant at St. Michael's, though his master was a loyal Anglican. Three days earlier the minister had buried Mrs. Anne Emroy, a Quaker.[175] There were some black deaths included in parish burials. These may have been greater in number than the records seem to admit. John, the son of John and Hannah Dally, was buried in St. Michael's in 1679. At his burial, it was noted that he was black. The parish clerk had noted that John and Hannah were black when they had baptized their daughter, Mary, in 1676, but not when they had been baptized themselves, with a son, Benjamin, the year before.[176]

The interior of the church was prescribed by status. The elite might be envaulted.[177] But the unclaimed "child out of the woods" was at least recorded in some way before being committed to the earth.[178] Even though he was never domiciled on the island, Captain John Tomms, as the commander of the *Agreement* of London, was also buried within St. Michael's.[179] George Lillington, as a former governor, could specify that he wished to be buried under the "common table" of St. Thomas's, thereby setting down a marker of both place and low-church belief, by not referring to an altar.[180] The status of Dame Ann, widow of the Right Honourable John, Lord Willoughby of Parham, entitled her to be buried in St. George's, Barbados, "according to my quality under my pew."[181] Governor Francis Russell died of fever while in office, providing a quandary for the Council since Russell seemed not to have started a will, nor to have land on the island (though they believed he had a grant in St. Christopher's), but they encased his body in lead and laid him in a vault next to Lady North, awaiting as close to a state funeral as Barbados could muster.[182] Also laid in lead was Sir Henry Pickering who, dying in Barbados, requested he be interred in Watton, Cambridgeshire, and therefore would be transported *post-mortem*.[183]

Registration, whether on paper or in stone, was a means to articulate a sentimentality of place, even if that meant linking near and far.[184] Parish registers do not survive, assuming they were kept, for the earliest years of settlement, but once they are produced there are disproportionately greater numbers of burials than baptisms, swelled by servants and mariners, who either quickly succumbed to heat and disease or were buried as soon as the bodies were disembarked. Sometimes wills were explicit about place, beyond the more usual phrases desiring a "decent" and occasionally "Christian" burial at the discretion of the executors.[185] Settlers, both humble and exalted, could allow for the possibility that they would die in a place other than that in which their roots and sentiments lay: Eleanor Brown, already a childless widow when she made her will in Port Royal in 1688, asked that if she died in the town, she be buried as close to her parents as possible, and Colonel John Hallett made provision for a simple burial, should he die "here in London," with as many bequests to kin, friends, and charity in Barbados as there were to those in Axmouth and Lyme Regis.[186] Expressing posthumous life in stone had to wait until the end of the century: Edward Chamberlain's memorial, despite establishing a family tradition of being buried in St. Michael's, Barbados, came not only with arms but also with reference to the English birth of both himself and his wife, Mary Butler.[187] After around 1730 they began to display the fashion for sentimental moral encomia and the arid ground allowed for the romanticization of interment within the West Indies.[188] William Barwick placed a blue marble slab in the church of St. James, Holetown, "To point out the Dust" of Barbadian-born Samuel senior, under which "the Ashes of Samuel the youngest Son reunites in one common Mass with those of his father."[189] The memorial to Ann, married in life to the Rev. Dudley Woodbridge, also of St. James's, called for a tear from those who grieved to be "bestow[ed] on the Dust that Sleepth near,/ That Dust, which animated did comprise/ The Fair, the Good, the Graceful": what should have ended "Wise," probably with the long-s, was chiseled "Wife" by the stonemason.[190] Her body, and thus the dust, was actually in the center of the nave. There are insufficient numbers to be certain, but the heat and dryness of the West Indies seemed to give rise to far more references to dust, than to earth and ashes.

Within Jewish profession, grave memorials, within enclosed burial ground, speak further of extraneous place. The merchants here made their mark with imported stone—most commonly, blue marble.[191] The register for the community of Bridgetown notes only names, and an occasional reference to either "Jew" or "Hebrew," but the tombstones, such as the elaborately carved memorial to David Joseph de Mercado, are larger and considerably more ornate than those of even the highest-church Anglican. Both his name and the inscription, in English and Portuguese, are testimony to his peripatetic life, as trader, foreigner, and exile.[192] Inscriptions in Hebraic script did not start to appear until after 1720, probably because the community could not read it. Several carry the motif of the hand of God felling the tree of life, beneath which the vegetation has a tropical look.[193]

In most cases, the plurality of colors, ethnicities, birthplaces, and belief systems complicated the identification of sentiment with place, but could reinforce it. The multifunctional building provided an excellent illustration: the storehouse was a dwelling; the dwelling was a meeting point; the intimate life of the individual was tied to the political life of a wider, often much wider, community. Domestic houses were used for worship. There might be insufficient means for a dedicated building; the difficulty or distance of travel might render a congregant's house a more regular center for worship; the possibility of persecution could render people unable to profess publicly; some believers eschewed formal structures as a matter of principle. Quakers met all these conditions: they gathered at a dwelling house, which often became acknowledged as a meeting house by the community, which further provided the location for a "Friends burying place."[194]

Irrespective of acreage or the affluence of its proprietor, the estate was a place to live, work, and die, but the bounds between public and private space were continually breached. Servants were recorded by name in parish registers, but buried on an estate: "John Child, in Feltons'; Captain Nicholas Stout, aged 55, who was freed from servitude by Captain John Williams, signed himself a gentleman when Williams' will was proved, but when Stout died 11 years later, he was buried on Mr. Frost's plantation.[195] Rev. William Leslie of St. John's, Barbados, noted that Daniel Clutterbuck was buried at Quintyne's, while in 1684 the parish coroner ordered that Hannah Tuffe, wife of Edward, be buried at John Millward's. Francis Seales was buried in situ because there were too few people to carry him to church.[196] It was usual for plantations to contain burial plots, with vaults, tombs, and memorials, so there could be multiple markers: a memorial in the (Anglican) church in Holetown reads "Sacred To the Memory of the Honorable William Holder who died the 11th of August 1705 aged 48 Years," his wife and grandson, "Who all were buried at the Family Estate of Black Rock in this Parish."[197] William was a cousin of the Quaker, John Holder, who stipulated that after his death, the house continue as a Meeting House.[198]

Buildings and place markers shaped a different place and a new identity. A presentment to the Grand Jury in Barbados called for the provision of schools, "Indispensibly Necessary" for "Unity Naturall Love and Affection which the Inhabitants have for the Places of their Nativity."[199] Robert Barrow's family was distressed that after he moved to Carolina he seemed not to want word from "thy Native Country old England."[200] Finding the commodity that flourished in local conditions could counteract any sense of alienation: Thomas Woodward applauded Sir John Colleton's plan to make wine in Albemarle, which demonstrated his "Zeale to this place." "Those that live upon a Place," he added, "are best able to Judge of the Place."[201]

John Ellis who had been in the West Indies over 20 years was "of Jamaica Esqr at present in the Kingdom of England," and George McKenzie left Darién for Jamaica and supplied the place name Far Enough, as in "far enough away from Courts and Kings."[202] There is also a Farenough in Old Providence. Moving in the other direction, (Sir) Samuel Husbands planned to leave the West Indies, "y^t Barbados security may become English," and to "fix" neighboring his Essex kinsman, Sir John Marshall.[203] Having maintained an active involvement in both places, we can study his language for sentiment.[204] Family affections propelled his resolve: the memory of his late wife induced gratitude; their daughter's duty toward her father provoked obligation. His new wife was excited by the prospect of a stately English dwelling house, betokened by a parcel of "this Country sweet-meats," as she chivvied her husband to add a marginal request for an "acc^t of the ffront of the [Essex] house, whither it be uniforme as also wither the rooms be lofty, & w^t rooms below staires & the heigth of ye Hall, & w^t manner of great parlor & little parlor, & whither the lights answere."[205] The Marshall family, all the while, continued to regard even continental Carolina as one of the "remote parts of the World."[206]

Society required both land and water to be traversed. In the smaller islands, settlement ribboned along coasts, individuals built storage facilities by the seaside, and ships sailed onto and off islands to suit the settlers. They communicated with each other along the coast, and, as the contiguous line of plots developed, parallel inland routes were created, such as our example of Mile and a Quarter, Barbados.[207] Lieutenant Richard Bayley, Gent., was established in Barbados by 1650.[208] By 1672, a councilor for St. Peter's—the only parish to stretch from east to west coast—his mill is shown near the sea on the windward northeast, connected by a road, via Mile and a Quarter, to "Coll Baylys well" just to the south of Speightstown on the west coast.[209] Edward Littleton was so impressed by vestry management of land and communication, that in the 1690s he recommended both the parish levy and Barbadian techniques of carriage and tree-felling as a means to extend, widen, level, and repair the roads in England. Since work would be carried out during summer, Barbados hoes would be much better than English spades for "pulling down Hills" of hard ground.[210] Despite Bridgetown's well-developed network of named streets, it retained a "broad path."[211] Jamaica was heavily wooded, so legislation for the "better amending and keeping clear the Common High-ways, and known broad Paths..., leading to Church and Market, and for laying out New High-ways, and turning Old High-ways, where it shall be needful," stipulated roads should be 60-feet wide in areas forested all around, 40-feet wide if forest was on one side only, and 20-feet wide in open ground, with instructions to plow through estates that cut across the chosen route.[212]

An important part of the English forces' plan to retake the mountainous Leeward Islands from the French involved making passage ways and keeping them clear through mountainous islands, but even in peace time the movement of peoples across the land had to be both facilitated and regulated.[213] Antigua was particularly backward in this respect and could not even claim mountainous and difficult terrain: highways were sorely neglected and "the Common Paths...allmost Impossible."[214] A threefold system of connection—private paths across estates, public paths, and highways—was born. The first, like Bayley's, was a socioeconomic resource in itself. One commentator on 1640s' Barbados offered the story of a planter more offended that a rider, taking a short-cut over his cornfield, refused repeated proffers of alcohol than that in trespassing he had damaged his crops.[215] Antiguan authorities attempted to create and control centralized markets and storage points, expanding from two to the so-called Six Towns: Falmouth, St. John's, Bridge Town, Carlisle Road, Bermudian Valley, and Parham Landing Place. They would regulate shipping, but freemen could dispose of personal property and merchandise anywhere.[216] The scheme was not popular, or even successful, but a relatively minor figure like Lawrence Crabb became empowered because his land was crossed by a path to Parham providing many with quicker and cheaper access to a port.[217] Other types of provision followed suit, with, for example, inland water sources—ponds and springs—or wharfs designated for public or private access.[218]

Continental colonies with inland waterways meant communication via water preceded that over land. When it fell to the Dutch, Surinam had few paths cleared through the jungle: connecting the towns of Tourarica and Paranam on the Surinam and Para Rivers respectively, and stretching around the south of Fort Willoughby and out to the "Sea Coastall drowned land."[219] This last was likely the route of "High Street," following the indigenous trail along higher ground—a pattern replicated on the north American mainland, at Charles Town, Carolina. Here, "Broad Path" ran to Goose Creek, and toward Virginia. It later became "Little Street," running northerly from Mrs. Mary Benson's Landing on the Ashley River.[220] John Stewart, who may have been one of the wharfingers in St. Michael's Barbados noted by Copen, subsequently diversified to Carolina.[221] In 1702 he extended his prime piece of Charles Town marshland, now marked in red ink on the Grand Model, with a further plot, next to "ye Creek or passage for boatts Left for publick," extending 15 feet from the middle of the creek.[222] Thus towns developed along rivers, catered for premises for those traveling in and out, and ended with the market at the waterside.[223]

Indigenous Americans seemed to travel with ease, displaying skills much admired by those who found any movement in an alien and hostile environment enervating. Europeans described small numbers traveling by *canoa*, while one mighty tree-trunk, hollowed, created a vessel holding 50 or 60 people: a *periago*.[224] The capacious *periago* facilitated travel between islands, and thus alliances between themselves and others. Courteen employed Guianan Kalinago to establish settlement and crops on Barbados, and Byam marshaled Surinam settlers against the Dutch by enlisting Kalinago to paddle the English up and down its rivers. Sir William Stapleton, on the other hand, who feared the indigenes above all, predicted a force of 2,500–3,000 in 50 *periagos* planned to attack Antigua, but islanders refused to pre-empt this unless all the Caribbean united in "national war."[225]

Islands were constructed as havens of stability (either Britons alone or in harmony with their American allies and African servants), besieged by hostile people (either Indians alone or directed by Europeans, harnessing their so-called "cruelties to eradicate their rivals). Barbadians who attempted to settle Tobago were attacked by a party from Trinidad, who happened to be following shoals, but it was conjectured that past experience of the Spanish had imbued them with an inveterate hatred of all white people.[226] During Sir Thomas Modyford's governorship of Jamaica, he complained against Francis, Lord Willoughby of Parham, for willfully attacking the indigenes of St. Lucia and St. Vincent, thereby alarming English people—more afraid of them than the French—in order to redirect the English to Willoughby's putative settlement on Antigua.[227] Twelve years later, the Kalinago attacked: "[T]hey have great opportunity to annoy the Leeward Islands, winds and currents making access easy, so that the English are forced to be always on their guard, and keep several files of men upon the watch; and three nights before and after the full moon (which gives the Indians light for their exploits) they are forced to double the guards, and make constant patrols of horse."[228]

This dialogue between expansive freedom and the danger of dispersal was repeated in Carolina.[229] Scattered people were more vulnerable to attack and less easy to control, and thus two governors were proposed: one for grand planters on one bank of the river and a second for lower-order religious sectaries on the other.[230] Later, the English made an alliance with the Cherokee to disperse the Yamasee from the "towns and settlements" in their midst, and it was suggested the "tract of land" called "The Yamasee settlement be parceled up and settled by migrants from elsewhere in the Caribbean, according to the customs that had developed in the country of Carolina."[231] Whitehall bureaucrats possessed a jaundiced view of settlement on the continent: "injurious to the nation, swallowing up great numbers of people" who were able "to produce food and raiment for their [own] livelihood." Smaller islands (therefore excepting Jamaica) were co-dependent, remaining tied by their size to the mother country.[232]

Between fixity and mobility lay the frontier: on the one side, escapees or rejects of the control, authority, and restriction synonymous with stable settlement; and on the other, those who had retreated beyond, or had yet to be brought under the control of settlement. Land frontiers were problematic in mainland colonies, such as Carolina's notorious buffer community at Goose Creek.[233] The malign influence of the Spanish in both Jamaica and Carolina was blamed for escaped-African concentrations of "towns" which created internal frontiers and it took less than ten years of English possession of Jamaica before the authorities expressed alarm at the disruption to both production and good order of domestic runaways, both white and "Blacks from Barbados" established on the north side of the island.[234] Therefore, the Jamaica Accord included measures to break the frontier: liberty for the

Spanish to trade slaves with the British, while the "free negroes" in the mountains were to enjoy all the rights and privileges of the English—including a militia regiment—provided they made submission, lived and spoke as the English.[235] Communication by slaves among themselves was controlled by tickets to travel if it stretched further than four miles beyond their estate.[236] In the following decade the authorities in St. Christopher's complained of runaways who had escaped to the mountains, and who robbed or fired plantations. Both black and white were encouraged to recover them, at a bounty of 500 pounds sugar alive and 300 pounds for a head.[237] Neighboring Antigua repaired and widened roads. The Assembly tried to halt moves to have runaways executed, but when clashes between runaway communities and troops escalated, they weakened, and attempted runaways would have a leg cut off. To execute runaways was not profitable.[238] The evidence of John Style of Jamaica illustrates the complexity. He had himself been imprisoned by the governor, whom he considered a "conquering" Cromwellian soldier planter. Post-Restoration, therefore, Style's measurement of community frontier became subscription to the royal Oath of Allegiance. He could appeal over the head of the Jamaican authorities, re-cast his jailers as those who breached the frontier, and slave runaways became insurgents into British politics, since, being drawn from the Indian, mulatto, and African communities, they had not taken the Oath either, thus creating a united internal enemy of those "foreign" to British values.[239] Runaways from Spanish settlements were not welcome evidence of the brutality of rivals, but a subversive enemy presence: Style also complained that slaves from Cuba were conspiring with a Jamaican jailer bewitched by republicanism.[240]

Autonomous communities were developing, particularly in places in which the terrain and relative sparseness of population made recapture more difficult. The dense rainforests of the Guianas offered the safest havens, and the marsh and islands of the Carolinas were also good for escape. Resistance in Jamaica was so strong during the wars of the 1730s that it is hard not to conclude that it was already well coalesced in the seventeenth century, with runaways from English settlements as well as those already present from the days of Spanish possession.[241] Under French control, St. Christopher's was described as having semi-clandestine assemblies of slaves, who came together in the woods to love and dance and then returned to their plantations; or those who were so brutally treated they ran away to establish permanent settlements in the woods and mountains "where they live like so many Beasts; then they are call'd *Marons,* that is to say, Savages."[242] The English preferred to stick with "runaways": dissidents were always abandoning their obligations, their fixity, their settlement. Servants shipped from Europe attempted to leave the process at various points, with proprietors and indenturers expected to pay additional costs to masters and agents to keep all the passengers together. There is, in fact, less evidence of slave runaways, because, particularly if they were able to establish themselves as autonomous communities, it highlighted a complete absence of social and economic control and thus of authority.[243]

Piracy also combined illicit movement—the rejection of prior obligations—with illicit fixity—the construction of alternative community. Only toward the end of the century were suppressive measures initiated, by individuals now sufficiently tied to British authority not to be as keen to circumvent regulation as anyone else, and with the British state having established infrastructures sufficiently robust to distinguish, determine, and police licit and illicit dealings. Early-century references to piracy therefore followed similar tropes to those for runaways—a practice carried out by others on English ships, goods, and individuals. Sir Thomas Lynch complained of Fitzgerald, a "renegade Irish rogue," and the pirate, Yhallahs. Fitzgerald hanged an Englishman because he ran away from Yhallahs but refused to rob his compatriots. Captain Francis Witherborn consorted with Yhallahs, the Spanish, and the French. In Nevis, Sir William Stapleton protested of the Dutch in Curaçao, and the Spanish who threatened his recipient of a commission to hunt pirates.[244] Transgressive behavior was that considered foreign. The other side of the coin was that pirates' indeterminate but ubiquitous presence provided a smokescreen for those who wished to create a life anew in the West Indies—the pretext that his ordination papers had been seized by Martinique pirates enabled Irishman, John Michell, to build a career as a minister of the church in Jamaica—or a catch-all term for anyone who might cloud one's bona fides.[245] The seas between territories made for fluidity on the water and constant escape and adventure. Read Elding, Deputy-Governor of the Bahamas, believing the West Indies infested with pirates, forbade any correspondence with the Scots at Darién, though at huge distance, and complained of Danish activity. Bahamas, Turks and Caicos, the sea islands, and the Outer Banks of Carolina formed a "frontier" of what Elding called "maroon islands," that is, uninhabited, ideal terrain to which pirates could escape, moor up, and establish an onshore community—a "ritual lodgment"—thereby inverting the language of war in which a lodgement was the secure enclave within territory captured from the enemy.[246] The following year Elding was arrested for the same crime.[247] Timothy Tynes of Bermuda conspired with mariner, Cradock Shellito, to seize the ship of a Frenchman serving the King of Spain, throw the captain overboard, and "repatriate" his ship, goods, and slave, Pedro, to Turks' Island, "a moroon key near the Bahama Islands."[248] The previous governor of Bermuda, John Hope, had been even clearer, and despaired of Bermudans' rejection of the benefits of fixity: "As a Reasonable Man prizes the Advantages & the Satisfaction that he enjoys in a well regulated Society; so the Great Good of these People is (what they call) a Maroon Life: This is wandering from one uninhabited Island to another (in their sloops), Fishing for Wrecks, & Trading with Pyrat's, & Living not like Animals that are indued with Reason." They loved a "Wandering Life and illegal Trade."[249]

Pirates pierced, subverted, and traversed the frontier and majority notions of place. Mooring his ship on a sandbar off Charles Town to blockade the port, "Blackbeard" Edward Teach and his crew paraded their "insolence," "publickly, in the Sight of all People; and tho' [the townsfolk] were fired with the utmost Indignation against them...they were forced to let the Villains pass with Impunity."[250] At Topsail, along the Outer Banks, feigning to clean his vessel, Teach ran it aground, "as if it had been done undesignedly, and by Accident" and thus captured the sloop on which he called for help.[251] The rest of the account of the activities of Teach and his fellows stressed first, that they were operating at both a territorial and intellectual/psychological frontier—"In the Month of July, these Adventurers came off the Capes"—while at the same time affording themselves an advantageous, transitory location, with ships leaving for Glasgow, Philadelphia, Bermuda, Antigua, Barbados, and Boston.[252] They maintained their motion to escape the authorities, but contained a community onboard ship or fixed at a mooring. One of Teach's voyages captured a Guinea Brigantine transporting 90 slaves. The pirates transferred the slaves to the vessel of one Yates, who it transpired, had been seeking an opportunity to abandon the pirate way of life, and so delivered the slaves and himself into harbor at North-Edisto River, south of Charles Town.[253] The authorities were in this instance "fortunate"—in itself an admission of transgression—but while this is an incidence of surrender, the pirates of the sand bars along the Carolina coast delivered Africans and escapees to places where they could exercise agency, either within autonomous communities or as crew. Several who sailed with Teach were black, and on their capture, the Virginia Council debated whether citizenship of the commonwealth of pirates superseded their chattel status in law, such that the fellowship of crew should now be tried with equity.[254] One of the tasks of authority was to secure and control place, and diverse individuals were rendered equal by refuting it, by operating parallel frontiers, communities, movement, and interconnectedness. Genuine freedom of movement was only possible when no one group asserted primacy.[255]

The pirate frontier was chronological: audacious stories of Captain Kidd, Blackbeard, Henry Morgan, and Woodes Rogers marked its death knell. The long seventeenth century was the era of freedom of movement, agency, and the avoidance of regulation. Into the eighteenth, the center reined in its wayward and diverse territories, imposed its imposts and taxes and duties, codified and rationalized law, and settled profitable land with loyal subjects. Freedom to traverse the Atlantic became a reward for loyalty from merchants, governors, or military. Goods could no longer be shipped from anywhere, but had to be signed out by a customs' official. Shipping orders became printed certificates, their wording increasingly standardized, requiring the goods to leave "in good order and well conditioned," to be subject only to the vagaries of the seas' conditions, and confirmed by three bills of lading, to ensure at least one could be attested.[256]

Merchants' lives were predicated on movement, along with anything or anyone with whom they traded. Goods unsold or debts uncollected tied one detrimentally to place.[257] In April 1675 Richard Worsam stood at Dover, watching ships pass and wondering if any came from Barbados, where his family had plantation interests. However, if he wished to receive news of them, it would have to follow his travel around the low countries.[258]

Traffic—constant movement—was secondary to the burgeoning communities of the Caribbean, but started to both define and undermine it. To "truck" barely escaped prejorative usage, invariably connoting a slight or unprincipled thing. It was often applied to the barter of good for good, and thus when applied to trade with indigenes came to define how trivially they regarded precious metals and gems, and increasingly defined trade with and in non-European people. Indigenous people were ever more excluded from community, but incorporated into the market in slave labor, to be shipped around the Americas, or transported to Europe as cultural curios.[259] Plantation slavery overshadowed the later century, with the Slave Trade determining movement between black and white, African and European.

As the century progressed, so trade, truck, and traffic were something to be fostered by the home government, such that the Caribbean became dependent, and therefore either exploited trade or was exploited by traders. The empire relied on customs, taxes, and duties, and the imperial administration did not focus on the land far away, not even on those who worked it or owned it, unless in profit and tax to be accrued back into markets, banks, and accounts in Britain. Within the torrid zone, administrations were at odds with the merchant, who flitted in and out of their purview. Governor Ashton tried to encourage "those that come to live by planting [and] not by pedling." "[A] man may be worth an Island to yo^w" was a view that had not changed at the end of the century, when Britons had still to be reminded that it was the people in the colonies who created the empire.[260] Trade across the Atlantic, to or fro, cut across Caribbean development, the stability of those who lived there, and the growth of local custom and law. As an illustration of the confusion, a ship's master, anchoring off Barbados, was accused of landing slaves illegally, because a doctor had not gone aboard to check for plague sores. The captain first denied, and sought to change, the place of the ship's embarkation, but was nevertheless accused of a breach of the Acts of Trade. The ship was marked and reported for prosecution to the Court of Admiralty in London. Meanwhile, the Judge of the Court of Common Pleas in Barbados, a "merchant of Bridgetown," connived with the captain to claim all creeks and bays to be integral to the lands of the Caribbean islands, such that judgment in such cases fell under local jurisdiction.[261]

The narrative of place in the Caribbean is convoluted, contested, and fluid. A multiplicity of human actors, with differing sets of cultural assumptions, was challenged by circumstance. Spatial and environmental awareness was shaped by soil type, rockiness, heat, aridity, vegetation, with the earth, the water, and the air agencies in themselves. Nature was a tool of a greater, extra-human force; whether the hurricane or drought signified the wrath of the Christian God, material objects formed the bridge between this life and the afterlife, or the spirits of the ancestors could be channeled through the monkey god. Everyone participated in a continuous dialogue between movement and rest. What distinguished European comment about the seventeenth-century Caribbean was the narrative of control. The English needed to know how human action might affect being under the control of the Christian God, how claims to the earth might be rationalized, or how the new world might be brought to serve the interests of individual representatives of the old. The desire to control could be viewed either as a grand, hundred-year narrative which posits as a start date the first footing of British people in the region and marks as the cutoff point that in which the control of the new world seemed to have been wrested back by the old; or one can hone in on an individual's personal struggle. What they have in common is the plan—the degree of deliberation which marks how much and what a person could control.

The former narrative is that in which the eighteenth-century empire was fueled by trade in luxury commodities and slaves. It is tempting to see an increasing imperial and mercantile mission in the second half of the seventeenth century engulfing the individual ambitions of settlers with dreams of a different and autonomous life. But for some, the light of ambition remained undimmed. In 1717, Ayrshire gentleman Sir Robert Montgomery could be explicit that his "Establishment Of a New Colony" was "design'd."[262] The "Correctness of this Model" was the "Margravate of Azilia," a perfect square—"You must suppose a level, dry, and fruitful Tract of Land"—of 256,000 acres, that is 400 square miles, divided into 116 "Squares, each of which has a House in the Middle...Every one a Mile on each side, or 640 Acres...bating only for the High Ways, which divide them" (Figure 1.1). Each gentleman would have the same allocation, with no opportunity to engross, and thus the only means to outdo their neighbors was to improve the land. It was designed to be self-contained, as the "Middle hollow Square" full of streets which crossed each other would be the city, surrounded by a "large void Space" which provided for a prospect of the metropolis. In its center would be the margrave's house "which is to be his constant residence, or the Residence of the Governor" to contain "all sorts of Edifices for Dispatch of Business." Montgomery published an engraving that was, indeed, the very model of correctness.[263]

Seven years later, Bishop George Berkeley of Cloyne published his plans for a college. Again, the requirement was for self-containment: but "necessary to pitch upon a place which maintains a constant intercourse with all the other colonies" the commerce of which lay not with Europe, but with America.[264] In later editions of his works was his plan for "The City of Bermuda Metropolis of the Summer Islands," based on a pentagon, reached by a principal street that carried through to the central "steeple" (physically separated from the classical-style church), and continuing with the classical themes, there would be academies, baths, porticos, and groves of cypress.[265] At the heart of the metropolis, Berkeley's plan included the most intimate of deliberative plots. Each building was to have its own enclosed garden (the word "yard" seldom used, not even for the area reserved as a burying place), and there were to be two "Publick parks and Groves into which back doors open from all the ajacent Gardens." The garden was the place in which one planted or gathered provision for personal subsistence. One of the earliest actions of the first settlers of Barbados was to designate a garden to feed

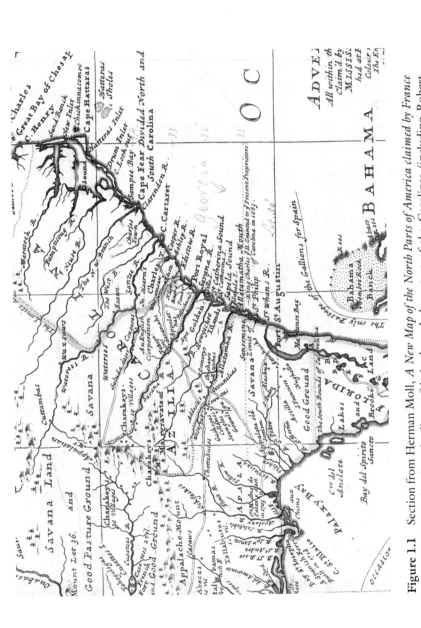

Figure 1.1 Section from Herman Moll, *A New Map of the North Parts of America claimed by France* (London, 1720), showing the lines of latitude and the extent of the Carolinas (including Robert Montgomery's buffer zone of Azilia), and the respective positions of Bermuda and the Bahamas. Courtesy of the John Carter Brown Library at Brown University.

the soldiers, and it acquired values of foundation, and of nurturing one's connection to place.[266] The Caribbean environment remained one that produced people with special qualities. Christopher Monck's martial prowess would be nurtured in Jamaica: for Berkeley, nature, sun, and "virgin earth" would produce an empire of wisdom, nobility, and virtue that would eclipse "barren" Europe. Montgomery referred to charming landscapes, unoccupied, except by indigenes, "all artless, and uncultivated, as the Soil, which fosters them."[267] The lord's task of managing the garden and the role of the people who tended it was important and acquired status.[268] Elisha Mellowes specified his desire for a Quaker burial, but made specific reference that he be buried near those children who had predeceased him, in "my garden."[269] In the discussion of burial location as a signifier of sentimental attachment to place, we encountered Robert Cunyngham, patriotic Scot more at home in Cayon, St. Christopher's. Cunyngham loved his garden there. He had a provision section, a potato piece, and grew "Budget Beans and Okara." In July 1729 he tended to the old fountain in the upper parterre, which presumes there was a new and a lower one.[270] It was the fashion to plant shady "walks" in lands so torrid; Cunyngham's were lined with olives. There were lemons and limes, plantains and bananas. Others planted walks of coffee bushes, but Cunyngham was gifted his coffee plants from neighbors and planted them in clusters either in the garden near the house or by the lower Cayon River.[271] The painstaking care with which Cunyngham kept his waste books, in his miniscule, neat, almost printed script is testimony to his sense of belonging. Nothing says it more eloquently, however, than the change of heart, whereby the younger man who had specified a wish to be buried at the foot of his parents in the kirk in Ayrshire, in his 70s, confined in Edinburgh, professed he was "Robert Cunyngham of Cayon in the Island of St Christophers in America" who bequeathed his soul to God, "who gave it, and my Body to the Earth. I desire it may be laid in my Garden" among the limes and the coffee and the olive groves.[272]

CHAPTER 2

Resource

"Provision grounds," gardens, and the loftiest ambitions of The Metropolis of Bermuda or the Margravate of Azilia possessed a common design to mix and diversify planting. "*Barmuda,...* possest by a Plantation of *English*," was a place that "agreeth well with their temper," producing "happinesse and prosperitie,...where they enjoy the meanes of true religion and salvation...where the government is good, without rigour and oppression, the place heathfull and temperate...they are freed from all extreme care and toyle...they have food in abundance...with other things needfull to the body...and...commodities meete for Trade, by which they may better and advance their estates."[1] Despite admitting that "gay Descriptions of new Countries raise a Doubt of their Sincerity...the *Picture* drawn beyond the *Life*," Carolina was to Robert Montgomery "*God's* own Choice" and "It were a Shame shou'd we confine the Fruitfulness of such a rich and lovely Country to some single Product" when there were so many others indigenous or "equally adapted to their Soil, and Climate."[2] A hundred years between the two, Britons retained a mission to plant man within a fertile, diverse Eden, but granted hindsight, warned that the reductive exploitation of monoculture would be their Fall.

In the West Indies, three narratives ran concurrently, described here as natural resource, exchange resource, and merchantable resource. Agents of the mother-state constructed these narratives sequentially. For them, the region was not a diverse collection of self-sustaining territories, but dependent nurseries, which produced the commodities, which raised the taxes, which fired the economy, which ran the empire of the court of the Stuart monarchs. In charting the change from seventeenth-century competition to eighteenth-century mercantile empire, historians relied on an account produced by a royalist exile who spent a few years in Barbados: Richard Ligon's *Trve & Exact History Of the Island of Barbados* was published in 1657. Its frontispiece laid out the early seventeenth-century footprint and set up the narratives of natural, exchange, and merchantable resource. First came history, "told me by the most ancient Planters...and what they had by tradition from their Predecessors": what was there when they came. This, they mastered through survey (a map, "as also the Principall Trees and Plants there"). Finally, Ligon revealed the means of transformation: "Together with the

Ingenio that makes the Sugar—[not sugar or sugars, but *the* sugar]—with the Plots of the severall Houses, Roomes, and other places, that are used in the whole processe of Sugar-making; *viz.* the Grinding-room, the Boyling-room, the Filling-room, the Curing-house, Still-house, and Furnaces."[3] Ligon had pictures (a rarity), placed Barbados at the heart of the region, and made sugar the aim of his narrative and foundation of the region's wealth and importance to Britain, which "makes that Spot of ground/ As rich, as any 'twixt the Poles." The civil wars and Interregnum were the turning point that created fortunes and gave birth to the Caribbean Empire.[4] Thus, Sir Dalby Thomas, writing around 1690, knew from Ligon that sugar was already present in the English Caribbean in the 1640s. Settlers had used it to make a refreshing drink, until James Drax persuaded the Dutch to divulge the "Art...to make it; since which time by the many ingenious men the last Civill war necessitated to seek their fortunes in that new world, there has been found out so many severall sorts of Mills, Coppers, Boylers, Stoves, Pots, and other Tools and Engins, for Planting and pressing the Canes, Boyling-up, Separating, Cleansing, and Purifying the Juice and Sugar, as well as for drawing Spirits of admirable use from the Mellasses, that we at present exceed all the Nations in the world in the true Improvement of that Noble Juice of the Cane."[5]

The traditional view, underpinned by Ligon's account, is therefore that a motley of civil-war exiles set up the engine of empire, but so exponential and unregulated was its production, that postwar regimes gradually regained political and economic control. The Navigation Ordinance (1651), and a series of Navigation Acts, which West Indians abbreviated portentously to "The Navigation," channeled trade into English shipping, ports, and markets.[6] Colonial revenue was tapped using taxes, duties, and levies: first in the Caribbean, then on entry into England; then goods reexported out of England were subject to a "drawback." Planters established before the Restoration regarded the Navigation and the customs' measures that gained pace under Charles II, managed by London-based aristocrats on the Board of Trade and Plantations, as the erosion of their liberty. Taxation accelerated under Charles's brother, James VII and II. When William of Orange overthrew James in 1688/1689, the colonies had to make their contribution to his foreign wars. The period from 1688 to the 1730s consolidated economics around the politics of Union, the Protestant Succession, and ensuring that Britannia ruled the waves: British resourcefulness perfected through inventiveness, enterprise, and industry.

But the alternative origin narrative, all naivety, innocence, and wonderment, survived, though it would increasingly struggle to be heard above the heat and the roar of the engines. Samuel Lee noted that the further mankind traveled, the more deliciousness was found on the hills of Canaan, rhapsodizing the Barbados pineapple "that supplies and transcends expectation with new and rasive flavours, and tunes our vocal Instruments for new Songs to bear a part with the harmony of Angels for ever."[7] "Vegetives...afford[ed] shape, taste, and delight/ To th'Sense," though they were "candied" into computations and designs for a sugar plantation. British commentators were not beyond idealization, assisted by the fact that so much of the Caribbean archipelago consisted of islands, as had been Sir Thomas More's "new Ile called Utopia."[8] Sir Francis Bacon's New Atlantis was "a great Island, which according to *Plato*, [had] perished in the Ocean," "[f]or it is the Model of a College to be Instituted by some King who philosophizeth, for the Interpreting of Nature, and the Improving of Arts. [Bacon] did (it seems) think of finishing this Fable, by adding to it a Frame of Laws, or a kind of *Vtopian* Commonwealth; but he was diverted by his desire of Collecting the Natural History which was first in his esteem."[9] It was edited by Bacon's secretary, chaplain, and literary executor, William Rawley, in whose 1658 version the benign governor speaks of "*this happy Island, where we now stood,...known to few, and yet knew most of the Nations of the World;...as if we thought this Land a Land of Magicians, that sent forth Spirits of the Ayr.*"[10] Bacon's Salomon's College of wise men, for "enlarging of the bounds of Human Empire, to the effecting of all things possible," predicated the island be inhabited, directly counter to the advice on place which he offered potential planters.[11]

Toward the end of this account of a lost ideal, we glimpse an island like that of the patriarch Prospero, who can summon spirits, enabling the bard to muse on nature, magic, conceptions of utopia and its opposites. He was probably inspired by stories of the wreck of the *Sea Adventurer* which resulted in the peopling of the "pure soil" of Bermuda. Various accounts of this place—rocks in the middle of the ocean—span the long seventeenth century, replete with idealistic visions of what the British empire could become.[12] In verses composed "upon those late-discovered isles," arch-royalist, Edmund Waller, was sure that Heaven had "kept this spot of earth uncursed,/ To show how all things were created first." But his utopian garden was subsequently spoilt by the English. They planted tobacco—"the blessed tenant feeds/ On precious fruit, and pays his rent in weeds"—and fought a ferocious battle of tide, tempest, and man against whales that beached onshore.[13] Andrew Marvell steered his account of Bermuda between pastoral and heroic and maybe also between garden paradise and puritan politics.[14]

The islands' windblown isolation produced a self-contained, semi-tropical garden of species unknown elsewhere.[15] The governor of Bermuda could therefore write to his Virginian counterpart: "Our Plantation commenceth a Commerce unto you: for by this Ship I have sent you suche of our prime fruicts, as (I heare) you have not, but assure my selfe you would have."[16] Their mastery of virgin soil also allowed the English to turn the Spaniards—"pilgrims, who in their peregrinations, being cast upon this mayden earth, fled from her embraces" and their devil's island—into a sexualized conquest of bed and board: the English "by the like accidents, comeing to have a sight and knowledge of her perfections, have accepted the offer, and taken her to wife (as it wer) by a willinge and ioyfull residence." Benign English husbandry introduced other West Indian plants and Governor Tucker was thus described as the creator of both a plantation and a garden, railed with fig trees.[17] As the actions of settlers and investors changed the purpose and the image of Bermuda, its reputation as an ideal nevertheless persisted. Berkeley proposed Bermuda as the site of his theological college because its isolation made it insusceptible to fleshly or financial temptations, and a century of accounts—Waller is named—rendered the islands "the most healthy and delightful that could be wished."[18]

The Anglophone narrative of natural resource had, in itself, two strands that ran in parallel. Both defined the region through lists of exotic fecundity: one assumed land and people to be self-contained and complete; the other, unfinished, and ripe for improvement. Allusions to the Bible, ancient philosophers, past voyages, and other locations were introduced as and when appropriate: these accounts must then be sifted for travelers' tales, tall stories, and the reading habits of audiences fascinated by extremes because they imbibed their color from the security of their domestic drabness. Many accounts were poesy: adventure, daring and legend; exotica, and sometimes erotica. Elysium, a term reserved for the heroic epics of the Heathens, by which were meant the Ancients, was not to be found in the Americas; Raleigh's Guiana possessed the only Arcadia.[19] In praise of the "project" of his friend, Captain John Smith, George Wither saw in the Virginias not perfection, but prospect. There was potential "To make more happie our Posterities," by "order[ing] *Nature's* fruitfulnesse a while/ In that rude *Garden,* you [Smith] *New England* stile;/ With present good, ther's hope in after-daies/ Thence to repair what *Time* and *Pride* decaies/ In this rich kingdome. And the spatious *West/* Beeing still more with *English* blood possest."[20]

Subsequent British descriptions of the American tropics pursued the practical application of incoming values in order to perceive the potential of an already rich and fruitful place to become more so. Narratives of resource to be improved tended to take others' descriptions and complain how little had been achieved. These tended to be the Christianized, and particularly Protestant accounts. Sir Francis Drake was their chosen one, summoning up the blood of Englishmen lest they fail in their projections, with rallying cries against Catholic enemies.[21] Drake's lesson was that it was the destiny of the English to grow rich from conquest. But this would not be achieved by planting; nor by the permanent settlement which engaged with West Indian resource. This would be accomplished by raiding, snatching, and exploitation for the benefit of those at home. In the previous chapter we encountered Sir Samuel Husbands, an Englishman who felt he had outstayed Barbados's resources. He was a conventional Anglican, and therefore had to attribute to divine Providence a life that had separated him from his extended family and kin back in England. When he described the West Indian ideal, therefore, he did so with irony. Writing to his kinsman that he was soon to quit "this paradize of the world," he was quoting directly the relief of the despairing Roanoke adventurers for whom Drake had provided a providential escape from failure and a ship back to England.[22]

Anglophone accounts of adventure in the West Indies, and descriptions of unfamiliar flora, fauna, and peoples, tend to be literary, though the source, intent, and audience of the few visual representations are similarly open to question. At the end of the sixteenth century, John White had produced exquisite watercolors of the Carolinian Algonquians, which were then adapted by the Liège Calvinist, Theodore de Bry, disseminated around Europe in printed engravings, and transformed from reportage into propaganda.[23] The "pictures of sondry things" were described as "counterfeited," meaning that as original watercolors they replicated something real in nature; but by the time de Bry's engravings appeared in print, in Hariot's account of the Roanoke voyages, or numerous subsequent images of indigenous life, the term had come to mean "fake."[24] White's illustrations of the Secoton and Pomeiooc settlements, various means to catch and cook fish, ceremonies and customs of death, authority or commemoration, and of flora and fauna are of the "natural life" of northern Carolina, and thus, while never free from the bias of the gaze, seem to represent interactions of people and environment which were sustainable, symbiotic, and circular. These are illustrations of the Algonquians' resourcefulness. By the time the illustrations were massproduced in print, these were accounts of resources to be exploited: in "the new found land of Virginia...the commodities there found and to be raysed, as well marchantable, as others for victuall, building and other necessarie vses for those that are and shalbe the planters there."[25] For visual representation of the elemental resourcefulness of indigenes—including *how* treetrunks were hollowed and stretched to make the *periago*; trapping parrots in Trinidad and Nicaragua; or scaring rabbits with fire to drive them into a hurdle fence called a *barbacone* where they were killed and skewered onto sticks—we must rely on a French account of the late sixteenth century.[26]

Did early colonial explorers encounter what two centuries later they would describe as a "noble savage"?[27] Accounts of presettled peoples throughout the Americas focused on customs, characteristics—whether their "tawny" skin was inherent, the result of exposure to the sun, their going about naked, or painting each other—and on their capacity for (European) civility, used to justify the mission to civilize.[28] British accounts of the peoples further south are subjective and superficial, but nevertheless discriminating and anthropological. John Scott's description of the Guianas between the Waini and Corentyne Rivers distinguished between the Arawak—the best humored, just and generous people—and the Warao, who did not share others' pleasure in diversions such as gardens, drinking or dancing, but were a people "blood Treacherous," best approached with weapons at the ready. Each description was articulated in terms of the indigenes, their health, and the commodities of the land; that is, of knowledge as a natural resource.[29] Thus the transfer of both plants and people from Guiana to Barbados, the latter uninhabited when Powell first set foot there, allowed the English to claim original right, with indigenes' plants, knowledge, and agency a resource, along with the Englishmen's labor.[30] Ligon's attempts to make a pie crust with cassava flour involved him in "trials" and "failings" until a woman passed on the "secret," and therefore it was to be left to "the *Indians*, whom we trust to make it, because they are best acquainted with it." He pedestrianized both exotic object and arcane knowledge: "I am too apt to flie out in extravagant digressions; for, the thing I went to speak of, was bread only."[31]

In the hands of a literary romancer, the flora and fauna of the Guianas were strange and "such as Art cannot imitate," and the natives were not those the British "make use of," but traded with on equal terms. Their features, color, flesh-piercing, and exposure were the cause of neither curiosity nor shame, "so like our first parents before the Fall."[32] Aphra Behn's indigenes had no conception of a lie, and "simple nature is [their] most harmless, inoffensive and vertuous Mistress. 'Tis she alone... that better instructs the World, than all the Inventions of Man: religion wou'd here but destroy that Tranquillity they possess by Ignorance; and Laws wou'd but teach 'em to know Offence, of which they have no Notion... They have a Native Justice, which knows no Fraud; and they understand no Vice, or Cunning, but when they are taught by the *White Men*." They embodied "an absolute *Idea* of the first State of Innocence, before Man knew how to sin."[33] Like Shakespeare in his study of Prospero's island visited by jaded European sophisticates, Behn created idealized types in order to explore European notions of nobility and cruelty, cognoscence and cunning.

Ethnohistory has attempted to restore the focus on indigenous peoples of the north American continent by eradicating from the discourse any terms which imply judgment by European values—civilized, advanced, primitive, savage, or barbarous—while presenting cultures and knowledge not only in parity with that of Europe, but similar in scope, structure, and manner.[34] We are given conflicting accounts of white peoples' intellect, wrestling with their fear and wonderment in order to understand an alien way of life, or glimpsing opportunities to shape the minds of receptive naïfs. But neither frees us from the narrative of resource. The intellect of the European visitor was a resource, stimulated in contact with new knowledge. The knowledge of the native was a resource, to be embraced and tapped as appropriate; shunned and condemned if expedient. Thus, in their new environment, Britons not only described natural resource, but how natural resource could be *used*. Thus the encounter between the natural resource of the old and the new worlds (old and new in themselves transposable depending on which side of the Atlantic one was standing) became an exchange. Britons developed their list of "necessaries." Exchange with indigenous people could be of knowledge, of things necessary for survival, or of objects that embedded contested attributions of esteem—pearls, beads, feathers, alcohol, guns—aiming to maintain that ideal which Behn described as "perfect Amity," but in fact introducing British ingenuity.[35] This was adding value. In White's watercolor of the ten-year-old daughter of a Pomieooc chief, she holds out to her mother the beaded necklace and the expensive English doll she has been given with what appears to be joy, a recognition not only that this was a high-status family within Pomieooc society, but that the English knew the equivalence of value judgments in their gifts.[36] One hundred years later, only £50 was allocated for "Indian trade" in South Carolina, of which the biggest single item was for 240 pounds of glass beads, along with agricultural tools and "10 Striped Suites at 10^s 6^d P sute."[37] Samuel Clarke gave a description of (important) tribute and grave goods among the natives of Virginia, but several English people were sent there specifically to make (unimportant) beads for the purposes of trade.[38]

With romantic idealism came a large dose of pragmatism: Britons required that which was necessary. This did not have to be expedient or pedestrian. Accounts were pregnant with colorful descriptions of the prerequisites for a good life. Indigenes could teach Britons what was good to eat, what grew in the conditions, how to build shelter so as to make the best of the climate and conditions, what predators to avoid; not only things, but also the ethics of value in this new world. It is difficult to illustrate this without producing lists: most contemporary accounts started with a catalogue. Nathaniel Butler said of Bermuda that its "soil by its nature produces a great variety of simples," that is, plants possessing inherent, unmixed, or unprepared medicinal properties.[39] A variety of other plants had yet to be given "name" or "use" and were thus temporarily deprived of "benefit," but "time and application" would reveal these and they began to be referenced—the prickly pear and the "poisonous weed"—according to their "effects."[40] "The sky has also done her share for these islands," and thus there were a variety of fowl, little birds, those with a ready supply of eggs, the gathering of which was immediately restricted so as to remain self-sustaining, and exotica sometimes rendered familiar: the longtail (*Phaeton lepturus catesbyi*) named the "tropic bird" for shying away from northern climes; and the night-active "pimlico," with a call reminding Londoners of the sounds from the taverns.[41] The seas were generous in yielding fish, familiar and not, shellfish, amphibians, turtles and tortoises, and fresh drinking water, wholesome when it filtered through the sands. While some of these effects had been named by "the Americans," the uninhabited and remote nature of the islands presupposed that stage two, consequent on that which nature or Providence provided, was the result of the resourcefulness of English people. God had left very few warnings for those who managed to land on Bermuda: plants that caused rashes or blisters were not seriously toxic; there were no poisonous creatures; and the only "unpleasant conditions" were wind and worms. Thus, the efforts required to render the bounty useful were "necessary antidotes to guard against idleness." The puritan mentality regarded the Land of Cockayne, where sleeping men gained nourishment from that which flew or swam unaided into the body, as a dystopia. It was necessary to the godly functioning of British people that they display endeavor, industry, and resourcefulness. "[B]esides these natural products of the earth, providence and work," they introduced "fig trees, numerous plantains, plenty of pomegranates many vines, oranges and lemon trees, wild olives, a profusion of mulberry trees, fine tobacco...Indian corn," tuberous sweet potatoes and yams, turkeys and hens, cows, pigs, and rabbits. Goats, geese, and doves fared less well. In setting the stage of English settlement in Bermuda, Butler took care to observe that this was no poetic fiction.[42] The accounts of increasing British presence in the region were defining their own hegemony, applying their ingenuity to the status quo, and imposing the values which they consider necessary and advantageous. Paralleling the way in which they had defined place through settlement, they began to apply design to the development of resource.

Seldom was there a representation of a golden age that could not be improved upon, or one that was only ruined by the addition of British industry and design in the transformation of commodity and trade. Such was exchange resource. The innate quality, condition, and therefore value of land, people, and things spoke of convenient and easy access; what William Bullock would describe as "natural commodities."[43] As the providence of the British West Indies did not seem destined to foster greed for gold as it had for Spain, estimations of value were borrowed from elsewhere within the Spanish experience. "Cacao, a fruit like Almonds," was "of great use and high esteem as well with the Spaniards as Natives... both to eat and drinke, but especially to drink, it yeelding a liquor exceeding wholsome and pleasant, with some composition they use maketh it no way inferior to high-country white-wine or Sherry-sack"; as was "*Piemente*, or *Jamaica Pepper*, a spice of the form of *East-India Pepper*, very Aromatical, and of a curious *Gousto*, having the mixt taste of divers Spices"—that is, allspice—which grew in Jamaica "in great plenty, wild in the *Mountains*. But the *Spaniards* did sett a high esteeme thereon, and exported it as a very choise *Commodity*, as indeed it is; and now it is begun to be planted by the *English*, and will become a good *Commodity*."[44] Thus there were tradable commodities, first between indigenes and newcomers; then among all of the newcomers to America. This effected and affected the balance between necessaries and commodities. A warning was issued against planting Jamaica with "Indian" (natural) commodities, for if the settlers of Jamaica were able to feed themselves, there would be no need of the New England trade, in which the privateers sold their precious booty cheaply to Jamaica merchants, who in turn bought high-quality wine, brandy, and foodstuffs.[45]

The keywords were "choice" and "curious": a premium on items possessed of rarity because they could only be produced in the torrid zone. Bermuda could distinguish itself from Virginia, as Nathaniel Butler had early realized, and nearly 100 years later, Sir Bevill Granville of Barbados could ingratiate himself with the governor of a "winter country" like New York with the "produce only of a warm Climate." Heat, so detrimental to the health, well-being, and temper of the newcomers, could be harvested and bring a piercing flash of burning sun to cold Britons: Granville's present to Cornbury traveled with a Colonel Harding, moving to cooler climes for the sake of his health. What was introduced to and consumed by Britons, as the indigenous production of the tropics, brought the outside in, naturalized the exotic, and tamed its magical, alien qualities into something utilitarian. It was commodious in its restorative value. Thus relationships could be sweetened, quarrels softened, inflammations brought down. Granville sent citron water—rough clear spirit flavored with lemon or lime—to those of "riper years." His standard gift, such as to Cornbury, consisted of citron water, sweetmeats, and pickles. The most rare, gorgeous, and visibly exclusive—parrots, monkeys, and black-skinned attendants—were dispatched so as to reflect the glamor, wealth, and exclusivity of the nobility. Granville sent these sorts of resource to his closest aristocratic relations who were in power sufficient to advance his escape from the Caribbean, as Husbands had had the same hopes of his not-quite-so-exalted Essex relations.[46] Presents of sugar and of candied fruits became the most apposite tokens dispatched from the West Indies, with confectioners active in Barbados and Jamaica by the 1680s, despite the ready availability of recipes at home.[47] By the end of the century, sugar had moved unequivocally away from any association with medicine and had joined the ranks of groceries.

All of the plants which were eventually developed as commodity crops in the West Indies came with their own interwoven narratives of natural, exchange, and merchantable resource. According to the first-footers on Barbados, transplanted from the Orinoco delta and the Guianas were cassava, pineapples, potatoes, maize, and sugarcanes. Henry Powell was specific in noting the combination of extraneousness and fundamental possession inherent in the process of planting: "Rootes plants, fowles tobacco Seeds, Sugger, Canes and other materialls together with thirty two Indians which hee carried to the said Islands for the Planting thereof which said Rootes Plants and other matterialls, were the first that were ever planted there."[48] In 1642 Robert Stallings and William Conisby had a tiny ten-acre plot in eastern St. Philip's, on which they grew "provision crops," probably potatoes, corn, and "tobacco crops." They had land "fallen" and "unfallen," and a supply of timber.[49] Later in the same decade, the Barbados plantation of 150 acres, planned by Sir Poynings More, valued land on which there was a good supply of timber at £3 per acre, though unfelled land proved slow to become profitable: by now the woodland which was reserved and managed was chiefly intended for burning.[50]

The Spanish cultivated indigo in Jamaica, therefore likely to have been the plant indigenous to South America, *Indigofera suffruticosa* (Guatemala Indigo). The English continued production, and by the 1680s it was estimated that 70 percent of English imported indigo came from Jamaica and as a commodity it had doubled in price. The crop was threatened, however. Its carriage and import was regulated by the Navigation Acts, and in 1670 the decision was made in England that Jamaica concentrate on sugar, imposing a duty of 3s 6d on indigo.[51] In the late 1680s, Jamaica merchants petitioned against the proposed transfer of indigo to West Africa.[52] Deponents from Powell's initial voyages to Barbados made no mention of it being an introduced crop, but it was widely grown on the island in the 1630s, the decade in which both Dutch and English East India Companies were importing Asian indigo into Europe, and thus the plant here may have been either the Guatemala strain carried from south America or that from India, *Indigofera tinctoria*.[53] By the 1640s Barbados indigo was usually a tiny proportion of mixed provision/commodity smallholdings, and even at the end of the decade, 10 acres of More's 150 was reserved for a mixture of indigo, cotton, ginger, and pepper.[54] At this time of postwar hiatus and the possibility of commonwealth rebuilding, lobbyists ventured moving these crops to the Roanoke-Carolina latitudes. However, they would not be staples "that must do the work" of recovering republican industry, because the islands had a head start in production, already reducing the price of indigo from 9s to 3s 6d per lb, producing the combination of oversupply and saturated market which West Indian producers referred to as a "drug."[55] Indigo production remained important in St. Christopher's into the 1670s, but doubts about its purpose or profitability remained. On the island, it operated as an exchange currency, worth 2s per pound current, to be exchanged for sugar (value: 1½d per lb) at an ounce of indigo to a pound of sugar, and, unlike sugar, its price in London (at least) continued to rise.[56] Among many tropical species of indigo, one was native to the Carolinas (*Indigofera caroliniana*), and the English cultivated it there in the 1660s, despite some claims that Carolina indigo had to be carried from Barbados.[57] By 1682 it had been abandoned.[58] Its revival and boom in the 1740s was due to the 16-year-old Eliza Lucas Pinckney, who introduced Barbados indigo to her Wapoo plantation in 1739.[59] It was being grown in the Leewards at the end of the century, and measures to regulate its merchantable quality were drawn up in Montserrat.[60] The Governor of St. Christopher, Christopher Codrington, was accused not only of manipulating the market in slaves for his own ends, but of using French prisoners and recaptured slaves to cultivate a private trade in indigo. In 1715 indigo was worth 140,000 pounds in official trade from the Caribbees and Jamaica.[61]

When the late-century projectors of the Carolinas suggested crops, they did not mention the cotton with which the southern mainland colonies would later become synonymous. The humble boll of cotton falls foul of the chasm that separates early Americas' history from its reinvention as the United States. Although grown in the Carolinas in the 1660s, it was characterized as little more than a "garden plant" (thus reversing the respective statuses of commodiousness and merchandise), and the industry has little information on its cultivation before the mid-eighteenth century.[62] Figures indicate that the years between the American Civil War and the present day saw a fivefold increase in yields, which would suggest a very low yield per acre in early Barbados.[63] References are invariably to bolls of cotton wool in a state fit to be merchandized: not only picked from the bush but also cleaned of stones, seeds, and pieces of leaf or earth. There is little mention of equipment with which to manage the cotton crop other than its storage in warehouses: a gin, a loom, or a "lift," presumably a simple crane to raise the cotton wool in bags made of linen or hessian.[64] Cotton often went hand in hand with tobacco, values being ascribed to one, the other, or both together. Tobacco usually needed to be merchantable or "well conditioned" and, unlike cotton, had undergone some element of process on the island, with inventories listing tobacco wheels and stipulating its exchange "in roll."[65]

Beyond this, it seems unlikely cotton wool and tobacco existed on the island in the quantities mentioned in deeds, but rather, acted as a measure of value that oiled the wheels of social and legal interaction rather than those of commerce. Sir Henry Colt commented in the 1630s that the prospect of cotton filled the planters with new hope for Barbados, but very soon there were fears of the fall in its price. The early deeds of Barbados made reference to significant poundages of cotton wool with no information from such early dates that the cotton wool was pressed. If it was, such presses would be relatively ineffective and thus storehouses would not be big enough—nor profits so great—for goods to sit long, waiting to be traded in kind.[66] There is little indication of domestic production of cloth or thread. The repeated requirement that cotton wool be set "at some convenient storehouse near the seaside" implies that large quantities of cotton wool could be produced with the intention of being shipped off the island to be converted into a monetary equivalent.[67] But how big a storehouse—which besides, doubled as a dwelling—would have been necessary for 20,000 pounds of un-pressed cotton wool bolls?

On the other hand, every aspect of a Barbados estate or of the interaction between settlers was valued according to its weight in cotton wool or tobacco. This could be the overall value of 10-acre lots—a contemporaneous indigo plantation was larger, 100 acres—furniture, equipment, stock, the remaining time on servants' indentures, bonds of compliance or assurance, payment of debts, or "protection money." Blacksmith Robert Powell was given contract in 1642 to serve fellow smith Edward Duff for two years, in all craftwork—therefore excluding "carrying of the bellows for a bear one mile and that he shall not turn over any of the bills of Edward Duff before they become due"—to which Powell made his mark and Duff agreed to pay Powell two installments of 600 pounds of cotton or tobacco.[68] People's service varied in value, but averaged around 100 pounds per person, man or woman, with an Irish servant worth rather less.[69] Only one indenture from these batches refers to a monetary bill of exchange: for £70 sterling Thomas Dubbs sold his half of an estate (around 45 acres) along with servants' indentures, but the transfer was nevertheless guaranteed with 20,000 pounds' weight of merchantable cotton.[70] Cotton operated as a medium of exchange within the islands, adding to the variations in value that certain goods possessed in situ but could never command in British markets: "[I]f...Captain Mathew Wood [mariner, resident in Barbados]...do pay...John Pennell [draper of the City of London, for whom an agent acted in the West Indies]...the full sum of twenty-six pounds and fifty shillings of lawful money of England, at or before the 20th day of May next ensuing the date hereof, with the interest of the said money, since the first time it was due, or the value of the said money and interest in cotton, here in the Barbados, to the said Joⁿ Penell,...then his bill of sale is to be delivered or returned and the said Matthew Wood to be discharged therefrom."[71] Passage to and fro across the Atlantic cost 2,600 pounds. All goods, supplies, or services required on an estate, including storage costs and constructing a lift within the storehouse, were valued in pounds of cotton, whereas an entire estate—for example, 20 acres in northerly St. Lucy's—could be valued at 6,000 pounds of merchantable tobacco.[72]

In England, people came early to view the West Indies through the fug of tobacco smoke. It made its first appearance in the accounts of Sir Francis Drake's voyages, while Raleigh's ventures to Guiana noted that the peoples of the northern banks of the Orinoco, who smoked the most, exchanged it for canoes in Trinidad.[73] Having established itself in Virginia, it made its way to Bermuda, where it quickly became apparent that growing tobacco was detrimental to the development of craft, and that in "Patents or Indentures of Grants of Lands, the Grantees shall couenant to imploy their people in reasonable sort in Staple Commodities, and not wholly or chiefly about Tobacco." It nevertheless remained the standard levy for the maintenance of a ministry.[74] Each tribe was to appoint two overseers—paid 2 pounds in every 100 of tobacco produced—who would survey and register the crops grown annually, and divide the produce in half between "owners" and Company, provided the tobacco was cured and rolled before the division was made.[75] Fines were to be paid in tobacco or "other goods," with the whole giving the impression that cultivation remained Bermudans' sole preoccupation despite exhortations to apply themselves to more "stabile and solid Commodities." Bermudans themselves complained of monoculture, such that they suffered under burdensome taxes and freight charges and could not exchange their crop in England for necessaries such as shoes and cloth. Rather, they were offered a ship on its way to Barbados, carrying salt and Madeira. Having produced nothing else for 30 years, Bermudan soil was exhausted and while tobacco returned sufficient to pay their dues, the "trading party" within the Company cared nothing for the planters' nakedness.[76]

The strain of tobacco introduced into Bermuda was presumably brought from Virginia. While that of Virginia (and Bermuda?) was regarded as "sweet" and commanded a good price in English markets, that which entered Britain from Barbados had a terrible reputation. Robert Harcourt, Sir Thomas Roe, and Roger North planned tobacco cultivation in Guiana in the first two decades of the century, and it was described as "Caracas," or, since the Dutch were active there, *cracostabak*.[77] In 1615 English people were advised that all their tobacco was bought from indigenes in Guiana, the southern islands of St. Lucia and St. Vincent, and Dominica: Thomas Parris was explicit in saying that Henry Powell carried tobacco seeds from Guiana to Barbados in 1626.[78] This then may have been *Nicotiana sylvestris*—woodland or wild tobacco—accounting for English people's poor assessment.[79] The perceived sweetness of more northerly production and the poor reputation acquired by tobacco from Barbados may also be related to relative air temperature, with implications for how quickly or gently the leaf would be cured in the open; hence Henry Winthrop's comment that Barbados tobacco was "ill conditioned, fowle, full of stalkes and evill coloured."[80]

British counterblasts against tobacco thundered in vain. James VI and I argued that barbarous countries were built on barbarous customs, and thus condemned a plant indigenous to the Americas, the people who used it, and presumably the ethical and customary right of possession of those same favorites to whom he granted charters to explore, settle, and trade.[81]

George Wither repeated that "The Indian Weed...Shews Thy decay, all Flesh is hay"; and an anonymous wit who designed an heraldic devise for tobacconists included a *"man reverst...or beast indeed,/ That doate to[o] much vpon this heathen weed,"* together with a Moor's head to show that "cursed Pagans did,/ Devise this stinke."[82] Another wit dedicated a tract against tobacco to the Lancashire republican Alexander Rigby by creating two satirical characters: a Bermudan, Boccacio Fumiganto, who bewailed the effect smoking had on the military prowess of the English gentry; and a Trinidadian, who countered that tobacco was "a weed, the wealth of many Ilands, and the delight of the Queene of Ilands."[83]

Tobacco, cotton, and other indigenous commodities were "country money": the medium of exchange produced in the country. Its price reflected natural, exchange, and merchantable resource. It varied in terms of internal use, domestic trade, and a third, lower value when measured against the cost of goods from Britain. Gradually (though very late), the goods themselves were replaced by bills of exchange or coin, also bearing the value of the country, to be exchanged at variable rates.[84] Bills of Exchange from the Caribbees, as late as 1730, were worth two thirds of their value in London: Jamaica, Chesapeake and New England even less. "Publick Paper credit" was distrusted on both sides of the Atlantic and issuing it a key complaint that brought down Governor Granville in Barbados. It eloquently displayed the disparity between impoverished settlers in the Caribbean on the one side, and those who represented the mother country's authority on the other. Local settlers thought of themselves trying not only to make a living but also to survive, flourish, and supply a family; while the mother country was represented by those trying to extract their dues, and supply West Indian commodities at the cheapest price in exchange for British-produced goods at exorbitant rates. The high cost of basic necessities was a constant refrain. Paper money indicated to the colonists, therefore, that their investment, costs, and industry would never be worth the paper it was written on. Debts would never be repaid. In the eighteenth century, mainland colonies ran up huge paper debts, claiming the difficulty of defending frontier outposts. They continued to have valuable merchandise to truck, but nevertheless breached public faith by not cancelling their bills.[85]

Nor did coin circulate much, and permissions to issue coinage were to encourage transatlantic trade. The earliest permission within the English Americas was granted to Richard Tucker of Bermuda in 1615, and a London mint produced cheap copper coins, washed with a thin coating of silver, to the value of two, three, six, and twelve pence. The reverse depicted a ship, probably the *Sea Adventurer*, and the obverse showed a wild pig and the legend "SOMMER ISLANDS": consequently, this was "hogge money."[86] The ratio of the weight of the coin to its value was based on that of tobacco, but even in the crudest of copper, the value of the metal was still greater than the equivalent commodity: the coin had passed out of use by 1624. We have little evidence to show that tokens circulated in the torrid zone, with the striking exception of two versions of a specific "Elephant Token" that bore the legend on the reverse: "GOD PRESERVE CAROLINA AND THE LORDS PROPRIETERS 1694" and its immediate replacement which corrected the spelling. Again, these were minted in England, at the Tower, and were more likely promotional than a medium of exchange. Governor Francis Russell of Barbados died possessed of a strong box, kept at William Rawlin's house, containing a bag, some other small pieces of gold, and small silver ingots: the only English money he kept, twenty-three guineas and one Jacobus. However, he had bags of Spanish money worth nearly £600, and 667 "checkeens," wrapped in papers or in a knitted purse.[87] This was clearly a consequence of trade—exchanging *reales* for Spanish slaves—and investment, savings, and insurance (he had (under) insured his life as a governor), but was not for spending.[88] These were the most often-used coinage around the English plantations: "pieces of eight," a coin of eight crowns supposed to correspond to the sterling equivalent of five shillings. Remitted to Britain, however, were "light pieces of eight," worth 4s 6d and *"heavy and light Pieces of Eight passed promiscuously*; and as it always happens, a bad Currency drove away the good Currency," so current money becoming lighter, heavy money became merchandise in itself, and debts were paid in light. After complaints from Jamaica merchants, orders were issued in 1709 that the weight be regulated throughout the colonies, but only in Barbados and Bermuda did the legislation carry any purchase.[89] Where direct exchange with the Spanish was maintained—either legitimately or as privateering, such as the cases of Jamaica or the Bahamas—pieces of eight dominated, so when John Bethell of the Bahamas died in 1722, his will provided for his family in house, lands, furniture, clothing, and in considerable saved wealth, all in pieces of eight.[90]

For the first half of the century, therefore, all taxes and levies were paid in pounds' weight of cotton or tobacco. In the disputed authority over Barbados, between Courteen and Carlisle, deponents decried the latter's universal poll tax: even sucking babes, it was claimed by some, were liable for 20 pounds of cotton or tobacco.[91] Among the arbitrary taxes levied in 1639 was ten pounds of cotton or tobacco per acre to anyone who wished to sell or alien their estate. They became obliged to take out a new patent, to be regulated by an Alienation Court, and topped by a fee of 25 pounds' cotton to the clerk of the court.[92] Captain Strong complained that

> When the tyme of the yeere came that Goods were ripe,...the Governors warrants directed to the Provost Marshall issued forth to every family with arrest upon their Goods not to dispose of them or carry them forth of their howses till the lord of Carliles and the Governors dutyes were first paid...he hath seene goods arrested as men have bin carrying them downe to the sea. Hath seene goods taken away towards and at the sea side, saith he hath heard that their bedds and ham[m]acks have bin distrained for want of Goods to pay their duties in Specie.[93]

It was this new requirement to pay to reregister estates, which resulted in the volumes of deeds kept on the island.[94] By the 1660s Barbados revenue was gathered from "divers kinds of Comoditis y^t pay Customs in spetie; as sugar, Indico, Cotten woll ginger, Tobacoe, fusticke, & strongwaters called Rum, [and] suckets." Nevertheless, Willoughby of Parham would pay the governor's moiety in sugar, to be exchanged for bills in London. Sugar at too high a price would be to the detriment of the king; too low, to that of Willoughby. It remained advantageous to those who wanted to function in British society to deal on the London markets, and not at Barbados values.[95] From the second half of the seventeenth century, general values were most likely to be measured in pounds' weight of sugar, not grown on a commercially viable scale until the 1650s. The precise curve of the spread of sugar cultivation, the engrossment of estates to cater to economies of scale, the increase in slave labor to manage production, and the profits to be earned are still to be determined. In the meantime, Richard Ligon remains the instigator of the concept of a sugar revolution, being told that not long before his arrival some planters had acquired canes from Pernambuco, grown sufficient to make it worth their while to build a small engine, but at this point produced "but bare Muscavadoes, and few of them Merchantable commodities; so moist, and full of molosses, and so ill cur'd, as they were hardly worth the bringing home for *England*."[96] Three years of trial and error and it was a viable commodity, and sugar's champion, James Drax, said on arrival to have been worth £300 sterling, was contemplating his return to England to purchase an estate worth £10,000 yearly.[97] However, Drax's contemporary, Sir Poynings More, doing his planning in Surrey, was expecting to plant "60 Acres of canes and to have 80 or 100 Acres of wood for boyling ye sugar and other occasions, now ye canes after ye first cutting may bee cutt every 14 months but will bee much better if they bee cutt at 18 Months, in wch time they will (wth gods usuall blessing) yeald 2000 waight of Sugar each Acre and more some 3000 so because ye Croppe must stand a yeare and halfe accompt but on 40 Acres yearly it will yeeld at least 40 tarces of Sugar, wch if it yeeld but 6 ye pound heere will come unto 2000 per Annum de claro."[98]

George Marten had a 259-acre, 250-slave estate on Barbados in the prime St. John's location, on the Cliff ridge that caught the winds. He also had the ability to refine his muscovado. But he was forced to mortgage his property to London merchants, and failed to make repayments.[99] Marten was a gentleman of the parish, a vestryman and churchwarden, and this vestry levied parish rates in sugar as early as 1653: one pound an acre to cover the cost of laying out the highways. Inhabitants took their sugar to designated storehouses, whose owners would issue receipts to be passed to the parish clerk, William Sernay, himself entitled to a commission of ten percent. After barely a year, however, overseers were claiming sugar in arrears, to be paid out to Sernay, the surveyor, the workers, and to cover the cost of provisions for them (25 pounds for fish). "[Y]^e Old William Wilson" received a pension of 520 pounds a year: how could this be to his benefit in Barbados? By 1682, the poor rates were calculated in sterling but Rev. Cryer was still being paid in muscovado.[100] St. Michael's, Barbados, imposed a rateable value calculated in sugar on the buildings of Bridgetown: John Jones paid 40 pounds on his house in James Street; the Royal African Company which rented it paid 600 pounds. Thomas Prothers had land in St. George's, but christened his son, John, in St. Michael's and paid 120 pounds for a house on fashionable High Street, which was rented by the parish in order to house "Irish Margaret."[101] Having announced the levy in St. Michael's church on three successive Sundays without objection, the parish in 1690, under the authority of Governor Edwin Stede, levied 26,782 pounds on all the houses in Bridgetown, 19,080 pounds on merchants, 8,000 pounds on Jews, 7,600 pounds on newcomers, and rated land at 3 pounds sugar per acre, thereby raising an additional 21,000 pounds. Maybe Drax was the only person to make such a quick profit. The reality for most Barbadians remained prosaic.

The by-products of sugar production corrupted home-grown virtue, not least because planters felt the need to diversify had been foisted on them. Sir William Stapleton restored and upgraded his plantations: this included converting the old boiling house into a still house and building a big cistern under the stanchions on the windward side of the lower boiling house in order to receive molasses.[102] In the early years of the century, molasses, as the "dregges or filth of Sugar," was painted onto tobacco leaves to give them the color which rendered them merchantable, or, to the shame of the Grocers' Company, became a means to disguise bad drugs.[103] In this second case, it was another word the meaning of which was sweetened as the century progressed, as the medicinal compound triacle was transformed into treacle. Christopher Merret, speaking for the "honest apothecary," described molasses, the syrupy "waste product" which ran, un-crystallized into a drip jar during the curing process, as "nauseous." His opinion that it was useless for medical practice was both denied and confirmed by recipe makers, who used it to sweeten rough spirits, adding spices and flavorings, but produced drinks, tonics, and cordials reckoned "good for the Stomach."[104] One of the earliest statutes of Charles II outlawed its use to adulterate wine, by darkening or sweetening.[105] In Scotland, imports of molasses were thought to threaten domestic grain production.[106]

Molasses was a vital component in distilling the by-products of sugar, so unfamiliar to British palates in the 1660s that it was felt necessary to explain this thing called "rum."[107] As it tended to be used primarily for quick drinking, it was likely to have been a clear liquor, the result of leaving standing for one day the "scummings" of the sugar boiling, fermented with the "lees" from a previous distillation, and then adding molasses and water and fermenting for a further five. The color associated with dark rum came as a result of storage in oak barrels, but was often faked by adding burned sugar or molasses again. Sir William Stapleton was shipping sugar and molasses and reserving rum to "buy provisions, and other Necessaryes for the plantations, thogh it may bee sold at an under rate, allowing the Negroes Drams in wet Wether."[108] Judging by the 60 barrels kept in the cellar of Thomasina Ellis's Port Royal tavern, it soon became the clichéd pirate drink of choice in Jamaica. It remained a commodity for domestic consumption, rarely for export.[109] The same could be said of Barbados, "the drinke of the Iland, which is made of the skimmings of the Coppers, that boyle the Sugar, which they call kill-Divell." Here, rum was sold as the standard drink: the West Indies' equivalent of running an alehouse without a license.[110]

A more refined spirit, suitable for gifts and bribes, and still redolent with place-specific exotica, could be produced by double distilling. The secret was that the liquor must be "proved" of sufficient alcohol content to flame or ignite gunpowder. Lawrence Crabb took advantage of his Antigua estate close to a creek to make a double-distilled product, considered worthy enough to sweeten the high and mighty men of the Committee for Trade and Plantations.[111] The most successful distilleries were those with access to spring water, accounting for the number of plantations which made eponymous reference to it. Access to fresh water was a vital resource in itself, and the existence of springs tended to mark out those who might benefit from rum production and those whose cane had to be sold on. In St. Christopher's, Robert Cunyngham noted careful "Directions for Distilling Rum had from W^m McKinen Esqr at Antigua," his son-in-law. Three cisterns of 600-gallon capacity, with 255 gallons of scummings and 96 of molasses, would produce 140 gallons of spirit: "When you Double, Wash the Still Head & the Worm carefully with clean warm water. Your Still of 300 Gallons may yield 100 Gallons of Proof Rum."[112]

Not only the product, but also the process went through the transition from natural, to exchange, to merchantable resource. Human action established and justified dominion over place via the law of nature. This involved selecting plants, preparing for planting, by for example clearing and manuring the ground, and planting a crop, however small or humble: "to till manure, and improve such Lands unto good husbandry and profitt, for the use of mann, which before lay wast, uncult, and untill'd, yeilding little or noe fruite, or benefitt, to the world at all."[113] Sir Poynings More's plans fell foul of the shift from subsistence to commodity—the "sugar-turn"—and now labor was required in advance of disembarkation and settlement. More envisaged 40 slaves "to cleare ye ground by Sep i," 20 "English servants," their clothes and tools, and a further 80 "servants" to build mills and curing plant.[114]

The processes of commodity production were then incorporated into the community customs of the locale and recast as evidence of manorial fealty.[115] The land itself and the processes required to prepare it were commodified. The distinction between the physical crop, the industry to produce it, and ultimately—with this role being turned over to field slaves—labor itself, and the bodies performing labor, were all commodified, reproducing the process by which indigenous knowledge and skill had been appropriated. Commodity became merchandise. The route taken in preparing, planting, harvesting, and consumption did not change: the value which Britons (particularly in Britain) attached to them collapsed. These were menial tasks, to be performed by laborers themselves reduced to a commodity. Lawrence Crabb believed himself under-resourced to establish himself in Antigua in 1690, because he had more land than could be manured using his existing laborers, and planned a specific Guinea voyage to augment the force to clear and manure ground and build plant.[116] In order to create a "brave estate" necessaries now included "erecting works, or replenishing the estate...with fresh stock."[117] Starting costs were huge, leaving many in "necessitous circumstances," but repayment was always expected from the produce of the estate.[118] Commodity prices fell; in part due to over-reliance on the crop and the volume of production. Sugar depleted the soil and clearing vegetation made areas prone to being washed into the seas in heavy rain. Ironically, the value of manure rose.

Aldworth Elbridge, who drafted a will in 1653 since he was about to undertake the perilous voyage to the West Indies, was a member of a wealthy Bristol merchant family which had pioneered sugar processing in the city.[119] He acquired servants in Barbados and went on to establish one of the eponymous "Spring Plantation's"—this one at Yallahs on the southeastern coast of Jamaica.[120] A daughter, christened Alldworth in St. Andrew's, confirms that Aldworth senior preferred to be known as Thomas, which, if correct, means he was in his late 20s when he and his wife Rebecca traveled out with their young family. He probably died on the island in 1680. Spring Plantation was said to have produced around 1,000 pounds of sugar a year in the 1680s. While not disputing that the Elbridges' involvement in sugar made them affluent members of society which fueled a wealth of Christian philanthropic projects, economic and ethical investment was exclusively in England. In Jamaica, the effects of continuous and intensive sugar production on the estates took its toll: "the Casse is Altered ye Reason is our Land ye Springe is wore out almost," the slaves old, the land in drought, and the accounts would show how burdensome was taxation: "all things Considered our Island is quite spoyld." Robert Elbridge had bought only 12 slaves since taking over the estate and, by 1720, was worth only 5,000 pounds, and the cattle were left with little pasture.[121]

The balance of trade was growing uneven, the new world increasingly controlled by the expectations of the old. Feeling settled in the West Indies relied on importing the familiar: making money in the mother countries depended on importing the exotic. There was a constant rumble of complaint about costs as merchants exploited the premium price they could charge for goods, services, and labor in short supply. The merchants of Cumberland expected sugar, cocoa, cotton, indigo, pepper, log wood, and cabinet wood from Jamaica, but the "Goods vendable at Jamaica from Whitehaven" were more basic and prosaic: coal, sheet lead and shot, and tallow; shirts, shoes, stockings, gloves, and hides; biscuit, butter, cheese, oatmeal, bacon, salt beef, and salted herrings, mackerel, cod and salmon; beer and hops, these last being low grade but at a price of seven or eight times the base price of Kentish best.[122] Lawrence Crabb informed his English suppliers that basic dry goods could earn the "verry preposterous" rate of 800 percent. He requested brass and pewter vessels; plates, ladles, skimmers, chocolate pots, and tea kettles. But his agent sent pewter chamber-pots, which remained unpleasant, unusable, and unsold.[123]

The exchange of locally produced commodity for over-priced British supply compromised American self-reliance. It was better for internal markets and social cohesion if supplies could be locally produced. In Carolina, locally made cheese was a shilling a pound cheaper than English—imported shoes approximately 15 percent more expensive. Hats which cost eight shillings and sixpence in England sold in Charles Town for five pounds, while the markup on cheap black cloth was even more shocking.[124] Thus the social, as much as the economic, values of trade were inverted. That considered pedestrian in Britain was rendered a luxury because it was imported: that which was the product of natural resource in the Americas, and thus exotic in Britain, was downgraded if it functioned only in internal American markets. Crabb sold his Antigua rum in Virginia (without receiving payment).[125] On the mainland, it could be a gift to be given to indigenes, and as much a means there to corrupt society and economy as it was in the island rum-houses. Newfoundlanders complained they were at the mercy of New England merchants who, predicting the fishing season, arrived with supplies that ought to have been received direct from England. If they purchased undercut provisions from the New Englanders, they were obliged to take a quantity of rum, which they sold on to the fishermen—who thus tarried in the Americas while their families became a burden to the parish—or to their servants who became its perpetually indebted bondsmen.[126] It became a regular staple of artisans' "wages," and a public resource which kept longer than beer, adopted by the Royal Navy and later fixed at half a pint a day.[127] Rum was a sweetener to be aimed at the lesser sort. Rather than stiffening the sinews, it was the gift that made one incapable. In addition, the internal market compromised relations between black and white, the former allowed to sell basic foodstuffs, or basic crafts, while at the same time, legislation continually tried to limit any interaction.[128]

The ability of people in the West Indies to exploit natural or exchange resource was always compromised by the need to produce "Merchantable Commodities" because they were defined by what the British markets were prepared to buy. In the early development of most fledgling settlements, traders on the American side were offered advantageous terms so as to promote "any necessary, laudable, useful or probable act, science, invention, trade, manufacture, husbandry, tillage, work or quality whatsoever not formerly in use" and to "sell, barter, send, export or transport the said manufacture, merchandises, land, commodities...whereby the commodity, trade, commerce or benefit...may be promoted, maintained, increased, or advantaged."[129] William Castell argued that those "who are sent away" to the Carolinas could soon recompense England—with "Silke, Vines, Cotton, Tobacco, Deere-skinnes, Goat-skinnes, rich Furre, and Beavers good store, Timber, Brasse, Iron, Pitch, Tarre, Rosin, and almost all things necessary for shipping"—which would be converted to a "store of silver and gold, pearls, and precious stones."[130] Despite initial portrayals of Bermuda as a land of milk and honey, offering self-sufficiency to its inhabitants, over the century the need to send commodity back to Britain changed the perception of this, and other territories' relative worth. In 1699 the islands and their inhabitants were deemed "wholy Useless to the king...for their Tobacco hath no Market in Europe therefore they plant only for the Islands use; and for any other of the productions as Potatoes, Pines & Hatts, made of Palmeta leaves."[131] The figures compiled in the 1710s by John Oxenford—who by 1726 was assistant to the Inspector General of Imports and Exports at the customs' houses in London—indicate the range of merchantable commodities arriving from the British West Indies (though we do not know the complete passage of these goods from their places of production via *entrepôts*), noted within columns of imports, exports, the customs which were payable on each item in the year 1688.[132] These are "Species," grouped into drugs, timber, and groceries, distinguished from "Goods sev[era]¹ Sorts," thereby noting the start of the specific separation of "engrossed" general goods from specific commodities.[133] "Grocery" referred in this instance to dry ginger, molasses, and brown and white sugar. Within a huge variety of goods, brown sugar was by some measure the greatest volume import, but also carried a colossal rate of customs on entering England: a duty of around £14 per pound weight, compared with £4 5s on white sugar and around £5 per gallon on rum. Nearly a quarter of the brown sugar was reexported, for refining elsewhere. There had been sugar bakeries in London since the mid-sixteenth century, but there remained relatively few throughout Britain in the seventeenth century, and sugar baking as a home industry started to expand around the accession of George I. Christopher Lowther of London, third baronet of Whitehaven, set up a sugar house there in 1712 and it was probably he who was the shipper of exotic imports from, and prosaic exports to, Jamaica.[134]

Oxenford's category of medicines included balsam, sarsaparilla, tamarind, chocolate, cordials flavored with citrus peel, liquorice, and allspice; the famous Peruvian bark (*Cortex peruvius* or *Cinchona*); resins such as that from the "torchwood tree" (*Amyris balsamifera*, described as *Hypocacania*); the *elemi* gum used as a digestive treatment; and *Cassia Fistularis*, an ounce of which, with "*Tamarinds half an Ounce, green Precipitate five Grains, Oil of Aniseeds four Drops; mix, and make a Bolus*...serves as a Stimulus, or Provoker," a diuretic, and treatment for gonorrhea.[135] Both the hardwood, *lignum vitae* (in the West Indies, "pockwood"), and *Gum Guiaci* provided treatments for syphilis.[136] Also imported were nearly 10,000 gallons of lime juice, snuff, platted straws and grasses, coconuts, tortoiseshell, deer and cow hides, indigo, potatoes, elephant ivory, and two feather beds. The timber was split into two types: more often "general"—eleven and a half loads in this case—and some specialist types such as fustic, redwood, and "sweetwood." Some woods for cabinet making—Brazil and Nicaragua woods, ebony and mahogany—were added in 1716. Rare survivals of English furniture employ Surinam's indigenous snakewood (*Piratinera guianensis*: "Specklewood" to the English), but these were items of the greatest rarity, for the most refined English taste.[137] Generally, Britons left furniture style and marquetry to the Dutch: within Governor Russell's house at Fontabelle were imported Dutch chairs and East Indies' japanning.[138] Russell kept several spice boxes: the West Indies continued to produce ginger—exported both dry and green—and aniseed, with the largest volume spice production in allspice. In 1715, 198,849 pounds of this "Jamaican pepper" was imported into London. Despite the volume production of the East Indies, nearly a million and a half pounds of cotton wool still came from the West.[139] Cargoes remained valuable to West Indians to the point at which they left their shores. By the time they reached the west-country peninsula, the economics had become more complex. Cornish tin production and internal shipping was growing with the production of all those prized dry goods. Its treacherous coastline, susceptibility to pirate attack, and the friability of many cargoes added value through exotic allure. Despite perishable cargoes, rich men claimed propriety over wrecks, after Admiralty-men had "seiz'd & seller'd what they could get off."[140] For the mercantilists of the region, stores of commodity formed part of their patrimony, as the land on which it grew and the slaves who produced it did for its West Indian suppliers.[141] From as early as 1630 sugar formed an important commercial element when it came to calibrating demand and manipulating the market, with Ezekiel Grosse, a lawyer so avaricious and an engrosser so ambitious he became a folk antihero, being sent "ten poun[ds] of shuger for [thi]s lenten P[ro]vicion, wch is the best Commodytie our Harbor at this time afordes" and "a pound of Tobaco, wch, I hope will like [thi]s last."[142] Doctors advised drinking chocolate and it was far better to obtain it in the west country than to wait for its price to hike and its quality to be compromised on its journey to London.[143] But while the price of tobacco continued to rise, between 1680 and 1715 that of sugar—except for "double refined loaf sugar" which could command 1s 3d per lb—remained flat.[144] West Indies' resource retained a value in home markets so long as it refined sour, bitter, medicinal commodities into polite entertainment. What for the seventeenth-century moment, at least, remained exotic for the people of Britain, would be tamed in the eighteenth century by American over-production and the rise of manufacturing at home.

Making resource merchantable turned anything and everything into a commodity, often against Caribbean local interests. In rudely formed Barbados in the 1630s and 1640s basic wooden buildings along the shipping coasts served for storage of goods and transportation off the island: access to the sea was at a premium and goods were shipped from "any Port, or Bay, or Creek; and at any time, either by day or by night."[145] As the century progressed, access to the sea remained vital, but could be sold and trucked in itself. Thus, Lawrence Crabb earned slaves from Christopher Codrington because crossing Crabb's was Codrington's quickest route to Parham port: Crabb exchanged slaves for free wharfage.[146] The distinction between privately and publicly owned wharfs in Bridgetown accounted for the case of Samuel Hanson, accused of stealing away guns from Barbados to supply his shipyard in New England. Hanson claimed permission to use Mr. Kendall's private wharf; Governor Dutton maintained he was exploiting public access.[147] Official approval, direct from the crown or its representative in the colonies, was required to erect and extend wharfs.[148] But the "public" was still interpreted by islanders to mean themselves: the governor, their servant. Francis Russell never earned Barbadians' trust or respect, with complaints of partiality toward the merchant community, sponsoring trading enterprises, profiting himself by sending trade off the island. In 1695 he commissioned resident engraver, Samuel Copen, to produce a prospect of Carlisle Bay, highlighting defenses, wharfs, and embankments, because the project of transforming them all would be for the benefit of trade.[149] He died the following year and his private papers revealed the extent of his mercantile (self)-interest (and the absence of personal or landed ties to the island): in "An acco^t of his Late Ex^{cys} Interest in Merchantdizeing in this Island" were shares in several ships and sloops trading cocoa, cotton wool, and firearms in a triangular trade with London and Madagascar.[150]

Few systematic public account books survive. The best served is the tiny Leeward island of Montserrat, for the years 1672–1680.[151] In the island's credit columns were various levies. At the core, a general island levy defrayed public charges, and additional duties and levies were issued on items such as imported alcohol—mainly brandy and Madeira—and a series of fines and licenses issued to individuals. A levy was charged on labor: 10 pounds of sugar each slave in 1672, but 60 pounds in every 100 on both Christians and slaves in 1678. This was part of the public stock enumerated at 2,636 "men, women and slaves," raising 158,160 pounds. In 1680, differential payments were charged: 30 pounds per Christian (1,680 in number) and 40 pounds per slave (993). Specific projects demanded an extraordinary charge, such as constructing a rum works on the island and a storage house for the pans of sugar.[152] In 1672 the total amounted to 100,350 pounds, but in 1678 Conrad Alers calculated the public stock at nearly three times that sum: 290,327 pounds of sugar; made up of levies on labor, waste land, rum works, tache house, fines for making corrupted indigo, and arrears.[153] In volume, this sounds a huge sum for a tiny island: but if the current price of sugar on the London markets was around 1½d, then the sterling value of Montserrat's public wealth in 1678 was less than £2,000.[154] In 1672 it had been only £630. A striking context is provided by an entry noting that 3,000 pounds sugar was compensated to an individual master of a runaway. Debits for 1672 almost exclusively itemize timber work on the fort; the only people paid or supplied, with food or nails, were carpenters and sawyers. A handful of masons repaired bastions and the munitions' building: gunners were paid between 2,000 and 3,500 pounds per annum.[155] Disproportionate effort was expended obtaining a flag. Work was undertaken on the sessions' house: there did not appear to be a public meeting house. So the island status of Montserrat condemned its settlers to raising funds from their own production and traffic in both basic necessities and life's little luxury glass of Madeira, to pay for their community's welfare, which essentially amounted to its defensive capabilities.

Montserrat was tiny, poor, and isolated and this did inform its reliance on traffic and truck which tied it to markets elsewhere, and ensured it could never develop a self-sustaining market of its own, but the relationships between political power, dependency, and merchant wealth predated even first footing in the Caribbean. It was reflected in King James's inability to prevent his reign from being usurped by tobacco, and his favorites fighting out their battles in distant merchandizing. Land was claimed in the name of political authority, but made possible by mercantile purchasing power. At the end of the reign of James VI and I, Secretary of State Sir John Coke and Sir Dudley Digges addressed the question of England's defense through an aggressive war against Spain, to be privately financed by West Indies' expansionism. Digges's scheme was for £200,000 a year over four years, creating a West India Company similar to that of the Dutch.[156] Sir Benjamin Rudyerd backed a "West Indie Association" with "Affection...Reason and...Iudgement," while admitting that "so shall a good part of my poore fortune" disappear should the project come to pass.[157] Others saw potential in the West Indies. In 1623, Ralph Merrifield sponsored plantings in St. Christopher's, Nevis and Montserrat, and three years later, Captain Henry Powell set sail in the *William and John* of London, co-owned by Sir William Courteen and Powell's brother John, "in Joint Stocke," in the first of three voyages "purposely for the Barbadoes to plant there." It cost £8,000, settled around 140 English, between two and ten black people taken as prize, and thirty or so Kalinago people from the Guianan coast.[158]

Robert Brenner's account of mercantile wealth focuses on the so-called puritan lords who tried to control British foreign policy using colonial shipping. The hopes of these anti-Spanish projectors for "a society of trade, plantation and defence" in the torrid zone, alluded to above, became corralled into the Bermuda and Providence Island Companies. But, on the contrary, for the majority of the region, development was generated through Crown patronage, as James VI and I and Charles I attempted to master their domestic affairs, and secured this by laying nominal claim to colonial territory. Thus proprietorship of "Carliola," or the Caribbee Islands, was awarded to Scottish favorite, James Hay, first earl of Carlisle. Carlisle's friend, James Ley first earl of Marlborough, who as Lord Treasurer had already "taken extraordinary paines and Care for the planting and protecting" of the Caribbees—maintaining a particular interest in Santa Cruz (St. Croix)—now joined with Hay in obtaining the proprietary patent.[159] This was all despite the preexistent claim (which all others parties said was unbeknownst to them) of Courteen and his party.

James Hay was a man of prodigious and lavish expenditure, in "chronic financial straits...jovially wasting...resources," but he could bring his court influence to bear on behalf of ambitious Citizens who became his investors. Benjamin Henshaw was a Merchant Taylor and may have been the "Captain Henshaw" who paid Carlisle's receivers, Mole and Havercamp, who in turn expended £2,200 to a broker and obtained bonds for the ship, *The Carlile*. Henshaw may have sailed for Barbados.[160] William Latham was a Draper; Edmund Edlin, a Salter; and John Johnston, a Scottish member of the Joiners' Company of London. These were no revolutionary capitalists.

Henshaw was employed as a tax farmer in the north, collecting for the king in the troubled year of 1628. Johnston in the 1640s and Edlin in the 1650s had tangential associations with nonroyal financing, but neither in a fashion that might exhibit either burgeoning mercantile capitalism or radical politics.[161] Of the receivers, Godfrey Havercamp, who followed the ship certainly as far as Gravesend, was one of the collectors of impost for the east-coast ports (Sandwich to Berwick but including Carlisle) and a sergeant to Charles I's carriage; and George Mole was probably a Stapler, who had been one of "his Majesty's subjects intending to deduce a Colony and make plantation in Virginia, and other territories in America...[and] divers other Islands...with other powers" incorporated as the London Company by Letters Patent of 1606, 1609, and 1612.[162] They obtained assurances totaling £1,000. Havercamp and Mole received £300 from Sir William Pitt, whom James VI had created Comptroller of the Household on his English accession, the MP for Wareham, founder of the mighty household at Stratfield Saye in Hampshire, and a shareholder in the Spanish Company.[163] "Mr Bland" who gave £500 was probably John Bland, "The Grosser."[164] His son, also John, emigrated to Virginia after his father's death. He was involved in the Spanish and Tangier trade as well as Virginia, and was a close friend of the only one named who would go on to have any truck with anti-royalist regimes, the entrepreneur, Thomas Povey.[165] The nature of Henshaw and Latham's trades brought them close to the persons of the royal family.

The voyage was to fulfill the commission "ffor the Settlinge a gouernmt in the Carebey ILands" and "ffurnishinge out the shipe Carlile," 30 "passengers"—which was scored out and replaced by "servants for my Lord"—"wth p[er]m[i]sions of all kinds for a hole yeare vizt vituells Clothes Amunitio[n] & tooles of all kinds fitting for the designe to the carabey Ilands." *The Carlile* transported 30 people at Carlisle's cost. Another 45 others paid six pounds "P[er] man" on their own behalf and that of family or servants, and a further three pounds per ton to ship goods. Pitt the shipwright expended nearly £3,000 on fitting out and equipping, including ordnance, £103 4s 6d for mariners' wages, and an allowance was made to a Mr. Hall to "keepe men taken up for my lords plantacon," that is, paying them not to run away. There were costs for victuals and for services, such as Mr. Ross the surgeon and Mr. Kirtland the chaplain who carried a Church Bible and two service books. There were services such as porterage, wharfage, lighterage, warehousing, boat hire, and "harbor beere." The ship sailed from Gravesend to the Downs where their passage was held up and they remained wind bound for three weeks in Plymouth, necessitating Thomas Davis to pay more money for food and to keep "my Lords men togeather untill they Could be shipt." Two planters who ran away were paid to return and *The Carlile* having sailed, they were sent on to St. Christopher's in *The Truelove*.[166] More esoteric items provided a flavor of Carlisle's design: £10 7s to Henry Harvey for a falcon; the great cabin was to have fine furniture and a carpet; and Carlisle seems to have anticipated the need to "win over" existing Barbados and St. Christopher's governors, since he took the incumbents carbines inlaid with pearl, and swords chased in gold. Havercamp and Mole paid out a total of £5,015 11s 1d, approximately half a million pounds in the modern day.

For ten years, the earls of Carlisle as Lords Proprietor of the Caribbees enjoyed the collection of all customs, subsidies, and imposts on trade, whether generated in English or Caribbean ports. The settlers in Barbados had agreed to pay Governor Charles Wolverston five percent on their produce, and Henry Hawley subsequently imposed a poll tax of 40 pounds of tobacco—half to the proprietor and half to the governor—with a similar but extended set of payments for fledgling St. Christopher's. Anchorage dues were imposed on foreign shipping. Allocations of land incurred a further levy. Having failed to secure an unlimited interest in the Caribbees' tobacco duties, Carlisle was awarded a pension of £3,000 per annum for 21 years, which, since tobacco duties were already going direct to the earl, constituted a levy on trade with colonies further afield.[167] In return, defense and security were the responsibility of a proprietor. Thus, in the case of the earl of Carlisle's patent, he was to supply the colonies with arms and ammunition, but at the un-reimbursed cost of creditors, and he was responsible for building fortifications, albeit, as was replicated in Montserrat 40 years later, at the colonists' expense.[168] In due course, colonists came to believe they had paid for their own security twice over: levies on their production disbursed to construct and maintain military building and personnel, after which all exchange between them, other parts of the Americas or across the Atlantic—of goods, information, servants, slaves, families—did not happen unless militarily protected from the enemies of their overlords.

The Carlisle claim to the Caribbees, even confined to its inception, serves to illuminate the confusions, complexities, and sources of endless disputation with which the region originated and from which it never escaped. One point of clarity to emerge is the enormity of the financial commitment, and its attendant risks. Behind Carlisle's ambitious and cavalier pretentions lay hubristic claim to aristocratic privilege and staggering levels of debt.[169] It was the opinion of Edward Hyde, who as earl of Clarendon would himself venture into West Indian and American colonialism, that Hay had "no bowels in the point of running in debt, or borrowing all he could. He was surely a man of the greatest expense in his person of any in the age he lived...having spent, in a very jovial life, above £400,000...he left not a house nor acre of land to be remembered by...he died with as much tranquillity of mind as used to attend a man of more severe exercise of virtue."[170] Colonial power was reliant on merchant investment; colonial settlement on its repayment; and the strange coupling gave birth to disharmonious relationships between settler and merchant, settler and governor, and production and merchandizing.[171] The link between money and land, mercantilism and settlement was at times symbiotic, at others interdependent, and often contested, but the nature of authority and power, in any sphere and at any level, was always compromised by economic insecurity.

The disputed Carlisle patent cast a shadow across the whole century. The personnel changed—many of the initial protagonists died, leaving their affairs to be settled by an army of family members, legatees, lawyers, and politicians—and the geographical focus of the dispute became increasingly blurred as parties traveled to Barbados and elsewhere in the Caribbean, to the American mainland, remained in Britain or Ireland (with attendant differences between their component parts), or migrated around all and far beyond, in and out of different jurisdictions. Although more evidence survives for those at the top of the social hierarchy (and then is confusing, incomplete, and sometimes unknowable), the enterprises involved everybody, from the king at the top of the great chain, down to the meanest servant, mariner, or slave. Every link was compromised by debt, dependence, and obligation—coiled, knotted, snagged, and fused across the globe, till the West Indies was not so much "settled," in all meanings of the term, as choked: the complexities beyond the wit of anyone to untangle. Suits for debt followed rapidly. Far from defending the Caribbees, Carlisle was charged with having surrendered St. Christopher's to the Spanish, setting in motion a chain of claims for loss of estate and investment. When the first earl died intestate in 1637—his personal estate a mere £5,000—the trustees for the second earl, led by kinsmen and namesakes the Hay earls of Kinnoull, were instructed to pay the creditors before any surplus went to Carlisle.[172] When these debts were not met, the creditors resorted to Chancery, which in 1644 ruled against the second earl of Carlisle who now owed (officially, at least) £40,000 for the initial Caribbee voyages: these, the earl and dowager countess tried to circumvent by claiming Lords' privilege.[173] The second earl's estates were sequestered for his support for the Stuarts, and so a release enabling him to send "a Commission over into the said Islands, for the regulating his Revenue, and settling the Inhabitants thereof in a more happy and secure Condition than at present they are in; and for the avoiding of all Doubts and Scruples which may any Ways arise in any of the Inhabitants of the said Islands, touching the said earl, or his Interest in the Premises" was delayed until September 1645.[174] Within the next 18 months, however, the Commons noted that "the several Plantations in Virginia, Bermudas, Barbados, and other places of America have been much beneficial to this Kingdome by the increase of Navigation, and the Customs arising from the commodities of the growth of those Plantations imported into this Kingdom" and extended three years' free trade on "Merchandizes, Goods, and necessaries for the better carrying on of the said Plantation."[175] The following month, Carlisle leased (for 21 years) the claim to the Caribbees—still loosely defined, but in essence, Barbados and the Leeward Islands—to Francis, Lord Willoughby of Parham, of whom decades later Carlisle's creditors would suggest was their nominee. It was in the creditors' interest to prevent Carlisle from traveling in person to Barbados, presumably because recovering money was made harder at a distance, and settlers whose investment in the region was starting to pay dividends were equally hostile: the burgeoning prosperity particularly of Barbados was the result of their efforts and expense, and should not be compromised by the export of British politicking.[176] With Britain mired in civil strife, Barbadians declared their neutrality, but for reasons more nuanced than being too busy making money to make war: they were questioning the foundation of civil authority and its economic reward and protecting themselves against the possibility that their industry would go to mask others' negligence or venality.[177] Royalist service also delayed Willoughby from leaving immediately for the Caribbean. He disembarked on Barbados on April 30, 1650, and found his authority was also questioned by fellow royalist Humphrey Walrond.[178]

Given both debtors' and creditors' intimacy with the persons of the Stuarts, it was with considerable irony that the disputants became reliant on the Commonwealth to decide their claims. The first official statement on how the colonies would return payment to their investors was obtained by the Carlisle creditors, with the ruling in December 1649 that Willoughby, his "heires executers [and] Administrators should collect gather [and] receive out of [and] from the sayde Province [and] Islands and all ye Planters [and] Inhabitants of [and] upon ye same All such Rentt impostes Customes dutyes profite paymente Sum and Sums of moneye whatsoever" due to the Proprietors of the Caribbees, and over the period of the lease—until Michaelmas 1668—divide the revenue in half, one moiety to repay Carlisle's long-suffering creditors.[179] It is difficult to disentangle statements because everyone felt forced to adopt two faces, looking at each other with frustrated, skeptical, and bitter scowls, and at their lords with the downcast eyes of supplicating vassals. Therefore, creditors claimed that Willoughby journeyed to the Caribbees and influenced the people of Barbados to agree to three heads: a levy of two and a half percent on their own goods; four percent on that of "strangers"; and to declare allegiance to the exiled prince, Charles Stuart. Most commentators adjudged the Willoughbys self-regarding bullies, rather than masters of the art of persuasion, and that anything was willingly undertaken at their new lord's urging is unlikely, especially since it triggered the dispatch of a Commonwealth fleet to reduce the island. Willoughby again failed to meet his financial obligations, and those in pursuit of the money accumulated a further £1,200 in legal fees.[180]

At the restoration of monarchy in England, the Crown received advice to rationalize competing claims to overseas' authority, territory, and trade, and those of the families, descendants, and trustees of the original progenitors of credit and debt. In March 1661, the newly ennobled earl of Clarendon, the Lord Chancellor, announced that all those with conflicting interests in the Caribbees, should they be prepared to submit their claims, would be compensated by the Crown. In Restoration London the creditors of Carlisle's original claim to the Caribbees were: William Latham and Oliver Browne (Merchants Taylor); Paul Panne of St. Martin in the Field, Taylor; Edmund Edlin (Salter); Robert English and James Gould, merchants; Gregory Philpot, citizen-clothworker; Richard Downing (Skinner); Richard Trevill (tallow-chandler); Godfrey Havercamp, now described as a gentleman of Petersham, Surrey; John Johnston (the Citizen-Joiner, also now a gentleman); and

Anne Henshaw, Benjamin's widow. Their most dogged champion would be Benjamin and Anne's son, the alchemist venturer, Thomas Henshaw, acting with Sir Henry Puckering and George Goodman.[181] The creditors regarded themselves as trusty Stuart loyalists, though "brought to great poverty...deplorable condition...[and] unable to ly any longer at charges here in london to attend the issue of their sigte [*recte*: ?suit]," but they relied on his majesty "that their drooping hearts may bee cheared and the necessities of many needy familys in due time relieved."[182] As Citizens, whose trades had furnished the voyages, they were therefore responsible for those artisans who had committed the labor and materials. Apparently annexed to the original settlement deed of 1649 was a schedule of these "diverse [and] sundrye other persons," whose case continued unresolved for another 40 years and more, but the active and elite petitioners usually professed to act for 80 or so others. In their case to the King-in-Council in 1664, they amended what had merely been the "great" distress suffered by those lower down the credit chain, to the "utter impoverishment" of "many hundred that are interessed [*sic*] in that debt many whereof are helples widows & orphans."[183]

On the debit side was a scroll of privileged aristocratic names. Taking over from the defunct lines of the Hay earls of Carlisle was their kinsman, William Hay, 4th earl of Kinnoull (d.1677), and his son, George, the 5th earl (d.1687); though during George's nonage the Kinnoull interest was in the hands of trustees, led by Mervin Tuchet, 4th earl of Castlehaven, who himself died in 1686. Carlisle's Lieutenant-General, Francis Lord Willoughby of Parham, continued embroiled until his death in 1666 and was succeeded by his brother, William, as 6th baron (and Francis's nephew, Henry, was also an acting governor). There was a further claim by James Ley, the 3rd earl of Marlborough (first creation, d.1665), former admiral of the royal fleet and founder of an English St. Croix, and his uncle, William, the 4th earl (d.1679). After James's death, Thomas Henshaw argued the Leys "never had any concernment in the s^d Islands."[184] Marlborough was written in as the trustee of the claim of Carlisle's original rival, the Courteen/Powell group, so it was hardly in the interests of those seeking repayment from Carlisle's patent to reopen the debate about its fundamental validity. The Willoughbys were the most active, at home and abroad, and the increasingly disempowered creditors noted their industrious extension of both military and political jurisdictions, which could be cast as making good the original description of the Caribbees, or defending English interests against the French, Spanish, Dutch, and Kalinago. Both cost: military activity involved additional and heavy expenditure; it got in the way of trade with foreign powers and enabled the Willoughbys to practice vacillation, disingenuousness, and guile when it came to returning others' investment.

It transpired that planters in the Caribbees had lobbied for the voiding of Carlisle's claim. The prospect of Francis Willoughby returning to his post in the Caribbean prompted many to point out that "ye Revenue of those Islands," now bolstered by possession of Surinam, "were too great to bee in[j]oyed by a Subiect and y^t it was a flower worthy to bee Stucke in ye Crown," so it suited the Privy Council to grant the planters' suit.[185] Charles II, before he took any revenue from the West Indies, would give satisfaction to the original investors, "as may consist wth equity and good conscience," and thus it was again proposed to divide the profits from the islands. Half went to Willoughby until his lease expired in 1668, with reversion to the Crown; the other half was itself divided equally in two, into annuities of £500 for life to James and then William, earls of Marlborough, and the other moiety to the earl of Kennoull until such time as the Carlisle creditors had been satisfied.[186] A further surprise was the ratification of the Commonwealth indenture of August 1649, possibly because at this point the creditors had agreed to abate one-third of their monies, reducing their total dues from £37,074 9s 6d to £24,716 6s 4d, to be "paid to them in Goods and Comodities upon the said Islands according to such rates & valuations as Merchants trading there do usually take off the same."

This levy was the cause of and shorthand for the most severe and permanent rift between those who managed resource in the Caribbean and those who hoped to profit from it in Britain. It charged a rate of four and a half percent on the production of the Leeward Islands and Barbados (i.e., that which constituted the de facto Lord Proprietorship of the Caribbees; minus the personal fiefdom of Surinam and the empty claims to authority over other islands which could not be realized). It marked the transition from the early period of colonization up to the fall of the Commonwealth: it consolidated the royal regime at the restoration of Charles II. It began codifying, rationalizing, and bringing to heel the distant settlements of the western Atlantic torrid zone, and as the mid-century was the period in which sugar was identified as a profitable resource, it consolidated the identification of these few islands as the geographical, cultural, and economic core of the region, ensuring they, and their sugar production, remained bound to the mother country. The focus of measurement of resource irreversibly shifted to London. Ironically, Carlisle's phenomenal debts finally ensured that the Caribbean islands remained vital to empire, as its mainland equivalents joined the campaigns for greater American independence.

Of this paradigm shift in the colonial–imperial relationship, there is remarkably little evidence. This may be because as far as London was concerned, it was just another mechanical expedient within a vast global network and there is a dearth of references in official documents, especially the "state papers." But in the West Indies it was a different story: this was the notorious, much-hated Four and a Half. Barbados tax farmers' accounts from 1670 to 1672 show the island was expected to pay an annual rent to the Crown of £7,000: of which it had managed just over £3,000, and the island's accountants had to admit a shortfall of £9,336 7s 1d.[187] Agents from Holetown and Bridgetown were produced to offer reasons for under-payment: suggestions included Barbadians' constant recourse to local customs and laws, adduced as the reason for not using Crown-approved beams, scales, or dockets; disagreement over the gross and net weights of a cask of sugar; and the wholesale abuse of officials. Production and shipping suffered during periods of instability, planters claimed, which in the form of war and plague was constant. The tax farmers batted aside all such excuses. There was as much sugar produced as ever; they informed their overlord, Thomas, earl of Danby, the Lord High Treasurer, but they battled to overcome resistant and obstructive locals, whether producers or customs' officers.[188]

Francis Willoughby took the credit, regarding the levy, the island of Barbados, and himself as the "Master Wheele" upon which the Caribbean empire revolved.[189] But Willoughby's creditors claimed he had gained the "Consent of [Barbados] and ye other Islands" to settle the Crown revenue "at 4½ P Cent: of all Commoditys to bee transported out of those Isl^s and farther prevailed wth ye Planters, to settle on himself (as he pretendeth) for ye support of his family during his Governement there, an ancient excise on duty uppon liquours worth about 3000^{ll} P ann, and wch alone in former time did use to defray the whole Charge of ye Government." All this, and "ye Ld Will: had covenanted wth ye King to receive for himself but one moytie of all profits whatsoever."[190] The supporters of Courteen argued that he had been and remained entitled to "the Servile Rents of *Sugar*, &c.... as absolute Proprietor by Original right of Discovery and Possession," but that these were "changed into a Duty of *4* and *½ per Cent*, payable by all Planters there to Your Majesty, and Your Grantees," which, in reality, became consumed by the cost of managing its levy.[191] As far as Treasury officials were concerned, the Crown had rendered the Four and a Half the legitimate tax of the Caribbean: it was ratified by Acts of the rate payers' assemblies, and was payable to and managed by their governor(s), their own, and the King's representative(s). It was to be levied "upon all dead commodities of the produce of those islands, and exported from thence," payable to the King, and managed by "the Lord Willoughby as chief Governor."[192] In specie, it amounted to 2s 8d out of every pound generated in Barbados and the Leeward Islands.

It is debatable whether the Four and a Half ever functioned as intended. The Willoughbys continued to claim the interruption of war, between England and the French, the Dutch and "the Caniball Indians": in 1668, William Willoughby explained that the duty had been suspended, and islands such as Antigua under conquest, but now his powers were reconfirmed, he had re-imposed the duty, in specie, on all "the native Comodities" of growth or production.[193] The issue, suspension, reissue, re-suspension, and further issue of the Four and a Half because of war mirrored genuine insecurity throughout the Caribbean, but provided a standing pretext why Carlisle's creditors had to renew their patience until threats to royal authority had been averted. From the reign of Charles II onward, war (pre)occupied the Crown, tying fast the Americas to the Metropole; while defense now came to consume the time and the resources of West Indian settlers, and confirming authority in the colonies became inexorably linked with consolidating territory and keeping it secure. There was always some new expenditure that could best be met from the Four and a Half: Barbados alone could raise around the same amount as the tithe on the Established clergy in England

and Wales.[194] If security were paramount, secret service costs, for example, could as easily be drawn from the Four and a Half as from domestic taxes.[195] The same could be said for the cost of sending and maintaining soldiers in the West Indies: in 1667, former Protectorate loyalist, Tobias Bridge, now knighted by the Restoration regime, arrived in Barbados with a regiment, and sought to increase Crown revenue, by receiving and disbursing the Four and a Half. The Council—"by wee know not what Surprise prevailed wth"— instructed William Willoughby to use the creditors' moiety to pay Bridge's regiment, and any others required for the defense of the islands.[196] Bridge's regiment was disbanded at the Treaty of Breda which ended the second Anglo-Dutch War in 1667, and was encouraged to establish as a permanent garrison, with allocations of Caribbean land commensurate with rank, but long after its commander died in the West Indies, neither his regiment, nor the state, had been recompensed for the cost, necessitating further application to the islands' customs.[197]

Future Captain-in-Chief and federal Leewards' Governor, Sir William Stapleton, arrived in the West Indies as part of Bridge's regiment, and he in turn, threatened by French and Kalinago raiders, expected the costs of the islands' defense to be met by the islanders, eventually remitted to London.[198] He and his fellow Caribbean governors would be assisted by a force coordinated by a trans-Atlantic committee: Commodore Lawrence Wright in England and Sirs Timothy Thornhill and Christopher Codrington in the West Indies supplemented by the Duke of Bolton's regiment of foot.[199] The inefficiency of this arrangement was the subject of complaint by the Commissioners of the Customs early in 1692.[200] The decision to pay Bolton's soldiers out of the Four and a Half benefited neither them nor the Crown, since the commodities sat months decaying in warehouses, compounded by considerable delay in turning payments in either direction into money.[201] At the end of the century, the planters' chorus of woes was summed up by former Assembly Speaker, Edward Littleton, publishing anonymously: "At the same time the Duty of four and a half *per Cent.* was extorted from us in *Barbados*, full sore against our Wills.... The uses of this Duty were pretended and express'd to be; For support of the Government, and for the publick Services of the Island. But the Duty was soon farmed out for Money payable in *England*." But while the planters in Barbados had paid their dues, they had seen "none of the Uses performed... So that we make and repair our Forts and Brest-works, we build our Magazines, we buy our great Guns and Ammunition; and are forced to lay great Taxes upon our selves, for defraying these and all other publick Charges. Moreover this *four and a half* is collected in such manner, that in the Judgment of all that have tried it, the Attendance and Slavery is a greater burden than the Duty."[202]

Though Francis Willoughby claimed the collection of the duty was a privilege confined to him, the Four and a Half became the standard means by which Caribbean governors were recompensed—a detail which Littleton had good reason to know as he had sailed to Barbados to act as William Willoughby's secretary.[203] The sum of £1,200 was paid to Governor Atkins toward a half-year's salary and his entertainment expenses.[204] During his term as governor of St. Christopher's, according to letters patent of September 23, 1672, Treasury Commissioners authorized John Loving, as a teller of the Exchequer, to pay Sir William Stapleton an allowance of £700 a year "out of the duty of 4 & ½ p Cent Barbadoes," operating two years in arrears.[205] Colonel Edwin Stede cost £600 per annum while Lieutenant-Governor and Commander-in-Chief of Barbados.[206] The Treasury paid salary arrears to Governor Christopher Codrington of £700 a year, although Codrington had more control over the resources of the Four and a Half than the state which employed him. He charged seven percent commission for changing commodity into specie, whereas the Board of Trade recommended that the customs' levy be sent to England as commodity and paid back to the state's servants in the colonies in light pieces of eight.[207]

Levies required infrastructure, personnel, and resources to collect them. In both mother countries and colonies hordes of farmers of customs' and tax revenue, their agents in the field, servants who engineered the operations of mercantilists—creditors or traders—who remained in Britain and sent lesser minions, beavered to engineer business. In every location a merchant, politician, or investor would have agents and factors. The two terms were almost interchangeable, meaning those who actually did the work—who possessed agency—as opposed to those who employed them, although factors tended to a more strictly economic remit than the more general agent, who could be engaged in business, the law, or politics. There was considerable overlap, however—particularly when so much of the empire rested on indebtedness, mortgage, and foreclosure: a factor was employed to manage sequestered or forfeited estates or lands in the hands of the bailiff.[208] These tended to be another rank of people who were absent from their families, temporary in their employment, who did not develop a permanent, fixed interest.[209] Thus, the most successful transitions to the Caribbean were made by those who established a reason to stay.

Agent for the Hay earls of Carlisle was William Powrey, one of several of the same name in Barbados, and quite directly related to his lord as the nephew of Archibald, the second son of Hay of Haystoun, Gentleman Usher of the Queen's Bedchamber in the time of Anne of Denmark.[210] The first William Powrey may have emigrated to Barbados before 1630 (one of Carlisle's original passengers?): he subsequently appears in the records in 1640 as one of the commissioners from Charles I to settle Carlisle's business with the Hawley brothers, Governor Henry, and his deputy, Captain William.[211] Powrey was also sent by uncle Archibald to purchase and manage Bridge Plantation, and from Bridgetown he traded in tobacco and cotton wool.[212] Not only was he swindled out of early shipments, but these sustained the poor reputation of Barbados tobacco production.[213] William seems to have been in regular residence in Barbados over the 1640s, and rose to be island secretary at the time of his death in 1651, which was also the year of the death of Archibald Hay, in the King's Bench debtors' prison.

It must therefore have been something of a coup that Carlisle's creditors retained the services of a new generation of William Powrey as their agent in Barbados, while their legal affairs in England were managed by Sir Robert Southwell, future Commissioner of Excise.[214] It was on Powrey's suggestion that the division of the customs' revenue into the Crown's and the Governor's moieties be rendered a material, physical process. The role of clerk or controller of the customs in Barbados would be held by two individuals, both of whom would sit in a receiving building—most islands designated storehouses for delivering and accepting public levies—possessed of a series of "casks" into which would be placed the specie for each commodity, daily apportioned between the two. The governor (William Willoughby) would be paid in sugar, and the controllers of the customs would receive £400, though it could not be agreed from which moiety their salaries should be drawn.[215] In fact, the person the creditors appointed to "control the customs" was William Boseman. Among Governor William Willoughby's vacillating tactics was to refuse to ratify Boseman as the Crown controller, denying all recollection of any letter of King-in-Council for dividing the customs, and claiming Boseman's instructions from Carlisle's creditors had miscarried. This was a great shame, professed the creditors, for in 1667 there would have been "very great shipping of sug^{r}s and Cottons very speedily, [we] have not in [our] time known more goods ready in this Island then now is."[216] Boseman persevered. He dug in and established his local credentials. By marrying a Barbados widow, Mrs. Judith Lovell, he extended mercantile networks between the Caribbean and New England.[217] He refused to accept Willoughby's professions of patronage unless and until the moiety went toward the creditors' restitution.[218]

Always, it seems, those whose task was to remit resource to London would stress the healthiness of production. Collectors of customs now had to be present when goods were shipped away, and the planters' inability to pay in specie allowed customs' officers to both reject goods as substandard and charge exorbitant rates.[219] In English ports, customs' houses were bureaucratic and subject to numerous claims of corruption, but there was officiousness aplenty and a veneer of efficiency and bustle. Here the state levied a further 12½ percent.[220] Thus, in the same fashion, the goods of the Caribbean must be rendered official, to an official building, rather than to the informal and domestic provision of individuals' storehouses.[221] The island of Barbados requested a dedicated customs' house early in 1666.[222] Still, Governor Atkins complained in 1680 that the island possessed neither building nor accounts, but rather, he signed around a thousand dockets a year for ships, the records of which ended up in the Naval Office section of the Board of Trade and Plantations. He made no income from these.[223] Stapleton's military reputation made him among the most popular of governors, able to federate the Leeward Islands, but when it came to levies that were Caribbee wide, the islands had to negotiate agreement between themselves. Throughout the 1680s they tried to have the Four and a Half commuted, for some other Imposition "wch may be more Advantagious or a Recompence att Least Equivelent to his Maj^{tie} and yett of more Ease and Conveniency of The Inhabitants of the Respective Islands."[224] Stapleton had been in charge of the Leewards for more than four years before he wrote back to London to inform them that Crown collectors having failed to arrive, he was ordering his own levy of the duty.[225] Ten years later the planters of Antigua requested that a second custom house be set up in Parham Town, that in St. John's being too distant for many (though the towns of St. John's and Parham were among the closest on the island), while delays, costs of transportation, storage, and bureaucracy were so burdensome and so liable to abuse that goods rotted. The custom remained unpaid, with the additional charges amounting to more than the goods, in perfect condition, would have been worth. The planters were meanwhile forced to import necessities at their own cost which nevertheless became liable for state duty.[226] Sir Robert Robinson was equally concerned at the absence of a customs' house in Bermuda, and of a multiplicity of ships able to transport tobacco off the island, which wasted 100,000 pounds of crop in a season. Bermudans, he protested, were further denied the liberty granted elsewhere in the region, whereby settlers could pay another fine to "allow" them to violate the Navigation Acts.[227] Gradually, inexorably, markets were closed off, including Scotland, which before the Act of Union had provided a means to avoid the Navigation. Isaac Richier, while in office, had used Bermuda sloops to send tea, sugar, and tobacco to Scotland, in avoidance of tax.[228]

There undoubtedly was a sugar revolution, but this is a different narrative from that we have come to expect. The spike in sugar's profitability in the 1650s provided the impetus behind the governments in London seeking to tap that wealth, while channeling political loyalty through the management of merchantable resource. In 1666, it was said, Barbados, the Leeward Islands, and Surinam had yearly sent more than £800,000 "value" to England.[229] The Four and a Half separated Barbados and the Leeward Islands from the rest of the region, defined them as the "sugar islands," and inexorably bound them to a reliance on cane, its derivatives, trade, slavery, plantation society, and empire. This was not the point of the Four and a Half's creation but it was the consequence of its application. It was the start of home-government levies that gathered pace in the reigns of the later Stuarts. Under Charles II the duty on "white" sugar produced in the colonies was tripled, while its price only doubled. Exporters still seemed able to ship large quantities so James II's governments raised duties again.[230] In the dying years of the seventeenth century, the interplay between Britain and the Caribbean, based on resource, became bombastic and coarse. Both had become dependent on sugar and each side blamed the other for their addiction. The market was glutted; the grocery was still a drug "as Ours is, and for ever will be."[231]

The process was not dissimilar in Jamaica where English planters gradually ran down the more diverse land use practiced by the Spanish and sought profit in sugar. The Helyar plantation and mercantile empire at Bybrook, St. Thomas in the Vale, kept far more copious and scrupulous records than most. Nevertheless, these reveal not the wealth of sugar but the crippling costs of its storage, carriage, freight, and duties. The returns did not cover the costs.[232] In 1685, William Helyar invested a fortune in buying the *Defiant Pinke* of Youghal. He increased its tonnage, made it ship shape, and relaunched it as the *Samuel* of Bristol. There, the city's leading merchant, John Napper, professed it the finest of its type in England, but a wasted investment, warning that the price of cotton wool was plummeting, all commodities were down, as were all drugs except tobacco and the best sherry.[233] As sugar took hold of Jamaica in the early years of the eighteenth century, hoping to capitalize on the larger island's economies of scale, it was declared "such a Drugg here [in London] y^t its hardly worth making."[234]

The natural resource of sugarcane was, in the final analysis, nothing more exotic than very tall grass. To become merchantable resource it demanded massive expenditure in capital, labor, and buildings. If the crop remained in the soil, for want of labor, because an estate became too indebted, or because its owner or manager absented themselves, it was "but of little Value": it had to be "ground into Sugar, Rum, or Molasses, which cannot be done but at great Charge."[235] Barbadians thought themselves at an advantage because they could refine sugar in situ using native clay, "temper[ing] it with Water to the thickness of Frumentry." This was poured on top of the curing taches, and left four months, such that when knocked out of the pots, the outsides remained muscovado, but the core was transformed. So began a further damaging dialogue between colonies and Metropole about what to call the bonanza commodity. The mother countries wished to attach to it the term "white": such as "perfect White, and excellent Lump Sugar" or "coarse white."[236] Colonists preferred the term "refined." They regarded it as the (re)finest sugar of all, dried under the sun, sweeter, and imparting less flavor than its British-produced equivalent, and branded those who boiled or baked sugar in England "a sort of Upstart People, of very little use to the Nation, in Comparison with the Plantations; Three Pound of whose refined Sugar will not sweeten much more than two Pound of Sugar Refined in *Barbadoes*, neither is it so Clean nor Wholsom as the *Barbadoes* Refined Sugar is."[237] The difference was not mere semantics. It was about the price that could be charged by any party. Colonists accused the British sugar bakers of wanting "to engross the whole Trade to themselves, of making Brown Sugars white, and fit for Use... being sole Buyers of the Browns, and sole Sellers of the Whites, they might buy and sell at their own Prices." To Caribbean planters, sugar bakers were sleight-of-hand monopolists, making themselves sole purveyors of "white sugar"—in the British sugar houses' interest to close down any attempts by West Indian producers to refine sugar in situ and sell it at a premium direct to British consumers. The Caribbean should supply the raw material. The British would make it refined. Thus the propaganda from refiners in Britain took the elite, cultivated pretensions of the Plantocracy and reduced them to coarse earth: they were "the *Clayers*, a Worm at the Root preying upon" Britain's interest.[238]

Caskage, freight, and other transportation costs were "ten shillings a Hundred." The land and "great and chargeable Buildings" were reckoned at nothing, because they had to be in place before any production was possible. The planter would "not get a Groat a day for his *Negroes* labour" which cost him £30 per person if the slaves had been seasoned, but every planter knew well enough that by 1700 the labor which produced resource to be transported to Britain was provided by slaves.[239] A supply of slaves tied planters to the Royal African Company (unless one was in thrall to Codrington), leaving Caribbean gentlemen of refinement to "scramble" in the slave market in a "shameful" manner. Transatlantic shipping was ruled by the Navigation; taxes and impositions sucked the marrow from planters' bones; and their markets were controlled by domestic manufacturing. The British maxim was "Production abroad and Manufacture at home," but ironically, if home markets did not want their produce, American colonies, Anglophone or otherwise, did.[240] Figures for the (official) cargoes carried to England, Guinea, and "the Plantations" respectively, over three months in 1711, expressed this graphically (see Table 2.1).

In the British West Indies, planters felt their ingenuity to improve was "baffled, and...Industry cut up by the roots." The proper order inverted, "the best Men in those Countries must in their own Persons submit to the Indignity," and in their "miseries" must all acknowledge that they were mired in debt. The English "make us savage: they make us forget all Rules of Decency."[241] Planters who tried to make their living in the torrid zone were forced to think about not being settlers, not being landowners, and, ironically, not being English. Families sold up, set on managers, became absentees. During 1694, 1,600 poorer planters were reputed to have gone over to the French, who, having seized land in the course of the Williamite wars, were developing their possessions by offering better terms for trade. The planter/settler who believed themselves at the very heart of "English Liberties" felt reduced to worse than a rack renter, because the English market was glutted by production and therefore commodity duties were turned into land taxes. They were, by their own government, "in effect made Forainers and Aliens."[242]

Their society debased and their role belittled, it was with sarcasm that it was suggested that "possibly we may have half a Score Weavers go to the *Plantations* and buy negroes, and weave the Cotton-Wool upon the Place, the Tobacco Strippers and Cutters go to *Virginia* and follow their Functions there." This would be an inversion of proper society.[243] Robert Montgomery

Table 2.1 Ships and their West Indian cargoes, distinguished by destination, compiled from data within TNA, CO 28/13, no.72ii.

	England	*Guinea*	*Plantations*
Ships	10	5	44
Sugar	1924 tons	165 tons	2133 tons
Molasses	12 hogsheads	----	529 hogsheads
Rum	0 hogsheads	72 hogsheads	2105 hogsheads

may have had grandiose feudal notions of aristocratic landlordism in the tropics, but he looked back over a century of his own and others' colonial ancestors' efforts and issued a warning to prospective settlers in the savannah lands of the Carolinas. Turning their precious virgin soils over to "some single Product" rendered resource "common, and the *being common* robs of Benefit. Thus *Sugar* in *Barbados*, *Rice* in *Carolina*, and *Tobacco* in *Virginia*, take up all the Labours of their People, over-stock the Markets, stifle the Demand, and make their Industry their Ruin."[244] In securing control of West Indian resource and resourcefulness, Britain had, by the end of the seventeenth century, destroyed planters' connection to an economy and a society it had taken them a century to create.

CHAPTER 3

Connection

In the summer of 1685, Jane Long gave birth to a daughter, christened Elizabeth in St. Philip's church in the southeast of Barbados. The father was not then named, but on December 4, Jane travelled west to Bridgetown, accompanied by Peter Perkins, to be married by Rev. James Faucett, minister of St. Michael's. They returned to St. Philip's, and conceived a son, Thomas, baptized on March 11, 1688. By 1692, they had moved to London, where Thomas was either rebaptized at St. Giles, Cripplegate, or they had lost their son and given another the same name. In 1698, the Quaker community in Southwark reported that a Peter Perkins, aged about 44, living in Allhallows, Barking, who had been working as a sugar broker, had died on October 29, probably from a fever. He was buried in the Park Quaker burial ground.[1]

Maybe the Rev. Job Brooks of St. Philip's had refused to marry a woman who had given birth to an illegitimate child, or maybe they sought community witness from congregants for whom this was an unrecognized man and woman embarking on a life of chaste union. Peter and Jane's desire to have their union witnessed by God, and in the face of a congregation, to be recognized within a wider community whose members otherwise set little store by church attendance, Christian mores, or observance, and their commitment to forging a family unit that cut across established societal bonds, bestows cultural capital on the intimate moment at which they joined hands; magnifying a personal connection into a political one. This single example of a marriage has such huge cultural capital because Jane Long was white; her husband, Peter Perkins, black. Other registers—for Pembroke tribe, Bermuda, virtually entire between 1645 and 1722; St. Andrew's, Jamaica, from 1666; or those sent home by Rev. Henry Pope, of St. George Gingerland, in Nevis—are silent about black participation within the white community.[2] The only examples to come even close, in more ethnically diverse Jamaica, are the marriage of Charles Benoit to the Arawak woman Uañah, and that of Robert Dakins to Sarah Dennis, a mulatto.[3]

This chapter explores the connections that created social bonds, albeit Eurocentric, and defined by British norms. Within the Anglican communion, this was the "mystical union that is betwixt Christ and his Church": Perkins acted "reverently, discreetly, advisedly, soberly, and in the fear of God, and duly considered the causes for which matrimony was ordained."[4]

He was also joining a number of British affinities: by inclination, toward Christianity and its expression in English; what Addison called an affinity to devotion, which, much more than reason, distinguished men from brute beasts; and of position, both by marriage and consanguinity. Peter Perkins and Jane Long had entered into a "Civil Bond of Persons...join'd together in one Body by Affinity."[5] However, the facts of Peter Perkins's color and the startling isolation of our example, allow us to glimpse a moment of basic connection, which we can isolate by stripping away as many possible ways in which we glimpse extraneous, ulterior, and instrumental ends. This is the closest we can get to a wedding that was most about the love between two people.

In terms of divining instrumentalism, we can explore Quakerism in the West Indies, because Quaker evidence is more explicit in identifying the instrumentalism that may lie behind connection, and articulating the only valid instrument to be the witness of the light. Theirs was a Society of Friends, the sense of fellowship shored up in three ways. Among themselves they had "holy Faith...and divine Support [which] bore up the Spirits," and the testimony they possessed against "Profaneness and Immorality...Superstition and Will-worship." Further, they endured the scorn, derision, beatings, buffetings, stonings, pinchings, kickings, dirtings, and pumpings from the "rabble"; the spoliation of their goods; and the stocks, whipping, imprisonment, banishment, and death from the magistrates. They became self-defining at the hands of others: their much-vaunted "sufferings."[6] They possessed a particular facility for mobility and dispersal, be it itinerant preaching, missions to spread the word, banishments, ejections, punishments, and transportations. Continual ejection was like being tossed on the oceans by the winds, "that a Rock, or Place to rest upon they have not known," and God's "chosen Vessels" would "run to and fro like Vagabonds" but neither sea nor land would separate their bonds of love.[7] William Brend, about to be transported from Newgate to Jamaica, chose not to identify with the saints' exodus in the Old Testament and the seed of Abraham, but to issue dark curses against the ship owners who would transport them, since this was the kind of merchandise the destruction of which had been foretold in Revelation.[8]

Quakers, therefore, combined the intimacy of shared values and beliefs within the meeting, feeling themselves beset by the torments of others' scorn and universal human frailty, while striving to sustain connection in new American locations. Life in the West Indies could be a continuation of their sufferings in pursuit of the truth: in Bermuda, one Robinson was "This poor Quaker" who was "hated by all the Rest for his being Soe honest."[9] Those who regarded the colonies as a sink of depravity, such as John Rous, for whom Barbados "excel[led] in wickedness, pride and covetousness, oppressing, cheating and cozening," saw Quakers as its victims, and there were worries that Caribbean society was too fraught with temptation to keep even Quakers true.[10] Frail humanity was cozened by the prospect of power or wealth.

Irishman, John Perrott, defined himself as "a Member of Truth, John, Who is called a Quaker," and published widely on both his sufferings and his prophesies. He fell into dispute with George Fox over a number of issues but in essence about who was guilty of allowing truth to be corrupted by worldliness. Fox had become a leader, such that "common people, that had honest minds, became wiser than their Teachers" because they were "without the Bias of carnal Interests or Passions."[11] Perrott took his preaching to Barbados, but in 1661, preempting his arrival, Fox warned Quakers that Perrott advocated that hats be worn during prayer, that he had taken a whore, and that he owned more in common with Presbyterians, Independents, Baptists, and Seekers than other Quakers. This last charge was also leveled at his supporter in Barbados, Robert Rich.[12] In Barbados, not only did Perrott identify connections with ungodly sects, he immersed himself in the flesh, wearing "a carnal Sword and a Staffe tipt with Gold, did wear Gorgeous Apparel, make a Feast and shoot off Guns."[13] The staff was a gift from Governor Sir Thomas Modyford, who thought him of "good Temper skill and knowledge in merchant affaires...great Cunning" and with a "searching and industrious spiritt." The degree to which he was accepted within West Indian society, and his willingness to call over his wife and children would serve Modyford to "take off much of the rude roughness of [Quakers'] temper" and Perrott's wide popularity among Quakers and others would prove useful in encouraging primary and secondary migration to the West Indies and promote the peopling of Jamaica, to which Perrott travelled in 1664.[14] Perrott retained his optimism that the West Indies offered "Glorious Glimmerings of the Life of Love, Unity, and pure Joy"; where he felt "that abundance of simple and single Love"; where "The Land is void of persecution." In future stretched "a clearer day of Amity and Vnity."[15] Thomas Pilgrim was a prominent Barbados man of business, "on whose integrity" the governor relied, who managed to ride out attempts to undermine either faith or networks. When Henry Clinkett made a will vesting guardianship of his three children to his brother-in-law, Pilgrim, and his father-in-law, fellow Quaker, Thomas Foster, both were denied for refusing to swear allegiance. Clinkett's widow remarried a non-Quaker who squandered the estate, such that the children might have been ruined had not Pilgrim been admitted their guardian "and by that Means, through disbursing much of his own Money, retrieved some Part of their Estate, and made it tenantable." Pilgrim sent the will of merchant, William Emblin, to the Prerogative Court in Canterbury, though himself excluded from administration on Barbados.[16]

James Fontleroy, a Friend in Ilminster in Somerset, confirmed to his brother, Richard Talbott, at least four years a merchant in Bridgetown, that Charles II's Restoration had produced "Tryinge, Apostatizing, [and] p[er]secutinge times" in which "those that conforme not to the prelatical worship may be forcd to Quitt theire English [Plan]tac[i]on[s]." Fontleroy sought to join Talbott in Barbados. "Bro: did yo[u] and my selfe minde heaven, more we should minde earth less, & be more willing to part with its choicest Treasure," counseled James, demonstrating how Quaker materialism was able to survive by connecting within and eschewing connection without: "however there is Comfort in that the sealed one shalbe enabled to hold out [and] not p[ar]take wth the Beast in neither Marke, name, or Number of his nam[e]."[17] Talbott died in 1668, but Fontleroy remained active within the Barbados Quakers and married a Rous.[18]

Others were prepared to emulate Perrott by taking up the sword. During 1663, the men of Jamaica drew up their wills in case they should be killed defending the island. Robert Clarke bequeathed his 90 acres at Port Morant to his wife Sarah and sons, John and Joseph, but if God should also take them, then "I freely bestow it upon the faithfull in ye Lord Called Quakers & thro mine estate wholley to be...executors unto the ministry."[19] James Kendall, as Governor of Barbados, was frustrated by the degree to which the Quakers did not completely shun the Beast of politico-economic power, but rather tamed it for their own purposes. They did not baptize their children, but they went to an Anglican service in the morning and a Quaker meeting in the afternoon. They obtained dispensations to take oaths and pull off their hats in order to "be more serviceable" to their party. They were industrious in lobbying for the election of sympathizers; whereas by their refusal to countenance war with the French "the Island is Extreamly weakned by itt; being a People wholly uselesse for the Defence and preservation of the Country."[20] He went as far as suggesting that their refusal to fight against France was because they were in league with William Penn, who was as absolute in his government of Quakers as Louis XIV was toward his "miserable subjects."

Despite attempts to dismantle their networks and their edifices, Quakers managed to root themselves. Domestic dwellings were used as meeting houses, but dedicated ground was committed to a Meeting in Tudor Street, Bridgetown, and a burial ground in St. Philip's.[21] In Nevis (1658), Quakers Peter Head, John Rous (probably the same as was active in Barbados) and Mary Fisher "found a friendly Reception" at the house of Humphrey Highwood, and when the ship carrying George Fox was forbidden to go ashore there, Friends gathered a meeting on board; while in Bermuda, from 1660, the itinerant preaching of George Rose and one other led to a meeting at the house of William Wilkinson in Paget's tribe.[22] Elizabeth Carter who had come from Barbados to visit "her Friends" in Bermuda, disturbed the divine service conducted by William Edwards in Devonshire's, and was shipped onward to New Providence.[23] A "Worship House" was built on Antigua in 1684; and there were regular gatherings in Carolina, with a meeting house and burial ground at Archdale Square.[24]

The Quaker community worked harder, and was more successful than most, at keeping connection between each other and across the oceans; formalized in the granting of certificates to travel, to marry, and to move between one meeting and another.[25] The printed certificates with which Quakers registered their marriages survive in the joining of the London merchant houses of Benthall and Eccleston, through the persons of their servants in the West Indies.[26] The combination of printed text and manuscript insertions (italics) announced that, "Having declared their Intentions of taking each other in Marriage before several publick Meetings of the People of God called QUAKERS in *Midd*^{x} according to the good Order used amongst them...at their publick Meeting-place at *Devonshire House in Lond*," Walter Benthall took Mercy Eccleston by the hand. He declared, "My friends in a true sense of the love of God, & before you whom I call to be my witnesses I take this my dear beloved friend Mercy Eccleston to be my wife, I Promising to be to her a faithfull constant & loving husband, as long as we shal both continue in this present World."[27] The wording was standardized, and increasingly so, but the sentiment behind it mediated by conscience.[28]

With the uncertainty of life itself exacerbated by sea-crossings and separation, Quakers searched within for evidence that God's constancy was witnessed through his servants. Thomas Holme, communicating from Swarthmoor, Westmorland, to Robert Barrow in Carolina, desired that the Lord would "preserve thee & Mee faithfull to y^t Measure or Talent wch hee hath bestowed upon us."[29] William Copp, in Barbados, feared that the separation of the seas would weaken the love of his childhood sweetheart, Jane Alexander, who, having been resident in Jamaica, had been sent by her father to Ann Travers's Quaker school in Chiswick.[30] He confided to Theodore Eccleston that he possessed "a Reall & unfained Love & Respect for her"; maybe because she was his first love: "ye Only & first P[er]son that I ever broke my mind to about any Such Concerne." He sent her ointment, chocolate, a wide-brimmed Bermudas' bonnet, and many romantic words:

> I could do no Less then to acquaint thee of my Welfare & of my Constancy in Love unfained towards thee, Tho removed a great Distance, Out of each Others Sight & Reach, yet thou art not nor cannot be Out of my remembrance not one hower in ye Day, but Still waiting to Receive Some releife or Comfort from thy Sweet hand, thou art still within the Horizon of my Love, always beholding of thee, with a Cheirfull Eye, and Desires nothing more in this World but to be in thy favour[. T]he Horizon of my Love is Large and Spacious it is boundless, as that of the Imagination, & where the Imagination Rangeth the Memory is still Bussey to Usher in, & present the desired Object it fixeth upon, it is Love that Setts them both at worke, & may be said to be the Highest Sphear, Whence they Receive their Motion. Thus thou appear unto me often in these fforraine Travells and that thou mayst beleive the Better, I send thee these lines as my Ambassadors to acquaint thee Accordingly Thoughts dureing the Time of our Separation, & Lett Our thoughts meet Some times by Intercourse of Letters; in which I shall Esteeme very much being the precious Effects of thy Love.[31]

Copp had reason for unease. Jane remained in London, and at Devonshire House on June 17, 1690, married instead Quaker John Stout, a malster of Hertford. Copp's friend Theodore Eccleston and his wife, Anne, were among Jane's witnesses.[32] Copp stayed in St. Thomas, Barbados, and married Elizabeth Ayshford, who died in 1704.[33] His estate, by custom, came to provide local Friends with a burial ground.[34]

The Quaker network of intermarriage was no less interconnected with commerce and settlement than non-Quakers. Tracing the names of the witnesses at Quaker marriages, such as the Benthalls, Ecclestons, Harts, and Ashfields connects people around the Caribbean, the Caribbean to the Chesapeake and across the Atlantic.[35] Ties of kinship and faith were continued through the generations, with monies bequeathed to ensure children were educated "among Friends," put to an "honest trade": and provision made for "poor Friends, that labor in the word of God."[36] Despite complaints of Quaker sufferings, the will of Richard Hoskins, a merchant of Pennsylvania, was overseen by three sets of Quaker executors: Theodore Eccleston in London; parties in Pennsylvania; and in Barbados, planter, Philip Collins, and John Groves, merchant, both of the island.[37] Quakers voluminously testified to maintaining a combination of intimacy and directness between peoples, which triumphed over the fracturing of place, tying economic, social, and moral values. Their resort to conscience made them mistrusted and trusted in equal measure while Quakers' connection to spirit, conscience, and witness minimized evidence of personal and intimate connection being corrupted.

It was more usual for the transatlantic passage to corrode family sentiment and the more humble the migrant the greater the breach. When Thurston and Jane Johnson departed Lancashire for Barbados, they left their 18-month old daughter with her maternal grandmother, with promises that they would send for her. But Thurston died, and Jane remarried in Barbados, leaving an increasingly elderly grandmother to raise a daughter who knew neither parent and was dependent on the parish.[38] James Forshaw told no one where he went, in 1634, when he walked out on his son, also 18 months old, but his family believed it was "into Barbados or to some place."[39] James senior had indeed been in Barbados.[40] When he wandered back into his now adult son's life, he was destitute, accompanied by a Barbados wife, and reliant on his son's financial support. James junior was the eldest son, and all the other lives on a lease of a tenement from the wealthy Faringtons of Worden being expired, he had tried to claim his birthright—albeit a humble one— but had been unable to pay the fine. When his father reappeared part way through the 16 years he had been given to pay, father and son agreed to divide the tenement in half during James senior's lifetime. But James senior not only refused to pay his half of the redemption money to the then tenant but also insisted that the new West Indian Mrs. Forshaw be paid an annuity from the property after her husband's death, and to seal their financial stake in England issued death threats against his son's wife and child.[41] Leonard Bezer destroyed the life of his son when he "intic[ed] and allur[ed]" his pregnant daughter-in-law, also about to inherit land, "to make merry a-shipp board" and sold her into indentured servitude in Barbados.[42]

It was not necessarily the extent of wealth or property on either side of the Atlantic that determined connection. Mary, a member of the Pole family of Derbyshire, which otherwise had little concern with West Indian affairs, tied herself firmly to Barbados by marrying there three times: to John Jones, a gentleman of St. Philip's; to merchant, Peter Legay; and to the Justice of St. John's, Thomas Quintyne.[43] Jones died of fever on February 1, 1671, having made a divided bequest between Mary and their child, leaving her "no freind here to assist me" in the "mutability" of her condition. She wrote to Derbyshire in the hope it would not seem strange to her family that God had restored her "to my former condition in the inioyment of a second loveing husband, one m^r peter legay a yonge marchant here...being a loveing man to mee of good repute and friends."[44] Her new husband familiarized himself to German Pole at Radbourne Hall as a former boarder at Winchester College at the same time as Judge Newdigate, who was his new wife's kinsman's wife's brother. He ingratiated himself by inviting German, or (initially) his wife, to be godparent to their child—a boy named German—conceived soon after their marriage, and baptized on the island as the Legays "intend to depute one in your place to stand for you."[45] On the loss of Peter, after fewer than four years together, she hoped that the "many crosses and misfortunes" she had "waided through" since "coming" (rather than going) to Barbados had been ended by marrying Thomas Quintyne.[46]

Mary rooted herself in Barbados and provided for herself and her children through successive marriages, but the letters from Barbados reveal her fear that her absence had eroded the mindfulness of those she had left in Derbyshire; her misfortunes revived "through the yelouseyes I have that some of you have forsaken this world or the remembrance of me haveing since I came from england not heard from any of my owne relations whose kindness was so great to me when with them that tyme nor place shall never make me forgett It."[47] With the officiousness of a judge, and as a public man concerned with the economics of inheritance, Thomas Quintyne angrily fought for his wife's family's remembrance, particularly as her first husband, John Jones, had been his cousin, and he clearly loathed Peter Legay's father, "the dipper," another charged with deliberately holding his son in Barbados so that he could seize his estate in England.[48]

The family was a forum in which ties of place first physically, and then sentimentally, divided the people. From the outset, isolated Bermudan inhabitants were exhorted not to scatter their settlements, but rather to group themselves into "families" of at least five, where they could "conueniently be, so to eate, and worke together."[49] Thomas Quintyne, related to the Mundys and the Pilgrims, both families disturbed by West Indian connection, was himself cemented there within his nuclear family.[50] By 1682, Mary had given birth to a third son, Thomas Quintyne junior; property and posterity buttressed by a "Plague of Building."[51] His mother, who had succeeded in marrying in the West Indies against the wishes of her family in England, suffered the loss of her husband and maybe others, which led her to develop greater empathy for those who struggled to forge connection in the tropics. Her response, however, was to talk about "goeing home": she would set on a manager in Barbados. Absence may have made William Copp fonder, but his sweetheart could get on with her life without him. John Atkins prefaced his long relation of his voyages to Africa and the West Indies with a warning to any who embarked, that there might be the danger of being lost at sea, of ending up a family without its breadwinner, and leaving behind those at the mercy of rogues who would steal away with the hearts of "wives and mistresses."[52]

In the testimony of Quakers, relatively poor white people, and (white) women, therefore, we have the best evidence of intimate connection determined by sentiment.[53] Peter Perkins remains the only black person whose story reveals something similar. The records of connection within the black community, including Perkins's marriage, are slippery because they are embedded within those of the white elite; in this case, church records. This is true of slave manifests in late seventeenth-century and eighteenth-century estate records. The copious records left by Thomas Thistlewood in both England and Jamaica date from the height of the plantation system in the mid-eighteenth century, in which all of the references to intimate relations with either black or white women are couched only in terms of (his) sexual gratification. Trevor Burnard has powerfully related Thistlewood's relationship with his (particularly female) slaves: all "to some extent, psychologically damaged by their experience...their community, to the extent that it existed, was one marked by personal devastation and social trauma...Slave women were workers, mothers, and sexual partners. Thistlewood interfered in all three areas and accentuated their trauma."[54]

Aphra Behn's *Oroonoko* was romantic confection, and her descriptions of love within the Kalinago community of Surinam, or between her black heroes, Oroonoko and Imoinda, at least while they were still in Africa, compromised by western notions of love and its prerequisites. The Kalinago went naked, but as witness to their natural state, not their sinfulness. They wooed only with modest eyes. The courtship of Oroonoko and Imoinda was similar, stressing Imoinda's modesty and beauty, each enhancing the other; and Oroonoko's warrior credentials, such that on their initial meeting Oroonoko, "having made his first Complements, and presented her an hundred and fifty Slaves in Fetters, he told her with his Eyes, that he was not insensible of her Charms," and Imoinda was "so glorious a Conquest...she understood that silent Language of new-born Love; and from that Moment, put on all her Additions to Beauty."[55] This love is further distinguished from that usually described, in that the sentiment between them was chaste, because "as he knew no Vice, his Flame aim'd at nothing but Honour, if such a distinction may be made in Love."[56] Their idealized and stylized connection was designed to mirror all the others. The beauty of Imoinda, Queen of Night and Black Venus, was admired by hundreds of white men, and she was the object of lust on the part of the Coromanti King. She so surpassed white women in beauty, grace, and modesty, that in Surinam, the governor's overseer, John Trefry, "who was naturally Amorous, and lov'd to talk of Love as well as any body" was captivated by Imoinda, in her mid-teens, whom he had renamed ("Christ'ned") Clemene, and thus became a love-rival of Oroonoko (renamed Caesar), the slave he had befriended and from whom he had earned respect and trust. Behn continued her metaphor of that purity of human connection that could be detected in and through the eyes: Oroonoko "saw a kind of Sincerity, and awful Truth in the Face of *Trefry*; he saw an Honesty in his Eyes, and he found him wise and witty enough to understand Honour."[57] Thus Behn set up a triangle in which men were enslaved by love, lust, and beauty. She contrasted the chastity of heroic love on the one hand, with the polygamy of African men: the Coromanti king had many wives and concubines and Oroonoko's singularity was unusual "in that Country, where Men take to themselves as many as they can maintain," and older wives came at length to serve the newcomers. This was designed to contrast bitterly with Behn's experience of white men; criminals, and sinners, who possessed many women only to abandon them in "Want, Shame and Misery."[58] Richard Ligon articulated the value system whereby planters allowed a "brave fellow" with "extraordinary qualities" up to three wives: but women only one husband.[59] This is a bleak view of the "daily changing of wives and mistresses"; the casual disregard for and discard of women (black and white) an incidental prize of planter strength.[60]

Polygamy among slaves in the West Indies was connived at by planters for reasons of economics and slave-management, but also because their own morals were so loose. Ministers, who were (in principle) charged with upholding Christian mores, complained of both the "Checker'd...Uncleanness" of those who "debauch themselves with their Infidel Slaves," but casually committed any children to bondage, and of the prevalence of polygamy within slave communities. And, contrary to Behn's apologia for the practice, the clergy were conditioned to see this as unchristian and immoral on its own terms because "the negroes take as many wifes as they please, and turn them off at their pleasure and take others."[61] No white commentator concerned themselves with either the sentiment of connection or the considered ceremonial that rendered a union recognized within the black community. The nearest we have is Bosman's description of Mina marriage (in Africa), in which goods were kept separate and the couple negotiated between themselves. Some kept concubines, whom "they several times prefer before their Wives, and take more care of them," though these children would be illegitimate. Bosman seemed as taken as Behn by the directness of the connection between man and woman "not over-loaded with Ceremonies, nor have they any Notion of a Previous Courtship to bring on the Match: here are no tedious Disputes on account of Marriage Settlements." All that was required was that a man "fix an eye" on a young woman, "(Virgin, I scarce dare say)."[62] The terms "marriage" and particularly "wife" were used regardless, as they were for other forms of union considered illegal or unsanctioned such as marriages conducted by dissenters.[63] Rev. Robert Robertson noted that polygamy was "permitted," but that it suppressed the birthrate, to Nevis's economic detriment.[64] In the modern era, Richard Sheridan conjectured that declining rates of African women and girls being imported also promoted polygamy.[65] The evidence for the earlier period is scant.[66]

In 1733 Robert Cunyngham listed 283 slaves on two Leewards' estates.[67] Of these, 112 were described as "Creol." There were "conventional" family groups, such as Doll, who, aged around 16, joined Basson Quaco, and they had at least five children together, ranging in age from Lubba (20, deaf and dumb) to Dick (9); three girls were in Michell's gang, and two boys in Little Gang. A question mark hangs over Esther (20), described as sister to "Dicky" of Little Gang, whose mother was named as Maria. Seventeen-year old Peggy is already described as "Swan's wife," Swan being a Mina slave of about 25. Izabeau (Moko, looking after the house and the pigs, aged 30) and Michell (driver, carter, and chief ganger, Creole, aged 31) had had three children together, over an eight-year period; while Joanton, who is not listed in her own right, provides a precise date for the birth of her two youngest children with Edenburgh, with whom she had also had a third, aged about 12.[68] It may be significant that although there are 41 different mothers listed, only 16 separate fathers are identified: Betty, an Igbo woman, had six children working at Cunyngham's, but no father given for any of them. The only possible identifiable polygamist was Clem (Igbo, gardener) because he is named as the father of ten-year-old Francois, with Louisa, still alive, and aged about 30 in 1733, and four- and one-year-old Clem and Scipio with Phibba.[69]

Cunyngham's slaves lived in relatively conventional European-style families, within slave-houses. At work, Cunyngham employed the usual subdivision into gangs, but when he purchased 21 Ghanaian slaves from Nicholas Gallway, he placed the newcomers in a scheme that crossed mentoring with apprenticeship. Thus one of the two Bambara men was renamed "London" and placed with "Doctor Ham," the surgeon from Kongo; an Awy called Accara "put wth Andrew to be a Cooper"; and three younger Awy boys, "Bristoll," "Codgeo" (Kojo), and "Piero" with "Will & the other Awy Young Negro men."[70] There was some, but not universal, sensitivity to language and culture, therefore, with other instrumental concerns such as the employment requirements of the estates, the age of senior workers, and their requirements for help. Similarly, Sir William Stapleton would place slaves in different employments if they displayed an aptitude for the work.[71]

On June 26, 1734—neat and precise—Robert Cunyngham named and enumerated (an important distinction) "The Number of my Family White and Black" as follows:

White Men	White Women		Negroes
Robert Cunyngham	Elizabeth Cunyngham & little Dau Eliz. Philadelphia	Men	124
Daniel Cunyngham	Jourdaina Cunyngham	Women	96
Charles Cunyngham	Elizabeth Arnold	Boyes	33
Simon Lanahan		Girles	25
Daniel Robinson			278

This simple list cross-references socioeconomic and sentimental connections.[72] The first is that "family" equates with "household," which was a connection confined to people, but only just: Cunyngham was as assiduous in noting the (very similar) names, values, and deaths of all livestock, its increase and decrease.[73] In this he was following custom, but his precision and detail allow us additional insights. All black people were enumerated within the category of "black family," but not all the white people eligible by affinity of marriage or consanguinity were named within "white family." Cunyngham referred to his relations with women as "ventures," and while there is no mention of his (presumably deceased) wife, Judith Elizabeth de Bonneson, there is of his mistress from London, Elizabeth Arnold, but not of the children she had borne him.[74] Three of Robert's and Judith's children are included: Daniel the heir, Charles, and Jourdaina; and also included was Daniel's wife, Elizabeth, and their daughter.[75] The (legitimate) children not included cannot be explained away by their having joined other households through marriage, and so we must assume that Cunyngham was employing a patriarchy of sentiment to include or exclude consanguinity. This is reinforced by the addition of Lanahan and Robinson, probably adopted by Cunyngham into his family, as he would "Mr James Hay in the Island of St Christophers whom I Brought up from a Child."[76] Elizabeth Arnold—later to be superseded (and bitterly) in Cunyngham's affections by the "Vile Jade," Mary Gainer, and their possible daughter together, "Susanna Cunyngham"—had a notion of the affinity of sentiment stronger than her patriarch: "I am sorry that you should think [so] much [of me] that you let me have the same Liberty that any Overseer has when I am the Mother of four as fine Chilldren to you as ever was born / and was a greater Slave then any you had besides the hardships you know I went under for you," and it is unclear whether in the phrase "it is very hard you should Maintain another Mans Bastards & let your own Want," she is referring to those children Cunyngham raised who had no blood ties to him, to the children that Mary Gainer had with Cunyngham, or the children they may have had together.[77]

A contemporary of Cunyngham in St. Christopher's felt compelled to inform the Bishop of London of the "truth" about the slaves. "Concern and Indignation at their being forced away from their Kindred, Acquaintance, and Country" necessitated the men, women, and children being separated from each other on voyages, which they had convinced themselves would result in their being fattened and eaten. On arrival, they ran away; many so "stupid" as to get a boat thinking it would return them to Africa. Those who remained were incapable of using a shovel, and proved at best but "Eye-Servants." While making rational conclusions from their treatment and legal categorization as chattel equivalents of livestock, therefore, the slaves were revealed to be all-too-human vehicles for sentiment. The sentiments of which they were deemed possessed, however, were entirely negative: fear—what Defoe would call "Slave-like Terror"—and "a peculiar Propensity to Theft, Idleness, and Lying." The attribution of these sentiments deemed them unable to form social bonds between themselves, for they were "void of the Seeds of Friendship, quarrelsom, foul-mouth'd, stubborn, revengeful, and Lovers of Strong-Drink."[78] Inability to form "proper" social bonds with the white community thus contributed to treatment on par with livestock.

Confusions of family, kin, and household were enshrined in the headright of Carolina: "To each Master or Mistress of a Family 50 Acres, and for every Son or Man-servant they carry 50 Acres more, and the like for each Daughter or Woman-Servant Marriageable, and for each Child, Man or Woman Servant under 16 Years. 40 Acres. and 50 Acres of Land to each Servant out of their Time."[79] So important was the household in the plantations that the Church of England was warned that if it was really serious about converting slaves, missionaries should devote themselves solely to that purpose (and not be led astray by any applause that sermons to their white flock might garner), and themselves travel and settle "without the Clog of a Wife, or Family."[80] Patriarchal terms, replete with the obligation to produce order through a balance of care and discipline, there may be slightly more paternalist sentiment and an admission that not all "Families" were as inclusive as his, in the description of a Leewards' cleric's hurricane shelter, which he would enter "(not without some Solemnity) with my whole Family, Black and White, and such of my poorer Neighbours as pleas'd to join with us."[81] It was unusual for Daniel Defoe not to tackle the effect of transporting notions across the Atlantic, but in a British context, he laid out the "Religious Oeconomy" of the family: one, fathers and children; two, masters and servants; three, husbands and wives.[82] By 1720 he had issued an amended version of the family instructor, which discussed the passions and their breach. Passion should play no part in the correction of children, he warned, but the instrumentalism involved in being obeyed and getting work done, determined that a master could have "no Love to his Slave's Person."[83]

In relations of marriage and consanguinity, how do we separate the connection of sentiment from that of economy? The language with which grants were expressed, suggested it was impossible. In the case of John Delbridge, merchant of Barnstaple in Devon, in granting his estate in Harrington tribe, Bermuda, to his son on the occasion of his forthcoming marriage, it acknowledged the recognition of "the naturall love and affection wch he hath and beareth to Richarde Delbridge his sonne and heire apparante And for the better pr[e]fermte of him...and his heires and for the p[er]formance of cer[t]en Covern[an]ts in that behalfe...in the marriadge of the sayde Richarde Delbridge."[84] In one instance, the transatlantic connection of marriage was maintained not by the partners, but through the ministry, as the rector of St. George's, Montserrat, sent a record—four years after the event—to his equivalent in Goathurst, Somerset, of the wedding of Colonel John Buncombe and Madam Mary Hodges. Buncombe, at least, was an important person in the society of Goathurst, but the more significant connection is that both ministers were called Allen, probably clerical brothers.[85] The disjuncture of the Atlantic was a liberation for Thomas Quintyne's mother, who married William Brickland, against the will of any of her children, and within the same family there were hopes that cousin Elizabeth Mundy's marriage to Mr. Taylor would be "happy [and] fortunate to her," choosing to score out that Taylor was a very honest man, and replacing it with his having a good estate.[86] Nevertheless, "Severall unhappy differences" between Thomas Simson and his wife of only 18 months, Anne, pushed them to live separate lives, Anne to sue for divorce, and Thomas to alienate his holding in Spring Garden Plantation, Port Morant, Jamaica, to cover the accruing debts.[87] Sir Bevill Granville was painfully frank in describing his marriage prospects in Barbados. There was a possible lady who had a good estate in England, but none of her own in Barbados, and though she managed land on the island for her son, opinion was divided as to whether it was encumbered. "If this shou'd be the true state of her Fortune" Sir Bevill was "affraid it will not doe my buisness."[88]

When Alice Gibbes married Captain James Thorpe on Barbados they joined two well-established and well-connected island families whose influence would then stretch to Carolina. Despite a network of wills and indentures, and careful accounts of children's marriages and children's children, it was from the "true bouells of tender Love that Relation of were Consun Guinity that runs in our vains for I have no Relation as I know of by my mothers side" that prompted Alice to write to her cousin, William Blathwayt.[89] She was born in Barbados, one of at least seven children, and she and James Thorpe had a further eight at least. Most formed part of an island network: her brother-in-law had been Samuel Barwick, onetime governor, and her daughters married into the merchant and military families of Randall, Wiltshire, and Hannay. Her nephews, Robert and Thomas, emigrated to Barbados as young men, attempted a failed settlement at Cape Fear, and continued to shuttle between Barbados and Carolina where Robert climbed the political ladder, not without difficulty or venality.[90]

The white elite, and perhaps not just the elite, therefore operated connections in three spheres, which I shall call household-family, neighborhood-family, and dynastic-family.[91] Cunyngham provides a classic example of the first. Household-family was that which pertained on the plantation, in situ in the West Indies, closest equated with the medieval notion of household, maintained through lordly duty. As a category, it had the advantage—for the patriarch—of being both capacious and fluid, but tightly bounded by his lordship and the borders of the fixed estate. It could accommodate all ethnicities, both genders, and consanguinity was not a prerequisite. This is the most difficult and painful distinction between sentiment and instrumentality, particularly on the part of the master, as patriarchy was the most active and forceful instrument of governance. Cunyngham loyally defended those in his household while they were in his household, but ruthlessly excluded Arnold when she overstepped his boundaries. By the mid-1730s, his old friend, former Leewards' Attorney General, Archibald Hutcheson, was advising him "surely it is high time in y^r advanced Age to correct that warmth in y^r Temper from wch you suffered so much," having, with his high-handed meddling, earned the ill will of those in and those out of power.[92] He expended care, attention, and money on the welfare of his slaves, carefully noting their deaths, illnesses, and childbirths, with a hint that this went beyond the initial category of stock, whose "increase" represented an income, or worth in laboring bodies, or a sense of pride in ownership, or even a belief that good treatment begot loyalty and industry. He might also have been exhibiting love, but so bound up with racism, brutality, and control that the historical record is choked.

Neighborhood-family is exhibited in the network of marriages that maintained the white presence within the colonies: of which Mary Pole's marriages to Jones, Legay, and Quintyne, and their kinship links with estates owned by the Mundys and Pilgrims; or Alice Gibbes's relations in Barbados and Carolina, are examples.[93] Note again that the sentiment of connection is provided by women's testimony, speaking of a love of place vested in people. Dynastic-family refers to the continued and continuing white connection of kinship across the Atlantic, particularly of closer members of a family, and particularly children.

The untimely deaths of the patriarchs rob us of the chance to trace miscegenated dynastic families. Jane Long's and Peter Perkins's family of both sentiment and inheritance, was cut short by the couple's poverty and Peter's death. The trail of the Perkins children goes cold. William Whaley, agent to the Helyars in Jamaica, was embarrassed at having to inform the family's English branch that a mulatta, now attending Modyford's daughter, had taken him to court, and he was now forced to reveal how in "these hott Cuntrys most men," including his former master, Cary Helyar, "are a little Veneriall given." In the late 1660s, Cary Helyar had lived with the woman who was the daughter of an African mother via slavery in Brazil, and a European father; the couple lawfully married in Barbados after at least seven years' cohabitation there. Their daughter had two sons with Cary Helyar, one of whom died, but on October 13, 1671, shortly before Governor Sir Thomas Lynch appointed him island treasurer, he married Priscilla Houghton, and then "hee turned away this wentch," allowing her a (subsequently disputed) pension.[94] Helyar died the following July, aged 39. The promise of a pension would seem genuine, therefore, since the woman sued in late 1675 for four year's arrears (and compensation). The family did not own an obligation to continue payments, "now since, the tymes have changed." Most connections of the Warner family are sketchy, both in Suffolk and the West Indies; not served by the relatively early death in St. Christopher's of Sir Thomas, not knowing whether his putative indigenous partner was Igneri or Kalinago, but after Sir Thomas's death, the man, Thomas, referred to by the English as "Indian Warner," was forced to choose between two sides of his shared heritage.[95] The untimely severance of family from patriarch not only stymied genealogical investigation, but also contemporaneously snatched away the sentimental link that outweighed color, and removed its protection from the next generation, allowing exclusionist white culture to reassert itself.

Caring for and raising children was the underpinning of dynastic-family sentiment. Education was the means. Thus, its absence in the West Indies was the major reason for the separation of children from their parents who aspired to retain or improve the family's fortunes, but remained outside the realm of possibility for those who lacked the means.[96] Usually, children of British heritage were sent away to school: Alice Thorpe's sons, aged 15 and 13, were to be educated in England, and placed in the trust of her nephew Samuel Barwick, son of the former governor.[97] Edward Chamberlaine's will of 1673 provided for two sons—Sagrave and Willoughby—and two daughters, the equally colorfully named (in the custom of turning a surname into a Christian name) Tanquerville and seven-year-old Butler, who were "to be educated as gentlewomen at some school in England." If this went ahead, Butler may have been a disappointment, for she returned to Barbados and, close to her twenty-fourth birthday, married the privateer/pirate, Thomas Hewetson.[98] Judge Thomas Quintyne professed it not worth his going to England, but neither would he fetch his cousin/son-in-law, Peter Jones, to come to him in Barbados, because education on the island was "but a fflash," so pointless that it overrode the difficulties of securing the costs of schooling in England when there was such a likelihood that directions, monies, or both would go astray.[99] Developing what a Barbados Grand Jury called "Publick Schools" on the island would have contributed to the prosperity of the West Indies, the character(s) of its next generation, and to developing bonds of place and society within the Americas. Those born on the island "when always Trained up" in love for their place of birth, "Seasoned with Virtue and Learning from their Youth," would find "noe ffriendship is more lasting or firme than that Contracted among Youth att Schoole which Com[m] only in Riper years Proves usefull and Servicable to the Publick."[100] The chief justice in receipt of this plea was the sympathetic George Lillington: he was not able to develop schooling on the island during his own children's lifetimes, but he did, at least, express his confidence in the wider future of the Americas, sending his third son, Edward, to school in New England.[101] The prospect of generations of families being able to reside, remain, and control their lives from within the West Indies was vital to the creation of a vernacular society.

The life led by the Crabbs, shuttling between Antigua and England, illustrated the destabilizing effect on children. They placed their eldest in schools in London, and found themselves increasingly unable either to cover the cost or guarantee the trust and protection owed to them. Eldest son, Isaac, had learned to read but not yet to write.[102] Remembrance was in objects. Sarah Crabb was anxious to receive samplers of daughter Katey's needlework, framed to hang on Antiguan walls, and on her husband's death, Sarah had to send a lock of his hair to be worn in her mourning ring. Their younger children continued to travel to and fro with their parents, and thus became the most susceptible carriers of disease. Youngest, Jamey, was transported across the Atlantic, to and from Nurse Peele in Smithfield, to the apothecary for medicines for a stomach ailment, for which the Crabbs could not pay. Neither could she afford a truss from the apothecary and had to make one herself. Jamey also had measles (as had several of the older children) and therefore could not return to Antigua. The family was trapped in

Portsmouth for some time before his parents were forced to embark without him. He died.[103]

Lawrence Crabb provides a good example of the way in which men, even about their children or inamoratas, were seldom free of the instrumentality of inheritance, obligation, danger or—particularly in a world in which people were commodities—possession. The private world of men was so seldom free from the intrusion of political economy.[104] A man's worth—his authority and his trust—was his credit. So many patriotic passions and merchant fortunes rested on the success of Darién and the outcome was such spectacular failure that we can plot the mutating ethical and economic discourse of "credit." Edinburgh merchant James Byres recounted his disagreements with projector, Thomas Drummond, in the following sequence: first to his friend, his correspondent in Edinburgh, his "account [would] bear its own evidence" so there would be no room to doubt how far his "credit and authority is to be trusted."[105] Drummond's "word of honour" on the whole venture was "the fund of credit he proposed," along with testimonials in his favor, which were "sufficient Funds of Credit," even though the correspondents were given "not the least Credit."[106] Byres's challenge was to seek (financial) credit in Jamaica—the venture short of provisions or the funds to acquire them—such that being sent out was "so much thin *gray paper*," and belittling of the Scots' efforts—"so many little *blew bonnets*"—that the colony would likely starve. Nevertheless, it was the Company that lacked credit, and he was besmirched by association.[107] Byres would return to Edinburgh to account for his time in the West Indies "knowing that they who are most guilty, are always ready to build their own reputation, on the ruine of other mens credit," while his account would do just that at the expense of Drummond, one who "whined, complained, boasted and appealed."[108] Similarly vilified was Roderick Mackenzie, the Company's secretary—a poor balladeer—who likened his own loss of moral credit to that of a woman who would complain that it was a hard thing to be called a whore and yet have none of the pleasure. He blamed the Company's lack of financial credit on those (Scottish) correspondents embedded in the English plantations who provided false or misleading testimony about Panamá.[109] The Darién scheme had been the brainchild of the banker and "Whimsical Projector," William Paterson, during his time in the Bahamas, supporting his projected new colony during 1698 and 1699 by his "Conduct and Credit."[110] Walter Harris, who sailed as a surgeon, would become one of Paterson's sternest critics, publishing one broadside which was "more than the *Darien* Gentlemen care to hear, or their Agents will suffer to pass for Sterling." They thought to "stifle his Credit" by further undermining his variety of Scottish patriotism, using "Teaguish [that is, Catholic and Irish] Artifice."[111]

Every indenture, deed, bond or will, was for men, a political expression, replete with the constraints of obligation, their histories as settlers in the British West Indies revealed in letters, interrogatories, depositions, and petitions that frequently accumulated in the Court of Chancery, endorsed, enumerated, and underscored by armies of lawyers, because their multiple levels of obligation were all regulated by financial debt. Benjamin Whitrow clearly felt emotional isolation when he arrived in Carolina in the summer of 1712, writing frequently and at length, but what he really lacked from England was "some Principall Modern book of Precedents of Chancery practice and pleadings."[112] "Obligation" represented both the act of constraining oneself and the paper on which liability was admitted. No degree of status conferred exemption. From kings and lords to the humblest person, the West Indies was built on debt, but the higher the social status, the more debt was overridden by other obligations, while the remove of the colonies allowed financial and moral debts to be overlooked.

Because of the arrival of the Europeans, the seventeenth century meant huge upheaval for all, couched in the language of the conquerors and filtered through preexistent hierarchies that sought to minimize the expression of extremes. Reports seldom reveal fear or despair; nor do they speak of elation. If the link with Britain was to be kept alive, it was imperative that despite it all, the Caribbean should not be represented in terms that were alien and alienating. Separating people, goods, and capital involved risk; retaining the link required webs of obligation. If someone took a risk for you—a servant or planter sent away; a factor who organized supply; a sweetheart, spouse, or child left behind; a merchant captain who shipped your commodities; a buyer who committed but did not pay; a promissory note that was never honored[113]—the natural order was distorted and taking a risk involved not only receiving the trust of another but also giving the power to the risktaker. Language reflected this difficult relationship.

The transmission of information was easily corrupted and the message distorted by rumor, scandal, and exaggeration. A reputation was, with one loose phrase, poisoned and the estate ruined. Captain Wyld was slandered by Mr. Wych, part-owner of his ship, who, meeting at the Exchange, threatened him with "all the mischeife that he could," and bid him "goe and look after his whore, or whores, or Bastard or Bastards in Jamaica."[114] Wyld was fortunate that the incident took place at the Exchange, and that in the safety of London were many friends and associates who came to his defense.[115] Much of the information about trade, shipping, and the situation in the West Indies was passed orally at the Exchange, where interested parties would stroll the Carolina, Jamaica, Barbadoes, or Virginia Walks, fronting Cattle Alley and Cornhill. Otherwise, they would pass news, gossip, and money, and hire passengers and servants, in the network of coffeehouses dedicated to West India business.

Information could more safely and honorably be transmitted if written down. Correspondence, whether carried by an ordinary, packet, merchant, or fleet ship, could be lost at sea through damage, shipwreck, or piracy, and information could be intercepted. Sir Bevill Granville felt isolated and abandoned in Barbados and relied on first Mr. Warr and then Mr. Ellis at the Treasury to send copies of "Gazetts, Votes of ye House of Commons when they sitt & a written news letter of such occurrences as are not in ye Prints."[116] Several copies were dispatched, recopied, and cross-referenced.

Benjamin Whitrow got into the habit of enclosing letters inside others "to p^{r}vent the Villanous practice of [Captain] Cole whose curious impertinence leads him to break open letters that come from hands whose concerns he hath a mind to be better acquainted with," destroying those which interfered with his own affairs "or disagrees to his humour."[117]

Therefore, one might imagine that printing material would confer authority on its contents. Indentures, deeds, bills, and orders acquired increasingly standardized formats, which provided business for printers in England (such items were not printed in the West Indies). Bills of Exchange remained handwritten in the seventeenth century. The survival of the originals is very rare, but they do, at least give a clear statement of sender, carrier, receiver, and to whose name the "risque" would fall.[118] Whether handwritten or printed, however, the extremes of Caribbean life distorted all. Petitions, which in first draft were feisty and demanding, were invariably moderated to reflect a tone of *noblesse oblige*. The requirement for agreements between parties to be accurate, precise, full, and binding could turn the most familial of connections into officious legalese.[119] "[W]ritten news letter[s] of such occurrences as are not in ye Prints," retained authority into the eighteenth century, but regular printing began with the weekly price lists of commodities that could be obtained from brokers. A broker was a go-between in any transaction, but introduced confused and mediated layers of communication and trust into transactions that could not be "plain dealing" across oceans. Not considered a respectable profession, brokers tended to retreat to the ale and coffeehouses encircling the Exchange.[120] Alongside statistical information was printed news, and as the seventeenth century progressed, the two increasingly overlapped. Sometimes relatively neutral tones—correspondents sent letters to the pro-government *Mercurius Politicus* that praised the Protectorate's commitment to supplying planting in Jamaica—most reports had more of the flavor of advertisement: such as the optimistic report from Carolina sent in 1682, more information on which could be gleaned from the ship's captain who at midday, every day, could be found at the Carolina coffeehouse in Birching Lane.[121] The *London Post* refused to believe a Jamaica correspondent who warned Darién was likely to collapse for want of supply, and proclaimed rather, that the Scots were gathering a formidable counter to the Spaniards.[122] The authorities could have "great influence" on hundreds of otherwise reluctant Quakers and sectaries—hostile to the persecutors and their values—"when they shall finde in the Newes books that...eminent preaching Quaker," John Perrott, "was Content for his Maties Service to appear in a Sattin sute w[i]th a Sword and Belt and to be Called Captain."[123]

But the line between confirmed and speculative; news and entertainment, was seldom clear-cut. The reliable choice (if not about Darién) for men of affairs was the *London Gazette*: Secretary to the Navy Board, Samuel Pepys, not above shenanigans himself, declared this organ devoid of "folly." However, the *Loyal Protestant and True Domestick Intelligence* related "news" of "our honest Neighbour *Merry Tom*," from "*St. Anns Lane Aug.*

24." Tom, "lately design'd to Transplant himself to *Carolina*, the Air of our Latitude not so well agreeing with him as formerly;) This day took an occasion to Trip to *Peggs*; how long he may stay there before he goes further on his Journey, is uncertain; And 'tis certain his Doxy has lost her Gallant, and credibly 'tis reported she hath got almost a 1000*l.* by the Exchange."[124] The *Intelligence* revealed more about its own bias than the life of Thomas Merry, who was lampooned elsewhere for his extremist Whig views and his license in both politics and love, in which his service to Anthony Ashley Cooper, Lord Shaftesbury, may have provided the potential escape from English politics to Carolina.[125] "News" could be the latest sailings to and fro, adverse weather conditions, or travelers' tales. The vivid colors of the Caribbean were a sales opportunity. Publishers seized on the expected bonanza, for example, to advertise Exquemelin's account of piracy.[126] Thus all stories could be embellished, magnified, and brightly painted for a British audience eager for scandal.

Pirates were a great sales' pitch, operating a society which in this respect was not inverse, but parallel. Social bonds were cemented with largesse, liberally dispersing pieces of eight to tavern keepers and prostitutes, and pouring drink down the throats of "companions." It was a charge leveled at the greatest pirate of them all, Sir Henry Morgan, in his administration of Jamaica, who had a "particular" club, debauching "(every day & night) with 5 or 6 little Sycophants."[127] The instrumentality of connection was expressed more coarsely here, to coerce women to do what men willed, or force reluctant people to a stupor of drunkenness and incapacity, resulting in financial bankruptcy that could be redeemed by the body, "seeing the Inhabitants there easily sell one another for Debt."[128] The lives of people within the underclasses were derided for their moral bankruptcy, in whose currency of exchange personal virtue and "dealings" would always be corrupted.[129]

West Indians were indebted for matters far more personal than specie. In Surinam, dissenting ministers such as Oxenbridge and Leverton, and sectaries persecuted in England, like Henry Adis, were beholden to the Lord Proprietor for his declaration of toleration, and thereby the opportunity to build a community of fellows. Leverton shared Lord Willoughby of Parham's religious sensibilities and made one of the few positive pronouncements on his behalf, since despite initial suspicions, he found him "a man of Learning, Ingenuity & of great Cyvility the famous nonconformist beyond all others." Further, "the governour & some others of Eminency" had been "very Civill to us[;] active for our Comfortable settlement, my wife hath already a Cow by ye Appoyntment of the Lord Willoughby." And so, down the line, Mr. Blight would carry away sugar and bring them other necessaries, on voyages "which would hardly defray his Charges had he not lived wth us on free Cost." Then, "I purpose to send A Parcell of sugar by [Blight] some to M^{rs}. Elford my exceeding dear friend & to M^{rs}. Johnson for ye Adventures they sent by him: & alsoe some for the use of my son Gersham to dispose of in some particular commoditi^{es} for us, And hereafter I hope to gratifie the rest of my dear friends."[130] His letter was to be communicated to "all my friends and acquaintance of the ministry."[131] If Willoughby's obligations were kept as ledger, the credit column might list: watering down the Anglican presence in his territories, maximizing settler-numbers, building family units, and basic economic provision.

In the corresponding debit column, Willoughby's settlers were beholden for opportunities to worship, advance their family's interests, and exercise patriarchal determinism. Leverton was anxious to marry off his daughter Jane and cousin Mary in Surinam, where "any woman would be of an Advantage here to themselves and those that have the dispose of them for Marriage and ordering househould affaires[:] I could wish some might be procured on my Account and sent to me" (which might explain why rumors circulated that his wife was prepared to poison him). Another example of marriage complicated and exaggerated by the materialism of Caribbean affairs is provided by the daughters of the Carlisle-appointee as Governor of Barbados, Henry Hawley. Hawley died in 1679, bequeathing his considerable estate in trust to his infant daughters, Susanna, and Mary, barely two years old.[132] Around ten years later an Act of Parliament was required to dispose of the Barbados assets; both because all of the girls' named guardians had died but also that they were now "Marriageable [and] bred up Protestants...if they dy before the yare of Age without issue ye s^d estate will goe to [a] Papist" and "The sale of this estate will be much to [the] Infants advantage besides their p^{r}tem^t [?preferment] in Marriage because they pay 16^l P Cent for every 100^l y^t is rec[eived] from Barbadoes [and] often meet with great losses by sea especially since ye Warr began."[133]

Friendship underwent the greatest test. To Lawrence and Sarah Crabb, the Sussex merchant George Moore had been a "bosome friend for many years." After two decades in the West Indies this had degenerated such that the lawyer who subsequently managed Moore's suit against the Crabbs thought these words worth underlining.[134] At the start of their connection, although they collaborated in business ventures, they possessed a bond forged by sentiment. By the time of Lawrence's death in Antigua in 1709, lawyers were measuring the obligation of each to the other in monetary terms. Witnesses were called to testify to the balance between Lawrence Crabb's personal integrity and status, and the monetary value to be placed upon it. The trust that Christopher Jeaffreson showed in Edward Thorne to manage Wingfield, St. Christopher's, proved misplaced. Thorne did not care for the plantation and exploited the workers and the land. He was too busy travelling to Boston, where he lived the high life and neglected everybody's business, so Jeaffreson lost profit in St. Christopher's—a place where it was unusual for merchants to be kind to absent debtors—and his good name among the merchants and shopkeepers in London, who had trusted him to recommend an agent.[135] Jeaffreson replaced Thorne with a Mr. Sedgwick, and slowly we see the bonds of first trust, and then as his new manager put right Thorne's "carelessnesse" and its "certaine compagnion...profusenesse"— the "two locusts [by which] my revenues are devoured"—Sedgwick is called a friend.[136] Nevertheless, we never learn the new agent's first name.

The language of connection ran parallel with that of business. When the seriousness of the breach between Jeaffreson and Thorne was articulated between them, Jeaffreson realized his repeated efforts at communication would not repair it, "as little [is] to be expected where beare cevilleties and friendly Correspondence is denyed and accompts refused wch are ye least and easiest part of yor duty but what yor unkindnesses...have beene to me I shall forbeare to ennumerate."[137] Agents, factors, and overseers were employed about business, their connections conducted at considerable distance and with consequent delay; there was ample opportunity for misunderstanding, and yet proprietors, operating from ignorance, had no alternative but to rely on their trustees, only for the connection to be shattered by reports of mismanagement, embezzlement, harsh-dealing, sharp practice, incompetence, or some unspecified knavery. Thomas Hobbes referred to "market friendships," declared inauthentic because the social bonds of love were replaced by those of commerce, traffic, or business: a phenomenon that Hobbes described as simple jealousy.[138] In a world of traffic, in which the meanings of love—trust, honor, credit, worth—by which people determined their relationships, had become corrupted, a system had been created and operated by merchant "men joined in one interest, or one business."[139] George Lillington, who embedded himself firmly within the fabric of Barbados society, warned both Britain and the West Indies of the exploitative connection of merchandizing. Merchants "speake the Language of those that Employ them."[140]

A dispatch from a West Indies' holding or a journey that presaged financial return also carried its weight in cultural capital. The little intimacies that signified connection were expressed in gifts and acknowledgments, such as Paschow Mooreshead in Barbados, soon bound for New England, Virginia, and home to Cornwall, but still distressed that he had had no word from his mother and no opportunity to send a token of his affection.[141] Senders and recipients could read into the words and the objects what they wished and measure how profound or nominal the symbolism, so with increasing formalism, it can be hard to detach the personal morals from mannered patterns. Letters offered health, prosperity, and "humble service." Sarah Crabb in an ill-formed hand and phonetic spelling, had been in Antigua for less than a year when she sent sweetmeats to George Moore, knowing no other means to "retaliate" for his kindness and friendship and "untill it be accomplisht my prayers shall be to the great god to make you happy and prosperous in all your undertakings."[142] Mary Quintyne offered three pieces of turtle shell: "as I get more you may expect them, be please to accept of thes as a thank offerring in remembrance of your unrecompencable ffavours."[143] George Marten lived his entire sojourn in Barbados on account, mostly supplied by his brother, Henry, who subsidized his high living with shipments of wine, George finding the alcohol of local production not to his refined tastes: "I will not promise you payment for it, but the next year I shall make white sug^r, and then if you find by youre Accompt, that the wine you send hether is Ballanst by the sug^r you receave from herer, I hope you will not be offended at it." His production was literally a handful.[144] At the same time, election to the assembly being unable to protect him from creditors, George was forced to mortgage his estate and, failing to make the payments, migrated to Surinam in 1658.[145] Based in Bristol, Elizabeth Nicklus acted as a hub for relatives around the West Indies, commenting in a postscript to her nephew, Edward Archer, "Inclosed you have Capt Isaac James Receip[ts] for one box Con[t] Two Silv[r] Tankerds & Twelve Silv[r] Spoones the Tankerd I sent you as a Presant is mark[td] $_E{}^A{}_E$. I Receivd by Cap[t] Isaac James on[e] small box of Sugar & Inclosed a small Kegg of Sweetmeats but have no acco[ts] whom it Came from."[146]

Slavery, in which both person and commodity functioned as the subject and object of exchange, is the most graphic illustration. At the top of the political hierarchy sat Christopher Codrington, who bequeathed his Barbados estate to the Society for the Promotion of the Gospel, for the conversion of the slaves and the maintenance of a ministry, the funding for which was provided by continuing the estates in slave-reliant sugar production. The other Codrington estates in Antigua—heavily encumbered—also promoted the work of the Society. Of Barbuda, "Colonel *Codrington* (to whom it belongs)...keeps [there] a large Family for its Defence," along with cattle, vessels "always Trading with the other *Caribe* Islands" and provisions "more than sufficient for the Consumption of its Inhabitants," which sounds dispassionate, but meant that Codrington bred slaves in order to buy friends' loyalty and obligation: more proper would be the pejorative term "creatures."[147] All were branded with his mark, and thus any supplied—given, rented, sold—to others, embodied/personified his largesse, his concern to develop the colony's economy, his business acumen, and his network of clients. Thus we have seen that Lawrence Crabb and Codrington exchanged passage and wharfage for slaves making Crabb "wholly devoted to the Governor," one of his "prevailing Scycophants," and ultimately a valuable testator against Codrington's enemies.[148]

Wills provide the clearest source about slaves as the subject and object of gifting. Eleanor Brown gave a woman, Sacia, to the executor of her will in part payment; Catalina, however, was manumitted.[149] John Lewis allowed his wife Anna the furniture in her chamber, one hundred pounds Jamaican, and the choice of three of the house slaves. His lands in St. James's, Barbados, were to be divided equally between his three married daughters, along with James, to Eliza; Duago,[150] to Sable; Phoebe and Phoebe's daughter Hannah, to Sarah; and "two Negro Men, on[e] boy and one Woman by names Jackie Gado Abell and Moll," to Mary. Grandsons were bequeathed a specific slave-boy each, whereas granddaughters received £50 Jamaican.[151] Thus it is difficult to separate the role of body as commodity and body as helpmeet. A will which made the distinction was that of John Hallett, who gave his daughter, Katherine Farmer, £100 "to be Layd out in Negroes for her"; and his wife, Anne, the house in which they had lived and its contents, along with Dennis, George, Patrick, Bess, Mary, and Jonny for her "Use Possession and Enjoyment."[152] In the upper echelons, the will of Lieutenant Governor Hender Molesworth named Mary Moore, a black servant to whom he bequeathed manumission, some clothes, £20 sterling, and a further £10 to carry her back to Jamaica should Molesworth die in England; whereas Mingo also was to have his freedom, and £5; Wakefield was to have all the apparel plus 12 holland shirts, except the blue lace cravat and silk waistcoats; and Molesworth's godson inherited the cocoa walk at Indico Plantation, St. George's, along with the man whom we must presume tended it, Golden Gloves.[153]

The distinction between intimacies of gift and acknowledgment, and those of will and bequest depended on an exercise of conscience, perhaps heightened by the imminence of death. During life, money or kind was levied to be used in public works, including being assigned by the churchwardens according to need and desert. The pound of sugar per acre specified for the relief of the poor demanded by the parish of St. John's, Barbados, in June 1655, signaled the expansion of parochial responsibilities from socioeconomic infrastructure to embrace socioethical concerns. William Wilson and Alexander Davies were paid a pension (520 pounds of sugar per annum); Thomas Bishop, who was old and lame, would be relieved out of the parish stock (ten pounds a week).[154] It also manufactured new disconnections of status, requiring regular meetings of "the Gentlemen Trustees" and the creation of Overseers for the Poor: new personnel—"worthies"—who made judgments on their fellows, or exercised charity by "entertaining" the needy, such as looking after the sick or arranging for rent to be covered.[155] Individual donors included Lieutenant-Colonel William Consett and his wife, Elizabeth, with their generous ten-year bequest of 1,000 pounds per annum toward the upkeep of the poor. They were stalwarts of the Church of England, and publicly minded citizens—William was a vestryman and trustee for St. John's for every year between 1649 and 1660—but the couple do not seem to have had any children or other relations for whose welfare they felt obligated.[156] Their deaths, within days of each other, transformed their charity from the personal into the political: the churchwardens hurried to retrieve copies of their wills from the Secretary's Office in order to spend their legacies on church plate and repairs to the chancel.[157] The parish of St. John decided to extend the policy of speculative accumulation, albeit for charitable ends:

> It being proposed by the Comm[t] For pious Donac[i]ons to the Vestry (that such Charitable Donac[i]ons in money as were found to remaine in any P[er]sons hand for the use of the poore of this P[ar]ish should be lett on at Interest for One yeare for the better Advantage of the poore, And that such p[er]son or persons that take the same at Interest enter into an Oblig[a]con for the paym[t] thereof with such Interest as the same shoud[?] be lett at to the Churchwarden for the time being and his Successor or Successors be with this provis[o] to be menc[i]ond in the Condition of such Obligac[i]on.[158]

Consett's Plantation was eventually incorporated into the St John's estates of the Society, and by 1724 two ministers were based there in missionary work, but both Consett's and Codrington's remained encumbered, sullying any purity of intent with indebtedness and litigation.[159]

Irrespective of confession—unless we could find reason to interpret manumission as an act of charity—the general pattern repeated the division into donations either to the poor or to the material structures of religious practice. On Barbados's west coast, John Hallett, devout, High-Church Anglican, who, "as I have Lived, soe I Continue in the belief, of the Catholick ffaith According to the church of England," whose will had made very particular individual provision for slaves, also made charitable bequests which connected him across the Atlantic.[160] £100 Barbados was for the upkeep of those of Bridgetown's poor not already in receipt of parish relief, while the rest of the estate—two plantations in St. Michael's and St. John's, Barbados, Lyme Regis in Dorset, and Axmouth, Devon—went to family and creditors, which included the Russia and East India Companies. The Quaker, Jane Alexander's father, Nicholas, had settled several plots around Yallahs, one of which—a dwelling house, smaller houses, and three acres—along with £40 a year was to accommodate Friends who traveled to attend the Meeting there. The residue, or all of his estate should either of his children die childless, was to go to the monthly Meeting for the support of widows and orphans.[161] Rowland Hilton was unusual: he made bequests to "ye poore people Amongst y^m called Quakers in this Illand... to be disposed Amongst y^m & none others as they shall bee needfull & requisite" but also named "poore Negroes," bequeathing a joint decision from beyond the grave between himself and his executors how to determine need and desert.[162]

High-minded puritan ideals drove the Lords behind the Somers' Island and Providence Island Companies, "not only under the awe of Religion," but with the "substance and power of it" in their hearts.[163] Covenanting, godly fellowship across the Atlantic and between settlers, provided a powerful discourse of connection. We cannot complete the web which bound James I's jeweler, Sir William Heyrick MP, to Thomas Harrison, writing to him from Bermuda in 1615, but it was expressed through shared puritan sensibilities, "because I have loved you from ayounge gentill man; [and] allways sithence/ [and] because I love you still; as well for discretion, as for truth [and] honestye."[164] Harrison counted on that love being "friend" to his "hope" and they shared their grief at the loss of "neighbours" with similar values to themselves, particularly John, Lord Harrington who, in departing "the world oute of our neighbourhood," may have left the fellowship of Christians, their godly circle, that of puritan patrons, the court of the late Prince Henry Stuart, London, Bermuda, or the wider Americas.[165] Similar satellites of less courtly orbit circled around clergymen Charles Morton, who wrote about the saints' service in the Americas as a new breed of ecclesiastical historians catalogued the trials of God's servants at home.[166] Nicholas Leverton and John Oxenbridge had hoped to entice him to Surinam. The former had served God in Barbados, Tobago, and Providence Island, before Guiana, while Oxenbridge had previously ministered in Bermuda, before serving two years in Barbados, and ending his days "chosen Pastor of the

Independent Church at *Boston*."[167] Morton's school for dissenters produced Daniel Defoe; Oxenbridge was a patron of Andrew Marvell.

During the first half of the seventeenth century, networks of interest and affinity, expressed within a puritan discourse, were described from without as rebellious cliques, which combined kin and kinship, marriage, patronage, friendship, financial support, geographical proximity, education, and travel to the Americas. "Wee have a Societtie" (in Providence), said Nathaniel Butler, of "Covenentinge Men," which turned meetings into means to plant contention, "dissentions and troubles," turn themselves into "parties and Judges," overawe their neighbors, and vent "splene and revenge."[168] Those values which made them respected for the plain dealing which bound them one to another, made them feared. We have already encountered Robinson the Quaker of Bermuda whose honesty created him and his circle a society within society. They made for honest merchants and storehouse keepers, but were widely blamed both as "eminently renowned men of Pretiousness and Saintship" who learned the "Pious fraud of the SAINTS" to set themselves up as banks to garner profits from others, and as low-class covenanters who murdered a king.[169] As the century progressed, covenanting turned into dissent, which became enthusiasm, and Rev. Alexander Garden, the Bishop of London's Commissary in South Carolina, was not alone in seeing in the rise of enthusiastic religion, a repeat of the impassioned forces of antisocial destruction which had caused civil war across the empire.[170]

There was scarcely anyone in Britain who aspired to any form of office holding who did not have some interest in the colonies: by the time engagement had formed within the American body politic, corruption was already in its marrow. Nevertheless, office holding involved some level of community choice about, or judgment on, status, respect, competence, or popularity: one's standing within male society, and one's masculinity. The insecurity, which physical separation brought to the connections of people across the Atlantic, fashioned heightened language. Failure to hear from family and friends spawned neediness. When those connections were politicized, the usual manners of deference, respect, and obligation collapsed into obsequiousness. Connections became parties, and parties turned into Party. The more tightly bound one became to a figure of worth, the more likely you were to be their creature. Gifts and tokens became bribes. Connection ceased to be something to be enjoyed and became something to be used: and thus itself commodified. Despite decades of delay and exasperation, the creditors of the earls of Carlisle remained just the right side of courteous in official correspondence. With each other they were more candid. In 1669 Sir Henry Puckering lamented of Thomas Henshaw's efforts, "Tis very sadd that No butter will stick to our bread": "And to the Patrone you speake of, I am...with you...to purchase such a one"; but not without further consultation, "in case such purchase must bee made by a considerable sum of ready mony, (wch is the thing rules all)".[171]

To add to the confusion, even loyalties clear-cut at home could not remain so once exposed to the sun. It became expedient to build barriers between you and your neighbor and to protect one's own interests and doing so involved daily decisions that converted principle into pragmatism. When every alliance involved instrumentalism, and with it, expediency, what price could be placed on loyalty when men's reputations could be destroyed and restored at will? Examples of principle are rare: John Michell asked to be excused from serving as Headborough of Camberwell in Surrey, because "altogether unfit for that Office" in that he was constantly between the City and Jamaica.[172]

Elections, no matter where they took place, were not edifying spectacles, and the few surviving descriptions of active political participation in the tropical Americas are little different from reports from New England, Chesapeake, or Britain. Writs were issued, voters canvassed, and results disputed. Sir Thomas Lynch issued writs for Clarendon parish, Jamaica, in February 1671, at which all freeholders were entitled to a voice, in choosing, in the standard phraseology, "two of the fittest and discreetest" of their fellows, in an election "freely and indifferently carried w^th^out ffaction or Interest."[173] This was tested the following year in the neighboring parish of St. Catherine's, centered on Spanish Town. There were attempts to have Assemblyman Humphrey Freeman overturned on the grounds that his election had not been "fair and equall." However, two very different rationales were offered. One was that the managers of the provincial election were not apprised of the writ, while it was also complained that Freeman was then in custody for speaking "certain seditious and contemptuous words of the present Authority and Governm^t^." It was a duality subsequently repeated: in questioning the "trick" of being denied election, Freeman was deemed to have continued his "seditious and mutinous Words." A third time, when it was argued that the two existing representatives for St. Catherine's relieved the need to exercise the franchise again, Spanish Town electors denied in a petition any stubbornness or obstinacy in choosing Freeman: they described his words and sentiments as a "crime," but they did not feel they or it disqualified him from sitting, whereupon Governor Lynch and his council took account of the "modesty of the Address" and Freeman's submission, and allowed his election to stand.[174]

The influence of the Quakers which caused Governor James Kendall to fear for the electoral process in Barbados combined ethical and material concerns. Assemblymen, he complained, were reluctant and vacillating in raising the levy to fight the French. He blamed the imminent expiry of their term, and noted that each man's prospects of being returned again were improved if they could avoid being labeled a tax-raiser.[175] Quakers' refusal to take oaths or take up arms, compromising their consciences, could disbar them from office holding and from serving in the militia. It marked them with dubious politics, lacking commitment to the fight against Versailles, and with greater loyalty to first, each other, and then, the wider Barbados community, than that which they failed to demonstrate toward Whitehall. Most Quakers returned were ejected again for their refusal to take the Oath of Supremacy, followed by Kendall's own form of a Test Act, which required

Assemblymen to have taken the sacraments in the Anglican Church within the previous 12 months.[176]

The second half of 1688 was a time of torrid politics in Britain, with the birth of James VII and II's son, James, on June 10, which would, in due course, precipitate the invasion of the Dutch fleet of William of Orange. But the Jamaica elections of August repeated only questions of process. The Governor, Albemarle, assured Whitehall that the Assemblymen were men loyal to James, but Councilor White had been removed because, like a lawyer, he had argued against the king's interest for a fee. Colonel Thomas Ivy, previously considered loyal, emerged as an agitator. The Clarendon elections were suspended with complaints of rioting, assault, abusive language, intimidation, and "treating."[177] On the 27th of the month, the Supreme Council issued fines, raising £3,340: Ivy's portion, at £300, was by no means the greatest, but two further fines were issued for contempt: Charles Sadler for being offensive toward the Chief Justice and John Towers for uttering the Ciceronian republican adage "*Salus populi, suprema lex.*" A jury did not deny that Towers had publicly said the words, at least twice, "but not maliciously or seditiously," so the judges, Colonel Needham, and Ralph Knights (significantly, "now in London") recalled the jury four times such that "they brought in a special Verdict That if the Words in themselves without any Relation did import Malice and Sedition against the Government, then they found [Towers] Guilty: Which, if not, then they found Not guilty."[178] In February 1687, Towers had requested permission to run his horse in a race against one owned by the governor, and had used the phrase in joshing fashion among friends that he was balancing the business of the house with that of the sport. Ivy, Towers, and others subsequently petitioned the Williamite regime and their fines were remitted: Towers later served on the Jamaica Council.[179]

Perhaps because, rather than in spite of, Carolina's reputation for wider political participation, people's conduct was the more notorious. From its inception, the colony's worthies complained of the behavior of people who supposedly constituted the backbone of the colony, whose profanity was not only against God, but to the "destitution of good Neighbourhood." But even without excluding such antisocial elements, the governor and council could find nowhere near sufficient freeholders to elect a Parliament. William Owen—who was not "a man of account"—in company with William Scrivener, attempted to "possesse the people" in order to circumvent the executive to exercise the franchise, "being moved, by the sd William Owen, in another Sphere then their owne."[180] There was some dispute about the status of some of those chosen—or as Owen had it, "their Elecon into dignity"—while Owen was accused of climbing aboard any issue which would draw attention; and Scrivener, of demagogy, in spiriting up anger when it seemed self-promotion might fail. Correspondents reassured Anthony Ashley Cooper that any elections to a representative body would be delayed until more ships, settlers, and plantations had generated electors and Assemblymen of the right sort.

The strategy was not successful. In 1684, a delay of 22 days between the elections for Berkeley and Colleton Counties compromised their fairness by facilitating the activity of itinerant agitators who intimidated voters.[181] Daniel Defoe, while far from a dispassionate source, drew attention to the persistence of similar issues when in November 1701, "a great number of servants and Poor and indigent Persons" voted early and often, as did "several free Negroes...taken for as good Electors as the best Freeholders in the Province." Such irregularities and compromises were deemed to scandalize Charles II's original patent and to be contrary to the principles required of English government.[182]

It could be argued that agitation, canvassing, and riot were the politicking of the disempowered and differed little from the networking, alliances, and leverage exercised by the elite, other than in the direction each party faced the tent. The better an incomer could embed themselves in the society and politics of the locality, the more secure their rise and hold on power would be. One of the most successful was the Irishman, Sir William Stapleton. A third son, his career began in the army—in itself an excellent place to display masculinity, fellowship, and connection—one of many who arrived in the West Indies commissioned in the regiment of Sir Tobias Bridge. Bridge demonstrated the value of marriage in situ: on Barbados he joined the prominent family of Hothersall, and could bequeath a sizable estate in St John's.[183] From Barbados, where Stapleton rose to the rank of lieutenant-colonel, serving with "great reputacon," "bred a Souldr from his cradle beyond Sea...a Gallant Man...good Comander," he was sent by William Willoughby to the Leeward Islands, where he married Anne, the daughter of Colonel Randal Russell, whose well-established family in Nevis brought him access to planter circles. He built up his own sugar fortune across the Leeward Islands, which engineered their political federation—"for the last twelve yeares Governo^r generall of all the Leeward Islands"—despite the opposition of vested interests in each.[184] He demonstrated unusual competence as a colonial administrator—his Celtic connections a boon in managing the disproportionately high Scottish and Irish communities of all stripes—and his service in the West Indies could be attested by King Charles II, James Duke of York, the Committee for Trade and Foreign Plantations, and the Irish West Indies' planter network. But thinking to return to Ireland on his retirement, he found that the degree to which he had embedded himself in West India service did not procure him a military position in Ireland: he would need to establish new connection to show "how fit it may be to make such a man" a "Creature" of the Duke of Ormond.[185] Isaac Richier provides an example of a governor unable to embed himself in his island community, or to buttress himself by joining island interests with those of neighbors. He was driven out of office, accused of venality. On return to England, he tried to rescue his reputation by projecting the economic recovery of the island as a bridge between trans-Caribbean and transatlantic trade. He waited six years before choosing to use the auspices of the Lowther family, whom he had not met, to advance his cause: "Yet I am no Stranger to Yor virtues Yor Innate Honor &

Justice."[186] His opinion of Bermuda was interesting: his attempt to generate connection entirely barren.

John Yeamans as lieutenant-governor of Antigua tried to undermine the Leewards' federation. A seemingly simple and benign proposal to build a new church for St. Philip's was supported by Governor Walter Hamilton, as a means to draw together divided congregations and increase the frequency of divine service. Yeamans opposed the move and, accused of being unable to prevail by authority, manipulated the election of vestrymen. Other objections were led by "one Skerret a Papist," and Yeamans was himself described as "a violent Jacobite." The minister, Samuel Orr, whose preferment had been at Hamilton's hands, was accused of minding his own interest before justice, and though described as a "Jack," an abusive term for Jacobite, he was one "on both sides." Equally polarized opinion about loyalty to either King James or King William was exercised about Hamilton. Family connection muddied opinion of Yeamans, tainted by his (obscure) relation to Sir John Yeamans of Barbados and Carolina, rumored to have been complicit in the murder of his partner, Benjamin Berrington, so as to acquire the whole estate through marriage to his widow. Therefore, Sir William Daines had only to mention that he was "Mr Barrington['s] Nephew's Grandfather" to damn Yeamans' lineage, character, and, thus, political opinion.[187]

It was probably during the last throes of the governorship of Sir Jonathan Atkins that a correspondent provided London with an account of the persons and principles of the men who sat on the council in Barbados:

1. Sr Peter Colleton Barn^t: Liver in England Viciously and under ye Conduct of my Ld: Shaltsbury [*sic*]
2. Henry Drax: Lives in England: and under ye Conduct of my Ld Lovelace
3. Henry Walrond: a goodman and of Right principles to ye Establi[shed] goverm^t
4. Sam: Newton. a quiet man but hardly stawe[188] his wife being a quaker
5. Tho: Wardall a good man
6. John Witham . a good man
7. John Peeres . a good man
8. John Stanfast a goodman
9. Richard Howell a goodman
10. Edwin Stede a goodman and of Right principles
11. Ben: Knight: very insignificant
12. Tho: Walrond a goodman –
    Coll^{ll} Tho: Colleton Sr Peters Broth good
    Majo^r John Hallet a goodman
    Tis said that/ one francis bond is likely to be one. and he is as good as Edward Bushell or Maurice Thompson: Reported a preacher heretofore./[189]

The list contains the names of two men who served as governor. Sir Peter Colleton was acting governor in the months prior to Atkins's arrival in 1674; Sir Edwin Stede would become governor in 1685. Sir Peter and his brother Thomas Colleton were Carolina landgraves. It is clear, however, that the correspondent's discrimination relates to the politics of London and not of Barbados or the wider West Indies. With the exception of the dissolute conduct attributed to Sir Peter Colleton, there is little judgment of the man within and more of the public alliances which resulted from communion within the Established Church—we have encountered the orthodox piety of John Hallett—loyalty to King Charles II and to the right of his brother, James, the Duke of York. Composed in the wake of the crisis of 1679, "right principles" meant support for James in the light of moves to have him excluded from the succession, led by Anthony Ashley Cooper, Lord Shaftesbury. The censure of Colleton and Drax is not that they were absent in England but that they were there to further the Exclusionists' Whig agenda. Those of low church principles could continue to act in the colonies provided they did so quietly and did not disturb the British polity. To be "under the conduct" was a curious phrase of Old Testament proportions.[190] While used negatively here to mean under the control of the Whig Exclusionists, Shaftesbury and Lovelace, it was usually employed to describe the benign paternalism ascribed to legitimate authority. It was command, direction, control, guidance, sway, protection, and channel. In the constitutional crises of Britain in the period between around 1670 and 1740, particularly that which cemented the Establishment in Church and State, it could define increasingly polarized politics.[191]

Barbados politics had always been a dirty business, fit only for the canniest and wariest. After the disputed authority of the Carlisle/Willoughby era came a series of governors, Sir Jonathan Atkins, Sir Richard Dutton, Sir Edwin Stede, James Kendall, Ralph Grey, Sir Bevill Granville, Mitford Crowe, and Robert Lowther, whose authority and conduct in office were contested within a context of politics in the mother country/countries which demanded the attribution of labels, parties, affinities, and postures.[192] Atkins has become renowned for his efforts to catalogue, codify, and enumerate the peoples of Barbados and their customs, for the benefit of Whitehall, noting wryly the partisan control they kept over their own domestic regulation.[193] Dutton's governorship was interposed with periods in which Sir John Witham—"a good man"—acted in his stead, but left a legacy of ill feeling between the two men. The Barbados Grand Jury welcomed the deliverance that Dutton's return signified.[194]

In 1702 the new governor named was career soldier, Sir Bevill Granville, who, not long in office, and his authority already weakened by his unfamiliarity with West-Indian business but over-familiarity with its fevers, attempted to legislate for a Barbados standing army. Another measure unpopular with the "Money'd Men" was a vote for £65,000 in paper credit: debtors were only too happy to be able to settle without producing either specie or kind.[195] George Lillington, indicted at a court of Oyer and Terminer for "reflecting on" Governor Sir Bevill Granville, wishing his death, by the hand of Thomas Lesly, a servant he had carried from an English jail, to shoot the governor, Benjamin Cryer for performing marriages without license from the governor, Cryer's brother-in-law George Ramsay, and Terrill, were declared unfit Councilors for encouraging faction.[196]

Having obtained leave from Queen Anne to return to England, Granville died during the passage, and was posthumously acquitted of arbitrary and tyrannical proceedings.[197] Nevertheless, brother George was unsuccessful in using the London press to rescue Bevill's reputation.[198] His replacement, Mitford Crowe, professed Barbados awash with faction and corruption, though it was far from clear whether Granville had been its contriver or sustainer: a hapless, sickly man out of his depth.[199] Lillington, returned to government and mobilized against those who "zealously and violently concurr with Sir B. Granville in ye oppression of ye honble. George Lillington," praising the now Chief Judge for restoring probity to political, military, financial, and judicial office.[200] Nevertheless, the factionalism continued, expressed in "scurrilous Billingsgate" language, beyond that which a gentleman might use toward a footman.[201] There was a wave of complaints about Scots' prominence.[202] Crowe was now recalled and Councilor William Sharpe wrote to the earl of Sunderland to express relief that the Lords of Trade and Plantations had saved Barbados from rebellion, the islanders from Crowe and Crowe from himself.[203] When he left the island in May 1710, George Lillington, as the senior Councilor, became acting governor.

Thus began Lillington's assault on London to establish (his) order. On August 3, he wrote two letters to men at the very top of the political hierarchy. Thomas Parker, first Baron Parker, had been Lord Chief Justice for five months when Lillington wrote to thank him for appearing on his behalf in Privy Council, hearing "Appeals from the Plantations." Any compromises which Lillington had made "I was induced to accept, that my Concerns might not be said to continue the unhappy Differences of this Country." Lillington felt he must "express my Joy in your Lordships succeeding...I humbly begg leave to congratulate Your Lordship thereupon, &...wish your Lordship an Addition (if it may be) to the Universall Honour & Applause which attended his late Lordship." He delivered a few bottles of citron water and a keg of sweetmeats, "Which if it meets Your Lordships favourable Acceptance, will answer the Ambition" of Parker's most humble, dutiful, and obedient servant.[204] A second letter probably went to the Lord High Chancellor, William Cowper, first Earl Cowper.[205] The "Heats & Animosities" in Barbados, Lillington averred, were rooted in the spirits of the people, beginning in Granville's time, but continued in Crowe's. To nip it in the bud, Lillington would have elected an entirely new assembly, but "such Elections are too apt to heighthen & inflame the Divisions", so he invoked Cowper's authority to secure a royal pronouncement on Barbados issues.[206] Factionalism, he maintained, was a domestic struggle within the island council, and his cure was to ensure that men who held offices such as treasurer should be a member of neither council nor assembly, "none but Men of the Clearest Estates and freest from Law Suits" sit on council, but, somewhat at odds with the foregoing, decisions should not be enacted without "giving the Gentlemen of Estates residing here an Oppertunity of Offering their Reasons upon the respective Subjects."[207]

Lillington's correspondents, Cowper and Parker, were sympathetic to radical deist and republican Whiggery.[208] While Cowper resigned as Lord High Chancellor and Parker refused the same office at the Tory landslide of 1710, the careers of all, including Lillington in Barbados, survived. With the accession of George I, Whigs returned to office, and Cowper was once again Lord High Chancellor of Great Britain. William Parker became regent between the death of Queen Anne and George's coronation, then Lord Chancellor, and earl of Macclesfield, only to be impeached in the House of Lords for having taken more than £100,000 in bribes.

On the other side, Sir Bevill Granville was part of a family of impeccable royalist credentials, who had little difficulty in faithful service to both James and William. Mitford Crowe moved in circles which included Tory skeptic, Jonathan Swift, but functioned in trade and diplomacy under successive governments. Hostility to the Scots was focused on the "Scotch colonel," the medic William Cleland, on whom Sir Bevill Granville was reliant, naming him to the council.[209] But in London, Cleland was a stereotype whose meanness meant Swift paid for the dinner at which he was courted by a man "who has a mind to be Governor of Barbados, and is laying these long traps for me and others, to engage our interests for him. He is a true Scotchman."[210] Possibly as part of his campaign, he published an account of the state of the West Indies, in which he declared that "[i]f the Governor be an honest Man, and when any Complaints are made by the People, they are redressed, there is little fear but the Law will have a due course in that Island, as well as in other Places," and he joined the ranks of those who supported the Establishment because it buttressed his own authority so far away.[211]

Scots were too firmly entrenched within the West Indies and fulminating was empty posturing. Governor Ralph Grey was alarmed at the distribution of pamphlets about Darién, new Scottish arrivals who would whip up Scottish nationalism, and councilors like Cryer queued up to make depositions against men such as William Duncan, who when drunk had proclaimed the Scottish as good as the English, of no allegiance to William III, and ready to bring about change.[212] Scottish Episcopalian, John Anderson, found St. Christopher's a place "of ye greatest Wildness [and] Licence," but earned the support of Lady Stapleton, which induced the governor (Scot, Walter Hamilton) to "more heartily [and] warmly espouse my Interest yn he had ever done y^t of any former Minister here," and among other "Instances of his Kindness" made him a present of a slave boy. This made the "principal persons" and the Governor's "Friends [and] Dependants," well-disposed toward him. In choosing a churchwarden who was good and active, he had "no occasion to entangle my self in ye secular affairs of calling in of Debts, shipping off of Sugars, &c ... And this besides ye Quiet [and] retirement y^t it gives me, does most happily rescue me from ye occasions [and] temptations of interfeering w^t ye Cross Humours [and] Interests of people, w^c is ye greatest snare [and] Inconvenience y^t lyes in ye way of Clergymen in ye West Indies." Dabbling in material business was the "first Beginning" of complaints against the clergy.[213]

The conflict between interest and materialism corrupted all connection. The dance of connections around the Caribbean or between Metropole and colonies was a tricky one if it was to look elegant and natural. The ultimate irony of a man such as Lillington, therefore, was that in making such extensive and firm connections within the West Indies, he was able to effectively exploit his position to obtain the support of Whitehall's great men. Friendships, marriages, hierarchies, networks, and affinities needed to be embedded within the West Indies. Lillington was a fixture in Barbados. He had been there for many years, with several estates in St. Thomas's; Spring Head, Bully Gibbons, and Page and Teague at Black Rock; a family burial plot; and a close network of kin by marriage (to Margaret Ayshford), consanguinity, and friendship.[214] He therefore had close links with the Quakers and was related by marriage to the lovesick William Copp.[215] He had been elected to the Barbados Council in 1698, sitting with several rivals, and became attorney general of the island, serving under Grey, whom he accounted "much in the good graces of the People...never any Governour was so well belov'd...a Man of Honour; his Soul noble as well as his Birth...not capable of doing any ill thing by them for his own Interest."[216]

If one were so well connected in the localities, one could afford to rise above faction, and (re)lay symbolic claim to impartiality. Lillington's opposition to the Paper Credit Act was that it would never work in a place where the people were litigious but the law expensive and slow, resulting in overvalued land and depleted coin. Despite the venom expressed toward Cleland the Scot, Lillington took pains to declare that both men opposed to the Paper Credit Act.[217] Both Granville and Lillington described Barbados's factions— "the two Partys in the Island violently sett against one another"—but these merely as "[t]hose that have a Majority of the Councell and Assembly and their Party against those who have not," or as "country" and "court" to describe those without or with power, the former morphing into the latter if successful.[218] Lillington died in office and requested that the minister of St. Thomas's, Adam Justice, inter him under the chancel table, and preach from the 25th verse of Psalm 73: "Whom have I in heaven but thee? and there is none upon earth that I desire beside thee."[219] His son, also George, would in his turn receive commendations for his justice from the Grand Jury, reminding him of the persecution suffered by his "patriot father," loyal to Barbados.[220] He had been, of course, reflecting personal concerns: he was a gentleman of estate. Authority should rest with him and those like him because they had interest in the land, but they maintained that their Caribbean patriotic sentiment was genuine because they were "not ingaged in the debts nor partys." He pitted the interest of Barbados—that its people not be obligated through debt or in providing a militia—against British factionalism.

On the other hand, one had to serve one's time in establishing local credit. Army officers turned administrators such as Bridge and Stapleton cultivated connection. Too aloof was Yorkshireman, Captain Henry Deane, who did not "expect ffriendshippe from any one" while he was in the Caribbean because the place was to him the worst of society. He became acting governor of St. Christopher's, but found the exercise of power compromised because

> few or none will doe another a kindnesse unlesse itt be to doe one to himself, there is noe such thing as areal Desire to promote any P[er]son, unlesse itt be to advance some by-ends, noe real intention in any man unlesse by some way or means Oblig'd, or the ambitious Temp[e]^r y^t hee may boast hee did such a thing, rais'd such a man, saved such a woman from ruine.

In such as way, he lamented, people would not be blessed with good society because they expected always to receive something in return—"soe loos[ing] ye blessing by expecting ye praises of men" and all natural affection and civil ties were thus buried beneath self-interest.[221]

Sir Bevill Granville did not develop connection within his administration of Barbados and his instrumental use of people was laid so bare that one could trace both West Indian and transatlantic destruction of connection. On his arrival in Barbados, he had tried to establish a "friendship" network based on an axis of gubernatorial authority, making common cause with his counterparts in Jamaica, the Leewards, and beyond.[222] He used William Cleland as his carrier, messenger, eyes, and ears. Sir Bevill was impeccably connected and as his close kin had brother George, Lord Bath, and the Carterets; his brother-in-law, Sir John Stanley, was the Lord Chamberlain's secretary. However, Granville's letters reveal his deployment of gifts and kinship to have been so devoid of sentiment that potential dispassion and neutrality tipped over into the jaws of corruption, such that every gesture of connection was calibrated as financial and political business. Gifts balanced worth against influence. Cleland was sent to Stanley to pre-empt the opposition to Granville which was "clamouring" in Barbados, for "I depend very much upon him & I desire he & his freinds may have ye countinance of mine, they intending to apply to you & it is my interest it should be soe: what I have done to apply to you & it is my interest it should be soe." It was Stanley who had provided the name of a potential Barbados widow for Sir Bevill to marry, but Granville's idea of domestic bliss was the exchange of the wherewithal to parade finery in public for a quiet life behind doors, and his potential, unnamed lady's role was thus to prove "a fortune sufficient for the occasions of us both...I hope she may [be] well satisy'd in what relats to her Else."[223] Should Granville become tied through her to Barbados, he became responsible for the estate of her children. Sir John took Granville's words and gifts amiss; hardly surprising when he was so candid in declaring: "I shall make you noe more presents if you receive them in soe wrong a sense[:] they are noe ways the mark of ye goodness of my Government, but

I intend they should be inducement to you to make it at least as good to me as it has bin to others."[224]

Granville may have been a Tory, trying to operate in a world of Whig ascendency, and he was certainly insufficiently politic in using connection, but his personal failure was far more simple. He did not build social bonds. He made no effort to forge connection with the society established in Barbados, and its people managed to exclude him and reject his political authority. It illustrated there survived a sufficient sense of loyalty within and among the Caribbean diaspora, and Lillington's far more fawning deployment of political connection produced effective lobbying on behalf of planter society. But the necessity or desire to retain or increase connection across the Atlantic mitigated against localism. It was not in Whitehall's interest to allow societal bonds within the Caribbean to assume such strength and self-containment that they functioned independently. It was not in the interests of those based in the mother countries to allow either land or industry not to make its returns to them. The wider debate was not about "control of the localities," or the imperial executive tightening its grip of garrison government in the Caribbean, but rather of indifference.[225] Affairs in the West Indies possessed all of the competitive venom of the mother countries, without the politics. West Indians replayed domestic broils—puritanism, the civil wars, Commonwealth and Protectorate, Exclusion Crisis, popish plots, Glorious Revolution, Whig and Tory, Jacobite and Williamite, and Anglo-Scottish Union—as regional repertory theater. Sir Henry Morgan, national hero in Britain for defending the empire, was a pantomime villain in Jamaica, where "(especially when drunk) the Dissenters were Cursed & Damn'd, & the whole Island provoked, & reflected on, by their assuming the Name of the Loyal Club, & People began to take notice, that it looked as if hee designed to be thought Head of the Toryes." But his clique withered as soon as it was realized it "had neither Sence, mony, nor Sobriety."[226] Politics practiced in the West Indies was operatic, with a dark and potentially lethal plot.

CHAPTER 4

Body

Sir Bevill Granville was a career soldier with a murky and violent past, who regarded the West Indies as an insulting appointment and tried to engineer patronage to the post in Virginia. So did Marlborough's aide-de-camp, Daniel Parke, to whom Queen Anne gave her miniature for bringing to London the news of the victory at Blenheim. Appointed instead Governor of the Leeward Islands, Parke wore it always. Parke took offence at the West Indies, and it at him; his unrefined soldiering language ran to crude physicality.[1] He was splenetic before he reached the Leewards—"I have had the Plague"; "I am almost crased wth the fateague, the Hott weather, and my feaver"—and if only he had not squandered the fortune his father had left him, and been "of a Saving temper, I need not at this time of day to be Sweating in Antigua."[2] There, he was described as "black and gloomy." In describing physical attack he invariably used the language of butchery in which animals were dispatched with a firm blow: "if I have my brains knockt Out the Queen must send some Other Unfortunate Divel here to be Roasted in the sun wthout the prospect of Getting any thing."[3] Scots, both former allies and enemies, would, in the heat "exhale all those crudities that makes them so troublesom" and "if I get them all knock'd on the head,...the English Nation will be no great loosers by it," whereas the Crown thought the Scots "good subjects and good Christians, too good to be knock'd on the head."[4]

Parke's masculine language was aimed at his planter-rivals, but the objects of its crudity were women. Like bashaws (pashas), planters' circles of women were called seraglios: exotic and foreign to virtue because he was alluding to sexual license between white men and black women.[5] His authority as incomer was compromised by the de facto presence of major planters "who live in profess'd adultrys and owne a mungrill race, the liveing wittnesses of their unnaturall and monstrous lusts, etc., not to mention their dissolute drunken actions" among their "paramours" of "the slaveish sooty race." "Sober" Collector of Customs, Edward Perry, who according to Parke was the wrong side of 50, had fathered a "Mollatta Bastard" by a slave on Colonel Long's estate that bounded that of the Perry brothers, "and now letts one Keate Attkinson live with him, who has all her Life time been a profligate woman and is another man's wife."[6] Edward bequeathed Edward

Atkinson's widow a silver tankard and 40 pistols.[7] Around 1689, John Perry was the subject of gossip that he kept an inn in St John's where he lived incestuously with another brother's widow.[8] Parke had tried and failed to civilize: "it is true wee have Stocks and Whipping post; and I got them to putt up a Ducking Stool, but it is only for forme Sake; but no Inhabitant was ever punished since I came; I saw two women fighting in the Street, and would have had them both Duck't, but one of them being a house Keeper's wife, tho[ugh] a notorious Jade, her person was Sacred, and not to be punished, but the other being a Soldiers Drabb, I had her Duck't."[9] The latter was Catherine Sullivan, Codrington's "Irish wench," who had "layd Two Bastards to him, but she Giving him the Pox, he turned her off."[10]

Parke arrived in the Leewards with a notorious sexual history of his own. But he aimed at elite white women and was soon peopling the islands with the bastards of "Gentlemen's Wives and Daughters."[11] In his lust for power, he attempted to "ravish" Madame Du Saussay, who informed her husband who worked at the customs' house: the latter was dismissed, and chased off the island, leaving his wife and three children destitute and at the mercy of payments from Parke to buy their silence.[12] Parke chose rather to couch it as political economy: "whether I have been a very good Husband for the Publick."[13] He had a sexual relationship with Lucia, wife of his chief defender, George French: Lucia was publicly whipped. He had a liaison with Elinor Martin, who then prostituted her daughter to him.[14] Margaret MacMahon, Alice Lawrence, and Elizabeth Sweegle, an "abandoned Strumpet," were "noted for their lewd and profligate Lives, and infamous Characters."[15] Catherine, wife of Edward Chester, senior, was, depending whose account one believed, saved from her brutal, volatile husband by Parke the guardian, or in turn "ravished" by the Governor.[16]

Here is a testimony of violence, seized possessions (the woman's body and the man's wife), and rape.[17] While Parke complained he could make no headway imposing authority on the inhabitants of small islands because they were all interrelated, now he had severed those relations and reattached them to himself.[18] The Perrys were old family friends, administrators of Parke's will: Du Saussay's family were dependent on him. The Frenches, MacMahon, and Sweegle testified in Parke's favor.[19] Parke's low opinion of Chief Justice Samuel Watkins did not prevent Parke's nephew from marrying Watkins' daughter.[20] Lucy—"that little bastard of Col. Parkes in Antigua"—and any husband she took—Thomas Dunbar—took the ancestral name of the Parkes of Essex.[21] There was so much evidence of Parke's priapic power it would "swell" any testimony and make the author a "grave Coxcomb" (as opposed to merely a merry one). What husband, his "Bed abus'd," would not contemplate murder?[22] Perry, putative member of the Calves' Head Club which celebrated the regicide of Charles I, was said to have threatened to remove the head of the Leewards' body politic.[23] It is also, therefore, a battle for the power of language, through a debate on the appropriate use of chattel.

In 1708, a shot missed its target and passed through Parke's arm, the bones of which were set and healed.[24] Attempting to find those guilty of conspiracy to murder was corporeally expressed: the internal poison of rumor and corruption, compared with the sudden, external danger of gunshot and blows.[25] Kate Sullivan's was the most prominent female testimony. Did the conspirators threaten to whip her and confiscate her slaves for having borne an illegitimate child, then bribe her with pistols, false promises and a marriage fashioned to rehabilitate her respectability, in order to push her to commit perjury?[26] Atkinson was to say that women had overheard Parke admit to sex with "the Dutchess" (of Marlborough?), sexualizing and in these terms degrading, Parke's court and royal patronage.[27] This was a mirror to the claims that Parke bribed people with guns to "beat the Gentlemen of the Country, promising them a Pistole for every one of them they...should beat" (five pistols if it be a particular named member of the "Country Party").[28] Metaphors for the dispatch of livestock continued through the discourse. In a monochrome cartoon Michael Ayon's party (in black jackets) foiled a Parke-inspired attempt to steal a beef carcass, guarded by slaves and belonging to "the Protestants," in Lanier's butcher's. Parke's party, in white jackets, claimed it was rescued from "negroes in the street."[29]

On December 7, 1710, during a volley of shots fired during an affray about meetings of the Assembly, Parke was hit in the thigh.[30] "Clem Lanier, a butcher, broke his back with a musquett": Parke was dragged around by "one Leg and one Arm (he being yet alive)...down a few Steps of Stone Stairs...and that his Head trailed from one Step to another, till they left him at last exposed to the scorching Sun in the open Street."[31] Turner, a lowly farrier, took the miniature: they took his clothes to sell in St John's. They took his papers and showed them abroad; several letters from women that could "breed ill blood in familys."[32] His body was taken to be tended by surgeon Goussé Bonnin, and nursed by Sarah Collings who packed the wound with flax and hemp rope but failed to stem the bleeding because the Governor thrashed about in his pain. Bonnin's and Collings's testimony was used to discredit both the report that Parke's body had been broken by musket-butt, kicking, or dragging, and the testimony of the unworthy women of Parke's acquaintance who claimed to witness his body stripped.[33] Women washed and shrouded his corpse, and "by a fearful and unhallowed death, he was sent with all his sins upon his head, to render in an account of his stewardship."[34]

The narrative of Parke's governorship illustrates the myriad approaches—in microcosm and macrocosm—that could be taken toward the body, and spews them back as endless torrents of contested rhetoric. Parke's replacement, Walter Hamilton, called for further depositions and testimonials to the events of his predecessor's death, but the allegations of each side mirrored the other, such that it was impossible (though no one tried very hard) to determine the truth and falsity of anyone's reputation and character. French, despite his loyalty, described Parke's assassination as an "unlucky Incident," and reflected on how free people were with ill-founded opinions—"so subtle, indeed, is the poysonous Quality of Detraction, that it soon diffus'd it self into the whole Mass, and became a Distemper almost Epidemical"—creating a body-language catalog of personal sleights: failure to doff one's hat, seizing an arm, using one's tongue to slander, rumor and swear; or paralleling physical assaults with verbal insinuations.[35] None revealed whether a specific and pointed violation of the body politic had been a calculated act of treason or a less-considered, more-chaotic clash of drunken and disorderly bodies that got out of hand: 11 government men were killed and 35 injured; four residents died, and eight were wounded. The Leewards' governor's name was appropriated as a verb: a "desperado or giddy mobb would Felton d' Witt or Parke."[36] There were tales of the abuse of, and by, black, white, male, female, healthy, sickly, noble, and ignoble bodies; human beings presented with their animal natures and reduced to carcasses. The bodily fluids of sex and violence flowed around, between and away from the body. Each body, and everybody, was a contested metaphor, until the carcass of a bullock was no more or less noble than that of the Lord's anointed.

Behn's romance of rebellion in Surinam was a black/white inversion of an assassination attempt on Francis, Lord Willoughby. John Allin first "smote at" the Lord Proprietor's head "with all his fury," and later at a gathering of the Council attempted to stab him.[37] The human body was an intimate thing, and graphic descriptions of its degradation could humanize lofty ideas and abstract concepts. The bodies of the rich and powerful were animal blood and bone too. Metaphorical allusion to the body politic is much rarer. This is Governor Sir Thomas Lynch, as he prorogued the Jamaica Assembly in 1682; one of the few overt references from the torrid zone to the body politic:

> You may believe the disorders of my Head, and misfortunes of my Voyage, are something alleviated, by the joy I have to see this Session so happily and suddenly ended; though God has been pleased to confer on me many great and signal Blessings, yet none of them methinks ever relisht like this, nor is it reasonable they should: they have been particular, and concerned my self onely. This is publick, and may, I hope, reach *White-hall*, and affect not onely us here, but every individual man in this great Island, and those that shall succeed us in it.
>
> We have, Gentlemen, fluctuated many years between Fears and Jealousies among our selves, and of our Governours...
>
> Like ill Sculptures, some would have made the Head too big, as others the Members, neither of them considering that the perfection and beauty of the Figure consists in the symetry and due proportion of the parts: for it's in the Body Politick as in the Natural; if the Head attracts too much nourishment, the Members become debile and weak; if the Body does it, the Head will be rendred incapable of exercising the Divine Function lodg'd in it.... Colonies that do not thrive, are like Scabs, they render nothing to, but draw nourishment from the Body.[38]

William Gordon reminded the people of Barbados that the essence of God could not be conjured by an "Imbodied Understanding" and if it could, its power "would Dissolve and Melt down our Tender Frame into Vapour and

Ashes."[39] Gordon's sermon, on man's ability to know God, was delivered over Easter 1710, and coincided with the funeral of Leewards' Governor, Christopher Codrington; and thus with the implication that the demise of his physical and political power was a parable of the Passion of Christ. The minister's account of this "Master-piece of Nature" was belied by the fact that when he died he was little older than 40: "NATURE had blessed him with vast capacious Parts exceedingly above the common Level of Mankind: He had a Great Soul of a fiery Genius, happily united to a Body of a subtle and flexible Composition, in which the Blood and Animal Spirits moved with Vigour and Rapidity, and render'd it rather a Spurr than a Hindrance to the Operations of his Mind. He had a quick and piercing Apprehension; a strong, solid, distinguishing Judgement; a retentive Memory; a warm Imagination; a fruitful sagacious Invention; a bold pregnant Wit; a sublime way of Thinking; a methodical perswasive way of Reasoning; and a Voluble distinct Utterance, upon the most unexpected Occasions." Gordon's embodiment, in perfect combination, of the *vita activa* and *vita contemplativa* is unconvincing: a man of loud, inopportune, gauche interventions, who certainly dominated as governor, but was not well-liked.[40]

The health and fitness of any governor was important to the exercise of authority, and the management of the health of the people key to the growth and stability of the settlement. Sir Bevill Granville corresponded with regular "Melancholy & long letters" updating his family about the deleterious climate and his body's failure to adapt to or cope with it, and Daniel Parke was a long and loud complainant. Two splenetic figures found it hindered their being accepted.[41] A combination of drink, heat, and disease took Governor of Jamaica, Christopher Monck, after less than a year's service.[42] Sir William Matthew's administration was regularly interrupted by his "indisposition," and he sent a final despairing communiqué to London via his wife. His deputy, John Johnson, reported his death in office less than three weeks later.[43] Francis Russell had already been recalled from Barbados when it "pleased Almighty God to deprive us on the 7th day of this last Month, having been taken with a Malignant ffeaver on the Monday before, the first Infection whereof (its' thought) he received on board the Bristoll where hee had been the weeke preceeding and Complained thereof soone after his returne a Shoare."[44]

Governor Henry Ashton held the prevalence of ague responsible for Antigua's slow development, with all the Leeward Islands frequently visited by epidemics and also under constant threat from the French, one weakening their resistance to the other. A particularly bad attack raged at the turn of the year 1690–1691, the fresh provisions required to feed the sick were spread thin, and the news of such heavy loss of life took nine months before it was noted by Whitehall.[45] Diseases ravaged the bodies of those in authority, and their office was undercut by their inability to keep their people healthy and well fed. The Governor of Providence appropriated the health and ability of those who served under him, in a puritan discourse of cowardice in authority that inverted the sentiments of Elizabeth I's address at Tilbury.

He "intercepted ye victualls wch o^r souldiers of the leaguer had formerly provided by their owne ca[re?] [and] cost, having left order to have it sent downe unto them: neverthelesse though they exceedingly needed it, being sore wearied by their painfull march [and] their great toyle in ye fight, he little considered them, who whiles they were falling in on their enemies he fell on their victualls, [and] in the very heate of the fight shewed his stomach wch was not to fight but to feed."[46]

Given the history of settlement in Virginia and the constant companionship of famine, malnutrition, and disease, there was remarkably little complaint about food.[47] Five pioneers in Bermuda became desperate, and James I's court was informed that rather than starve, they had built themselves a boat the size of a double wherry in order to sail back to England.[48] However, while local food represented change, it was not necessarily a hardship. Rev. Nicholas Leverton recounted his adventures around the region, and the times when food was scarce, but, given that his mission was to explain the blessings of Providence, he gave more attention to the wild provision of Tobago, where the ship could stock up on goat and game, and of the indigenes of the Leewards, with whom they were able to barter brandy for meat, fish, and maize-corn.[49] Henry Adis claimed he did not miss that of England, and although he was now an old man, he fared as well on the provisions available in Surinam as he had in his youth.[50] Much about the diet was better than at home, with ample hogs—the planters' food, often reserved in deeds so that they could come and go in the knowledge that food would remain available to them[51]—cattle, sheep, goats, fowl, fish, turtles—"to furnish the inferior sort of people with good Food, at an easie and moderate price"[52]—and fruit. Jamaica was described as a land of seven million acres in which every acre would yield food or fodder for man or beast.[53]

Those with a public role, clergymen or soldiers, for example, would expect to be provided for; in part as a signal of their status, but also as a means to ensure that they could and would fulfill their duties, thus normalizing life in the Caribbean. The provision accorded to ministers, either in terms of what church or state stipulated or what their flocks would allow them, gradually improved across the century. Anglican ministers were usually expected to hold glebe lands, but seldom did; were expected to earn a salary, but seldom did; and often had to exchange food for the soul for some for their bodies.[54] They were entitled to a christening or marriage feast, though this was dependent on the affluence and largesse of the hosts, who, in the case of christenings, for example, often waited to baptize several children together, often as adults, and thus provide only one dinner. By the end of the century, the otherwise moaning demeanor of Antigua Anglican, James Field, boasted that a single man as a minister could eat well from such sacramental feasting and the entertainment of wealthy merchants. This was unlikely to have been true: he was desperate to be replaced.[55]

A well-provisioned ministry, though seldom achieved, was considered vital in improving the morals and behavior of the European settlers. An ill-provisioned soldiery was a further threat. Caribbean settlers were ambivalent toward soldiers; reluctant to incorporate them, but mindful that only a professional soldiery and navy could guard their territory and their ships from enemy attack. The presence of soldiers—sometimes as planters, other times as temporary guards—often on small and crowded islands, still ill-developed, represented a major drain on resources. Supply devolved onto the hard-pressed island authorities, so if resources were not forthcoming, islands had to feed and house their guards and their families.[56] Otherwise, soldiers were quartered in private houses. In the midst of a smallpox crisis, a shortage of able men to serve in the militia, and the consequent effect on artisan labor and the costs of servants' food and clothing, Barbadians struggled to persuade London to restrict to three months the time for which soldiers could be billeted on a family.[57] The emaciated and disheveled appearance of its soldiers brought the English forces in St Christopher's into disrepute before they met the French.[58]

Food was integral to indenture, in return for service and as part of the journey. George Mole paid for the provisions of *The Carlile*: Mr. Shether the London butcher; Houghton the fishmonger; Bishop for cider; Major for cheese, butter, and beef; salt, sugar, rice, and other grocery provisions for the ship's use. Mr. Ashley was the ship's cook. Since it took the ships such a long time before they were in a position to sail across the Atlantic, further provisions had to be taken on along the way, and passengers kept on board the venture, while not actually at sea: this was the task given to Thomas Davis, who paid £6 at the Frying Man in Gravesend to entertain the passengers and keep them in one place.[59] Sir Thomas Warner's passage to St Christopher's was hampered by the loss of his ships' victuals, the deaths of many of his passengers, and the obstinacy on the part of Henry Hawley in Barbados to assist with either.[60] Merchants could turn the tables, professing themselves reluctant to carry servants if they suspected them of falsely demanding their entitlement to food and clothing by subsequently claiming they had been spirited abroad.[61] Once colonies started to amass a sustainable population, recruits to people new settlements could be enticed into repeated migrations by the prospect of victual and raiment. About 60 English who were driven off Bermuda to Eleutheria, where they were denied clothes and provisions, could be encouraged to migrate again to Jamaica if given provisions sufficient to "provide for themselves."[62] The wages, raw materials, and provisions for artisans engaged in public work, such as those repairing the forts and public buildings of Montserrat, could constitute the island's entire expenditure. The diet of some was paid in sugar. John Adams and Samuel Robinson were working on the Sessions' House (Adams clapboarding it): Tielman van Vleck, who was employing John Roach to work on gun carriages, received 96 pounds sugar for what he had paid out for his diet. Other, unnamed artisans—sawyers, carpenters, and masons—ate bread, beef, and rum.[63] As a treat, there was occasional herring or mutton.[64] The meat and fish was invariably salted, and fresh meat was at a premium, requiring the prices to be regulated.[65] Bermuda's position as a northerly, but strategic, isolated garden of plenty was not indisputable. The Bishop of London questioned George

Berkeley's choice of the island for his college (suggesting Albany instead), because the Bermudans were too busy being seafarers and had to import all their food.[66] But, Isaac Richier suggested that the island could act as the region's larder:

> It is well knowne why the Scotts Deserted Darian: vizt for want of provision and health; supposeing they had been possesst of Bermuda those two ffatall Evills had been most infallibly remedied especially the first and att a farr lesse Charge and much better provisions then is possible to have from Scotland att that distance, for instead of being forced to ffeede on Beefe that has been a yeare or more in Salt they might have itt monthly from thence, and oftner if Occasion required, And also Hoggs Sheepe Poultry &^{c} alive, And what cannot be sent thither from Scotland as Maiz Cabadges Onions Potatoes Pumkins Cassava Bread &^{c}.[67]

Safeguarding local foodstuffs was important. Plantations continued to grow provision crops ("Indian provisions" to denote their indigenous origins) either for their own use or the internal market, and livestock kept for food had to be protected against rustling.[68]

Descriptions of indigenous peoples, focusing on their connection with nature, conflated external and internal aspects of the body. Samuel Clarke described the people of the Leeward Islands as "the Islands of the *Caribes*, or Canibals," who "eat mans flesh, and...hunt for men as others do for beasts." When resting with their own, "they only cover their privities, but in war they use many Ornaments: they are nimble, beardlesse, shoot poisoned arrows, bore holes in their ears, and nostrils, for bravery, which the richer sort deck with gold, the poorer with shels, and make their teeth black, which never ake nor rot." Those further south, in those islands such as St. Vincent and St. Lucia, claimed by the Lord Proprietor as part of the Caribbees, were peopled by natives who "paint themselves, to keep off the Muskitoes, wear their hair long, cut their skins in diverse works, worship the Devil, and poison their arrows."[69] Europeans were also aware of the poison of such plants as the Manchineel, with its deceptive apple-like fruits, but of how an unsuspecting Briton, in search of food, shade, and soothing sappy balms, might rest beneath its spreading boughs, and would "feel some indisposition in himself...his head and face will swell, and his eye-lids in a short time be closed up" though the fruit so sweet "that scarse any man, especially that is a stranger, but would be induced to taste of it," albeit indigenes made an almost invariably fatal human poison from it, such that this was likely to be the "unhappie fruit which deceived our first parents in Paradise."[70]

When it came to the diet of slaves, white settlers demonstrated all the confusion of wanting to keep costs as low as possible, both in terms of estate budgets and of the slaves as a commodity in themselves; while at the same time, recognizing that these were both fellow human beings and members of their wider household (in a way in which livestock was not), over whom they possessed a duty of care. There was also a contest between difference and liberty, between foods "natural" or "special" to the African diet, and those which were similar to that of Europeans, albeit of lesser quality. Sir Hans Sloane expressed amazement to find indigenous and African people eating "cossi" or Cotton-Tree Worms, and the poisonous root of cassava, dried and ground into flour to make a bread, although it had long since been imported into the white settlers' diet.[71] In Sierra Leone, Britons described eating manatee—white like veal, without a fishy taste, and "boiled, stewed, or roasted... is as acceptable a Treat [in the opinion of a man from Plaistow] as Venison to Cockneighs"—while its skin was exported to the Caribbean, where "West Indians" used it in the cats-o'-nine-tails with which they punished their slaves.[72] However, in New England, catches of cod and pollock, if good, were "merchantisable," and if not, "refuse fish," to be landed in the Caribbean to feed slaves.[73] A cow that died would be divided up: the servants would be given the meat; the slaves, the skin, head, and offal. If a horse died, the slaves would be given the whole carcass, "a high Feast, with which poor souls were never better contented."[74] Sir William Stapleton would "allow the Negroes fish, or flesh at Christmas, or other festivals": overseers and agents should continue this practice during his absence but he would not then allow the keeping of pigs, sheep, and turkeys, which would divert slave labor from the fields.[75] Beyond cultural revulsion directed either at the type of foodstuff eaten by Africans, or its quality; or the dichotomy of amity/enmity embedded in Britons' attitude toward indigenes and food supply, few made any comment about the holistic nature of the good life, requiring a spiritual, mental, and corporeal element. One who did was the mystic and merchant, Thomas Tryon, who, having already developed his philosophy of asceticism—eschewing both meat and alcohol—thinking to try his hand in Barbados, was horrified by the inhumane expression of patriarchy in the West Indies and offered the following exposition:

> The same is to be understood when any particular Person or Family has awakned the *poysonous Wrath*, it doth powerfully attract the male Influences, whence Sickness, waste of Estate, and many other great Troubles & Miseries, both to the Body and Mind follow; the truth of this daily Experience doth testifie; how many of our great Masters have by their *Vitiousness, Vncleanness, Intemperance, Violence* and *Oppressions* both to Man and Beast, whom they have had the Government over, fallen into great Disorders, Distempers, Losses, Crosses, Troubles and Vexations, so that their Children that were kept so fine and choice, that they would hardly suffer the Air to blow on them or their Legs to carry them whilst they lived in Prosperity, are many of them come to nothing[ ] some forced to work hard for their Bread, others have taken worse Courses, and have been immaturely cut off.[76]

The poison used by the white elite was self-interest, which provoked anger; the providential effect of abusing their own bodies and those of their servants and livestock, loss of estate, health, and life. Tryon did not quite condemn behavior as wrong in itself, but did advance a connection between living a good life and making a good living.

The most poisonous substance in the West Indies was the drink.[77] Alcohol funded administrations: the vast majority of import duties raising money for struggling island economies came from the levies raised from "pipes" of Madeira, brandy, and to a lesser extent, beer and ale.[78] Madeira or Canary wines, in particular, were the drink of choice for the planter who laid claim to a refined palate and a social status—"that I may not in drinkinge yowre health lose my owne"—though by the early years of the eighteenth century, the coffeehouse had made an appearance in the islands.[79] Barbados, where this refined palette resided, was more associated with kill-devil rum, stronger than brandy.[80] The planters seldom went thirsty, but would overheat their bodies by working in the sun and further dehydrate themselves with "*English* spirits, or *French* brandy, or the drink of the *Island*," though they could make a number of drinks. Some would "fly up into the head"; others were more temperate: from potatoes (mobby); cassava; sugar cane and water (punch); plums; plantains; orange-juice, sugar, and water (beverage); and pineapples (the "best sort of Drink which the World affords").[81] Excessive drinking was a basic social lubricant between white people otherwise strangers to each other. More than one person related the story that travelers or neighbors were judged according to whether they accepted the hospitality of their hosts. One continued, "the merry planter, or freeman to give him a Carecter, I cann call him noe otherwise then a German for his drinking, and a Welshman for his welcome"; another, Henry Whistler, travelling in the Western Design expedition to Jamaica, was generally fulsome in his descriptions of the land and its potential, but scathing about the characters of the people who lived there, including plying every passerby with strong drink.[82] The planters wished to be known for their "very Generus fashion," and to be able both to brag and to demonstrate how well they could entertain with a mixture of meats, fish, fruits, and drinks, either expensively imported or exotically domestic.[83] The overall impression, however, was that the people who lived in the West Indies were coarser than the average: the rubbish cast on a dunghill, according to Whistler, who added that "a rodge in England will hardly make a cheater heare: a baud brought over puts on a demour comportment, a whore if hansume makes a wife for sume rich planter." Even without the descriptions of pirates pouring rum down the throats of all and sundry, a tavern inventory from Port Royal could provide a flavor of Jamaica in the seventeenth century. That on Queen Street was kept by John and Tomasine Ellis: it had a ground floor room fronting the street, bedrooms, a billiard room; 60 gallons of rum and 21 of wine in the cellar, debts "hopeful doubtful and Desperate," and only the help of an "old decrepid" black woman.[84]

Once in the West Indies, everyone (except Thomas Tryon) drank prodigiously, making it impossible for commentators to tell whether the West Indies attracted drunkards and sots, or conditions created them. Alcohol was the nemesis of respect. The Established Church despaired at its inability to plant roots in the "Foreign Plantations" of the tropics, because the lack of sober servants exposed it to the "scoffers of religion."[85] Christopher

Jeaffreson offered advice to Mr. Sedgwick, an incoming estate manager: "be sure to shew a good example of sobriety [which] will get you Esteeme amongst ye better sort [and] respect from inferiors (yea even from ye verry drunkards them selves)." Strong drink was the "Epidemick distemper" of St Christopher's, and Jeaffreson showed some awareness of its poisonous effect on people's good character. Alcohol was the servant of time; "he is on ye plantation to inveigle ye slaves y^t will be so long in his power." Slaves who showed Sedgwick loyalty were to be encouraged, whereas the previous manager had acted with "too great severity where wth Mr Thorne Created them well in aw."[86] Ensign Edward Thorne was accused elsewhere of carelessness and "profuseness" and the implication is that drink provoked laziness in himself and violence toward the slaves, who themselves retreated into drink.[87] Slaves took rum medicinally when they were "sick" or "inwardly distempered," but this nugget came within a narrative of slaves' cowardly natures, such that if threatened with punishment they would hang themselves, or if suffering "bruises or strains" would soothe their skins with oil, and drink, in which context the causes of their fear, sickness, and injury sound more malign.[88]

Rum required careful control and allocation: Samuel Clarke's account of a slave "feast" cautioned that they drank only water, while Sir William Stapleton doled out drams during wet weather. Strong drink in the hands of black people conjured up multiple fears in the minds of their white counterparts. Drink provoked laziness, insubordination, and violence, which were all examples of assertive liberty resulting from slaves' incapacity to serve: it would reduce productivity at best and incite murder and rebellion at worst. Masters of families, therefore, were responsible for the regulation of alcohol within the private confines of estates. Drink available publically, showing no respect to race or status, was a social lubricant between black and white: drinking together was the initial stage of terrible disruption to the social order. While all of the Acts passed in one session in Montserrat in 1683 were designed to order people to their allotted place, two in particular spoke to how much more difficult that became when alcohol was involved. "An act restraineing christians ffrom confederateing wth negroes" was designed to preclude Christians' debauchery by "drineking, playeing, or conver[sing]" with non-Christians. The same day, steps were taken to stop the regular practice in Montserrat whereby seamen were concealed and detained from their ships until they had been sucked into debt by keepers of the "tapp-house or other...Mast^r or Mistresse of houses of entertainm^t."[89]

No one could agree whether their corner of the region was healthy or not. Carolina, furthest from the equator, "developed a dual identity both as a paradise and a morgue."[90] Surinam, closest, was enveloped by malign vapors during the night, where sleeping in a hammock left the body dangerously exposed. Indigenous people lit a fire under themselves as they slept, and Europeans kept themselves covered.[91] In the mid-century Barbados was described as a healthy place, you "may wth pleasure live heere." It was impossible to move around during the day without sweating, but was apparently not the fainting, tiring sweats familiar in England. The air was pure and English appetites for food healthy, while—contrary to the mid-seventeenth century accounts of Barbados above—islanders' appetite for Bacchus and Venus was said to be on the wane.[92] Many considered the Bahamas the pinnacle, and Bermuda was generally regarded as a healthy place, combining a more northerly aspect with the cooling, fresh breezes of an isolated island. There, people could live to be one hundred, and died of old age rather than disease, with poor people's humble diet held up as a key component of their longevity.[93] Thus former governor Isaac Richier, selling the island as a regional hub excellent in all things, could offer it as a convalescence-*entrepôt*, noting the "[s]ad undoubted truth that those who goe from England to Barbados Jamaica &c and happen to Live; yett generally they become Diseased weake and Languid." There was "Scurvy and other Maladies insident to Sea" and "the infection of the Southerne Islands." Barbadians, afflicted by the Iliac Passion, "(or dry Belly Ach)," which was severe constipation with an obstructed or twisted bowel, were cured on Bermuda; better than a dose of indigenous purgative, drawn from the "negro-oil bush": castor oil.[94] Richier's predecessor as governor had, along with his men, many of whom had been thrown overboard, arrived very sick. As soon as their ship was aired and cleaned and the men had spent three weeks in Bermuda, "their Lame Limbs" were "made sound and they have often returned in...two Months strong and vigorous."[95] Illnesses were generally described in terms similar to the climate, producing torridness in the body. In 1671, "god hath bin pleased to inflict...a very great mallignancy, where of in this bridge towne I doe not know of any family hath escaped, or indeed few p[er]sons but did more or less tast of its visitt."[96]

There was imperative need for a "good stomach."[97] The extremes of temperature, weather conditions, the passage over the Atlantic (seasickness described as being "stomach-sick"), and seesawing perceptions of glut and dearth, combined to ensure that the stomach retained its rhetorical and descriptive powers in the Caribbean long after it had been superseded in Britain by the heart or bodily mechanics. It was used metaphorically and literally, and could mean good diet or the absence of gastric diseases. At the corporeal core, it took in the nourishment required to show valor or worth, or to toil; and under attack from difficult conditions, often spewed it forth again. Extreme Caribbean environments could usually be ridden out or managed. The great enemy was immoderation. "It hath been experimentally found," opined Richard Blome, "that there is no such Antipathy betwixt the constitutions of the *English*, and this clime, for the occasioning Sickness to be Mortal or Contageous, more than in other parts; for if a good *Dyet*, and moderate Exercises are used, without excess of *Drinking* they may enjoy a competent measure of Health." The moral laxity of incomers was inclined to produce "*Dropsies* (occasioned often by ill *diet*, *drunkeness*, and *slothfulness*)" and "*Calentures* too frequently the product of *Surfits*."[98] A calenture, was in itself, a tropical creation, being the name for a light fever, sometimes accompanied by fainting or delirium, brought on by the heat: sunstroke perhaps.

When it was so difficult to distinguish between the different consequences of excess, how could one tell whether individuals had died of natural causes, albeit in an unusual climate, or had been speeded on their way? The alacrity with which bereaved spouses remarried put fuel on the fire. Infamy followed the name of Yeamans from Barbados to Carolina, via Antigua. John Yeamans started as partner to Councilor Lieutenant Colonel Benjamin Berringer, building up an estate of over 500 acres in St. Andrew's and St. Philip's.[99] When the otherwise active Berringer died in 1660, during his wife Margaret's pregnancy (she gave birth to a daughter, also Margaret), she quickly married Yeamans. They travelled in the first fleet to the new colony of Charles Town, Carolina, but under the clouds cast on Margaret junior's paternity, the cause of Berringer's death, and Yeamans's role in both.[100] Poison was suspected. Over in St John's, Barbados, Henry Willoughby was taken ill at the house of his rival, Christopher Codrington, and it was intimated that the latter had attempted poison, over the magnificent estate left to Elizabeth, the widow of Lieutenant-Colonel William Consett.[101] Presumably, Codrington's power, influence, and noisy bombast silenced the rumors and won the dispute, as the Consett estate joined that of Codrington himself as part of the patrimony of the Society for the Propagation of the Gospel.[102] Such suspicions were not confined to the inheritance or the patrimony of the wealthy. Ambitt Rener, who married Rev. Nicholas Leverton in Bermuda in 1640, blossomed in the tropical air. Her husband offered one explanation:

> M^{r}s: Lev: who was in England thick fatt and unweldy was in A short space become Active and very beautifull, as ye young man Affermed who Came from them and like a maid (as he said) of 18 years of Age, Tis strange I say & yet some reason may be rendred for it, for I have heard m^r Lev: say y^t when he first married her in Barmudas she was so slender that he could wth his hands span about her waist, but afterwards in England by the could stopping her pores she was as it were blown up & troubled wth many distempers but when she came into a warmer Aire and y^t congeniall to her nature, in Barmudas it soon unlocked the pores Breathed out those humours & might well make a sudden alteration in her for ye better.

Nevertheless, when Reverend Leverton died in Surinam, there was a story "that he was removed not without...Suspition of poyson, By some: who had A Minde to have his wife after him: tis true that women in that Plantation were very scarce...she was quickly married after her husbands death to a person of Quality in the countrey: one Mr Bovell Rouden [Bevill Rawdon]."[103] An unedifying battle was fought over the unworthy carcass of Robert Cunyngham, but while she was living with him in St. Christopher's, Elizabeth Arnold advanced as proof that they were married, the idea that if news of it had become public knowledge in the West Indies, his children by his first marriage would have incited the slaves to poison her.[104] The role of house slaves, particularly in the kitchen, was one of such intimate trust in this respect, that it is amazing that there were not frequent accusations of poisonings, whether as a means to throw suspicion away from the real culprits, or as a covert but effective expression of resistance.[105]

Provision of food, management of disease, and hygiene were issues of acute public concern, but steps to control public health were not taken until the very end of the century. In Nevis, the danger of fire in Charlestown's combustible buildings stretched not only to the requirement to have a separated brick or stone chimney, but also limited boiling and dressing food in the streets. The town was built almost on top of its port, and given the Leewards' reputation for agues, ships that could carry disease had to be cordoned off from public food displays.[106] The Lords' Proprietors of Carolina stipulated within their instructions of 1692 that buildings be erected on ground high enough that cellars would not be wet and "(if possible) far from marshes, swamps, or standing water."[107] Steps were eventually taken to isolate contagious disease from people and contagious people from each other. The provincial legislature of Charles Town began formulating public health measures that year, and from 1698, incoming vessels were required to show that they were not carrying infectious disease before they were allowed to land. This did not stop the first outbreak of yellow fever the following year: "this contagious distemper...which is verry mortall" killed around 5 percent of the town, including the minister of St Philip's, Samuel Marshall, who "fell sick of a light feaver...[which]...soon turned to a pestilentiall feaver and a Calenture attended with a perpetuall fflux and vometing...his vometts turned black as Ink and his pulse Grew so low and Irregular attended with cold Clammy sweats...There was the utmost endeavours used to have brought him to A sweat but it was not possible...and...he yealded up his soul to God."[108] In 1707, Charles Town built a brick pest house on Sullivan's Island, and the contagious were isolated, but four years later there were more reports of "small Pox, Pestilential ffeavers, Pleurisies and fflux's" which killed without discriminating color, class, or ethnicity.[109] The following year, the legislature created a Commissioner with responsibility for public health, but the position lasted only as long as its first and sole incumbent.[110] High mortality and fever hung over Bridgetown for longer than usual in the summer of 1700. Responsibility was quite literally laid at the doors of named individuals: sweaty sheets had not been burnt, bad masters had fed rotten meat to their slaves, housekeepers and scavengers had not cleared the dirt from the thresholds of houses, and new building and neglect had stopped up other waterways. Individual effort and public works would be necessary to cleanse the city.[111]

Personal health details—such as the suffering of Rev. Marshall above—disgorge rich and colorful testimony, in which lie dangers of interpretation. Statements of "how I am feeling" rely on the historian being able to read and judge personality from a 300-year remove. Francis Le Jau described his fellow minister in Carolina, Gideon Johnston, as robust and active (reminding London that he was busy about his spiritual task), whereas Johnston's own letters are a depressive catalog of the illnesses of himself or his flock. Christopher Jeaffreson's romantic and positive image of St. Christopher's was unusual, but also made him more tolerant of the heat of the West Indies than of the English winter, mortal to folks of "riper years."[112] All comments come back to the heat and activity in the heat. Johnston informed the Society for the Propagation of the Gospel in 1710 that he was always busy "visiting the sick, of which there is always Numbers here; and the burying of the dead, which in the hot Weather is no small work, and oftentimes very Nauseaus."[113] Carolina was a later foundation, but throughout the region comments come from the end of the century, and the contemporaneous interest in experimental science. Experiment, empiricism, and experience operated as synonyms, and the stomach-churning accounts were not only to inspire terror, sympathy, or the reformation of manners, but also a prerequisite of accurate and complete description.

The imperative for graphic and precise description of symptoms and effects was not confined to those with specialist training or interest and flirted with gratuitousness and grossness. It spoke to the ways in which people "at home" had to be apprised of what was different, alien, and exotic about life in the tropics. The unhealthiness of a place could turn English gentlemen into "walking shadows."[114] Henry Ashton's report to the Earl of Carlisle on the state of the Caribbees reported that in Antigua, by 1641, "the Ague and the Indians are the onely Gorgons pʳsented in their most terrible formes to all that looke this wayes."[115] The language was, at one and the same time, both precise and generalized: impossible to be certain of the correlation between contemporary description and modern diagnosis, but nevertheless, discriminating. Poxes were manifest on the skin; as were yaws of (literally) yawning, open, and suppurating pustules: vomit was expelled from the mouth and flux evacuated below. Others could be determined by their actions on the body, such as fevers, or agues (similar), but acute and violent, accompanied by fitting or quaking. Malaria was usually identified as ague, particularly in its delirious, fitful, initial stages.[116] Dropsy referred to swelling, usually containing fluid. Edema could be fatal, in children or adults, though in the case of slave deaths it is hard not to surmise that what brought about the swelling was the more likely cause of death.[117] Some illnesses were considered indigenous or particular constitutions more susceptible. Smallpox was deemed imported from Africa.[118] Scott was quite specific about locations along the Wild Coast of Guiana, imputing different susceptibilities to illness to the peoples as he moved south, all on the basis of observation.[119] The health of a body in an alien environment was dependent on the season of its arrival, and a newly arrived body needed to acclimatize. William Byam noted how English constitutions were more robust than those of the Dutch in Guiana, because the latter were "no planters" and presumably given their propensity to trade rather than settle, were more liable to land newcomers on the Wild Coast, whom, "sad souls for suffering any hardship," would die of "fever and ague, belly-ache and yawes."[120] Again, statements concerning seasoning appear only in the final 30 years of the century. Benjamin Whitrow described it to his brother:

> Since my last [July] I have undergone the Comon fate of that they call here a Seasoning to the Country, [and] this is the fifth day since it has been upon Me, I was first taken with a Sickness at my Stomack, which soon turned to a fflux attended with some blood I was thereupon imediately bleeded, and the next day purged, which removed some violent griping pains I before laboured under, & I bless God, I this day find myself quite free of pains as well as purging.[121]

In Jamaica, mid-May to mid-September was hot and wet, leading to fever, and seasoned Jamaica-watchers predicted that around half of those who landed then would die.[122] Maurice Berkeley, of Gloucestershire, married a Tobin (of an Irish family that had moved to the Isle of Man), born in Nevis. The pair went out to St Christopher's, "when he did not long encounter the climate," while she was presumably inured to the heat.[123] A body once seasoned would be able to engage in strenuous or physical work, which was a fillip to secondary migration. Christopher Codrington recommended that seasoned men raised in Barbados be used in any attempts to buy, take, and mine silver in Dominica, and experienced and seasoned settlers from Surinam were considered four times as valuable in terms of productivity than labor shipped from Britain.[124] Seasoning was deemed vital in semitropical as well as equatorial climes, so several projectors suggested importing citizen-soldiery to protect Carolina from the Spanish in Florida and the French on the Mississippi, who in times of peace could produce pitch, tar, and maize, but be ready to fight if necessary.[125] Captain James Norton was successful in a suit to become Lieutenant-Governor of St Christopher's, because, among his qualifications, his frequent travel to the Caribbean meant he had acclimatized.[126]

Kiple's account of slave bodies is replete with detail about susceptibility or resistance to disease, but most of his references to the seventeenth century are to the white population and there is no mention of seasoning slaves.[127] Studies have been done for later periods.[128] Peter Kalm provides one of the few early eighteenth-century accounts of black bodies needing to be seasoned but in this case he referred to the Delaware valley and the shock of the cold.[129] Richard Sheridan referenced the seasoning of slaves and the tragically high mortality figures among new arrivals, but there are no references earlier than 1732.[130] Reverend Robert Robertson of Nevis estimated that approximately two out of every five slaves imported from Africa died during seasoning.[131] In the seventeenth century, while settlers were wary that bodies from Africa might harbor disease, it was generally felt that Africans were possessed of a robust constitution that could work in Caribbean conditions. But we know that there was at least an economic awareness of the value of seasoning black bodies because Edward Littleton complained that slave labor could only be hired out for less than a groat a day, while a seasoned slave cost £30 to buy.[132]

In recovering the black body of the seventeenth century, historians are faced with a shocking paucity of both evidence and analysis.[133] The remains of slave bodies, some of which must date from the seventeenth century, have been the object of archaeological and anthropological study, but they come from burial grounds that were in continuous use for three centuries and keep their silence as to change over time. As a starting point, Britons in the early seventeenth century regarded sub-Saharan Africans to be constituted similarly to themselves, except for the color of their skin: "that all the people in generall to the South, lying with[in] the *Zona Torrida*, are not onely blackish like the Moor, but are exceeding blacke...so at this day they are named Negro's, as then whom no men are blacker."[134] The spectrum of skin color in which the pallor of northern Europe was at the opposite end to the black of the equator provided opportunities both to equate the black form with ugliness and to romanticize the extremity of the blackness.[135]

Violence toward the body was, as far as the British were concerned, a means to distinguish alien from intrinsic, "natural" values. The French used the violent Kalinago to attack British settlements: in Antigua in 1666, and 15 years later, when Kalinago brought onto the island via Guiana, Tobago, St. Vincent and St. Lucia formed a fifth column, and Britons contemplated the extirpation of an entire people.[136] The practice of violating the bodies of captive enemies distinguished between those indigenes who lived in the area from Virginia northward, who scalped their victims, and those in the torrid zone, whose name was synonymous with consuming them.[137] Britons needed no excuse to add to Spain's black legend. Peter Dyer was taken prisoner by the Spanish, and having purchased his freedom, was asked by the Committee of Trade and Plantations to catalog Spanish practice toward English prisoners, and did so with (disturbing) gusto.[138] Soldiers and sailors were dispatched cruelly on all occasions, "smother'd and one kill'd by a pistoll ball, a Cruelty which a great many others have sufferd which for Brevitys sake I omit." The sadism toward the wife of the governor, however, was "unparalleled": "having first defil'd her...they took her & beded her, & y^n took rum & set on fire [and] put it in her private parts and to make their spleen appear still greater they Cut of a piece of the same," which as a trope of Spanish barbarity, particularly on Providence Island, was still deemed beyond what tongue or pen could relate.[139] The Spaniard was notoriously promiscuous, having spread syphilis through the Americas; "too free of his Flesh to be combined within his own Nation."[140] Despite and because of the extremity of the language it was deemed possible to relate in the case of rape by foreigners, the individual female body (and in this case her gentle status), because the governor's wife symbolized and abstracted the victimization of English political values; while at the same time allowing for a sado-sexualized discourse to both shock and titillate the gentlemen of the Committee. A rape committed by an indigenous man could be the pretext for war or stand for generalized brutality on the part of slaves who attacked their oppressors. A slave convicted of rape would be executed, the master of the slave compensated financially for the loss of a worker, as was the case if one slave killed another.[141] Pirate torture would involve burning with matches, dismemberment, and popping out their captives' eyes ("woolding"); during an attack launched from Jamaica on Puerto Belo, "a woman there was by some set bare upon a baking stone and roasted."[142]

Given a combination of the desire to assert dominion and the fear of losing control, it is hardly surprising that descriptions of violations of the body are reserved for punishments.[143] Absence of proper authority defined the violation, not the act itself. This is generally true whatever the ethnicity of the "guilty," as one of the ways in which white prisoners made a case for their wrongful conviction, imprisonment, innocence, or oppression was to describe in bloody detail and heightened language the indignities they had suffered. This was, of course, part of the same trend by which all violations carried out by foreign enemies were bloody, brutal, and unnatural. There was also a relationship, irrespective of the ethnicity or gender of either punisher or punished, between the incarceration and binding of the body, its violation through physical trauma, and the public shame attached to acts of such intimate physicality. This is not to say that punishment (as with most aspects of the Caribbean) was not, or did not become, a racialized category. Once more, however, the evidence on which historians can make assertions tends to come from the later decades, because by then, actions had been articulated and could be measured against official legal pronouncements. There were frequent codifications of laws, aimed at forms of refractory behavior that expressed willful resistance to authority, some of which applied to black and white, but specified differential chastisement. As unfree, and therefore chattel property, responsibility for the punishment of slaves usually lay with the master/owner. Codifications of individual, variant practice did not begin until the second half of the century, and then slowly. The so-called Slave Codes represented the separation of Acts for "the good governing of Servants, and ordering the Rights between Masters and Servants," from those for the government of slaves. The latter were constantly issued, reissued, expired, and were supplemented, such that it becomes difficult to trace variation around the West Indies or across time. Considerable emphasis has fallen on Barbados, where we know there was a slave code of 1661 and 1664, which developed the notion of slave courts and "status offences," a category of offence confined to slaves. Thus Barbados became the model on which other British colonies were subsequently to draw. This was very much an official record of practice already in place, and too much emphasis can be placed on the Codes as punctuations of establishment.[144] When "official" statements of the laws in place in a particular location were published, what appeared to acquire a veneer of respectability, foundation, and legacy, was, in fact, only the latest statement, all previous legislation on the same topic having been superseded or rescinded. William Rawlin's codification of the laws of Barbados, therefore includes a full text of only one piece of legislation on the government of slaves—that of August 8, 1688: that is, the law in effect at the time of publication.[145]

Whipping was among the most physical of attacks on the body, commonly and widely applied. It was not confined within social parameters, but did represent a very graphic and immediate juxtaposition of the power to impose versus the humiliation of receiving corporal abuse that resort to the whip and the post became a means to articulate contested authority. It was a symbol of the (corrupted) authority of Hawley and Huncks in Barbados that there was a whipping post in the center of Bridgetown for the humiliation of recalcitrant settlers. Some of those associated with Powell's initial voyages to Barbados and St. Christopher's appeared before the courts in England to testify to the arbitrary physical restraint and punishment under which they suffered under the Carlisle patent. Governor John Powell was usurped by Henry Hawley, by being inveigled onboard a ship for breakfast, seized, clapped in irons, tied to the mainmast and carried to St. Christopher's, taken prisoner by the Spanish, and dying in the Indies as a consequence of his ill-treatment. Captain Peter Strong did not know why he or the vestry of Christchurch had been imprisoned, but guessed it was for "not doeing things" or doing things contrary to the judgment of Hawley or Huncks, "because they would not submit to their yoake."[146] A separate section on "Whippinge," "Pillouringe," Stigmatizinge and cuttinge off Eares' stressed not only arbitrariness, but added to the calculated extremes that could be called viciousness. James Astrey reported several whippings in 1629 or 1630, including a Frenchman who was punished for speaking against the Calvinist Archbishop of Canterbury, George Abbot, and forced to wear a stigmatizing message in his hat, but more vividly, was whipped for four days running. Captain James Futter was also sentenced to wear a message in his hat, but "stood on the Pillory an houre, in a violent hot day betweene twelve and one of the Clocke without his hat, it beinge then soe parchinge hot that the sunne peirced his skull."[147] Futter had certainly proven refractory in questioning the authority of the Earl of Carlisle, and in this case, the two sides bandied accusations of physical corruptions one against the other: Futter was charged with contempt of court for saying that all the magistrates were whoremasters and that the Earl himself "was somewhat too much given to drinke."[148] It was reported that John Wiborne (accused of libel) stood in the pillory for two hours at sunset, naked, so that he was attacked by midges: Wiborne himself testified that he did not stand that long, but was whipped with his doublet off, and stigmatized for calling the governor and council traitors. He made no complaint that his ears were hammered to the pillory, but was scathing that it was done using "ten penny nailes."[149] Early stages of settlement seemed to maintain what Larry Gragg would call the "tough guy" motifs. Forty years later in fledgling South Carolina, Governor Joseph West told settlers that punishments for swearing and blaspheming would be meted out irrespective of status and the same punishment—beating and gagging—was that to which any lord of England was subject. It was objected that there was no law of gagging in England.[150]

Times of contested authority allowed for the intimate testing of the body politic in microcosm: individual character against corporal chastisement. The period of questioned or questionable loyalties surrounding the accession and deposition of James VII and II produced confusion and fear. Captain

Thomas Hewetson carved out a swashbuckling life attempting in 1688 to adventure to the Pacific coast of South America, getting no further than Tobago. He learnt of James's deposition in this year, and in Bermuda (1689) he obtained a commission from Governor Sir Robert Robinson, and in April 1690, a further one in Barbados, as a privateer, employed to "protect" English settlements in the West Indies in the fight against the French. He commended the bravery of William Kidd (and, for his pains, had his ship stolen and diverted to a life of piracy), and was widely employed by Christopher Codrington to plunder French ships in the Leewards.[151] Within the midst of this service, however, at the height of regional unease over disputed allegiance to King James or King William, his trustworthiness was called into question. It was claimed that he had ordered his chaplain, Mr. Boureman, to pray for the old king and queen, rather than for the new. It was also alleged he had embezzled from ships lost or captured at sea. All this was recounted in over four huge pages about the Catholic/Jacobite/Irish threat, but that which confirmed the truth about Hewetson was confined to a postscript: "One of his Seamen, a lusty ffellow, of about One and twenty yeares of Age" had been a petitioner against Hewetson's hard usage. Hewetson coming to hear of this "hee threatned them all to hang them, every third man with a Petition about their Neck…and swore he would have this young ffellow Whipt to Death, which was very narrowly persued, for after hee was seized to the Capston barr, and One of the Officers of the ship ordered to Whipp him to death; Capt Hewetson stood by to see the Execution done, with a broad sword in his hand Drawn, to Cut the Execution^r if hee did not p[er]^{r}forme his p[ar]t." The victim's body was "Bloody and Raw as a peice of Beefe to be broyled," before he had the further misfortune to develop malnutrition, "ffeaver and Ague and fflux," and was transferred to *The Hunter* that was blown up. But this was all recounted to demonstrate Hewetson's causeless "Inhumane Cruelty."[152]

Governor Lowther of Barbados was accused of conniving with two other gentlemen to indict Bernard Cook for impugning the modesty of the gentlemen's wives, for which Cook was whipped with "twice thirty nine lashes on his bare back," by the "common whipper of slaves in an inhuman, cruell and barbarous manner the [petitioner] considers as the least part of his punishment when he reflects upon the infamy and scandall thereby brought upon himself and his posterity."[153] Subsequently, he complained that his own wife had been sentenced to stand in the pillory "three severall times when she was big with Child."[154] The threat of the whip could also be an (albeit) rare form of raising public funds: when Daniel Daly saved a "wench" from a whipping in Montserrat in 1673 he did so by paying a fine into the public levy.[155] Enacting punishment combined terror and humiliation to reduce the status of the body to that of a considerably subordinate creature that could be of the same ethnicity, lowlier status, a lower-status ethnicity, or a beast of the field. The body of Surinam rebel, John Allin, who had taken his own life rather than be captured, was dismembered, disembowelled, beheaded and quartered, "dry-barbicued or dry-roasted, after the *Indian* manner, his Head...[was]...stuck on a pole at *Parham*, and his Quarters...put up at the most eminent places of the Colony."[156] The body of Bernard Cook was brought down because it was scarified by the man who beat the slaves. Female bodies were simultaneously brutalized and sexualized. Sarah Cook was a landholder in her own right but was paraded heavily pregnant. Women caught making off with a canoe were whipped on their bare backs, which would thus expose white breasts.[157]

Whippings—"their *Shrieks* and *Howls*...were loud and lamentable"— were meted out to slaves with the permission of the owner.[158] William Harriot Jr. and Johosophat Leacraft were indicted before the Bermuda Council for "unreasonable whipping A Moalta Man belonging to Mrs. Ellen Burch, Widow contrary to the knowledge of his Mistress or without an order from authority." They were each fined twenty shillings for the public use.[159] This example provides an insight into the difficulty of unraveling these cases. There are two aspects. One must have the authority to administer a whipping, which in the case of a slave refers back to the ownership of one person over another, but there is the further inference that the punishment must be of "reasonable" nature and extent: unreasonable could be lacking the authority, or could exceed the "proportionate" or stipulated severity of the punishment. There was a bounty, literally, on the heads of escaped slaves, so public accounts of fines and levies were punctuated with gory human commodity: "March [1673]: To Mathew Doe, P ye Generals ord^r for bringing in a negros head: 300 [lbs sugar]."[160] Proposals from the Assembly of Nevis to keep order on the island, restricted to fines punishment for verbal abuse within the white community, whereas black people who aimed abusive words at white would be punished with 30 lashes at the whipping post. A black hand that struck or threw something at a white person would be severed. A first offence of theft of black from white would result in losing an ear; the second offence would lose the other, or 60 lashes; death for the third.[161] While unpredictability constituted for the white community, the very definition of illegal punishment; arbitrariness could be a tool of punishment in itself when directed at the black. In an example from Montserrat, one slave found guilty of stealing a cow was burned to death, while two others, for the same offence, drew lots: the loser being executed and the other severely whipped.[162] The most clear statement of deliberation—the "consideration" given to the punishment of a black body, which we would term sadism—is provided by Sir Hans Sloane, who described late-century Jamaica: for rebellion—"nailing them down...with crooked Sticks on every Limb, and applying the Fire by degrees from the Feet and Hands, burning them gradually up to the Head, whereby their pains are extravagant"; for lesser crimes—dismemberment ("suffered by them with great Constancy"); running away, "they put Iron Rings of great weight on their Ankles, or Pottocks about their Necks...or a Spur in the Mouth"; negligence—whipping "till they are Raw" often followed by salt, pepper, or hot wax on the wounds "to make them smart...and several exquisite Torments." "[T]hough they appear harsh," there were several qualifiers to justify sadism as authoritative punishment. The treatment offered by the British was "easier" than that meted out in Guinea, the East Indies, or by other Europeans; and was proportionate (therefore not arbitrary) because, for example, manatee-hide whips were outlawed by Jamaica custom for being "too cruel"; punishments rarely equaled the nature of the crime, and were sometimes merited by "the Blacks, who are a very perverse Generation of People."[163] Aphra Behn ascribed a similar fate to her fictional rebel hero: he stoically smoked his pipe, while he was first dismembered, then had his nose and ears cut off—with an "ill-favoured Knife"—then an arm; finally collapsing when the second arm was severed. Parts of his quartered torso were sent out around Surinam's plantations to cow other slaves into submission.[164]

When black bodies became violated through accident or injury, the absence of direct causation by the white community precipitated a twofold process in which causation was thrust back on the slaves themselves—as a result of intercommunity altercations—and provided a means to be clinical: to acquire medical information. Rev. James Field—who had a reputation as a brutal slave owner—was able to describe the surgeon's art of stitching internal wounds when a row over plantains escalated and resulted in the stabbings of a slave man and his father-in-law. The incident took place in about 1705, and Field sounded triumphant when he reported over 15 years later that both "were perfectly cured, and have been very well ever since."[165] Richard Lloyd, a planter in Jamaica, petitioned for pardon on behalf of "Sherry," sentenced to transportation for poisoning a (slave) child on a neighboring plantation, on the grounds that although there was nothing substantive in the way of evidence, as a wheelwright and carpenter his value was to his estate.[166] Relations between Robert Cunyngham and his Cayon neighbor, Chief Justice John Spooner, were poor, so when Traveller, of Cunyngham's, caught Bristol, from Spooner's, stealing corn, "the said Bristoll struck at him with a Bill upon which Traveller with his Cutlass cutt Bristoll across his Arm which was Cutt off by John Dixon an unskillfull person no way qualified for that operation, and after six dayes being in a fair way of recovery was let to ketch cold which threw him into convulsion fits of which he dyed."[167] Traveller was tried for killing Bristol, but Cunyngham lay the blame at Spooner's door, for conniving at theft, and failing in his obligations to treat Bristol's injuries with due care. As a surgeon, presumably confined to his own estates, Cunyngham employed a middle-aged Kongo man with the given name of Ham (though he had no greater value than a carpenter); and Marot, a Creole woman, attended sick slaves, but he also retained a Dr. May, at £60 a year, to take care of his plantation, and later John Maddox, who cured a young girl of a canker.[168] Though the numbers must have been legion, there is precious little evidence of injuries and deaths sustained in plantation work. Also from Cunyngham's is one of the few examples of a slave killed by sugar burns, at which point Cunyngham had taken to entering "N.Dead" (or variations) in the margins of the waste books.[169] The intimate physical corporeality of these examples of damage contrasts starkly with the prosaic clinical abstraction of empirical investigation.

At the other extreme were descriptions of prodigious black bodies. They were, however, parallel examples of the reductive distancing of white from black. Aphra Behn used the dark skins of both her male and female heroes as an inversion-trope, in order to inspire admiration and empathy for the runaway slave prince, Oroonoko, and his wife, Imoinda. She was "the beautiful *Black Venus*" and "fair Queen of Night," who captivated white men. He was brave and noble because royal blood flowed in his veins, and he possessed an awesome, outstanding physique, but not because he was typical of Africans. On the contrary:

> He was pretty tall, but of a Shape the most exact that can be fansy'd...His Face was not of that brown, rusty Black which most of that Nation are, but of perfect Ebony, or polish'd Jett. His Eyes were the most awful that cou'd be seen, and very piercing; the White of 'em being like Snow, as were his Teeth. His Nose was rising and *Roman*, instead of *African* and flat. His Mouth the finest shap'd that cou'd be seen; far from those great turn'd Lips which are so natural to the rest of the *Negroes*. The whole Proportion and Air of his Face was so Nobly and Exactly form'd that, *bating his Colour*, there cou'd be nothing in Nature more beautiful, agreeable, and handsome:...His Hair came down to his Shoulders, by the Aids of Art, which was by pulling it out with a Quill, and keeping it comb'd; of which he took particular Care.[170]

In other words, Oroonoko was an exemplar for a handsome, chivalrous, puissant white man, whose external corpus reflected inner character, contained within a black skin.[171] Former slave, John Talbot Compo-bell, impersonated by Robert Robertson of Nevis, wondered how anyone could privilege "*pale, sickly* Whiteness" ahead of "Majestick Glossiness."[172] A doctor in Barbados explained how skin color was not the result of being scorched by the sun, but more likely "the[ir] Blackness...is likely to be inherent in them," because their blood was the same color as their skin, so easily demonstrated to be faulty logic by empirical observation.[173] From Virginia, came evidence of vitiligo.[174] The Royal Society got to hear of a black woman who had carried a fetus for 18 months, before a surgeon delivered it through the woman's ulcerated navel. The "Importunity of the Master" may have hinted at a nervous father and/or an owner potentially losing an investment, but the woman recovered from the operation and later carried a child to term.[175] The story of Dick Rivers, as told to Benjamin Whitrow soon after his arrival in Carolina, did not reach the curious virtuosi in Europe. The family thought better of it; maybe incredulous of "a thick round shoulder'd bandy leg'd fellow," born around 1689, who by the age of three had reached a (small) adult's height, could carry tremendous loads, married at four and fathered a child by five.[176]

Human skin provided a canvas. Behn described Kalinago who had inserted "any shining Trinket" through their noses, lips, or ears, and painted their faces with pretty flowers or specks.[177] John White presented warriors who painted themselves in preparation for hunting or feasting, women with tattooed upper arms, and the Timucuan chief and his wife with extensive body tattoos as a sign of high status. None of this visually survives in de Bry's engravings, though Hariot made textual reference.[178] Neither did these illustrations approach the outlandishness of the tattooed and painted illustrations of ancient Picts, which Hariot and de Bry included as an appendix to the *Briefe and true Report*, "to showe how that the Inhabitants of the great Bretannie haue bin in time past as sauuage as those of Virginia."[179] Evidence for Europeans adopting the deliberate marking of skin as a badge of pride is virtually nonexistent.[180] Welshman Lionel Wafer was a ship's surgeon, who after sailing in the South Seas, settled in Jamaica in 1677. After two years, however, he joined a series of privateering expeditions, during one of which he was marooned on the Darién peninsula and stayed with the Kuna. He describes going naked as they did "and was painted by their Women; but I would not suffer them to prick my Skin, to rub the Paint in, as they use to do, but only to lay it on in little Specks." The women used primary colors, and lay on the pigment with sticks, gnawed soft like a brush at one end. The color dried hard and it took Wafer a month to wash it off, layers of skin coming away with it.[181] "Finer Figures," by "greater Artists" were sketched in, and then pricked with a thorn "till the Blood gushes out," though only a small minority were indelibly marked, confirming this to be a sign of high status: not by Europeans, wary of being permanently inked. Wafer had struggled to clean his pigmented skin, and his companion, Bullman, had been tattooed on the cheek "by the *Negroes*," which despite repeated scarifying and stripping of the skin, Wafer could not remove.[182]

This suggests that in the seventeenth century, pirates and hard-bitten seamen had not yet adopted permanently marked skin as badges of identity; taking high status, inverting it, and readopting it as a symbol of defiance, bravery, and character of a different sort. In the seventeenth century, indelibly marking white skin still meant shame. The practice of branding had long been common punishment for both men and women in Britain, convicted of felonies such as theft, burglary, and coin-clipping, though most cases heard at the Old Bailey suggest it was an ineffective deterrent.[183] Stigmatic punishments were incorporated into the criminal codes in New England, including the recognition that moral offences were as punishable as criminal.[184] Branding was often a lesser punishment for those who successfully claimed benefit of clergy and an alternative to transportation, so it is an interesting speculation how many white branded people ended up in the West Indies.[185] In Bermuda in 1673, Edward Pearman was found guilty of abusing military officers, sentenced to be whipped, and to have his hair cut off. The sentence was pronounced by Councilor William Peniston, whom a future governor of the island, Colonel Richard Coney, would claim to be one of the Fifth Monarchist sectaries active against authority on the island; which fact he could prove by the brand on his shoulder which Peniston had carried from England.[186] In Jamaica, magistrates attempted to determine the person responsible for the death of Henry Westond. One possibility was William Heb, because he had had a number of altercations with Westond;

but held equally guilty of manslaughter was "respectable" planter, Richard Taylor, whom Westond had challenged to try his hand at wrestling. Should the punishment of branding on the hand be carried out on him, Taylor believed it would be "a mark of infamy to a sober minded person as grievous as death."[187]

Branding of cattle and horses to mark ownership was regular, but not universal, British practice, whereas in their desire to describe, delimit, and contain their new world, English people marked everything: trees that bounded plots; documents; the wooden cases in which goods were shipped to and from the Americas; and the nature of the mark, its origin, and its recipient carefully itemized in correspondence.[188] Thus, the branding of slaves conflated the categories of property and stigma, and in a parallel process, the politics and intimacy of branding. Little evidence survives for the practice from the seventeenth century. But there is enough to indicate its profound cultural power. Antigua privateers captured and sold men, women, and children from Guadeloupe—a mix of freed and enslaved—revealing that some but not all bore a mark; whereas Christopher Codrington branded all of his slaves, stamping them with intimate, *ad personam* possession. This ranked his personal power higher than loyalty to his nation or state: Codrington was accused of using the brand to bring captured runaways into his patrimony, using the excuse that he would use them to fight against the French.[189] Codrington was a slave broker, and therefore needed to distinguish slaves from his plantations from those supplied by trading companies. Robert Cunyngham sent his brand to his silversmiths, Craig and Wickes of London, to make ebony handles and alter "a Negro mark."[190] A brand in silver cost 16s.[191] Skin was preprepared with palm oil, and various balms soothed the wounds that followed. There was thus painful consideration and understanding—deliberation—of the contact point of shared human skin, inseparable from the deliberate action to treat it rather as the hide of an animal. Thus, in that same moment, was signified utter detachment from the possession of color.

Identity on the skin, be it chosen or imposed, required it to be on public display, but the ability to cover the body signaled social hierarchy within the West Indies in a way which mirrored that of the skin beneath, and identity through clothing could be, at one and the same time, both blatant and subtle. Among the elite, it signaled the ability to afford that considered most appropriate in London and ship it to hotter climes. The Earl of Carlisle was advised to pack robust items, but sparingly: "plaine habitt, stout of Lynnen," but to pay no heed to exaggerations, for once used to it "the Clymate...will beare for back or bed whatsoever is Comonly used in England."[192] Charles II was also informed that the climate on Barbados enabled men to be as "thick clothed" as in an English summer.[193] Christopher Jeaffreson disagreed, and from St. Christopher's sent to London for sufficient to keep out the chill when he disembarked.[194] As refinement developed, so fashion and status commanded greater attention. There was some confusion as to the requirements of drapery. Jeaffreson's imported serge was considered too coarse, whereas "Irish frieze," which was a coarse, napped woolen cloth often used for coats and waistcoats, was "too fyne yt beeing a wore here only for negroes or poore people who can not reach the price" of, presumably, the serge.[195] Shopping for clothing fabrics in London, which Mr. Shippy would measure and tailor into a black coat, Lawrence Crabb viewed only the "finest & thinest" fabrics, to sport in Antigua. When he died on the island the following year, his widow did not let uncertainty over either the value or direction of his estate deter her from ordering 20 yards of black silk and a number of expensive pieces of mourning jewelry.[196] At the end of the century, most outposts of the tropical empire boasted local seamstresses and tailors; but these, such as Sarah Prentis, mantua-maker, and tailors, Benjamin Chezzus and Richard Waters, all in Nevis, were invariably humble, and catered to an ordinary market.[197] Nevertheless, resident tailors were in short supply, and a hardworking man like Joseph Demure, could make a good living on St. Christopher's.[198] Gentlemen who aspired—Christopher Jeaffreson was courting the 15-year-old Frances Russell—combined a taste for fashion with their tropical requirements. It was important that his sister accompany anyone shopping for clothes for him in London because she lived at the modish end of town, but they could get him a "demi-castor" hat (partially rabbit-felt), "wch if good will doe allmost as much credit as a bever in this Island," and other hide items such as his belt or jacket pockets tended to perish quickly. He also requested "A good Perrewig / A Laced Cravatt [and] Cuffs / As much broach cloth as will make me a fashionable suite [4¼ yards]," lined in any color except yellow or blue; and while he required lace and ribbon for collars and cuffs, and gold and silver laces for his hat, he also hoped he would not outlive three pairs of shoes and required his stockings to be stronger than those he had previously been sent.[199]

Indigenes on St. Christopher's etched the image of a tricorn hat into the rock. Was that evidence of it being worn by the high and mighty men of the English ships, or might it have been gifted them as a symbol of authority, as some decades later King Jeremy of the Miskitu kept by him a "crown and commission" from Governor Albemarle of Jamaica "which is but a lac'd hat, and a ridiculous piece of writing."[200] To protect their heads from the wind and the sun, it was more usual for ordinary British sailors to wear a "Monmouth cap," after the Welsh town that became famous for its manufacture, but developing into a generic name for a knitted hat.[201] As increasing numbers of people sailed to and fro across the Atlantic, the Monmouth cap migrated onto land as general wear and began to distinguish between those required to labor at the height of the day and those whose leisured means afforded them shade.[202] William Bullock outlined servants' clothing for the semitropical Carolinas: each should be kitted with a cloth suit, canvas suit, woolen draws and waistcoat, three shirts, two pairs each of shoes and stockings, three neckerchiefs, and a Monmouth cap.[203] Thus it was imported into the Caribbean as part of the clothing to be provided for indentured servants. As it was the duty of an employer to provide clothing and victuals for those contracted, how soon did wearing a Monmouth cap become a means to distinguish between one who had the means to contract labor, and the badge of one who had been contracted?

In the earlier period, the economic attraction of employing servants rather than slaves was illustrated by the fact that a slave would cost twenty-two pounds each, whereas each artisan would cost a mere ten, to include the costs of "taking up, apparralling transporting and buying tooles."[204] The first Earl of Carlisle's expedition to the Caribbees intended to transport the material for making suits, and the means to do so, at a cost of just over £200, along with £36 5s paid to a Holmes and Chester for shoes and hides.[205] The Committee for Providence Island was advised that only shoes, hats, and linen clothes would be necessary, and in due course it was arranged that in order to transport 150 men, bills be issued for 200 dozen shoes, 1,200 shirts, a similar number of linen suits, and 60 dozen stockings.[206] By the 1730s, Robert Cunyngham contracted Gabriel Adrian for four years as a distiller, "I to find him Cloathes Meat Drink Washing & Lodging and Twenty Pounds Sterling Wages P annum"; his servants' attire to include double-thread stockings at seven shillings a pair and a hat costing sixpence.[207] The inventories of relatively humble white settlers, such as that of an Irishman who died possessed of nine and a half acres in Antigua, show he owned little else but his clothes—jacket, two shirts fastened by sliders, gloves, stockings, neck-cloths and a handkerchief—and a chest in which to keep them.[208]

There was seldom an express stipulation that slaves—uncontracted—should be provided with clothes, and European commentators noted that field slaves, male and female, went naked: the men with possibly a small apron to cover their modesty; the women suckling children on pendulous breasts (because they went naked) as they worked.[209] Those who feature carrying canes on the "Blathwayt map" of Montserrat, probably drawn by Sir William Stapleton himself, are entirely naked.[210] It was a widespread belief that black skins and constitutions were more able to work in direct sun for long periods, but pre-scorched canes sliced open skin that became prey to venomous creatures. Slaves certainly went barefoot, with concern for the effect of chiggers attacking their feet.[211] As the seventeenth century turned into the eighteenth, apologists for slavery stressed the (moral) obligation on masters to provide clothes for slaves: the chief evildoers in the slave trade were those who sold their compatriots into slavery and sent them out of Africa naked, and thus providing clothing was an act of British compassion.[212] Among the advantages claimed for Carolina, which could not be said of English colonies north of the torrid zone, was that the bodies of slaves would not have to endure cold winters and thus would thrive within, and need less clothing without, "which is a great charge saved."[213]

House slaves, on the other hand, had to be provided with decorous clothing: most orders are for jackets. Robert Cunyngham spent prodigiously on all the accoutrements of "family," including livery; all designed to brand "Cunyngham" as prominently and comprehensively as possible, acutely aware of his position within a minor but aspiring and pretentious branch of a noble clan. Included within statements of status and prominence were: the number of his slaves; their loyalty, service, and labor; and how well they reflected his largesse and disposable income. In 1720, he spent £8 10s. 6d. on livery suits for Jack and Phoenix. He also had a collar made in silver for another houseboy, to the weight of two ounces and twelve pennyweight, costing £1 4s. Silverware was a particular means by which the name of Cunyngham was displayed in the domestic sphere. Tableware, candlesticks, and sconces were all engraved with his arms, sent to Craig who made his brand.[214] It was inconceivable that items of domestic silver slaveware were not themselves similarly marked to affix possession more securely to his human property.

Branding his women was more complex. Elizabeth Arnold, Cunyngham's companion in Cayon, was spurned two or three years before he died, but had expected to be (and claimed she was) the second Mrs. Cunyngham. She felt compelled to humiliate herself in order to demonstrate the contribution she had made toward the ease of her man and how little he had given in return. Particular weight rested on "head clothes": she "never had but one sute of Head Close of your byeing." Even the lace for her mob cap she had purchased for herself, using a guinea she had won at cards.[215] She was forced to show that she had prostituted herself to his lusts and demands, but not in the formal sense of being bought, particularly in counter to an array of witnesses to her (putative) first career. Her version of their first union (in London) had come about because he locked her in her room, stripped her naked, and put her on the bed; but according to Arnold, Cunyngham had to wait nearly a month before she had sex with him. Clothes for Arnold were a means both to cover the body, which Cunyngham designed to incorporate sexually into his "white and black family," and to assert her identity. A parallel example was provided by naval captain, John Bear, commissioned by Sir William Stapleton. But Bear turned pirate, and claimed he married a noblewoman in Havana. Bear's own treacherous corruption allowed free rein to Jamaica's Lieutenant Governor to reassure London that every aspect of Bear's life was an inversion: in fact, the woman was a "strumpet," the daughter of a rum-punch seller in Port Royal, and sailed with Bear on the pirate ship, wearing men's clothes.[216]

One of "Mrs Bear"'s inversions was that she had not only donned man's attire but had also dressed for utility. Within the West Indies, at least, cloth in the masculine world, those who worked it, and the service it rendered, were utilitarian. Hemp canvas was used as protective wrapping for items to be shipped (including those as large as a carriage), and for sails for ships or mills, all still fashioned by a tailor.[217] Lace was a luxury status item, on both sides of the Atlantic, as Elizabeth Arnold's mob cap so poignantly illustrated, but in the gritty environment of the tropics it was key to a feminized means to compute wealth and connection on the one hand, and affluent display on the other. Katherine Waller arrived in Antigua as a result of the emigration of her husband, Leonard, a medic, who carried with him a box of lace.[218] When Leonard died, Katherine remarried John Greenway, and the pair was sued for those of Waller's goods they had failed to declare on the inventory of his possessions, which included the box of lace. Compelled to explain what had happened to it, they commodified the lace into economic utility. Waller had sold much of it in Antigua, they said. Only 14 or 15 pieces had been used by Katherine for herself and her children so she stressed to the court their lack of value, either because they were narrow, or because three or four further pieces were personalized, being a gift from Waller's mother to Katherine and her children.[219]

Displays of refractoriness, therefore, could be both without and within, but with the norm set by British men, bodily excess was most likely ascribed to some other. Sir Hans Sloane, whose account of the illnesses, complaints and cures of the West Indies is otherwise more evenhanded between white and black than most, gave specific examples from within a sexualized black community: pubic lice; a man whose excessive drinking gave him stomach cramps and fits, relieved because he "suckt of two *Negro* Womens Milk"; and "*Gonorrhaeas* of all sorts amongst Men and Women...very common here, especially in Plantations amongst *Negroes*." Sloane held to the view common in Europe that venereal diseases were more easily cured in the West Indies than in Europe, but when he saw the place for himself he realized "the Disease was propagated there the same way, and had the same Symptoms and Course amongst *Europeans, Indians* and *Negroes*," so all should be treated alike.[220]

White men did not take responsibility for sexual health since they did not own themselves the origin of venereal disease, deemed "native" to the West Indies because it was the land of the "animal Indians," subsequently peopled by "the cursed [African] posterity of the naked *Cham*" [Ham]. Thomas Trapham concluded with an origin for venereal disease in bestiality with lesser primates—monkeys, baboons, and gorillas in Africa or marmosets in the Americas—carried by worms in discharge from the vagina or penis, or in urine. Those worms not thus expelled from the body remained to pierce viscera and bore into bone.[221] He observed Guinea worms in the sores of black children and assumed, by their size and length, evidence of greater levels of both promiscuity and venereal disease in slave societies, while the otherwise active, healthy appearance of white people masked the "intestine enemy [which] approaches the very bone, and thereby violent intrusion separates the sensible *Periostium*."[222]

Given the characterization of venereal disease as inherent to the tropical environments of Africa and America, it did not seem to strike any as odd that it was better treated by exposing the body to warm, dry climates. Even as late as 1718, a surgeon, William Beckett, felt compelled to publish a paper to "attempt to prove" that venereal disease had a presence in Europe long before Europeans contracted the clap in the Americas.[223] Cold weather caused humans to "harden their skin," forcing worms to drill inward, whereas it had been observed in the West Indies that "if these quickned Executioners take their course outward towards the skin, they then worst themselves there, and by forcing themselves through the dry skin dy and ly buried in the crusting Scabs easily known by the eye of each due observer, which last apparent discharge i^s most usually in the Indies."[224] In the case of "those pernicious Animals, Common Pockie and Incurable Prostitutes," there was an additional benefit of transportation to the West Indies, beyond removing excess population far away. Sending them "back" to the source of the disease and to the dry, hot climate, might in this case, render the incurable cured.[225] At least people who lived in the West Indies had the (dubious) advantage of not having to kill parasites, germs, and diseases with mercury, but rather to take regular purgatives. Ingesting antimony to this effect was barely any healthier, but may account for the early and ubiquitous presence in the West Indies of Dr. Lockyer's miracle pills. Their main active—a better word would be destructive—ingredient poisoned parasites in the gut. The pills themselves spawned an epidemic commodity in the seventeenth and eighteenth centuries. Christopher Jeaffreson received a consignment in St. Christopher's in 1681, but was unable to shift them all, as even in the sink of debauchery, the drugs out-glutted the parasites.[226]

Despite it being widely believed that most white women who went to the West Indies started life in prostitution, they were, once they arrived, credited with more generally circumscribed behavior. Clorosis (a form of anemia, which gave a bilious tinge to the skin, and was therefore known as "green sickness") was thought to affect women before they became sexually active, and thus fornication was often suggested as a cure: thus it was no surprise that Thomas Trapham detected its prevalence among the boarding school girls on Bermuda, where "this uncomfortable Distemper...made them uneasie to themselves, and unpleasant to their Relations."[227] Women who were unwell could be led to consider that they looked unattractive and therefore be induced through vanity to view themselves in a corrective mirror of either others' example or one's own reflection: "parting with the golden State of Health and Ease for so babling a looking-Glass of their own misery."[228] More importantly, it was the duty of women to bear healthy and legitimate children, and thus it was indignation on the part of Bermudans, charged with being among the most licentious of people, that led them to repudiate their "profaneness, drunkenness, uncleanness, and other licentious courses of life." "[M]oreover," they went on, we "cannot but conclude that the terming us as irreligious and irrational, profane, and refractory, and the hopeful-issues of our bodies, which are dearer to us than our lives, we mean the youth of our country, opprobriously nicknamed spawns and young fry, is no less than a Machiavellian design of some interested persons to wrap us in a bear's skin and with the dogs of cruelty to devour us."[229]

Dry heat was also considered "propitious to Child-bearing Women" on account of its capacity to speed labor, because women were "not so subject to Miscarriages, Distempers, Pains or Difficulties before, at or after Delivery, as they are in *England*," such that there was, apparently, scarcely time for a woman to cry out to the goddess of childbirth for assistance. In Jamaica, women required a mere three days' recovery and would be busy "about House" within the week. It is unclear whether this refers to white housewives, black domestic slaves, or both; "nay some *Negro* Women are at work in the Field the same or next day."[230] Sloane, however, noted that it was common for women of all ethnicities to rise from their beds quickly after childbirth, but that some white women could damage themselves by pretending to a custom not practiced in Britain.[231] Few allowances were made for any woman in labor. When references were made to women being pregnant, the pregnancy itself was rhetorical and served to emphasize a different point: this could be the illegality and proportionality of a punishment; or the barbarity of a foreign invader evidenced by their seeking out of the most vulnerable, "bigge wth childe, others wth Infants hanging upon the brest, [and] little ones in their hands."[232] One might expect masters or the authorities to display a level of emotional detachment when female slaves gave birth: the body of the mother reduced to a mechanism for carrying a new generation of labor.[233] The Bermuda Company, in renting out a female slave while she was pregnant, had to petition for ownership of the boy "borne of ye body of their negro woman when she was lett out to service," since it was her labor which was leased, while propriety over her body remained with the Company.[234] The lists of births recorded by Robert Cunyngham in his St. Christopher's ledgers preferred "delivered of," but given his obsession with possession, refer more to his workforce's "increase" than to anything that might imply sentiment:

> Dec 11 [1728] My Negro Woman Lubba died she was valued at £20. Ster
> Dec 15 My Negrowoman Izabeau Michells wife del^d of a Da^u Lucinda
> 6 [July 1729] Icany my Negro Cooper Andrew his wife del^d last night of a Daughter Dinah
> 9 [July 1729] My Negro Boy Sam Irwin's son dyed of the Cramp.[235]

Evidence provided by Robert Cunyngham points to the likelihood that childbirth for either black or white women was little eased by excessive temperatures and had small effect on the life-chances of the babies they bore. His first wife went through 14 pregnancies in 21 years (of which there is record): Richard (number two) died at 16 weeks; a second Richard, born the following year, died within hours of birth; Bonneton (number nine, born in 1706), and Barat, the tenth child, born on Shrove Tuesday 1708, were merely listed "D"; twin sons born on October 24, 1710, "died presently"; followed by William (born September 30, 1711, "D"); and a daughter "born dead" on December 29, 1715.[236] His mistress, Elizabeth Arnold, measured her value ("valey") to him "having had so many children by you," claiming Cunyngham gifted her a (silver) saucepan on the birth of her first, and a candle-cup at her last. Only one child survived.[237] Women's agency in childbirth is not noted, but Sloane made reference to the usefulness of hammocks, in which pregnant women could guard against miscarriage by raising their feet to the level of their heads.[238]

Commentators among the French and Dutch recorded American and African women using the seeds of the "Peacock flower" (*Poinciana pulcherrima* or *Caesalpinia pulcherrima*) as an abortifacient. So did Sir Hans Sloane.[239] He did not discriminate the ethnicity of the women seeking to terminate a pregnancy (or of the fathers), but endowed them with knowing agency, saying that they feigned different illnesses in the hope that they would be given a powerful-enough emetic to induce miscarriage. Maria Sibylla Merian in her travels in Suriname in the early eighteenth century noted that female slaves told her of the plant's abortifacient properties and concluded that abortion, suicide, and self-harm were forms of resistance to slavery. It seems plausible that female slaves would use abstinence, abortion, and infanticide as acts of resistance but even in the late eighteenth century, statements to this effect—with the exception of Merian about Dutch Suriname—are poorly evidenced.[240]

Nurses for babies and small children were not unknown, but were more likely to be employed as medical help rather than as wet nurses. Wet nurses seem to have been employed in Britain (Elizabeth Arnold's child in London in 1739 was put to a nurse),[241] but less so in the West Indies. Black nursemaids were engaged, but not in planter families, for fear that criminality might be an "infection," though Sloane was sure that "a Blacks milk comes much nearer the Mothers than that of a Cow."[242] West Indian women's appetite for drink lessened the attractiveness of employing any servant given charge of children. What evidence we have seems to point to settler-women throughout the early colonial period, of any social standing, suckling their own children: Mary Quintyne, wife of the Chief Justice of Barbados, did so; as did "spare," "lean," and 35-year-old Mrs. Aylmer in Jamaica.[243] There has been considerable scholarly debate, albeit reductive, about the relative ages at which children were weaned, with most concluding along with the commentator of 1712, that slaves in the seventeenth-century Caribbean were likely to follow the African pattern of later weaning, perhaps at the age of two or three.[244]

Exoticism and physical difference allowed the elite to interpret the appearance and behavior of anyone beneath them as prodigious; provoking wonder, astonishment, and awe; the subject of admiration, fear, repulsion, curiosity, and temptation. If the prodigious were considered monstrous and animal, their role as temptation to the godly demanded good and evil be kept apart; while if inherent qualities, there was no point in attempting a reform of manners. Despite constant complaints about the depravity of the West Indies, practical reforms there were few.[245] Bermudans had a reputation for puritan zeal but the island failed to shake off its image as an isolated refuge for tenants, rebels, dissenters, and king-killers, all revealed in licentious behavior. Jamaica, initially the home of Cromwellian soldiers and pirates, also suffered from the perceived connection between political and personal license. Witnessing prodigality could be a portent, heralding divine retribution on the wicked. The earth, a natural body in itself, created by God, would swallow or suck malefactors into its bowels. Port Royal sank beneath the waves. The behavior of the dregs of the earth in this most wicked of places was punished by a specific example of God's awesome power, but its warning was aimed at everyone. In Edinburgh, a fiery bombast suggested that the depraved lusts of Port Royal was a prodigious manifestation of Scotland's political debate over allegiance to the Jacobite or Orangist cause: "Earth open its mouth, gainst people bad, / (Because to Heav'n. no mouths these people had) / And, weary of it's Bur[den] did enclose / Them in it's hollow womb; There to disclose / The real darkness, which their Sins did love, / And En'mity against the Powers above."[246] Bridgetown, consumed by flames, would cause inhabitants to "be sensible of his severe displeasure."

Corruptions of the body could stem from inherent bestiality in certain kinds of human being or its willful embrace on the part of wicked individuals. The Rev. Dr. Anthony Horneck was tutor to Christopher Monck, future second Duke of Albemarle, Lord Proprietor of Carolina, and eventual governor of Jamaica, though Horneck confined his service to Exeter, and did not himself travel to the tropics. Subsequently patronized by his former pupil, he dedicated to Monck a philosophical study of "consideration." Horneck implied that sin stemmed from the (Hobbesian) state of nature, but that the decision to corrupt the godly human form was one which man took for himself, "as if the World were return'd to its former Barbarism, and we had once more to do with Infidels, as if men had divested themselves of Humanity, put on the nature of Beasts, and were sent into the World to understand no more, but the *matter*, and *motion* of the *Malmsbury Philosophy*."[247] Sin was an act or idea that could take many forms, and another learned theologian, Rev. Dr. John Wilkins, Dean of Ripon, meditated on a philosophy of character, during which he offered a schema for understanding the various manifestations of "corruption." It could be

- *Primary* and proper, [which] doth denote the *Being*, or *Making* of a *thing, evil*, or *worse*, whether by
  - *Admixtion* with that which is bad, and then it is of the same importance with the word *Defiling*.
  - *Privation*, as to a thing
    - *Being*, so corruption is *destroying*.
    - *Vsefulness*, so corruption is *spoiling*.

- *Secondary*, as applied to things
  - *Natural*, so Corruption will denote according to the Degree of it, either *Infection*, or *Decay*, or *Putrefaction*.
  - *Moral*, whether more
    - *General*, so it denotes the Evilness of the mind or manners, *Vnholiness, Viciousness*.
    - *Special*, so 'tis peculiarly applied to *Vnchastity* and *Bribery*.[248]

Therefore, rather than drawing a (possibly modernist) demarcation between emotion and materialism, these seventeenth-century philosophers expressed the sense in which the collapse of mind, morals, body, society, or estate, by whatever manner of sin, corruption, or rejection of values, stemmed from mankind's willful rejection of God's creation.

Henry Whistler acknowledged that sinful Britons, dumped on the West Indies' dunghill, took the opportunity of transformation in their new environment, but did so not by atonement, but by adapting their facade, as a prostitute would dress to match the status of her client. Christopher Jeaffreson was more forgiving of the cause of putative settlers' poor behavior in Britain, and admiring of what they managed to make of themselves in the tropics. How many "broken traders, miserable debtors, pennilesse spendthrifts, discontented persons, travelling heads, [and] scatter brains" had previously been sent out, he opined, who had eagerly seized the chance to "shun their greedy creditors [and] loathsome Gaoles...to fill theire bellies though with ye bread of affliction,...to leave an unkinde mistresse a dishonest wife or it may be something worse then either...to satisfie fond cureosety," or "cross his friends [and] seeke his fortune." These were personalities, actions, and motives that "first peopled ye indies [and] made it then a kinde of a Bedlam for a short tyme," but "from such brain sick humours came many sollid [and] sober men." The ingenious and industrious could raise their fortunes in any part of the West Indies: "men raised from little or nothing to vast estates [and] I can assure you o^r slaves live as well now as ye servants did formerly." Such advancement was in the hands of indenturers provided they were not "too refractory": that is, they exercised self-will to the point at which they might be deemed stubborn. Thus, for Jeaffreson, no jailbird was incorrigible, but any British servants were preferable to the Irish, who were "good for Nothing but mischeife."[249] The administration of Governor Edwin Stede of Barbados had the opposite experience. It was agreed that servants were liable to be brutalized on arrival, being the product of jails in which they were starved, inured to crime, and unused to work. Thus in the West Indies, they resorted to insolence, embezzlement, theft, and escape; were not averse to beating overseers and masters, and a ruling that masters ought not to break the skin of a servant only emboldened them to goad masters into striking or whipping them.[250] Thomas Trapham referred to "implanted inclinations," which could be moderated, even in the face of tropical excess, but this seemed to be at odds with his opinion that Jamaica was year-round like England in June, so a healthy, prosperous life was in prospect "for sober temperate persons, who have command of themselves, especially at first arrival, and can moderately drink one third Wine with two thirds Water."[251]

Christopher Jeaffreson's manager, Thorne, who took "a great deale of liberty at home and abroad" in "Bachanalian festivalls and veneriall revellings" was the subject of considerable gossip. It also made him careless: Jeaffreson was angered that ten slaves and four horses had died in the summer of 1683, and half the slaves were sick or lame. Thomas Tryon, in commenting on viciousness toward man or beast was also referring to that trope in which human slave bodies fell within the same chattel classification as livestock animal bodies. Tropes, like clichés, become such for a reason, but a psychology deserves greater exploration in which white settlers could express compassion, concern, and care, and empathize with fellow human beings, while at the same time possess humans, enumerating them in inventories together with livestock, and treating them with brutal, calculated viciousness. Within Sir William Stapleton's instructions to his attorneys, as he prepared his Nevis estates for his absence, how are we to interpret the juxtaposition of the following?: "To Incourage Some of the Negroes to get in the two Runawayes Mingo, and Jn° Salmon; to procure Maligeto, and Negro Oyle, [scored out—to bee kept in stockhouse?] & verdigrees and salves to bee kept in ye house."[252] "Loyal" slaves were to find those who had run away and a variety of medicaments were to be obtained, with some thought being given to whether they were stored with the stock or in the house. Is this to be read, therefore, that the balms and oils were to be used to treat slaves who were injured or sick, as a preparation before branding in case they absconded or to treat wounds given the punished runaways?

In addressing the body, actions of the body, and actions on the body, commentators also explored the mind. Discrimination and judgment was necessary to put "difference between the scorner and simple, seducers and seduced."[253] A refractory person enjoyed a carnal or fleshly life, with no concern for their spiritual welfare or their judgment in the afterlife because the first Adam's perfect relationship with creation was forever compromised when in overreaching for primal status he usurped his own Creator.[254] Tryon had been more explicit about the carnal corruption of self-interest, which in more modern times might be termed "solipsism" and absence of sympathy and empathy. Vice could be any carnal, corrupting, fleshly exercise of self; applied to one's own body, to the bodies of others, or to the psychophysical malady with which white West Indians were afflicted: this was "viciousness." It stemmed from too high a sense of one's own dominion.

CHAPTER 5

Will

The first colonial governor of Carolina, William Sayle, was a veteran of traveling around, settling, and exercising authority in the West Indies. His first post was as governor of Bermuda in 1643. Four years later, he led 70 Bermudans to the Bahamas, subsequently obtaining the charter to settle the island of Segatoo, which was renamed Eleutheria, from the Greek to mean "liberty."[1] The 1647 founders noted that all attempts to impose uniformity and conformity caused dispute and discord, and "[t]hat there are both babes and strongmen in *Christ*: And that every Member who holds the head is of the body of *Jesus Christ*, hath not the same place and office, nor the same measure of light, who yet desire and endeavour daily to increase in knowledge." Sayle and his fellows framed a charter of respect: "no names of distinction or reproach" or "difference in judgement"; instead, the jurisdiction of the magistracy—here termed the "Officers of the Republike"—would extend only "to men as men." No person would be reprimanded for holding an opinion, nor for the "opinion it self."[2] For the next 20 years Sayle traveled between Bermuda, Eleutheria, and, in 1669, to Carolina, on a Bermudan ship that bore the new colony's name.[3] By this time Sayle was in his eighties; frail, and responding poorly to the humors of the Carolina low country and struggled "for severall reasons" to exercise authority. He "Inclyn[ed] much to the lettergie dropsie and other deseases, that what small reason he had is almost taken from him in soe much that...he is hardly Compas montes." Within months he had died, "P[ar]tly with age and P[ar]tlie with a kind of a Lethargicall distemper."[4] He succumbed just short of the first anniversary of his "appointment."

"Feeling authority creeping over him," as his predecessor was interred, the commercial manager of the voyages, Joseph West—the "storekeeper"— chosen governor by the worthies of the local council, broadcast his intent. As he willed, so Carolinians would act. He would punish swearing and profanity but he uttered not a word of encouragement to industry and planting.[5] London continued exasperated that colonists relied on proprietary storehouses without planting their own provisions. Sir John Yeamans began to inveigle to himself the means to control; providing provisions cheap, and other goods profitably. He was already vastly landed, and would be awarded a title—landgrave, nobleman-manqué. Replacing West, he took up his commission in April 1672, while Lord Proprietor Anthony Ashley Cooper, and his secretary, John Locke, remained concerned that none of the figures invested with the power to establish, mold, and develop the fledgling colony were, in fact, suitable.[6] People of such diverse backgrounds, conditions, histories, opinions, expectations, and personalities came to share the already varied Americas, that coming to rest on a sense of settlement proved a skill hard-won. Everyone questioned everyone else's idea of the Indies: too old, too sickly; too haughty, too ambitious, too dissolute, too indebted; too highborn, too low-born; parochial, remote; too cowardly, too gung-ho; too low-church, too high-church. As those placed in government judged the actions and intent of the governed, so it was as likely to happen vice versa, with how innate and natural a person's authority might be, revealed in the degree of deference paid. From Barbados in 1700, Thomas Hodges looked back and concluded two maxims: that "in process of time, as the Plantations and their Trade increased, Controversies multiplied," and that it had "grown a Proverb with the English Merchants, that tho a Man goes over never so honest... yet the very Air there does change him in a short time."[7] Neither authority nor deference were provisions that travelled well, as constant disputation made hypocrites of pious Christians and advocates of liberty.[8]

British people were constructing or reconstructing their world in the Americas from scratch, so established ideas were challenged by practical reality, with ancient performance recreated or reconceptualized to take account of new times and new environments. That action—more particularly, the act of labor—could establish propriety had been asserted by the famous jurist, Sir Edward Coke, himself applying common law precepts to ancient formulations. At the start of the seventeenth century, he noted that "a man may make a Title by vsage": by its end, the adage would have been cemented as a cornerstone of the British way through the work of the secretary to the Lords Proprietors of Carolina and Committee for Trade and Plantations, John Locke.[9] The connection between authoritative proprietorship in the land and the action of claim, was in English, found in planting. To plant was to establish a foundation, as guns, garrisons, and religion were also planted on a global stage.[10] Tending to land and its products was deemed God's providential gift, granted to those who were identified by their right action: "O what a noble acte that were for an husbande or houswyfe, to purchase suche a royall place in heuen... [through]... what thynge pleaseth god most, that we myght do it."[11]

Authority, vested in the highest magistrates, was assumed, but needed also to be claimed and realized, particularly in situations of fresh establishment (or reestablishment overseas). Its discourse reached dizzying heights when referring to the empire's chief actors; lieutenants who were "under God...the foundation and essence of the colony."[12] The prospect of being in control of vast territories, far outweighing in size and potential profit, those of the English overlord in whose name they acted, puffed up individual pretentions and addressed notions of feudalism that had long come under attack at home.[13] The words and actions exhibited by the Lords Proprietor,

James Hay, Earl of Carlisle, and Francis, Lord Willoughby of Parham, given the status of Palatine lords of the Caribbees or Carliola; the governorship of Daniel Parke; or, on a smaller scale, the St. Christopher's planter, Robert Cunyngham or the Carolina adventurers Sir John Yeamans and Sir Robert Montgomery, reveal passionate commitment to aristocracy, status, and deference, and a responsibility for lands, people, and possessions that accorded with feudal lordship.[14] Patriarchy, patronage, and paternalism were inextricably bound. They believed that their pronouncements and actions accorded with Medieval notions of good stewardship, manifest in the supreme control and direction of every aspect of the political, personal, and intimate sphere. Offensive to modern ears, Master knew best.

If Willoughby, Parke, and Cunyngham carried in their heads a manual for the Americas, it was Sir Robert Filmer's *Patriarcha*.[15] Masters—sovereigns of state, church, household, family, or dwelling—possessed either in reality, or in a series of devolved parallels, the power of the first father, Adam.[16] Filmer countered those, such as the republicans of the civil war period during which he was composing *Patriarcha*, or Locke, writing contemporaneously with its publication, who accepted that power, universal and absolute, "was from God but its distribution on earth the choice of the people."[17] Rather, he maintained that the absolute sovereignty of Adam passed through the patriarchs to Noah, who was the first husbandman, and his sons and their progeny (particularly Nimrod, the great-grandson of Noah, through his son, Ham) peopled the world.[18] In the 1730s, a Scottish cleric in Nevis could relate an account of the Jamaica Coromanti slave uprising of 40 years earlier, through the character of a freed Christian black man who explained Britons' enslavement of Africans as their "*Perfect Servitude*...from the Days of *Noah*, or of *Nimrod*."[19] "The first society" was "made of many houses in a village, which seems most naturally to be a colony of families or foster brethren of children and children's children."[20] Another clergyman who retrospectively examined the expropriation and forcible relocation of Kalinago in Dominica and Cherokee in Carolina concluded that they were naïve people, "naked and poor as the Worm of the Earth." The Cherokee had their own king but now recognized "the Great King *George* as the Sun, and as our Father," recognizable as such because while they had only broken ropes to bind their slaves, the English had iron chains. Thus, said Rev. William Smith, "the powerful and great Nation of the *Cherrokees*" was merely the latest in a long line of American people who submitted to the monarchy/tyranny of Nimrod.[21]

The right of dominion, vested in the white man, was that corruption represented by Nimrod and lurked in the breast of every white man, was the right of dominion in which being "Patrons of Mankind" was manifested in conquest, triumph, manslaughter, and destruction.[22] But the indigenous peoples of the Americas had original authority over the land, which by force or trick, the Europeans now graciously granted them back.[23] Pitted against the facility of Nimrod, therefore, was "native right." Smith's letter asserting indigenous rights is remarkable. So too was a debate that took place during the Interregnum over the right to the Caribbees.[24] This is usually expressed as a battle between rival aristocratic sponsors (Philip Herbert, first Earl of Montgomery versus James Ley, third Earl of Marlborough); their respective claimants to the patent for the Caribbees (Courteen versus Carlisle); and their respective appointees as Governor (in Barbados, Henry Powell against Charles Wolverston). The Crown was forced to issue a letter to Wolverston confirming his authority in Barbados "by what name or names soever the same then was reputed, taken or knowne, or vulgarly named, within the 10. and 20. degrees of the Northern Latitude" (Carlisle would place it "neere the thirteenth degree").[25] Barbados famously became such a locus of disputation because each claimant sent passengers to settle an island that they had found uninhabited, and could thus claim the perfection of plantation as defined by Sir Francis Bacon through first-footing right of possession, and thus when the Courteen/Powell faction challenged the rights of the Carlisles, they stressed Barbados's uninhabited status before the fundamental "First Plantacon of Barbadoes" when Captain Henry Powell "set out of England purposely for the Barbadoes to plant there" and "that they were the first people wch setled in the Barbadoes, and that there was noe plantacon then or before, to their knowledge nor any people heathen or Christian."[26] The phrase used to refer to St. Christopher's, part of the Caribbees settled prior to Barbados but inhabited by indigenous peoples when the English arrived, was that the first English settlers were "primitive" planters. One such was John Jeaffreson, father of Christopher, who travelled with the intention of establishing right on the island.[27]

The dispute over the rights to the Caribbees developed a complex and tortuous history, but some of the more remarkable statements emerge during the Interregnum, when the right of ownership and governorship was recast as the rights of the settlers. William Steele, of Gray's Inn, pronounced that "[i]f savadge Lands be tamed by others by the price of their blood and purses, they and not the Kinge have right to it."[28] James Winstanley, also of Gray's, cited the existence of planters prior to the Carlisle claim, and thus the Biblical tyranny of the Earl who was granted power "too greate for a subiect." "Nimrods tyranny, and in the next chapter his contraction," determined Winstanley, "applyed to the Earles takinge and exerciseinge a greater power, then he ought by lawe" and a baleful message was also delivered to Judah, in Jeremiah, chapter 22: "woe to them that erect the howses by unrightousness ec and for erectinge Manno^{rs} or creatinge tenures, 'tis more then the king can graunt, nay more then he can doe himselfe."[29] Plain speaking was exercised by Mr. Philips. "Englsh subiects discover, and plant without licence," was the core of his case, and therefore, even though the Earl of Carlisle maintained that plantation had been at his charge (borrowed, and never repaid, but that was the subject of other litigation), it was the action of the original settlers in first-footing and initial planting that established their right. The planting of those landed by Powell was a de facto act which, was also, in essence, de jure, and voided any subsequent patent to Carlisle from the Crown, since "the kinge cannot graunt what his subiects got before."[30] That Powell had established a republic was the most startling statement, but

Philips went on to further degrade the value of Carlisle's patents. The second patent was misdated; a combination of lack of knowledge of the region and confusion of names and places meant "the Graunt as to Barbadoes is not good, for it is noe parte of the Caribee Islands"; and if the region were defined by latitude, "[t]he mathematicall words are generall are soe not good, as if the Kinge graunts all his lands under the moone or other Planet."[31]

On February 17, in the twenty-second year of his reign, Charles I confirmed the transfer of the patent for the Caribbees (listed at length and accounting for the English claim to all of the islands' archipelago), on a 21-year lease from the second Earl of Carlisle to Francis, Lord Willoughby of Parham.[32] The lease period was interrupted, ignored, and intermittently voided by civil war and republican government, but he was reappointed as Proprietor of the Caribbees at Charles II's English restoration, following dispute about whether it should also include the Guianas and lands of 1,200 by 600 miles' scope in Surinam: unprecedented proprietary power for one subject. Willoughby was a man whose purchase of a fiefdom entitled him to deal "rigorously" with his "stubborn" people, "for my back is att the wall, And I find good words, & meeke carriage begets little but contempt, where no other can bee used amongst A people, who have beene rough bred, & not used to the Yoake."[33] His opponents would have preferred to restrict his title to "General," which denoted dependency, but Willoughby's (American) patriarchy gave him superiority over aristocrats whose status in England would otherwise be higher than his own.[34] In England, this was a challenge to the power of men such as Edward Hyde, Earl of Clarendon, but in America, Willoughby was enabled to direct every detail, such as his management of an allocation to Sir Robert Harley of land in Surinam.[35] This was not a plat, first-footing possession that established autonomous liberty for a settler to plant, harvest, and dwell, but a Domesday projection of a 40-acre fief, in which every action, seed, and laborer was specified in advance.[36] This overbearing management and oversight was a key characteristic of patriarchy. The "English"/Cherokee peace treaty of 1730 was drafted by Alured Popple, to read that all of the peoples who lived in that part of Carolina were "Children of one Family," whose "kind, and loving Father" had "given his Land on both sides of the great Mountains to his own Children the English, so he now gives to the Cerrokee Indians the Priviledge of living where they please" provided it was at a designated side of the mountain, with all trade and routes through it maintained by the Cherokee for the benefit of the British.[37] On the scale of an individual estate, Robert Cunyngham possessed an exaggerated pride in aristocratic heritage, drawing up his own Scottish pedigree, and then replicated that degree of detail and personal oversight in the waste books for his Kittitian estates. His closest friend despaired his deferential service to "superiors," describing a "Knight Errant."[38]

When John Locke, with his vast practical knowledge of American colonialism, published his *Two Treatises of Government*, he explicitly countered Filmer.[39] The oft-cited passage deemed to refer obliquely to America in which he "disproved" Filmer's notion of "paternal sovereignty," lies in section 115:

> For there are no Examples so frequent in History...as those of Men withdrawing themselves, and their Obedience, from the Jurisdiction they were born under, and the Family or Community they were bred up in, and setting up new Governments in other places...and which always multiplied as long as there was room enough...All which are so many testimonies against paternal Soveraingty, and plainly prove, That it was not the natural right of theFather [*sic*] descending to his Heirs, that made Governments in the beginning; since it was impossible, upon that ground, there should have been so many little Kingdoms, but only one universal Monarchy, if men had not been at liberty to separate themselves from their Families and their Government.[40]

The concept of "room enough" was often implied, but it was used to establish not only liberty from a higher patriarchal authority but also the autonomy to act the patriarch oneself. It was Willoughby's reason why his authority should *not* be bounded by decisions made in London; Parke's justification for his failure to exercise authority because he was chasing his subjects around the islands as they flitted to avoid traditional patriarchal limitations. Robert Cunyngham engineered a global network, in which rule over his "white and black family" spanned the Atlantic, the Americas, and several locations in Britain and Ireland. It was a freeholder's right and duty to master their family: kin, affinity, servants, and slaves.

With Britons' belief in their own status came the corresponding expectation of deference. Whitehall functioned with the anticipation that those who lived in the Caribbean would follow the constitution; maintain loyalty to the government of the mother country—and to its agents in the new world; advance the rule of law; behave with Christian decency and mores; and respect power. The extant correspondence that passed through official channels divides into occasional over-breezy reassurances that all was well, drowned by a deluge of plaintive wails relating deference unforthcoming. Carolina's Fundamental Constitutions operated Byzantine checks and balances that echoed the republican model of Harrington's *Oceana* a generation earlier, but together with a parallel politics of hierarchy and deference enshrined in the creation of titles relating to landownership, complete with gradations. Among the eight Lords' Proprietors, palatinate status devolved onto the eldest, and the Proprietors would always hold the offices of admiral, chamberlain, chancellor, constable, chief-justice, high-steward, and treasurer.[41] Of the land, the "province" was subdivided into "counties," eight seigneuries, and baronies; four "precincts"; each of six "colonies"; and clause four added that "[e]ach signiory, barony, and colony, shall consist of twelve thousand acres; the eight signories being the share of the eight proprietors, and the eight baronies of the nobility; both which shares, being each of them one fifth part of the whole, are to be perpetually annexed, the one to the proprietors, the other to the hereditary nobility, leaving the colonies, being three fifths, amongst the people: that so in setting out and planting the lands, the balance of the government may be preserved."[42] Other "dignities," assumed rather than specified in the Constitutions, were the noble titles of baron, cassique, and landgrave, essentially establishing "lords of the manor." In all, the first 60 of the constitutional statements established the dignities of hierarchy and office, and the 120 items that formed the "sacred and unalterable form and rule of government of Carolina for ever" were ended with a further 11 "Rules of Precedency" that reiterated proprietary, age, and gender hierarchy.

In an example from 1701, land was transferred from King, to Lords' Palatine; to local governors with the feudal title of landgrave; to individual landholder, "Carolina settler and controversalist," John Stewart, via,

> his Excellency John Earl of Bath Palatine, George Lord Carteret, Sr John Colleton, Bar^{nt} Thomas Amy and William Thornburgh Esqr true and Absolute Lords [and] Props of ye Province of Carolina by their Comission under their hands [and] Seals bearing Date ye Sixteenth day of August Anno D^o 1698[;] Have Impower'ed us ye hono[ra]^{ble} Joseph Blake Esqr one of the true [and] absolute Lords [and] Prop^r of ye Province of Carolina and late Governor of South Carolina James Moore Esqr Present Governor Landg^r Joseph Morton Landg^r Edmund Bellinger Coll Robert Daniell John Ely Esqr.[43]

Fifteen years later, when Sir Robert Montgomery of Skelmorlie proposed an even greater Carolina estate he followed his ancestor, who had been "purposely created" a knight by James VI and I to the end of planting Nova Scotia, so when sacked by the French it fell to his ilk to make good the Montgomery form of "Service of their Country" in which the "humour" of colonialism was carried in noble blood. Bacon provided motivation: "Plantations of new Countries... *are among the Primitive, and most Heroick Works of Man*," in that "*Religiously*... they illuminate the Souls of Heathens through the darkness of their Ignorance, and *Politically*,... they strengthen the Dominion."[44] Montgomery would erect "a distinct Province, with proper Jurisdictions, Priviledges, Prerogatives, and Franchises, Independent of, and not subject to the Laws of *South Carolina*": foreign enemies had not been to blame for the historic failure to root in America, but "want of full Powers, and distinct Jurisdiction."[45] In Azilia (after a Pyrenean Mesolithic culture of around 10,000 BCE), he would be Margrave, thereby instituting for himself a title between Palatine and Landgrave, which reflected the size, frontier status, and militarism of his holding. He would people his lands with soldiers, who would turn farmer: in essence, the feu: land to farm in return for military service.[46]

Our Anglophone and Christo-centric examples refer to the relationship between "*meum* and *tuum*" and between "man and God," in determining codes of behavior, behavioral relationships, and whether they were defined and articulated in ethics, law, or both. In the King James' Bible, Genesis 1.26 was rendered: "And God said, Let us make man in our image, after our likeness: and let them have dominion over the fish of the sea, and over the fowl of the air, and over the cattle, and over all the earth, and over every creeping thing that creepeth upon the earth."[47] At the end of the sixth day of Creation, God gave to everything that lived on the earth "every green herb for meat." But there was as yet "not man to till the ground," and therefore God made it rain, and "planted a garden eastward in Eden" that man was to "dress" and "keep." He showed it to Adam, who named all living things. But Adam had no helpmeet, so God placed Adam into a deep sleep, took one of his ribs and created what Adam called "bone of my bones, and flesh of my flesh: she shall be called Woman, because she was taken out of Man."[48] This was the Old Testament, prelapsarian "Covenant of Works" (*foedus operum*), which in Christian societies formed the basis of a worldview that dictated the nature of future biblical covenants (the so-called Covenant of Grace, made between God and post-Fall man, in which salvation was not earned or merited), and the relationship between the Old and New Testaments—Law and Gospel. In anglicized meaning it defined "obligation," which could be of an "imperfect" nature, between God and man (ethics), or "perfect obligation" (law and institution).[49] Analysis of Reformed theology emerging at the end of the sixteenth century, has pointed to God's covenant with Moses, and the codification of the relationship between man and God and man and man in the two tablets of the Decalogue, and that with Noah, which distinguished between different branches of the people of Israel and produced the cursed children of Ham and the tyranny of Nimrod.[50]

In tracing the development of covenant theology within the seventeenth-century Reformed churches of England and Scotland, and the rise of "puritanism," scholars have paid close attention to the transfer of puritan ideologies to America, but with particular concern for puritanism's heartland, radiating out from New England. But, in setting out the nature and delineation of land, in the origin of tillage and planting; the fundamentals of a human being; and that which distinguished between human beings, and from other sentient creatures, the Creation provided a blueprint for colonialism and empire. Further, dominion was expressed in the discourse of law, and thus provided definitions of that over which man had dominion—his property—and of what dominion consisted.[51] The conflation and confusion of ethics and law appeared in determining what was good, for there could be goods of mind, spirit, or quality, and goods of property and possession. Increasingly, in the singular, it became a word for the judgment of quality, and in the plural, for property and possessions. Property was divided into that which was non-moveable (land, and by extension, the buildings erected on it), and movables, over which one could have "fee" ("feu" in Scotland, from the Latin, *feudum*). The word "goods" applied generally to all such, and then more particularly to moveable property, and then "goods and cattle" or "goods and chattels," to reflect a distinction between livestock and dead-stock.[52] In law there was a distinction between personal chattels and real chattels, which could be things such as leases or wardships. A ward, therefore, "during the time of his minority, suffers much bondage," which according to the Apostle Paul, did not differ from that of a servant, "as hauing free hold in law, though as yet not free hold in deede," but was very much different from a slave "who was in old time no person in law, but a meere chattell, and as it were of the nature of cattell."[53] In 1684, Sir Richard Dutton, his Council and Assembly, debated the following divisions of dominion: "An Act for serviceing the possession of Negroes and Slaves...An Act for more speedy remedy of distresses takeing damage ffeasant, and trespass[es] done by Horses, Cattle, and other liveing Chattells...And an Act Entituled, How pirates, and felonyes due upon the Sea, shall be tried and punished."[54]

British ecclesiastical and civil polities disputed with increasing gusto and bitterness the fundamental nature of man, the relationship between *meum* and *tuum*, and in whom and over what dominion lay. When they set foot in new worlds, should they return to first principles, bring their formed English ideas to a new environment and apply them as fixed, or should they be molded and adapted to suit changed circumstance? A descendant of Sir Edward Coke, one Roger Coke, claimed that "From the Principles of Authority" came religion, manners, judgment between right and wrong, civil justice that restrained and punished those who offend against religion or manners, and "From these Principles man derives his property in his Lands and Goods...his Life, estate and good name; and from hence Humane Society and Converse is guarded and encouraged."[55] During the last 30 years of the seventeenth century, Coke also mused on the history of the English state from the Interregnum; the extension of England's dominion over trade, the seas, land and its improvement; the legitimacy of chattel, and of slavery, and the rights of the East India and West African Companies.[56] There was ample opportunity in the Americas, particularly in the raw version of it represented by the tropics, to return to the Covenant of Works and define the first Adam.[57]

What of Eve? We have noted that women in the tropics tended to be longer lived (and better behaved) than their menfolk, and it has been suggested—largely from the evidence of wills—that there was autonomy and self-determination open to women in the early-modern Americas, at least in the Chesapeake.[58] From the evidence from the West Indies, however, while some women benefited from wills and there was increased partible inheritance among both male and female kin, the status of women was described in the absolute possessive language of patriarchy. The power of fathers of families, be they at the level of state or estate, was gendered and sexual. Daniel Parke governed uppity Leeward Islands' men by laying sovereign possession over their wives and daughters, while accusing them of abdicating good (and goods) by having sex with black women. His opponents paralleled their loss of (justified) authority through his forcible assertion of (unjustified/unjustifiable) power: "His unparallel'd lewdness was carried on by his authority, [and] was equally fatal to the relacons of the parties both w[h]ere his lust found success, [and] w[h]ere it was Disappointed, where their chastity resisted, he attempted to ravish them, found means to deprive their husbands of their imployments, Harrass'd them by warrants, imprisonments, and excessive bail."[59] Robert Cunyngham's conquest of Elizabeth Arnold was an event of which she implored him "to reflect in what Manner you took to rob me of all that is dear to Woman."[60] Her subsequent service to her man was nevertheless unstinting and unquestioning, even after she had been cast aside, but the contribution she and her daughter made to his propriety, ultimately negligible.

Cara Anzilotti has identified other such women who indefatigably acted to shape the torrid zone, while gender excluded them from participation in the public political sphere.[61] She focuses on the story of Affra Harleston, one of 600 women identified running estates in the Carolinas. Harleston traveled alone on *The Carolina* in 1670, meeting and marrying two years later, Henry Brayne's mate, John Coming.[62] They established themselves on the upper Cooper River: John was often away at sea, the couple were childless, nephews failed to join her in America, and John died in 1694, leaving the whole estate to his wife. "A lady of eminent piety and liberality," she took in orphans and donated to the parish of St. Philip the land on which the church was built. She "molded Comingtee out of the wilderness," refused to return to England, and acquired status (and land) by widowhood; but still the name, title, and the dream followed the patronymic, because in her heart, her husband had been the best in the world.[63] When she died in 1699 she left the estate to those nephews who had not helped her "forlorn" state, listing both, even John Harleston of Dublin, as the heirs of John Coming.[64]

There remains considerable work to be done on the role of women in the early colonial Americas. Anzilotti's portraits of colonial Carolinan women are drawn from a wide remit stretching way beyond the Revolutionary Period, do not compare beyond the Carolina low country, and therefore insufficiently convince that women connived at, or actively complied with, male expectations and norms.[65] But there is further evidence. What may seem empathetic expressions of charity and humanity—not carrying out punishment of runaways themselves or branding animals but not slaves—betokened acceptance that despite practicing de facto autonomy, the idea of proprietary authority lay elsewhere.[66] If we separate idea (intent?) from action, we can accord individual weight to an action, irrespective of the status of the actor, who nevertheless remains determined by the idea (law). Actions in the private sphere (at the level of the personal and the intimate), made a major contribution to the development of the torrid zone, and, because contained within the family, were not incorporated within or appropriated by the public political sphere. We have a dispute about mastery and those who were mastered. As might be expected, this debate was ported across the Atlantic and expected to operate as it had in Britain; but under the strain of translation and interpretation at new hands, was challenged, distorted, and in some cases, blown apart in its new American environment.[67]

Susan Staves has addressed some difficulties in defining and adapting value-sets in a world transfiguring from feudal roots, in which the relationship between sovereign and subject power was "natural," to the mercantilist, early-modern state "concerned with...colonization," in which the relationship became increasingly negotiable, voluntary, and contractual.[68] The complexities and (re)negotiations that took place in early eighteenth-century Britain, affected by mercantile trade, colonization, and new categories of Britishness, had been established in tropical America in the century before, having navigated greater confusion. The seventeenth-century Americas were not an ill-, partially formed version of its eighteenth-century manifestation, formed by Whitehall, from where British identity was honed through negotiated interactions. Rather, British eighteenth-century identity was being inched into life in seventeenth-century America.[69]

Personal certainties under threat, contestation, and renegotiation in Britain, were subject to phenomenal pressures crossing the Atlantic. Within the white world, the norm in which (barring war) men outlived women was subverted by physical license, both to journey and debauch. Women acquired status through widowhood (often quickly relinquished, sometimes by nefarious means), and male and female partible inheritance kept colonial land within the family, by dividing among branches rather than concentrating it in male primogeniture. This was reinforced by the increasingly frequent practice in the Americas of codifying the changing of surnames to buttress inheritance, the adoption of surnames as middle names, and the increasingly frequent use of former surnames as newly adopted Christian names, to keep tradition alive. Wills display the complexities of adaptation. One example concerns the Pollington family. John Pollington was born around 1560 in the Weald of Sussex and in his sixties involved himself in transporting goods and settlers to Virginia, and was there a representative burgess, and a signatory of a heartrending account of the colony's failures.[70] John Pollington's second of three children, and elder son, was Alexander, born in 1585. Either he, or his son, also Alexander, developed an estate in Montserrat, and committed 3,000 pounds (commodity unrecorded) to two more called Body and Fig-Tree in Antigua, in which process he lost his five sons: John (died before 1658); William and Richard who died on the island in 1658; Samuel and Moses in 1666.[71] Nevertheless, he continued to support adventurism and migration to Virginia.[72] Alexander, Citizen and Haberdasher of London, educated all of his children at Merchants' Taylors' School and died in 1672, directing his relict, Dorothie, to sell the three estates, and take the proceeds in slave-bodies to develop his other estates in Antigua. His son, also Alexander, described as a haberdasher of hats, would inherit the management of West India affairs; the estate, "Knowls" (Nowells/Newells) in Sussex; the shop, the Three Bells in Lombard Street; and a house in Threadneedle Street, near the Royal Exchange.[73] Alexander successfully sued for the recovery of Body and Fig-Tree in 1685, but in his will he took patriarchal direction to another level. Of his three children, his "Most Dutifull Daughter Elizabeth" was to be his executrix, manage his estates, particularly those in Antigua, aided by his friends, "In whose great prudence and fidelity I place a great deal of Confidence."[74] Elizabeth was to have sole control, independent of any man she might marry. His other daughter, Martha, was entitled to something from the estate, provided she did not marry Pollington's journeyman, Thomas Ruff.

Alexander's third child was a son, the third Alexander, with whom there appeared to have been some rift, expected to renounce his claims to the estate, and accept what was settled on him. His sister Elizabeth would use the profits and rents from Nowells to ensure that Alexander's son John, and any other sons, be educated until the age of eight, ten, or twelve, "[a]ccording to the Discipline of the Church of England as Now Established by Law And also to read English perfectly well And after that to be taught to Write fair hands And to be well Instructed in Arithmetick as far as may be usefull for them," and when they were "of Sufficient growth and Stature," they would learn navigation. Elizabeth would consequently place them with "good honest and sober Men and good Artists being Masters of Ships Tradeing to Barbados and the Leward Islands in America." Should the children refuse to follow the path of West India merchantmen, by their own choice or under the advice of their parents, they too would lose any advantage of the bequest. So clearly was this a patriarchal means to shape the structure of his family that Alexander senior referred overtly to his "design," before he thought better of it and decided to substitute "desires."[75] He designed and determined to affect the gendered status of both daughters; the locale, focus, and personnel of the family business; the harmony of his family; and from the grave to reward or penalize character.

Sir Joshua Child listed those Britons destined for a term of service in the West Indies, thereby rescued from the consequences of their circumstance, character, and activity, or often, inactivity: "*loose vagrant People*, vicious and destitute of means to live at home, (being either unfit for labour, or such as could find none to employ themselves about, or had so mis-behaved themselves by Whoreing, Thieving, or other Debauchery." They were either saved by Spirits who scooped them off the streets, or benefited from the commutation of death sentences. Others "betook themselves" after "our late Civil Wars, when the worsted party, by the fate of War," were "deprived of their Estates." Some of these had "never been bred to labour," while others were "made unfit for it by the lazy habit of a Soldiers life." "*Scotch Soldiers* of his *Majesty*'s Army, after *Worcester Fight*" (1651) were sent there by the victors; joined at the Restoration by the very people who had vanquished them, now themselves deprived of title, estate, and means; along with those who could not live under the restoration of the Established Church, or Quakers, dealt with as a separate refractory group who met only under the pretence of religious worship, and consequently were banished, forced to transport themselves, or sell themselves to be transported by others.[76]

Most famous/notorious were the West-Country royalists sent to Barbados, and their (self)publicists, Marcellus Rivers and Oxenbridge Foyle, who lashed out at the Commonwealth rhetoric of liberty and declared themselves to be prime examples of "England's slavery." They had been deported without trial or conviction, sold for an average of 1,550 pounds sugar by a power that was arbitrary to them, continually bought and sold between planters, and set to hard labor, "grinding at the Mills attending the Fornaces, or digging in this scorching Island, having nothing to feed on...but Potatoe Roots" and nothing to drink but mobby ("water, with such roots masht in it").[77] The terms of transportation offered to the vanquished of the Monmouth/Campbell rebellion (1685) specifically allocated fixed-term service (10 years, without commutation), subject to the direction to "be held, Compelled and Obleidged to Serve and Obey." Ensuring they served a full term fell to their masters, while the rebels retained ownership of that character that had propelled the action that brought them to the West Indies: "that they may become fully Liable unto, and beare the foresaid marke of their monstrous Villany." Up to this point, the mark was figurative. After this point, any rebels attempting to escape would be exposed in the marketplace, receive 39 lashes on their "bare body," spend an hour in the pillory, and be branded "T" for "ffugitive Traytor." This represented the extension to new lands of the corruption of British character, rather than recognition that they possessed no inherent ability to serve any master.[78] They would not benefit from any of the customary laws of Barbados, including that which would otherwise manumit their service should they marry a free woman on the island. Rather, the woman would be penalized £200 and suffer six-months' imprisonment. The Act was repealed (though the customs of the country were still not to be held out to rebels) in 1691.[79]

Differences of both nature and degree have been attributed to Irish labor sent to the Plantations, a precedent for transportation having been suggested to the Virginia Company in 1607: removing 700–800 "Idle persons" of "unlawfull propigation," who were "base, apt to follow factions," "live allwaies by yr spoyle, and will never be brought to other Conformitie there," would spend "tyme elsewhere" and the harshness of the conditions would either "eate them oute or amend them."[80] A further request was made in 1620.[81] At the ideological level, distrust of the Irish rested in their Catholicism; at a personal level, it was more dependent on a character assessment, as they were branded with idleness, intransigence, slander, and profanity.[82] A statement about the rebelliousness of the Irish in Barbados made by Governor Daniel Searle conflates several aspects: that they were of no fixed location, and thus acted free from both propriety and service; they lived lives judged to be of poor character: "dissolute, leud, and slothful"; committed actions against normative values, relying on theft rather than honest work; they actively and passively encouraged others to follow their lead; and had menaced "several of the inhabitants of this place." Cumulatively, these actions had led them to "a condition of power," in which they had acquired arms, physically resisted control, and they were now the ones able to "design," though theirs would be "wicked and malicious."[83] Their transportation as prisoners could only lead to negative views of the Irish being confirmed. Abraham Studd thought fit to write a letter, by way of an ad hoc will, to be delivered to London by his brother, after a party of Irish transportees had attempted to seize *The Meteor* on June 21, 1642, on its passage to Barbados.[84] Many Barbados inhabitants may have carried with them prejudices against the character, actions, and intent of the Irish. Examples of Irish behavior observed or projected in Ireland, often confirmed by example of the passage or life in the colonies, set the normative, British values—patriarchal design, manifested in behavior that revealed authority on one side and deference on the other—against antinormative determination, in that within the West Indies, the Irish designed for themselves the power to subvert.[85]

Influencing how one might determine or be determined, therefore, was a combination of circumstances at home, the resultant character displayed at home, whether character traits exhibited or entrenched at home were carried to the Plantations, who made the decision to travel to the colonies, who carried them and under what circumstances, and the degree of autonomous action they could claim once in the New World. The relative authoritativeness with which fixity (proprietary interest versus sloth) or movement (transporters contra vagrants, pirates) defined a person would determine judgments between governors and governed, and whether such judgments were arbitrary and tyrannical or lawful and reasonable. This was summed up by the description of the usage of servants made by Richard Ligon, that it was "much as the Master is, merciful or cruel."[86] The Irish described by Searle, were freemen and women, and as such could have chosen to work within normative values. They were invested with inherent determinism, and made choices that gradually formed into normative judgments against them, and while they may have been affected by English or settler mistrust, these were formed, confirmed and sometimes repudiated by their actions within the West Indies. That penalties fell on masters or women who married Monmouth rebels indicates a lack of autonomous determinism: the character of servants here was determined at home, the consequences of which were played out in their service punishment abroad. The mark of "T" was treachery already committed, authorized by London; the action committed in the West Indies, the attempt to escape punishment; so the mark of villainy was already upon them, made manifest to all should they deny their punishment. Servants, therefore, were, irrespective of the behavior they had exhibited either before or after their indenture, incorporated within patriarchal structures of allegiance.

Under certain circumstances, when loyalty and incorporation into the "English community" was of paramount concern, specifically non-English people could display sufficient adherence to and assimilation of normative values to warrant inclusion. An earlier statement by Searle, in the years of Commonwealth rule in England, embedded within an arbitration between masters and servants who disputed the lengths of their terms of indenture, the extension of English rights to those "late Prisoners of War and all others of the *Scottish* Nation" who had taken an oath of loyalty assenting to "the Union...that *Scotland* be incorporated into, and made one Commonwealth with *England*."[87] In the later period, Christopher Jeaffreson, instrumental in creating the legislation that enabled the shipping of "malefactors" "in order to ye peopleing his Majesties Collons [*sic*] on St Christophers Island wth English Subjects," was alarmed that it might be interpreted strictly by the letter to exclude Huguenot refugees. The French were now "necessitated to be faithfull to those amongst whom they find safty and refuge and so...his Majesties Collony is by ye Protection of these men (who in one age will be perfect Englishmen in Interest religion and language) peopled and streangthed [*sic*] by so many new subjects who in all probabelety will be as faithfull to his Majestie as his owne naturall borne subjects."[88]

Much of the manner with which relations between man and man were regulated and adjudged was codified in 1661. Thomas Hodges described justice having been done in a "summary" fashion, up to this point, and he referred to courts being "erected in imitation of those in *England*" because trade had increased; but in fact the Restoration postwar regime was harnessing and controlling the state of the increasingly variant world of the Caribbean.[89] In Barbados, such sorting of regulations applied to the status of service, applying to origin, means of transportation, role of ship's master, role of Barbados masters, and "rights" of servants, reflecting on the tendency of servants to "unruliness, obstinacy, and refractoriness...bold extravagancy...[and] wandering."[90] Children under 14 were not yet considered to possess autonomous will, and those spirited onboard ships without their agreement were given 50 days to complain and turn the weight of judgment against the master. A freeman who made a serving woman pregnant would forfeit two years of his labor to recompense the parish for the child's upkeep: the woman, for getting with child, would serve an additional two years. Should the woman die in childbirth, the man would serve all of the woman's remaining time. Autonomously acting indenturers who married without their masters' consent would serve additional time. A determination would be made between those servants who became sick and were the responsibility of the master to keep well, and those who became unable to work through their own willful misbehavior. Should a servant attempt to run away, it could "justly be *presumed*, that the said Servant *intended* and *prepared* to escape," thereby judging degrees of authoritative action.[91]

The point is not purely nominal that for Britons in the seventeenth century the term "slavery" referred to something most grievously suffered by themselves, deprived of their freedom of will, and therefore of their ability to act autonomously, and of liberty itself. This was most explicitly expressed against the actions of Barbary pirates who seized mariners off the southwest coast of England, on their way to and from the West Indies, and kept them in "miserable Captivity [and] slavery under those cruel Enimies of our Saviour Christ"; "subjugated [and] exposed to a most wretched [and] remedilesse Slavery."[92] Usually, slavery was used as a means to define a legal status that had been corrupted by (foreign), arbitrary and tyrannical power. During the years of civil war, this was oftentimes Catholicism and the papacy, or the oppressions of monopolies or apprenticeships and other such that deprived English men in particular of their "liberties." Its heightened language rendered it poetic or polemical. Balladeers sang of men's enslavement to love, for which "A Hen-peck'd Husband's like a Slave, who wears / His Masters Fetters."[93] Apprentices, subject to sumptuary laws could rightly complain that "*London* is no *Algier*, where the captive slaves have their several badges by which they are to be known, though it may be presumed the rigidnesse of some Masters cared not even in this City if there were Brands put upon Servants as they do upon Horses, to showe their absoluteness and Propriety."[94] The word "slavery" was engrained within the dichotomous discourse of politically aware British people: religious conflict, in making a choice between Protestant liberty or papal slavery; relations with foreign powers were, given their Catholicism or Islam, about delivering good Christians from anti-Christian slavery; monopolies and apprenticeships were enslavement to those who would rather level citizens; factions and Parties accused opponents of slavish subservience or slavish arbitrariness; the Scots, Irish, and English variously accused each other of wanting to enslave free peoples within their islands.[95]

On the flip side were constructions of the danger and exoticism of life outside English norms, romanticized into tales of captive sailors enslaved in the galleys of foreign powers, or the juxtaposition of English liberties and the black-skinned inhabitants of Africa. Fenlander, Job Hortop, wrote about the third triangular trading voyage of England's first slaver, Sir John Hawkins, in which African people were defined by their skin color and by their exceptional resourcefulness. One man, taken in a fight at Cape Verde, advised of a cure for Hawkins, who had been wounded by a poisoned arrow; they constituted the other parties in a series of trades; they were described hunting hippopotamus; and in Sierra Leone comprised a force of fifteen thousand, many of whom were slain, and a town burnt. Hortop's account of Africa is largely incidental—his major focus was on the "Indian voyage" in which the crew traded their human and other cargo in the Spanish Caribbean—but this is not a narrative of the cruelty of English enslavement of Africans, but of the black legend of the Spanish. They were brutal toward indigenous Americans, each other, and the English sailors taken prisoner. Although difficult to read the poor Gothic imprint, it would appear that the English prisoners, having escaped the fire of the Inquisition, "were sent to carde woolle, like as the Indians doo that are slaves to the Spaniards, which we could not abide and therefore every one of us consulted to beat our Keepers." Thereby the autocratic tyranny of Spain, expressed as cruelty and injustice, justified dissentient action on the part of the English. What in fact they did, was to turn to the other perceived aspect of Spanish injustice—their superstition—and use it against them: they earned their freedom by persuading their captors that they were devils.[96]

The debate about whether the character, ideas, and actions of British, Irish, indigenous American, or conformist peoples from elsewhere within Europe could be part of a native right that could be transferred to the Plantations was never accorded to Africans. Patriarchy constructed the natures of the communities for inclusion or exclusion of rights, and as such, early apologias for African slavery were not of markedly different construction from those which questioned it. Consider in the following, the interweave of active political patriarchy: "I cannot but think it charitable and commendable, as well as lawful Undertaking to buy a Slave in Guinea where the severity of his Government has subjected him to a Discipline, that Flesh and Blood can scarce go thro," argued a proponent of the rights of independent traders (as opposed to the Royal African Company) in Africa. In the West Indies "he retains the Name of Slave but performs only the work and Business of a Servant...he becomes useful and profitable to his Master and beneficial to the Publick." Or: "they change their Country only, and not their Condition, unless it be for the better." Individuals would be given a new opportunity for agency in the West Indies, by being "more free, and have more Ease" than English servants would have in England. The monopoly held by the Royal African Company was also deemed to recognize agency among Africans who traded with (and in) their fellows in Africa, who "impos'd upon [the Company] what Prices and Delays they pleased," thus complaining it was the Company which was denuded of political capital.[97] White people in the West Indies were spared having to make moral judgments about their own motivations and actions: they did not have to question any instigation of slavery, any design to enslave, because the incoming Africans were already enslaved. Neither did they need to ask themselves why. There was an implication that the incoming slaves would remain outside the bounds of English law, not only or solely because they were not free, but because they remained "foreign" and were therefore not encompassed by "native right."[98]

Throughout the seventeenth century ran a series of dichotomous definitions, for people of "black" skin tone in the Anglophone Caribbean. They were rarely—particularly in official discourse—referred to as directly and unambiguously as "slave." They could be free, freed, chattel, domestic servant, enslaved, movable property, attached to land; born in Africa; born in Africa but distinguished by more specific place, people, or language; born onboard ship; born in the Americas; traded, exchanged, rented from a neighbor; bought from a chartered British Company; bought as contraband; or used as credit and patronage.[99] Where there is explicit identification of people of non-British ethnicity with slavery, therefore, we must carefully dissect why. A Barbados Act of 1652 required runaways to be notified to Mr. James Beak, who was storehouse-keeper to James Drax: those who returned slaves to their masters would receive a reward.[100] A subsequent Act "against the stealing away of Negroes from off this Island...by specious pretence of promising them Freedom in another Countrey" established a punishment for this offence, where no prior legislation had existed and referred to persuading "any Negroes to leave their Masters service (to whom they are Slaves)." The Act to prevent "Servants and Negro[e]s" from wandering Barbados when they were not working, causing mischief to "Masters of Families" was glossed as "Servants and Slaves," until such time as different punishments were enacted for servants (additional time), or slaves (to be apprehended, whipped, returned under guard to the master or to Drax's agent, as before). Payments to those who brought in runaway slaves were increased, as the previous Act had been ineffectual in this regard.[101] In 1656, Colonel William Hilliard, having returned to England from Barbados, made a settlement for the "Marriage agreed uppon [and] shortly by Gods grace to be solempnized" between his daughter, Meliora, and his Barbados factor, Ferdinando Gorges (who operated a company with Drax), included in which were the Hilliard lands of "Henley" in St. John's, buildings, sugar pots, utensils, household stuff, cattle, Christian servants for their terms, and "Negroes Indians [and] other slaves." Here is confirmed that indigenous as well as African peoples were not only being used as slaves on Barbados, as was also the case in late-century Jamaica, but were called such.[102]

But at the very end of the century, William Rawlin of the Middle Temple, clerk to the Barbados Assembly, took it upon himself to publish a compendium of island legislation. Here, all which related to slaves and slavery was indexed under "N." This illuminated a definition that had always distinguished between, on the one hand, those who were free, had once been free and could become free again, and those who voluntarily gave up their freedoms for a limited period; and on the other, those who had never been conceived of as free or possessed of inherent freedoms. "An Act for Governing of Negroes" was followed by "An Additional Act concerning Slaves" for the purposes of inheritance and estate. The Act, brought in under William Willoughby, created slaves as real estate, with such a confusion of proprieties that Willoughby was required to clarify his meaning.[103] When slaves were "deemed real Estate and not Chattels" this did not disallow the practice of issuing personal actions for debt, for which purposes "negroes continue Chattels."[104] One of the chief ways in which commentators distinguished customary legislation in the West Indies from that which had developed "since time immemorial" in England, was by the different island customs pertaining to slaves' status as real or personal property and the differences that developed on account of the levels of colonists' debt.

Therefore, most key statements that explicitly refer to "slaves" come from the Commonwealth period. Because the liberal/republican/commonwealth tradition was concerned with expanding the number of free individuals, to include those who forged their liberty through their adventure and labor in the colonies, it was more likely to be explicit and unapologetic about invoking patriarchalism to establish the privilege of skin and openly delineating why some were excluded from that community. When Locke came to codify those liberties in his philosophical tomes and American constitutional frameworks, he was tacitly repeating the stark message that his forebears had made explicit: Britons knew that Africans were as possessed of the human "light of nature" as themselves, but chose to deny it.[105] Locke could place in print the maxim that it was the labor on the land that justified property because by the time of publication, white freeholders had been spared having to justify whose labor then created and maintained their estates.[106] And classifying people by means other than their actions, could bypass not only the debate about labor, but also that about disposition. If Africans who arrived in the West Indies were already slaves, and the children of slaves were born into slavery, it was not necessary to have a debate about character. That human liberties, given status in law, would never be held out to slaves had early on been made explicit.[107]

The Barbados Slave Code of 1661 is infamous for describing Africans as "an heathenish, brutish and an uncertain kind of people" but it was the later "Act for the Governing of Negroes" of 1688, under Lieutenant Governor Edwin Stede, that specified that limitations were required to be placed upon an enslaved person because of the character of the person, rather than that he or she was a slave per se.[108] It held that "the said Negroes and other Slaves brought unto the People of this Island for that purpose are of barbarous, wild and salvage natures, and such as renders them wholly unqualified, to be governed by the Laws, Customs and Practices of our Nations," they being "naturally prone and inclined" to "Disorders, Rapines and Inhumanities."[109] Regarding human beings as property enabled another side step. Slaves were so ungovernable that they could not be contained within the law, but by the second half of the century numbers had grown to the point at which the economies of the West Indies could not function without them. Now, financial motives so suppressed edification, exemplar, cultural assimilation, theories of cultural or behavioral difference, or rules of morality, that unedifying behavior was both expected and connived at. A house-slave, educated enough to say the catechism and trained in domestic service, but who burgled a blind, bedridden white woman; and three field-workers who robbed a plantation owned by a freed slave, escaped the stipulated punishments for slaves because their execution would devastate the labor force to the detriment of the sugar economy.[110] The economic imperative enabled white commentators to disregard any debate about whether behavior was natural and inherent, and it also enabled them to ignore whether the refractory behavior—"Laziness, Stealing, Lying, Drunkenness...Murmuring, Stubbornness, Disaffection...and Designs"—might be a reactive response to white people's character and actions.[111]

Even those West Indian commentators who wished to emphasize humanity shared by all still predicated bondage on a mercenary relationship, in which obedience could be exchanged for just dues.[112] Unable to persuade West Indians to abandon either the economic imperative or the color-conscious legal and ethical frameworks that they had constructed to buttress it, instead they applied their reforming zeal to the relatively conservative end of educating Britons. Morgan Godwyn saw an opportunity with the accession of James II to appeal to the king's overt professions of piety to call for the conversion of heathens in his majesty's wide dominions. But in reality, he was publishing a sermon delivered in Westminster Abbey, and that "Trade [was] preferr'd before Religion, and *Christ* made to give place to *Mammon*" was expressed in the relatively constrained ambition of baptizing house-slaves working in England.[113] Their impersonation narratives were homilies on the golden rule—"all things whatsoever ye would that men should do to you, do ye so to them" (Matt.7.1)—with three characteristics that distinguished an African-heritage life from the other inhabitants of the West Indies: the former had been forcibly separated from their native country; they were engaged in sweated labor through which they could never advance their own economic or social fortunes; but their labor contributed to the ease and luxury of others.[114] They created an edifying black man: stoical and industrious, whose virtues were usurped by their masters. Impersonation narratives began to appear at the end of the seventeenth century. They provide valuable information about the big and small actions of black protagonists in the West Indies, Africa, and on the Atlantic-crossing, but must be approached with caution, for they remain the words of a white elite: an alternative view; paternalist, but no less patriarchal.

The power of Aphra Behn's narrative of slave rebellion in English Surinam lay in her taking the story of the attempted tyrannicide by, and subsequent capture, torture, and execution of, a white settler; retelling it as that of an African, whose features, education, and royalty gave him characteristics that were recognizably English. Personification narratives could induce empathy for the treatment of Africans in the West Indies, but only by denying their difference and emphasizing the degree to which they had assimilated commendable aspects of English culture. The black character that fulminated against the hypocrisy of the advocates of liberty, was the fictional freed-slave created by Rev. Robert Robertson. He has him say that under the Commonwealth "[n]othing was to be heard every where but *Liberty*, the *Law* of *Nature*, the *natural Rights of Mankind*, whereof *Liberty* is one, *which* (`tis said) *they might be robbed of, but could never forfeit*, . . . and *the bringing any of the* Human Race *into* Slavery *was pronounc'd execrable.*"[115] The former slave could also characterize European politics as unseemly squabbles akin to those of African nations, but in the case of Europe they were about the merits and demerits of Protestantism or Catholicism. Irrespective of the divisive principles that were believed to guide action within Europe, all European peoples agreed that whenever there was interstate rivalry "whichever Side gets the better in any Part of the *West-Indies*, the Conqueror (be he *Protestant*, be he *Papist*, or of the same Communion with the conquer'd, `tis all one) instantly seizes all his Adversaries *Negroe-Slaves*. . . and carries them to *slave it* anew in a Colony of his own, or sells them to the highest Bidders in open market."[116]

Irrespective of the ideas that the white population of the West Indies or the mother countries held about themselves, their approach to their black counterparts never escaped the capacious bounds of patriarchy. Africans could be incorporated within household, family, or congregation; or be the objects of sadism, brutality, pity, compassion, empathy, rescue, or negligence, without ever deviating from the dictum of "master knows best." Some believed Africans to have called down wrath upon themselves, such that either conversion to Christianity was impossible, or did and could not wipe clean the sins of those, who according to Virginia legislation, in a personal inversion of English first-footing rights, "at the first purchase were Infidels."[117] Others held out that all humanity was possessed of the "light of nature" and the subject of wrath or pity. Both remained in the service of patriarchy, as was the transformative mortification of the flesh meted out to slaves, even as planters abused their own refractory bodies, and brought the wrath of God upon themselves.[118] The phrase chosen by the authorities to describe black people who attended Quaker meetings, redolent of meaning in giving the Quakers the privilege of acting, with those who accompanied them denied voluntary will, was that they "have been *suffered to remain* at the Meetings of the *Quakers* as *Hearers* of their Doctrine."[119] Would slaves be capable within an atmosphere in which white behavior was far from edifying, of determining the truth of the Gospel? Non-Christians had noted the contempt in which the Christian ministry was held.[120] Bishop Berkeley, in his plans for a seminary on Bermuda, concurred that "though the surest means to reform the morals, and soften the behaviour of men, be, to preach to them the pure uncorrupt doctrine of the gospel, yet...the success of preaching dependeth...on the character and skill of the preacher" because man was "more apt to copy characters than to practise precepts." He reiterated that owning a person was not in itself anti-Christian: rather it would be to planters' advantage "to have slaves who should *obey in all things their masters according to the flesh, not with eye-service as men-pleasers, but, in singleness of heart as fearing God*: that gospel liberty consists with temporal servitude; and that their slaves would only become better slaves by being christian."[121]

The most remarkable white commentary on the behavior and character of slaves was made about the Akan-Coromanti. Modern commentators have attributed, through a combination of the study of the ethical and sociological belief systems pertaining in Africa, and action taken by Coromanti slaves in early colonial America, an explanation for the nature of leadership among African-born slaves within the West Indies, albeit "politically parochial and ethnically particularistic," and their assertions of freedom, albeit as a "withdrawal from society."[122] This ascribes a linear history of Africans becoming African-Americans to parallel that about the degree to which European culture migrated across the Atlantic and was either developed with continuity or radically transformed in the light of new experience.[123] Studies in anthropology and African history have identified a distinctive attitude toward slavery within Africa among the Akan communities, and within them a particularist difference among Asante. They note that slavery was a position that accorded some honor; that the work undertaken by slaves had standing; and that slaves were such for a determinate and limited length of service. They have suggested, therefore, that the positive acts of Coromanti resistance in the Americas in the seventeenth century reflected their rejection of the humiliation, violence, and lifelong, generational servitude associated with British chattel slavery.[124] Thus was noted, both by contemporaries and modern scholars, the predominance of Coromanti within maroon communities.

As the descriptions of the maroons has shown, however, the nature of their withdrawal from (colonial) society was regarded as the most unwarranted assertion of positive liberty, and was emphasized by the most brutal(ized) descriptions of their violent actions, tyrannical and arbitrary self-government, language, and customs. George Gamble was struck with fear which he said went deep into his soul when he recounted to Governor Christopher Codrington, then about business in Nevis, the news of the attack by 15 Coromanti men on Samuel Martin's estate in Antigua. At around eight in the morning, on December 27, 1701, the men approached Martin at the door of his bedroom and laid into him with bills and knives. They then cut off his head, washed it with rum, and "triumphed over it" (subsequently retold as having used the skull as a celebratory drinking cup). Gamble reiterated how the people of Antigua had been surprised by this attack, and the planters, desperately short of weapons, continued to fear should there be an invasion by the French.[125]

Codrington had only Gamble's account of the rising when he enclosed it in his letter to the Council of Trade and Plantations. He produced one of the few accounts of human character, as revealed by action, which addressed both white and black. Of Major Samuel Martin, he was sorry to lose a "useful" man, who had been an active public servant. He did not accuse Martin of having been an habitually brutal and "severe" slave master, but imputed to him "some unusual act of severity, or rather some indignity towards the Corramantes," to have precipitated the attack, because

> [t]hey are not only the best and most faithful of our slaves, but are really all born Heroes. There is a difference between them and all other negroes... There never was a raskal or coward of yt nation, intrepid to the last degree, not a man of them but will stand to be cut to pieces without a sigh or groan, grateful and obedient to a kind master, but implacably revengeful when ill-treated. My father [Christopher Codrington senior], who had studied the genius and temper of all kinds of negroes 45 years with a very nice observation, would say, Noe man deserved a Corramante that would not treat him like a Friend rather than a Slave, and all my Corramantes preserve that love and veneration for him that they constantly visit his grave, make their libations upon it, hold up their hands to heaven with violent lamentations, and promise when they have done working for his son they will come to him and be his faithful slaves in the other world.[126]

Ironically, in his will, Codrington requested that the body of his father be exhumed from its resting place at Betty's Hope and reinterred in Westminster Abbey.[127] Gamble, he concluded, must have been in such consternation of fear and grief for his friend to have described the rebellion as he did, for clearly they had made a limited and specific attack on Samuel Martin alone, which must have explained and even justified their response.[128] Aphra Behn's romance of Oroonoko was a commentary on the warrior nobility of Coromanti stoicism, bravery, and principle. Although the model for her hero was a white planter, and her description of Oroonoko was careful to Europeanize him in all except his very dark skin, her story was published in 1688 and thus predated the first major Akan risings in Jamaica and further suggests that the English were aware of the existence of maroon communities in Surinam from quite an early period.

Codrington remained someone who believed that Christianity may (or should) have precluded some behaviors among its adherents and may even have required people to do as they would be done by, but was not incompatible with the *idea* of slavery. He controlled the provision and ownership of slaves by universal branding, breeding Creole slaves on Barbuda to circumvent the Royal African Company trade; and engineered patronage and power among settlers under his command by extending them credit, in the form of slaves, to develop their own plantations. William Gordon lauded him as one who "hath set a Noble PATTERN to all those, whom providence hath Blessed with Plentiful Fortunes, arising from their Commerce with the *yet Dark and Unbelieving Parts of the World*," encouraging others to follow Codrington's example and "consecrate" part of their estate "to the Conversion and Instruction of those *Infidels*, to whose Labour, under Providence, they owe their Wealth and Affluence."[129] His enemy, Parke, described him as a "Couvettous" hoarder who rooted his authority in bribery, corruption, and patronage.[130] Neither the labor of slaves nor their Christian profession would negate their status and Codrington's (along with Consett's, so hard fought over) created a center for the training of missionaries to serve in the Foreign Plantations. There should be care for both the body and soul of slaves; education and instruction. Codrington College would therefore have "three hundred negros at least Kept always thereon" and "a [c]onvenient number" of scholars who would practice divinity, medicine, and surgery.[131]

Richard Ligon had not believed that by the custom of Barbados, a basically good human being whose skin was black—"as ingenious, as honest, and as good a natur[ ]d poor soul, as ever wore black, or eat green" [*sic*]—anxious to be a Christian, would cease to be a slave.[132] For Richard Baxter, those who took slaves were "the common enemies of mankind," but slavery itself was justified as a punishment or a voluntary agreement; while Morgan Godwyn separated the condition of slavery from religious identity and inclusion within the Christian family. Whether the "family" was household, congregation, or humanity, white people determined black people's inclusion as much as their exclusion.[133] The bishops had claimed to stand against the merchandising of people as a matter of principle but Berkeley was still persuading the Society in the 1730s that the conversion of the heathen should start with promoting proper knowledge and respect for the Gospel among the planters, and that (admittedly referring chiefly to Rhode Island) early planters had held an "antient Antipathy" toward indigenous peoples, "together with an irrational Contempt of the Blacks, as Creatures of another Species, who had no Right to be instructed or admitted to the Sacraments." But still they were of an "erroneous Notion" that "being Baptized is inconsistent with a State of Slavery."[134]

So, the white communities managed to delude themselves that neither bondage nor the feudal order per se were against God's Law, but those actions that transgressed it. There developed codes of behavior and punishments for transgression, and some slippage in the changed environment and conditions of the West Indies that might explain, excuse, or even justify behavior considered unacceptable "at home." Drinking to excess, virtually universal practice, was the subject of frequent comment, but seldom censure. Contact between black or indigenous and white, across a spectrum from rape, merchandising, to companionable familiarity, was widespread, and legislation to prevent miscegenation powerless.[135] Planters showed no conscience about committing generations of mulattos, mestizos, and Creoles to slavery, even though their existence which demonstrated their ability to reproduce, proved them no monsters outside the principles of God's Creation, and if the English did not recognize the humanity they shared with their "*English Off-spring*, we should one Day have too much cause to repent of our large Discoveries in these Parts, which of *Men*, (by their being Transplanted hither) must so inevitably make them to degenerate into Brutes."[136] Both planters and clergy excused themselves that baptism was too great an expense but the planters did not scruple to "cheapen Religion" and read a- and antireligious books. Christians and Jews connived with slaves to ensure that enterprise was a seven-day activity, and slaves "want[ed] proper means [and] Opportunities" for conversion.[137] Clergymen were seldom exemplars in that drunkenness was a frequent charge: ministers kept black slaves as workers, and as sexual partners, mothers for their children and companions. Rev. William Lesley of St. John's, Barbados, was married to Ann, but his will provided for several children with a black bondswoman.[138] Rev. James Cruikshank held himself to be alone in his "study to make my own life regular, so as not to give any wilfull offence either to Christians or Heathens."[139]

There was nothing edifying in the British tropical Americas, neither literally nor metaphorically. Within Europe, cultures had evolved so as to inculcate and remind those living there of its normative values: one was born into, grew up, and lived within, a self-referential environment. Catholic colonists had been considerably more successful in building awe-inspiring cathedrals, monasteries and palaces, towns and churches, and filling them with works of art and craft that reinforced the majesty of church and state. Among the litany of complaints from British-born clergymen was that they lived too remotely from their flock, that the journey to unite minister with congregant was hot, dusty, and fatiguing, that services were held in the claustrophobic back rooms of houses, and that they possessed no surplices, plate, or bibles, laboring "under ye want of a suitable place for ye exercise of devotions agreeable to ye christian religion."[140] Ministers in St. Christopher's were willing to admit that the French had built a church of "splendor," but impious hands burnt it down during the war. Ambitions went unrealized. Thomas, Lord Windsor's instructions were "to take Care that Drunkenness and Debauchery be discountenanced and Punished,... none to be admitted to Publick Trust, or Employments, whose ill Conversation may bring Scandal thereupon," and to ensure that the Church of England "may have a due Reverence & Exercise among you." Twenty years later, Sir Thomas Lynch was merely enjoined to ensure that all ministers exercising the Anglican communion were in possession of a license.[141] Sir Richard Dutton's efforts to make ceremonial practice and education conformable to Anglican rites were thrown back at him as examples of his arbitrary power. He was said to have ordered an additional prayer for the welfare of himself and the Council to be inserted into the

Communion service, ahead of that for the bishops. Dutton responded that he had attempted to ensure that the ministry, particularly schooling, was in the hands of those loyal to the Church of England, and had therefore ejected those who refused the oaths of allegiance and supremacy. The prayer, he maintained, was inserted, had the approval of the clergy, and was based on that used in Ireland, changing only those things that made it suitable for this occasion.[142]

Sir Jonathan Atkins noted the value of edification, but he was being optimistic (and self-regarding) when he related that his own regular church attendance had resulted in all the Barbados churches following full Anglican rites.[143] Rev. John Blair described the inhabitants of North Carolina thus: Quakers who did not know what they believed; those who called themselves Quakers if it allowed them to lead a less "moral life than they are willing to comply to"; a sort of Presbyterian acting as itinerant lay preachers; and Anglicans whose elite socioreligious status would make for good governance if only they were not swamped by the greater numbers of the other three.[144] Thomas Bray surveyed the colonies' lack of Christian edification as the Society for the Propagation of the Gospel was extended to the southern Americas. He noted that when Muslims planted their creed in a place, they built a mosque and placed a symbol of their faith atop it "to intimate that his Religion shall increase."[145] But after 20 years of Codrington College, Bishop Edmund of London received one "sad acc^t of ye Place" from Rev. Arthur Holt and another from schoolmaster Thomas Wilkie. Holt praised Governor Henry Worsley as a pious, wise, and equitable administrator, "yet they"—"those of our own Complexion"—"can not or they will not see it."[146]

In what a bind were ill-resourced Protestants in the West Indies placed? They could not overawe their flock with imitations of the grandeur and loftiness of (as they saw it) legitimate power. They could not resort to icons, images, statuary or display to demonstrate legitimate authority's loftier values. In puritan-leaning Bermuda, attempts were made to have ministers use "decent ceremony" and congregants "reverent posture," to little effect.[147] Attempts by the Scottish Episcopalians, Governor Archibald Hamilton and Rev. Commissary Richard Tabor, to furnish St. Catherine's, Jamaica, with £5,000-worth of statuary and images of Moses and Aaron, merely meant "several weak but well-meaning people would not approach the Altar for fear of bowing to those Images" and they "were so gaudy that they occasioned a great avocation of the mind and desecration of thought in the time of Divine Worship."[148] Not Hamilton, nor any of his predecessors in gubernatorial office, had any faith in the servants of religion in the West Indies, who, charged with asserting and maintaining authority could not be relied upon to practice the imitation of Christ and neither could any of the ordinary people who were supposed to be created in God's image.

The golden rule could have little purchase in a society in which no one behaved well and it could be argued that what was encouraged was spiraling levels of negative emulation. Action was determined by mental capacity; decisions by reasoning; and both must be possessed of meaning. Britons believed that even the most stupid of people could perform by rote or "incautious [and] unwary persons" be led astray by artifice.[149] And so they tied themselves in knots of hypocrisy, dissimulation, and self-delusion. Rev. Arthur Holt contradicted himself. His experience of black people in British Barbados, Virginia, and Maryland, and also the example of the French in Martinique, showed him "that many of them are capable of Information," but that there were nevertheless "unhappy Creatures" from particular parts of Africa, from whose "Incapacity" "seem rather to be Idiots"; so longer-term acculturation of Europeanism revealed intelligence, reason, and inner (Christian) light, but alien and heathen ideas and the languages in which they were expressed did not.[150] Thomas Wilkie noted a dichotomy. Younger slaves were "very docile & capable to learn any thing": "five or six of them...can spell very prettily and repeat ye Creed & Lords prayer."[151] As soon as they reached an age, however, they were put to work, lacked time for learning and hid from their teacher, which merely buttressed planters' scorn for religion because it had failed to reveal, inculcate, or impose normative values, merely highlighted rejection of them. It continued refractory behavior, either by nature or as acts of resistance, considering slave "numbers, Subtilty, savageness, and proneness to run away from their Masters." Wilkie was preparing two slaves for baptism; (almost) able to repeat the Creed, Lords' Prayer, and Ten Commandments, spending every Sunday afternoon in school, and they "tell me they'll content themselves with one wife." Despite his commitment to education, and Robert Robertson's conviction that every man was possessed of soul and conscience, they nevertheless exposed their prejudice that slave Christianity was not innate belief, but skin-deep observance. Hence, reformers accelerated and reiterated their pleas to the church and state at home, some going so far as to say that there was such great need for reformation at home as not to "waste" good people in America.[152] And the consequence, possibly unwitting, was increasing imperial oversight.

The numbers of slave baptisms during the seventeenth century made Christian reformers pessimistic and discouraged anything other than a conservative approach. But it could equally be argued, as in the case of the cultural capital acquired by the black and white wedding of Peter Perkins and Jane Long, that the outstandingly small numbers served to emphasize the profundity of the conversion process for those who undertook it. In Barbados were nine (recorded, "Anglican") "black" baptisms at St. Michael's, Bridgetown, between 1682 and 1685, and 36 in St. Philip's before 1715.[153] Free, slave, mulatto, old, and young came for baptism and clearly not by way of reward for, or expectation of, their freedom. Hannah chose to be baptized before going to Carolina in 1682, though whether she traveled with her master, Captain Walley, is unclear.[154] Several couples chose to baptize their children without evidence they were themselves baptized; Margaret Cary was christened at the same time as her daughter, Mary; and Rose, a free mulatta in St. Philip's, baptized seven children on two separate occasions, about a year after she had herself become Christian.[155] The entries do not indicate that new names were taken at baptism, and there are odd entries that seem to show that even "Africanized" names were retained, confirming that names, whether they were of a European or an African type, after place-names, or reflective of character traits, were invariably given and not taken.[156] Not choosing to change their name, however, detracts little from a decision taken by those few who seem by their very scarcity, to have demonstrated understanding and appreciation of the meaning behind the symbolism of baptism and not to have undertaken an action for instrumental or incidental reasons. It should have encouraged and pacified the establishment. Instead, the isolated actions of these few offered a challenge of such profound moral consequences to its worldview that it dare not embrace them. Instead, choosing baptism was audacity that merited a whipping.[157]

In a general account of burial practice, Sir Jonathan Atkins noted of Barbados, that slaves buried their own in the ground of the plantation where they died and thus owned a place that was distinctively theirs, but "not without ceremonies of their own."[158] Arthur Holt complained of the noisy rites performed over slave graves to guard the community against the haunting of the dead.[159] The only entries that might indicate black people buried at a church is "Leeds," the only name entered for a burial on March 30, 1706, under the auspices of rector Gilbert Wharton, and Charles Cunningham's burial of "Darby a Man from Gen¹ Codrington's."[160] In these two examples, the most perplexing aspect of the evidence is the absence of a note that they were black, since details of people, particularly at burial, could be quite specific.[161] With the tantalizing glimpses of ceremony that kept African belief systems intact, and the triumph in death of a home within the Caribbean soil, in other respects black burial practice did not much vary, in Atkins' eyes, from Baptists, Quakers, other sectaries, or Jews.[162] The dispersal of Jamaican communities far from a church determined local interment, without rites of burial; the sacraments secularized and patriarchalized by having "masters of families" responsible for delivering to a JP details of births and deaths in any in their families.[163]

Ceremonial in the civil realm was infrequent and it seems generally unwelcome, unappreciated, and ineffective. Under Francis Lord Willoughby of Parham, the pro-Charles Stuart "rebellion broke out" on May 1, 1650, and on the seventh, trumpeters announced Charles's kingship, for which the governor awarded them as much wine as they could drink.[164] Despite advice from William Hilliard that the island should "reduce itself," the Commonwealth eventually sent a retaliatory fleet. When the monarchy was eventually restored, the arms of the Commonwealth were removed from public buildings and replaced by those of the king, the only evidence that Caribbean buildings displayed arms.[165] Willoughby appointed Sir Robert Harley to the office of keeper of the seals of Barbados and the Caribbee Islands, with all the pomp of a feudal commission, but it is difficult to see how, in Surinam in particular, the office or the objects carried any authority.[166] Copies of the *Gazette* were sent to the West Indies to inform people of the death of Charles II in February 1685, though the ceremonial was "pompous" but "private," and "notwithstanding the distinction in the governments," the sovereignty of James VII and II was proclaimed in the Americas.[167] The death of the Duke of Albemarle in Jamaica in October 1688 coincided with the preparations of William of Orange and his Protestant force to sail against James to England, but the subsequent attempt to proclaim William king "with all possible ceremony," was not the problem that faced new acting governor Sir Francis Watson, but the fact that he had sought to assume his own title without the support of his council, and therefore he was without authority to manage what in the West Indies, was reduced from political rebellion to posturing faction.[168] While the body of Governor Francis Russell, who died in Barbados, was repatriated to Britain with a ceremony of drums, trumpets, and colors, Commodore Robert Wilmot, sailing out of Jamaica to counter the French, stood too much on his own authority according to the Governor, Sir William Beeston, and was denied a royal salute as his ship entered Port Royal harbor.[169] Later Beeston further revealed the futility of pomp, as a patent of William III, probably affirming that his government superseded that of the pirates, was the only one recorded as having been announced "with all the ceremony the places [Port Royal and presumably, Spanish Town] could afford," the standard phraseology deployed in the tropics to admit a deficit of both authority and money.[170] Those at the height of the political ladder were as hidebound by the cannibalistic relationship between action and intent as the meanest. The less authority one possessed, the more noise with which one announced it, and governors who claimed they were insufficiently supported in their "Honour and Dignity" provided an example for their underlings of avarice and faction.[171]

The contrast between empty ceremony and forceful action explains Rev. Holt's dismissal of the noise with which slaves warded off the spirits of the dead. It was also employed in descriptions of indigenous communities, in which Britons reduced the performance of peace and war to the acceptance of ceremony. Robert Sanford, one of the first English people to reconnoiter the area of the "Ashley and Cooper Rivers," gave us a description of Tuscacora amity in presenting tribute, being stroked on the shoulder by the palm of the hand while sucking in air through their teeth.[172] Richard Baxter warned against providing to those indigenous American children whose parents were not Christian the means to convert, for they would remain indifferent and regard baptism as instrumental.[173] Descriptions of violence on the part of nonwhites were so exaggeratedly stylized that action tipped into performance and back again to casual ritual. Dominican and St. Vincentian Kalinago did not only attack Montserrat and Antigua but consumed the land with fire and the people with acts of torture, rape, and cannibalism.[174] Crab Island was lost to a Spanish force that contained English, Irish, French, Turks, and a number of black people, among whom, one who detained a woman to ask directions, shot her twice in the belly.[175] Retrospective commentary on Jamaica divided the black population into those who had escaped slavery during the rule of the Spanish, saltwater slaves newly imported by the British, and Creoles born on the island during English rule. Taking over from the Akan to this last group was attributed the most ruthless and brutal violence in establishing de facto free maroon communities in the mountains:

> Monsters in Wickedness, Devils incarnate, Murders, Ravishers, Robbers, such as have wilfully set Fire to Houses, or to the growing *Sugar* Canes; and these being cunninger than you [other black people on Jamaica], and well acquainted in every Creek and Corner of the Island, lead you forth in all your Sallies on the *Whites*, and have assum'd the ruling and ordering of you in all other Matters. I need not say what worse than brutal Rulers they are, how they lie with your Wives, and ravish your Daughters before your Eyes, and how in their Wrath, or their Rum, they will plunge their Knives in your Bosoms or Bellies.[176]

That same patriarchy against which Jamaica maroons railed was ascribed in greater measure to them: internecine quarrels, domineering over children and the elderly, seducing or raping "the weaker and more ignorant Sort," vilifying the form of liberty exercised by maroons.[177] In the debate about English liberties, a distinction was being drawn between freedom to act within the bounds set by authority without restraint or coercion and the freedom to act as one willed. The laws, constitutional frameworks, rituals, and ceremonials by which the former was performed were not acquired without struggle but were increasingly lauded as the positive benefit of English/British rule. The latter was increasingly associated with license and regarded negatively. The maroons posed such a threat because they represented a 180-degree inversion of slavery to perform perfect liberty, and thus their freedom to act had to be rendered as immoral as possible.

In response to black revolt in Providence in 1639, settlers were urged to work their slaves harder.[178] The Governor, Nathaniel Butler, was already concerned that the numbers of black settlers would outnumber (and overpower) the white.[179] According to impersonation narratives, "designs" to kill the crew and escape slavery were formed during the Atlantic passage, despite the mix of peoples and languages aboard. It was possible to work hands free of shackles, using them to knock the shackles from the hands of others. Crew were killed and tossed into the sea: slaves were killed or chose to jump overboard.[180] In 1683, a man who was an officer in the militia in Barbados related to London the rumors of slave insurrection circulating on the island. The correspondent had been woken in the night by a messenger informing him that the whole leeward side of the island was in revolt. The correspondent mustered his men to Bridgetown, but was subsequently told by a cavalry major from a different regiment, that he

> could find no cause for the alarm; the negroes were quiet and had no arms. On inquiry, nothing could be made out against the negroes except four or five bold insolent blacks, who were well whipped as an example, and one old negro belonging to Madam Sharp, who frightened his mistress by saying of some Christians, who were beating negroes, that the negroes ere long would serve the Christians so. For which he was sentenced to be burnt alive, and was put

to death. Since this some foolish mischievous persons have scattered about the enclosed paper and others like it, forgetting that negroes are not able to read. If we could find out the authors of these papers, it would be right that they should be punished.[181]

An island-wide insurrection was reduced to the insolence of an old man cursing a woman; the disproportionate punishment of isolated individuals, who spat in the face of authority, stoked by planter pamphleteers. The aim was not to paint a human picture of the protagonists but to reassure Whitehall that Barbados continued controlled.

Overt references to black action as "rebellion," therefore, are rare.[182] Similarly, William Whaley started his account of an hundred-strong insurrection in north Jamaica with the news that they had "killed Seaverall white Men, Burnt and destroyed most of the Plantacons in St Maryes parrish," but everything that followed was designed to downplay it.[183] It meant a loss to their own plantation and those of their neighbors in St. Thomas in the Vale of six to ten men. As if to further explain the concept of runaways, the report added that a further three men had run away, but only in order to steal chickens, and then to use them in religious ritual. How then are we to distinguish between the escape and rebellion of larger numbers together and the gradual establishment of small groups on the fringes of an estate to collect provisions and kinsfolk, slowly engrossing family units until self-sufficient village communities were viable? Larger numbers escaped in St. Ann's Jamaica in 1673, to which Whaley alluded above (usually numbered at 200) or during the Coromanti rebellion at Sutton's, Clarendon, in 1690 (400); but this made more difficult the logistics of establishing villages that were both coherent and independent.[184] Planters were more exercised by the cost of putting down rebellion, leading to disagreements between the assembly that proposed a Poll Bill and Lieutenant-Governor Molesworth, who charged them with the hypocrisy of wanting all except themselves to pay.[185] Molesworth informed Blathwayt that these maroon communities were between 40 and 100 people, largely formed from slaves shipwrecked early in the 1670s, whose continued "mischief" made it difficult for the poorer settlers to flourish and pushed them off the island.[186] There was unrest in Antigua during 1687, with violent clashes between a party of runaways who built bulwarks and palisades. One in particular, later identified as George, "bid Defyance" to Captain Carden's troopers, and was "Chosen Governor of that Quarter," and the dissent was expressed in a rival ceremony of authority in which slaves gathered to see him "Jnstated" in office.[187] George had been carried shoulder-high around plantations as the chosen "grandy man," and on his home plantation, Smith's, had knocked the pipe from Thomas Smith's mouth for which he was beaten over the head. When he complained to the master, Robert Smith, George threatened the Smiths with burning down their plantation.[188] Deponents were sworn who gave evidence of George's usurpation of authority. Richard Borraston's 16-year-old son, Joseph, said it was only his mother's persuasion that had prevented him from reporting that

George threatened to push him into a copper of boiling sugar.[189] George's wife, Bess, then slapped Joseph Borraston's face, and George hit him in the chest, saying "in his negro Language, I^t was not for strength hee knocked his wife Bess."[190] George had come before the authorities before. In 1684, he had near-fatally stabbed Richard Lynch, who was clearing the highway to Rendezvous Bay, although Lynch seemed to have causelessly struck George first.[191] The Council meeting on March 24, 1687, just days after the aborted rebellion, concluded that Richard Lynch was a Christian man who would himself have been killed had not other slaves prevented it. George's other "outrages" would result in his being "Burnt To ashes."[192] Philip, one of the Governor's slaves who had offered support to the rebels, would, if his master subsequently saw fit, have his tongue cut out "that he might remaine as a Liveing Example." But he would lose a leg immediately. From the turn of the year 1702/1703 comes a lone mention of the "Cockling Pond gang," led by "Bulley," whose wife was being persuaded by Colonel Sadler to give evidence, and was to be reassured that even if she had contact with the rebels, if she were able to effect Bulley's capture, she should receive a free pardon.[193] These accounts credit slaves with choice, intent, and deliberation in their rejection of white authority, whether that be the assertion of authority itself, the actions to establish the character of that authority, mocking the ceremonial with which it was performed, or the language—African or Creole—in which it was expressed. The English account of the incidents use several constructions with which again to negate it. The numbers of the disgruntled are minimized, and their power and authority further undermined, because the fear they provoked disproportionately targeted the weak and vulnerable, or ridiculed and derided them for acting tyrannically among their fellows.

The Assembly in Nevis, asked to comment on the emigration of (white) people to Crab Island, Antigua, and elsewhere, blamed "the great Thefts and Insolencies of Negroes," demanded a "verry Severe Act" against it, and blamed the lack of a planting provision all over the Caribbean. Acts were subsequently drawn up "for preventing the Thefts and Insolencies of Negroes"; "against Negroes Committing Riotts or meeting in Great Compa[nie]s"; for preventing running away; and for planting provisions proportionate to the number of slaves. The authorities in the West Indies thought fit to send these to James II along with an encomium about the new-born "Prince of Wales Sprung from your Jllusterous loynes…to Govern the Brittish Empier."[194] In Montserrat, Governor Blakiston and his council noted the slaves had become "more Insolent than ever" with robberies and "other misdemeanours" committed by those who had "absented themselves" from their masters' plantations. The Assembly responded that legislation remained on the island "unsent home," and that in the absence of ratified legislation there was both defiance of authority and derision toward its authors, though the Assembly made no mention whether the defiance was from white, black, or both.[195] The same applied to curbing activity that in other circumstances would be wholly embraced by the community: in Barbados in 1680, black people were forbidden to learn a trade.[196]

White people's emphasis on the economic losses consequent on any activity further diminished the human aspect inherent in any self-assertion. Slaves working on an estate were tied to place just as tightly as they were bound to people: family and estate, one and the same, codified in the laws that regulated the consequences of their actions. They were denied the protection of the laws of English liberty and could only be granted "freedom" by their master. Rebellion could not be recognized and donoting that slaves were outside the law ensured that for the white planters, legitimate uprisings by black people did not exist, but only confirmation of their characterization as "heathenish, brutish and...uncertain." The threat from others operating outside English discourse—the Irish, (certain types of) Scots, runaways, pirates, maroons, those working with Britain's enemies—were, ironically, incorporated into the laws of English liberties because they operated from a place outside them.[197] Even on tiny Bermuda, when slaves were freed, they were obliged to leave the islands, or enter upon new bondage as slaves of the king.[198] There was evidence of design within the black community, but they were denied the opportunity to invest it with contemporaneous meaning. Even "harmless" activity, such as practicing a trade, would be dangerous in providing the means to autonomous action, or, ironically, as was the case on Robert Cunyngham's estate in which slaves were given tasks of some skill and learning, bound them closer to the family. In civil society, slaves were deemed incapable of emulating edifying behavior, only of inverting it.

In circumstances in which there was nothing awe-inspiring about power, it was apt to be imposed; claimed by force, violence, or insistence. In the white community, loss of control and self-mastery laid one open to charges of abandoned reason and abnegated authority. The greater the loss of control, the more incumbent it became to appear to demonstrate the contrary, and whether at the level of the household, government, territory, or empire, there was a battle to assert authority. In remote, unstable, and infant colonies, the need for a firm and steady hand frequently became a hefty slap. It put great trust in the self-restraint of the governor and thereby in his ability to restrain others. Some of the greatest critics of the powers claimed by Charles I held an interest in Providence, but whereas Charles would lose his head by exercising, over-exercising, and seeking to continue a power of veto, the island's governor was granted an absolute negative voice with little demurrer.[199] The only person to speak out was the minister Hope Sherrard, who pitted his own power to excommunicate against that of the governor to exercise the "rotten principle" of making the people "his absolute slaves and vassals," "that whatever he Commands be it either lawful or unlawful yet we must yield an absolute and active obedience...without any questioning power."[200] Those who pioneered settlement in south Carolina waited anxiously for Proprietor Ashley Cooper to send a governor, because in the words of William Owen, a governor "will suddenly drawe multitudes to this place besides those from New England [and] other p[ar]^{ts} who are alreadie fitting for this Countrey and as many p[er]sons Come from those sev^{r}all places soe it is not otherwise to be thought but that they wilbe of different Iudgem^{ts}

and as well pleased with ye Constitutions of ye Govr n^mt when Managd with a tempered and Vnderstanding person." Office required "prudent Manag^mt" by a man "of able parts soe he should be noe overgrowne zelote."[201] Prudent action and edificatory behavior was the order of the day, which was not a principle that would level men, any of whom could display prudence without having fortune, but rather was a mark of distinction and character. It was necessary to determine between "chimerical and practical politics...[and] to deal with such different characters in the same species as those of freemen and slaves, that they who command have a just sense of human nature itself, by which they can temper the haughtiness of the master, and soften the servitude of the slave." This was a characterization made of General Robert Hunter, who considered himself an opponent of the willfulness of enthusiasm. Self-restraint then was a cardinal virtue for a person in authority, but it was not necessarily one that needed to be applied to all aspects of a man's life.[202] Rather, it was a means to deal evenhandedly, cautiously, and politically, with all those who fell under that authority, such that one was trusted to determine between man and man. If one were in authority and yet a hypocrite, the secret was either not to get caught, or to elevate one's control to the level of unimpeachable.

The degree to which power was deemed to have tipped the balance into tyranny was dependent on who was making the judgment. Migrants who were shipped as prisoners of civil broils at home planted a captive and restless presence abroad, and sought escape from or compensation for their hurts. At the restoration of the monarchy in England, in 1660, Whitehall received floods of petitions on behalf of those who cited the Caribbean as a punishment they had not sought. Soldiers, not only from the ranks, "beareing too visible a stampe of loyalty," sent by the usurper Cromwell to the West Indies in 1654 should not be shipped back to England without their arrears.[203] Thomas Woodward lost his place in the assay office because he had refused his assent to the Engagement of loyalty to the Commonwealth in 1649 and went to Virginia, where he vowed to remain until the king's return. His son, John, successfully sued for his place at the Mint, but Thomas is likely to have remained, becoming the Lords Proprietors' surveyor of Albemarle County, Carolina, and an exponent of the theories of planting espoused by Sir Francis Bacon.[204] Henry Hastings claimed 60 acres and stock in Barbados. The original planter was St. George's Anthony Strange, who had fled, his lands forfeited after the murder of Captain Bowers in 1657. The land had been bought for £300 from "the late usurper Crumwell" but claimed that having served royalists faithfully in wars it should be conferred on Hastings.[205] For whatever reason they arrived in the Caribbean, there remained a symbol of residual loyalty to domestic politics which it remained necessary either to reaffirm—"I am here because I was despatched here by a good/evil power"— or became necessary to exaggerate—"everything under the sun is chaotic, run by usurpers/charlatans/fools and we must needs turn the Caribbean into Britain." Rev. William May of Kingston, Jamaica, summed up this second approach: "To be short and plain...they have no maxims of Church or State but what are absolutely anarchical." As such, (particularly) British men, whose politics already sat at the extremes of the spectra, arrived in the Caribbean and operated cheek-by-jowl with their diametric opposites.

The domestic debates about Church government of the 1620s and 1630s, which made puritan pilgrims in New England, also caused considerable internal unrest in Bermuda and Providence Island, and remained contagious in the ostensibly godless Caribbean because administrators equated orthodoxy with order and dissent or religious toleration with licentious anarchy. Attracting settlers with religious promises came with dangers. "Our desire," according to the Council of State to Daniel Gookin, transporting secondary migrants to newly acquired Jamaica, "is [t]hat this place...may be inhabited [by those] who know the Lord and walke in his ffeare that by their light they may enlighten the parts about them which was a heigher end of our undertaking this Design, and might alsoe from amongst them have persons fit for Rulers and Magistrates who may be an encouragem^t to the good and a terro^r to the evil doers."[206] Willoughby and Ashley Cooper did not offer religious toleration in mainland Surinam or Carolina because they believed in liberty of conscience (other than as a right for such as themselves) but because it would populate mainland areas quickly, drawing not only settlers from the mother countries but also those disenchanted with the prospects for faith elsewhere in the Caribbean.[207] Willoughby, who could also have been writing about himself, thought "the people of these parts, as they are nearer the Sun, so they grow more productive of theire ill humours, & dangerous practises which drive them out hither to seeke A Lively hood, when they could not bee admitted, for the evils they had done, to enjoy any being elsewhere."[208] Nicholas Leverton (a puritan Calvinist who operated both within and without the Anglican communion) and Henry Adis (a sort of General Baptist) praised Willoughby for his largesse, but most, including Adis, detected more license than liberty.

Carolina remained of concern to the Establishment of Church and State because it still migrated "the Scum of the Earth, and Refuse of Mankind," to balance out the Anglican loyalist incomers.[209] Robert Robertson had distilled all the politics of the region into Royalist versus Republican, placing the thought in the head of his black character, Compo-bell; a theme taken up by the antiquarian Nicholas Darnell Davis, whose history of Barbados was peopled by "Cavaliers and Roundheads," in which the legacy of the civil wars was polarized and fractious communities across the British Caribbean. Monarchical loyalists who involved themselves in American affairs tended to be extremists, pushed to greater declarations of patriarchy because their experience of letting people loose in a world in the state of nature confirmed Hobbes's most nightmarish visions. While monarchists Francis Willoughby and Humphrey Walrond became rivals in Barbados, they were also battling with their political opposites. One such, Samuel Farmer, chosen speaker of the Assembly, alarmed both Willoughby and Charles II, as the latest in a line of revolutionary levelers: "A very dangerous fellow; A great magna=Charta=man, and petition of right maker; the first that started upp, that kind of language here, which tooke so with the people;...a beginning to dance after the long Parliaments pipe, assuming to themselves the imitation of itt by the stile and title of the best of Parliam[ts] which was the Doctrine...John Cade...spread amongst the people."[210] The politics of Bermuda were already dyspeptic when the Commonwealth government in London saw fit not only to invest its government in a select group of republicans, but also to allocate to them land and shares, such that 50 years later Isaac Richier still referred to the "Regicides Land."[211] Championing commonwealth-style liberties in Surinam were: George, brother of the republican leader Henry Marten; Marten's friend Thomas Westrop; and minister and patron of Andrew Marvell, John Oxenbridge. Were the activists in the tropics, Robert Sanford who sailed for Carolina and John Allin who traded in Curaçao with the Dutch, libertarian-pioneers or traitors?[212]

It was therefore not only the need to impose order, but also to distance oneself from any person whose ideas and their effects were refractory, which pushed figures into controlling demonstrations of conservative patriarchy. He may have settled his patrimony with sectaries, republicans, and Jews, but Willoughby had made explicit that he planned to create an aristocratic West Indies to substitute that which he had lost in England. Christopher Monck, Lieutenant-Governor of Jamaica, was "sensible of the great Hono[r] and favours that his Ma[tie] did bestowe," on his father, George, whose title as Duke of Albemarle had been earned because he crossed over from commander of the Parliamentarian armies to architect of Charles II's restoration. Albemarle left its mark on place-names throughout the region, but with Christopher, the title became extinct. Shame had infected the household through "soe ungratefull and soe dishono[ble] a discent," because Christopher's heir "at law" "was married to the sonne of one of them that had a hand in that horrid murder of that blessed Martyr King Charles the first of blessed memory And therefore the said Duke cannot out of his duty to God allmighty or to his Ma[tie] permitt the Children of any discended from any Regicide to enioy any part of his Late ffather's Estate."[213] The history in Britain of Ashley Cooper as Earl of Shaftesbury continued to be difficult and antagonistic toward the monarchical regime when it slipped from its promise to promote religious toleration and he ended his days in the Netherlands in order to escape prosecution for High Treason. He patronized the philosopher of liberty and architect of the Fundamental Constitutions, John Locke, but Charles Woodmason was mistaken in attributing any residual, stubborn anti-Establishment fire in Carolina to the "Republican Spirit...the Old Leaven of Lord Shaftsbury and other the 1st principal Settlers," like Albemarle, or Landgrave Locke. Carolina was a feudal patriarchy.[214]

New world realities were still expressed in the discourses of the old, with reference to Charles I's misrule, the High Court of Justice, Charles' execution, Cromwell's usurpation, and later Stuart reenactments.[215] Using epithets drawn from the British broils of 1649, 1689, or 1707, rivals were accused of being republicans, sectaries, Whigs, Tories, or Jacobites, but their new identity was literally mundane. It could change from day to day. We have encountered Governor Kendall of Barbados, the reductionist who accused the Quakers of pacifism, gerrymandering, Jacobitism, Catholicism, being in league with Pennsylvania, and being lovers of French autocracy.[216] Often expressed as rumor, gossip, or diverting entertainment, it had disruptive—and sometimes fatal—consequences, without ever attaching ideology to practice. As illustrated by the accounts of the assassination of Daniel Parke, the ideas held by all the protagonists, and the actions they provoked, were related in such polarized and violent exchanges of metaphor, that reality becomes irrecoverable. It was white Britons' vacuous ceremony. At the time of the Monmouth Rebellion, the Governor of Bermuda kept a close eye on his dissident people: "Strange Whisperings went about ye Country; As, that now was the time, or never. the Right of the Crown was in the Duke of Monmouth; and y^t he was no Papist; that ye Protestant Religion now profest in Eng was Popery; and y^t the Pope was the Whore of Babilon, and was Drunk with ye Blood of ye Saints: with much more such like stuff."[217] In Jamaica, Governor Lynch had accused Sir Henry Morgan of masterminding a drinking clique, calling it the "Loyal Club," themselves Tories, and Lynch a Whig, which amounted to no more than six dipsomaniacs.[218] William Waddington produced his wife, 12 inhabitants of Barbados, and 32 former neighbors from Billingsgate to attest that he was no roundhead, and was never disaffected toward Charles II, and should be excused for having uttered in a house in Bridgetown the notion that the king ruled only by election and could be tried by the people, because drink had so dissociated his mouth from his brain that the idea floated airily and did not presage any action.[219] At Christ Church College, Oxford, the student Christopher Codrington had deviated just once and briefly from his anti-Catholic friends, to write a Latin encomium on the birth of James VII and II's son, James Stuart, the future Old Pretender.[220] His service to William of Orange in the West Indies, however, was unquestionable, except by Admiral Neville, whose best evidence that he was a Jacobite, came from his supposed "intrigue" with a knave, an incestuous person, a taphouse keeper, plunderers, and pirates.[221] The coarse sound of accusation lingered on the air, without ever forming itself in the mouth of a particular speaker.

Intentions for a new world gave rise to projections of grandiose ambition, and small ideas that might be contained at home went on flights of fancy. People trying to survive and flourish in the West Indies were expected to restrain them and act only in the greater interests of the ultimate sovereign power, but were diminished by how little was possible. Ideas of governance, authority, liberty, and servitude underwent serious reevaluation in the circumstances of new world realities, where every aspect of one's life could be used by a competitor against you, within an environment in which the stakes were raised but the repercussions could be sidestepped. Allegiances that functioned in the mother countries required jettisoning abroad. The region invited ideas to be pushed to extremes, in which Governor Daniel Parke, or George, the slave on Smith's Plantation, could be egregious or heroic by turns and to conflicting audiences. The Caribbean surely was Hobbes's state of nature, in which people acted with license and this a study of the inauthenticity of and mismatch between intent and action.[222] And thus the tropical colonies became victims of a grand irony: that while London politicians strove for greater control over the Americas, best achieved by uniformity and centralization, those trying to act in the tropics constantly devolved control to smaller and smaller units. The basic unit of authority was the household: a private sphere.[223] There were hierarchies of status—governors, citizens, servants, slaves—and within those, hierarchies of gender, ethnicity, and birthplace. In the household, the individual planter was both patriarch and freeman, with powers that included the right to determine the degrees of autonomy and autonomous action allowed to those who served.[224] In the public sphere, households were writ large, as congregations, parishes, or assemblies. Africans, almost from the start, indigenous peoples gradually, and Europeans by experience, were denied the opportunity to express the self-mastery, reason, and control that denoted liberty and inclusion, through law and citizenship within the community. They could not be part of the design: they could not be designers.

Conclusion: Design

When in 1671, John Ogilby, Charles II's "*Cosmographer, Geographick Printer*, and Master of the *Revels* in the Kingdom of *Ireland*," surveyed in 674 dense pages over 200 years of activity by rival Europeans to possess the lands and peoples of America, he used the word "design" 154 times. These were generally the public projections of individuals onto the lands and peoples of two continents: their place on the globe was "(as if design'd) for Transportation to *America*."[1] Cromwell's Western Design to humiliate the Spanish in the Greater Antilles evidenced the grand political deliberations of Whitehall and its servants, in an epithet coined by the pen of General Robert Venables to identify the mismatch between those "wholly cast…in the management of this western design" whose "pikes prove[d] too short."[2] It thereby excused poor human execution of God's Design: Jamaica was the prize for English sin. At a personal level, everyone who set off on a venture, a risk, or voyage; or who formulated a plan, speculated, described, surveyed and delineated; who made a bequest; built, cultivated, or destroyed, was about the business of designing and designating. Every action taken and every decision made, no matter how intimate, was the consequence of deliberation: what differed was the degree to which hegemonies, structures, and power curtailed many from fulfilling their designs. What resulted was vivid and cacophonous, hard to credit as the conscious creation of its actors, and running throughout are parallel narratives that are seemingly at odds. Exploring individual agency credits everybody with some degree of construction, turning the Caribbean world into competing designs and perpetual unease. But the long seventeenth century was not a detachable unsavory episode. The nastiness of their world may have encouraged emigration from it, in favor of imperial oversight from the comfort and leisure of that grand lifestyle that colonial adventurism and the labor of others enabled and maintained, but it created both nonetheless.

That the Caribbean remained loud, clamorous, and disputatious, despite parallel development and change, was noted by contemporaries who, after several decades of British activity, questioned what had been achieved. In 1704, the Anglican minister of St. Thomas's, Barbados, Samuel Fullwood, was told by "a very honest man" that "those of this generation are hastening the prediction of the first Grave settlers of this island,…lamenting the present state and management of affairs, that if the second did not ruin this island, the third would."[3] The principles of planting in virgin earth, described by Sir Francis Bacon at the start of our period as the pinnacle of heroic nobility, had by its end eroded to reveal a viciously corrupt plantocracy. Twenty years later, the new Treasurer of Barbados, George Plaxton, arrived from England and confirmed that the Caribbean contained "much the worst people, as to meum and tuum."[4] In other respects, however, he still possessed hope. Barbados had "the best Govern^r [in Henry Worsley] and the best Crop that ever was seen upon it."[5] Further, within one generation, Plaxton could make statements (in private at least) that formerly would have earmarked him and his master as the source of the rot. In the treasury, he could boast that "I am Judge and Jury, [and] issue Executions upon all defalters."[6] Crucially, he could effect designs that once would have signaled unwarranted interference in settlers' liberties. Plaxton addressed the dearth of currency and introduced paper money: he drew up each bill's design for his brother to take to a respected copperplater.[7] Charging an additional tax on each slave, at 7s 6d per person, on top of 2s 6d in duty already paid, would clear the debts of the island: Plaxton awarded himself a healthy commission of 1s 3d. His masters in Whitehall had embraced place and patronage to increase the control its servants had over its colonial limbs, which represented good governance if one had trust in one's agents and, ironically, the Plaxtons were under the influence of the Granville family, for whom Bevill had been such a disappointment. The Granvilles were now safely under the wing of the Hanoverians, and Worsley was with Plaxton's patron, John, Lord Carteret, at George I's German court, where he secured the further post of Controller of Customs— "worth 700li. P ann this mony"—to replace John Stevens, "a native of Barbados...of late much out of Order." This job he could depute to an underling and still "put something into my pocket when I leave ye Country."[8] When resident in the West Indies, Worsley represented a new breed of magistrate, who "covets very little Comp[a]^n[y] never drinks, diverts himself in planting variety of fruits and amuses himself in the gardens as much as the heat will give him leave."[9] The island levy raised £11,000 per annum to finance government, of which £7,000 maintained the person of the governor and the aloof dignity of the office, enabling its incumbent to design tranquil cultivated formality, removed from the disputation down the hill from Government House.

In 1610, survivors of the Bermuda shipwreck had represented the island as God's providential blessing and envisaged a colony as the Tree of Life, planted and watered by ancient patriarchs and nurtured by God's light in the original garden.[10] The destiny of the Bermuda survivors—Fullwood's "first Grave settlers," or "primitive" planters as John Jeaffreson had it—was, literally, to root themselves in the ground. The garden was established as teleological signifier of increasing cultivation: first primitive "Indian gardens" produced "Indian provisions," which were then gifted to, bartered with, or aped by new settlers, then measured individual proprietors' control over their plot, to become the ultimate designed place of leisure, refinement, and eternal rest.[11] At the "end" of the process of becoming cultivated, the garden marked manorial demesne, the patriarch's cool and shade, quiet and detachment from economic production, without departing from Eden's utopian ideal. Worsley appeared to be one of the first governors able to enjoy such a remove, but the early eighteenth-century examples of Cunyngham and Montgomery illustrate that the garden remained a metaphor for original mixed and self-sufficient planting.

Across the period, the free will to control one's own place was afforded to fewer people, increasingly divided along ethnic lines, determined from the mother country by economic, legal, or political interests of state or family, which accelerated the withdrawal of capital, leaving land and labor to be overseen by managers, who in turn bridled at reins held in England.[12] Possession of a colonial holding became a means to recoup debts, and the aphorism of empire, "production abroad; manufacture at home," turned the land from being the end and good in itself to become the instrument of a status and worth increasingly judged in Britain. In this process, the state was key, as colonial land became a means to cement executive power, and the (usually) smaller-scale finances of the plantocracy were the means for the Crown to recover its debts, through measures such as the Four and a Half, Royal African Company, and the customs' duties that financed the wars of the later Stuart period. Stymieing the development of self-contained island states was the mother country's price for economically productive commodities, and the sinews of tax and customs went into Whitehall's treasury, not those of Basseterre, Bridgetown, or Charlestown. For the "small island" of Britain to command a "large empire," production abroad and manufacture at home was cemented by naval and mercantile control of the Atlantic (then the South Sea) and the flow of people and goods upon it and around the globe.[13] Efficient centralized collection of revenue "saw the beginnings of an imperial administration slowly take shape."[14] Around 1714, it was still taking shape, but sufficiently formed to determine our retrospective image of Caribbean monoculture, plantation society, and slave labor. The "groans" of men like Littleton were those of a resident planter elite for whom these were the object of London's design.[15]

In the wake of the 1715 rising to restore a Stuart to the throne, the Council of Jamaica lamented that the "Lies and Stories" concocted about the island could not be countered without a vernacular press.[16] This was rectified in 1718 with the publication of the weekly *Jamaica Courant*.[17] When descriptions of the Caribbean were located in and directed from Britain, the more detached, removed, graphic, colorful, exotic, fantastical, and false they became. The West Indies was the subject of open-mouthed incredulity, with minimal attempts to uncover "the truth" at the time, and a consequent dilemma for the historian. Connection was increasingly directed by extraneous interests, and it became harder to develop intra-regional links. For the white community, family, friends, middlemen, agents, education, news, and markets were located in Britain: these became the links that mattered. Proponents of locally based networks struggled in vain against the view that self-regulation meant subversion.[18] Empiricism was no less commodified than any other aspect of the region. Peter Perkins and Jane Long, our sole example of a black/white connection sanctioned by law and faith, felt compelled to move to London. So did planters if they wanted to enjoy the fruits of their patrimony: even merchants born in the West Indies looked for ways to relocate to Britain.[19]

Intentions came into conflict with others' designs. People learnt that there was not "room enough" and individual designs became competitive and consequently hierarchical rather than cooperative. This was a process that rapidly marginalized indigenous peoples, and increased in speed and effectiveness as the century advanced, to relegate Africans and those of African heritage to the lowest, and in many cases at law, outside the hierarchy of humanity altogether. Thomas Tryon, who wrestled with the worst excesses of patriarchy, could not halt its degradation of the bodies of both black and white. Those of slaves were objectified: the white view that slaves lacked self-control. When the white community exhibited an absence of self-control, all the more reason for the firm hand of authority to impose order and civility from above, often sanctioning violence under the law, from Britain, when necessary.

Autonomy is expressed as will. It could be articulated in writing, as directive statements made as death approached, in government decrees, or in philosophical tracts to explain the human condition. It could be expressed in thought and deed. Allocating the responsibility to punish (or reward), or identifying another human being by livery, collar, or brand expressed individual will beyond structural determinants of behavior. Choosing to believe that Christianity was not incompatible with slavery placed the determinism of conscience or the consciousness that the flesh that they branded was human, in balance scales that calculatedly deliberated that it be outweighed by economic competitiveness. All thoughts and acts of defiance were autonomous deliberations too; the majority invisible at the time, many expunged from the record. In the hierarchy of agency, defiance came to personify refractoriness and thus disorder, while patriarchy was the measure of harmony. A history of the Caribbean world during the seventeenth century is made up from those expressions of will and agency that can be recovered. They sat within a spectrum of behavior and belief ranging from those who wanted to keep their lives exactly as they had been before their encounter with the region or the others who came to invade their space, to those who saw a chance to model an entirely new reality; with millions of compromised, competitive, cooperative, acculturated, obliterated positions in-between. The dichotomy of the Stuart Caribbean was that it fitted neither the British imperial narrative, nor the American narrative of independence which gave rise to 1776. It was a world of itself: and yet it gave rise to both. Whitehall, the Great Agent, slowly wrested control, quashing the libertarian designs of its Caribbean offspring and the grand design which won out was the imperial project. On the mainland of North America, its sons and daughters continued uppity and unruly, but in the Caribbean, disputatiousness had been their undoing.

Notes

Introduction: Disputation

1. E. A. Reitan, "From Revenue to Civil List, 1689–1702: The Revolution Settlement and the 'Mixed and Balanced Constitution,'" *Historical Journal* 13.4 (1970): 571–588; Allan Blackstock, *Loyalism in Ireland, 1789–1829* (London: Boydell Press, 2007); John M. Murrin, "Gordon S. Wood and the Search for Liberal America," *WMQ* 44.3 (1987): 597–601.
2. Baptista B[oazio], *The Famouse West Indian voyadge* ([Leiden], [1589]): JCB Map Collection, Cabinet B589/1.
3. Thomas Gage, *The English-American His Travail by Sea and Land: Or, A New Survey of the West-India's* (London, 1648).
4. Thomas Chaloner, "Upon This Worthy Work," in Gage, *New Survey*, A.
5. Richard Blome, *A Description Of the Island of Jamaica: With the other Isles and Territories in America, to which the English are Related* (London, 1672); and *A New & Exact Mapp of yͤ Isle of Iamaica* (London, 1671).
6. Her[man] Moll, *A Map of the West-Indies or the Islands of America* ([London], [1709]): JCB Map Collection, Z M726 1709/1/3-SIZE; H[erman] Moll, *A New Map of the North Parts of America claimed by France* ([London], 1720): JCB Map Collection, Cabinet C720/2; TNA, C66/2501: Patent Roll 5 Charles I, pt.5/no.5; "Modern Engineers Marvel at 17th-Century Boundary," *Lexington Herald-Leader* July 28, 1990; Royal Colonial Boundary, American Society of Civil Engineers (ASCE), http://cms.asce.org/People-and-Projects/Projects/Landmarks/Royal-Colonial-Boundary-of-1665/ (retrieved July 8, 2013) Ralph J. Gillis, *Navigational Servitudes: Sources, Applications, Paradigms* (Brill: Martinus Nijhoff, 2007), 65.
7. Sebastian Münster, *A Treatyse of the Newe India* (London, 1553); Sir Humphrey Gilbert, *A Discourse of a Discouerie for a New Passage to Cataia* (London, 1576); Pedro de Medina translated by John Frampton, *The Arte of Nauigation* (London, 1581); George Abbot, *A Briefe Description of the Whole World* (London, 1664).
8. Anguilla's Arawak name, *Malliouhana*, like its Spanish equivalent, referred to the serpent-/eel-like shape of the island. St. Christopher's was *Liamuiga* (fertile land); Nevis, *Oualie* (land of beautiful water); Montserrat *Alliouagana* (land of the prickly bush); Barbuda and Redonda *Wa'omoni* and *Ocananmanrou* (meanings unknown); and Antigua *Waladli* (land of fish oil).
9. TCD, MS 736, p. 187; César de Rochefort, *The History of the Caribby-Islands* (London, 1666); TNA, CO 1/19, no. 97, ff. 217–218ᵛ.
10. Thomas Glave, *Among the Bloodpeople: Politics & Flesh* (New York: Akashic Books, 2013); "*Among the Bloodpeople*, contains all the power and daring of his earlier writing but ventures even further into the political, the personal, and the secret."

11. Raymond A. Bauer and Alice H. Bauer, "Day to Day Resistance to Slavery," *Journal of Negro History* 27.4 (1942): 388–419; Sidney W. Mintz, "Enduring Substances, Trying Theories: the Caribbean Region as *Oikoumené*," *Journal of the Royal Anthropological Institute* 2.2 (1996): 289–311.
12. David Eltis, Frank D. Lewis, and David Richardson, "Slave Prices, the African Slave Trade, and Productivity in the Caribbean, 1674–1807," *Economic History Review*, New Series 58.4 (2005): 673–700; Alden T. Vaughan, "The Origins Debate: Slavery and Racism in Seventeenth-Century Virginia," *Virginia Magazine of History and Biography*, 97.3 (1989): 311–354.
13. Katherine Frank, "Agency," *Anthropological Theory* 6.3 (2006): 281–302; Paul Kockelman, "Agency: The Relation between Meaning, Power, and Knowledge," *Current Anthropology* 48.3 (2007): 375–401.
14. As differentiated by Isaiah Berlin, *Two Concepts of Liberty* (Oxford: Clarendon Press, 1958).
15. Fernand Braudel, *La Méditerranée et le Monde Méditerranéen à l'Epoque de Philippe II* 3 vols. (Paris: Armand Colin, 1949); Samuel Kinser, "Annaliste Paradigm? The Geohistorical Structuralism of Fernand Braudel," *American Historical Review* 86.1 (1981): 63–105; Jan de Vries, "The Return from the Return to Narrative," Max Weber Lecture no. 2013/01, *European University Institute, Florence: Max Weber Programme* (2013), 3. See also Jan de Vries, "Great Expectations: Early Modern History and the Social Sciences," *Review* 22.2 (1999): 121–149.

1 Place

1. William Alingham, *A Short Account of The Nature and Use of Maps* (London, 1703), pp. 41, 43.
2. "Philotheos Physiologus" [Thomas Tryon], *Friendly Advice to The Gentlemen-Planters of the East and West Indies* (n.p., 1684), pp. 68–69.
3. Examples of fallen and unfallen (sometimes standing/immovable and fallen); see BDA, RB 3/1, pp. 108, 109, 118, 121, 122, 126, 127.
4. TNA, CO 31/4, pp. 133–138.
5. Joseph Moxon, *A Tutor to Astronomie and Geographie* (London, 1670), Pref. sig.A3; W. Eland, *A Tutor to Astrologie* (6th edn., printed by Joseph Moxon, London, 1670), n.p.
6. John Locke, *Second Treatise on Government* (London, 1690); J. P. Day, "Locke on property," *Philosophical Quarterly* 16.64 (1966): 207–220; Karl Olivecrona, "Appropriation in the state of nature: Locke on the origin of property," *Journal of the History of Ideas* 35.2 (1974): 211–230; Barbara Arneil, *John Locke and America: the Defence of English Colonialism* (Oxford: Oxford University Press, 1996). See chapter 5.
7. TNA, CO 152/6, no. 63.
8. LancashireRO, DDF/2/5.
9. Robert Sanford, *Surinam Justice* (London, 1662), pp. 6–7.
10. GA, D7006/2/2.
11. LancashireRO, DDF/2/5.
12. NAAB Roe Book, box 187; TNA, C110/175.
13. CumbriaRO, Carlisle, D/LONS/L1/1/41/29.
14. NAS, GD34/933/1, unfol.,f.c.
15. NAS, GD297/159, unfol.; TNA, CO 1/22, no. 8.

16. TNA, CO 31/1, pp. 103–119.
17. CumbriaRO, Carlisle, D/LONS/L1/1/41/29a.
18. UMJRL, STP 2/3.
19. "Discription of the Coleny of Surranan," 1667; Copen "Prospect," 1695.
20. TCD, MS 736, pp. 100–101.
21. UMJRL, STP 2/3, f. 13.
22. TNA, CO 153/3, pp. 80–83.
23. GA, D1610/C1a.
24. ROLLR, DG7 Box 4982, ff. 2–10, 3.
25. [Borland], *Memoirs*, p. 10.
26. ROLLR, DG7 Box 4982, f. 4.
27. BLARS, L 29/164, [1], [2].
28. Memorial of Governor Haskett in answer to the deposition of the People of Providence and Michael Cole (1702): TNA, CO 5/1261, no. 126.
29. Sarah Barber, "Power in the English Caribbean: the proprietorship of Lord Willoughby of Parham" in L. H. Roper and B. Van Ruymbeke (eds.), *Constructing Early Modern Empires: Proprietary Ventures in the Atlantic World, 1500–1750* (Leiden: Brill, 2007), pp. 189–212.
30. "Description of Surranam," BL, Sloane 3662, ff. 27–49: "Lieut Gen[ll] Byams Journall of Guiana from 1665 to 1667." He referred to "Natives, [and] each other Nation." Sir Robert Harcourt, *A Relation of a Voyage to Guiana* (London: printed by John Beale for W. Welby, 1613); TNA, CO 1/67, no. 36c.
31. BL, Sloane 3662, ff. 27–49, f. 37.
32. TNA, CO 1/17, no. 88.
33. GA, D2700/PA1/9.
34. GA, D2700/PA1/9, f.b[v]; D2700/PA2/23.
35. CUL, Political Papers/85/7, *versus* TNA, PC1/58/B2A/Pt1.
36. Sir Francis Bacon, "On plantations," *The Essays or Counsels, Civil and Moral* (London, 1625), p. 198.
37. It was claimed that the woman was called Barbe and was Igneri (Arawak): Jean Baptiste du Tertre, *Histoire Generale des Antilles Habitees Par Les Francois* (2 vols.) (Paris, 1667).
38. Ordnance Survey for the Government of St. Christopher's and Nevis, Series E803 (DOS 343), 1:25,000. The Pelham River is also known as the Stone Fort River. Around 100 petroglyphs are located up-stream. Larger, more obvious stone engravings, referred to as the Wingfield Petroglyphs, are a mile up the coast from Bloody Point, toward the English capital at Old Road Town.
39. HC, BLAC, Jeaffreson Box 1, M3b.
40. ROLLR, DG7 Box 4982, f. 8.
41. Thomas F. Thornton, "Anthropological studies of native American place naming," *The American Indian Quarterly*, 21.2 (1997): 209–228; William S. Pollitzer, *The Gullah People and Their African Heritage* (University of Georgia Press, 2005), pp. 121–126; Clifton Ellis and Rebecca Ginsburg (eds.), *Cabin, Quarter, Plantation: Architecture and Landscapes of North American Slavery* (New Haven, CT: Yale University Press, 2010).
42. Alexander de Lavaux, "Map of the province of Surinam," ink on silk, 1737, Rijksmuseum, Amsterdam, NG-539.
43. TNA, PROB 20/671.

44. NAS, GD34/933/1, f.e.
45. Bernard Bailyn, "Politics and social structure in Virginia," in J. Morton Smith (ed.), *Seventeenth-century America: Essays in Colonial History* (Chapel Hill: University of North Carolina Press, 1959), pp. 90–115; Trevor Burnard, *Creole Gentlemen. The Maryland Elite, 1691–1776* (London and New York: Routledge, 2002); François-Joseph Ruggiu, "Extraction, wealth and industry: the ideas of noblesse and gentility in the English and French Atlantics (17th–18th centuries)," *History of European Ideas* 34 (2008): 444–455. I do not agree with Ruggiu or Michael Braddick on the imposition of civil social institutions on this particular frontier (p. 448).
46. [Vere Langford Oliver], *Caribbeana* (7 vols.) ii, Preface, p. vii.
47. CUL, Ch(H) Papers 84, 58: "The Case of Robert Johnson Esqr."
48. C. F. E. Hollis Hallett (ed.), *Butler's History of the Bermudas* (Bermuda: Bermuda Maritime Museum Press, 2007), pp. 91–93.
49. Douglas Watt, *The Price of Scotland: Darien, Union and the Wealth of Nations* (Edinburgh: Luath Press, 2007), p. 187.
50. The wording here is taken from the author's own transcription, edition, and modernization of the nineteenth-century transcription of BDA, RB 3/1, p. 56.
51. UMJRL, STP 1/1 [undocumented minutes].
52. LPL, FP xix, ff. 22–32^v.
53. LPL, FP xix, f. 22.
54. BDA, St. John's vestry minutes; Copen, "Prospect," 1695.
55. E. M. Shilstone, *Monumental Inscriptions in the Jewish Synagogue at Bridgetown Barbados* (London: Macmillan, 1988), pp. x, xxiv.
56. Norwood's survey published in *JBMHS*, vol. xv.2 (1948); Shilstone, *Monumental Inscriptions*, p. xxv.
57. As portrayed on the so-called "Robinson Painting," depicting a procession traveling into Bridgetown, thought to be Sir Thomas Robinson (Governor 1742–1747), painter unknown, in the collection of the Barbados Museum; Karl Watson, "The Sephardic Jews of Bridgetown," in Woodville Marshall and Pedro Welch (eds.), *Beyond the Bridge: A Series of Lectures to commemorate the 375th Anniversary of Bridgetown* (Bridgetown: Barbados Museum and Historical Society/UWI, Cave Hill, 2005), p. 41.
58. Edward Harris, "Look out for the Sawed Stone Jack," *Heritage Matters* ii (2008): 84–85.
59. John Smith, *The Generall Historie of Virginia, New-England, and the Summer Isles* (London, 1624), after p. 96.
60. Philip Lea, *A New Map of the Island of Barbadoes* (London, n.d. [c. 1700?]); Robert B. Potter, "Spatial inequalities in Barbados, West Indies," *Transactions of the Institute of British Geographers* new ser. 11.2 (1986): 183–198, 193.
61. UMJRL, STP 1/1 [undocumented minutes], [unfol.].
62. TNA, PRO 30/24/48/68.
63. TNA, CO 138/10, pp. 439–450; 137/5 no. 102; 137/45, no. 44; 138/10, pp. 451–457.
64. Pedro L. V. Welch, *Slave Society in the City: Bridgetown, Barbados 1680–1834* (Kingston, Ian Randle, 2003); Marshall and Welch (eds.), *Beyond the Bridge*; Robert F. Marx, *Port Royal Rediscovered* (n.p.: New English Library,

n.d. [1973]); Donny L. Hamilton (Texas A&M University), "The Port Royal Project," http://nautarch.tamu.edu/portroyal/index.htm (retrieved December 27, 2012); Michael Pawson and David Buisseret, *Port Royal, Jamaica* (Kingston, Jamaica: University of the West Indies Press, 2000).
65. James Robertson, *Gone Is the Ancient City: Spanish Town, Jamaica, 1534–2000* (Kingston: Ian Randle, 2005), pp. 52–53.
66. Richard Stafford, "Extracts of three letters," *Philosophical Transactions* iii (1668): pp. 791–796, p. 795; Phyllis Allen, "The Royal Society and Latin America as Reflected in the Philosophical Transactions 1665–1730," *Isis* 37.3/4 (1947): 132–138.
67. Michael Jarvis, *Bermuda's Architectural Heritage: St. George's* (Hamilton: Bermuda National Trust, 1998), pp. 118, 59–60.
68. TNA, CO 1/49, no. 23.
69. TNA, CO 1/47, no. 7.
70. BDA, St. John's Vestry Minutes, ff. 47–52.
71. BDA, St. John's Vestry Minutes, f. 51.
72. TNA C110/175, fragment.
73. NAS, CS96/3103; UMJRL, STP 2/8/1 [a]. Ward Barrett, "Caribbean sugar-production standards in the seventeenth and eighteenth centuries," in John Parker (ed.), *Merchants and Scholars: Essays in the History of Exploration and Trade* (Minneapolis: University of Minnesota Press, 1965), pp. 147–170.
74. NAS, CS96/3104, unfol.
75. D. W. Meinig, *The Shaping of America: A Geographical Perspective on 500 Years of History, Volume i: Atlantic America, 1492–1800* (New Haven, CT: Yale University, 1986); p. 68, "Transatlantic Interaction: Fixation Phases."
76. Brent Fortenberry, "The life of a church and the eventual death of a State House: public space in St. George's Bermuda," Unpublished PhD dissertation, Boston University, 2013.
77. Jarvis, *St George's*, pp. 16–17.
78. TNA, CO 124/1, p. 90; 124/1, pp. 114–117.
79. TNA, CO 31/2, pp. 388, 390, June 1680; Oliver, *Monumental Inscriptions*, p. 144; BDA, RB 6/13, p. 243; 6/12, p. 168; Larry Gragg, *Englishmen Transplanted the English Colonization of Barbados, 1627–1660* (Oxford: Oxford University Press, 2003), pp. 136, 170.
80. TNA, CO 31/2, p. 447.
81. TNA, CO 31/1, pp. 458–463, 472–478; 31/4, pp. 1–12, January 26, 1687.
82. TNA, CO 31/3, pp. 349, 350.
83. TNA, CO 1/57, no. 96, April 22, 1685, apparently the day before James' coronation in London.
84. TNA, CO 29/3, pp. 402–4; CO 31/1, pp. 715–718.
85. TNA, CO 31/4, pp. 479–84; TNA, CO 31/5, pp. 16–20, 72, 123–127; SCLA, DR73/2/Box 98/500, 501, 503.
86. SCLA, DR 37/2/Box 98/479.
87. TNA, PRO 30/26/90, p. 45: Schomburgk, *History of Barbados*, pp. 242–243; Larry Gragg, *The Quaker Community on Barbados: Challenging the Culture of the Planter Class* (Columbia: University of Missouri Press, 2009), p. 153; TNA, CO 28/10, no. 80; TNA, CO 29/11, p. 209.
88. TNA, CO 1/34, no. 110.

89. *A Brief and True Remonstrance of the Illegal Proceedings of Roger Osburn* (n.p., [?London], 1654), broadsheet; Howard A. Fergus, *Montserrat: History of a Caribbean Colony* (London: Macmillan, 1994); JCB, Cabinet Blathwayt 30, "Monserrat Insula Entire and in 4 parts herein Inclosed," the map of Montserrat from the "Blathwayt Atlas" (1673); Lydia Mihelic Pulsipher, "Assessing the usefulness of a cartographic curiosity: the 1673 map of a sugar island," *Annals of the Association of American Geographers* 77.3 (1987): 408–422.
90. UMJRL, STP 2/3; William Nelson (ed.), *Archives of the State of New Jersey*, 1st series, vol. xxi (Paterson, NJ: 1899); Jane van Vleck, *Ancestry and Descendants of Tielman van Vleek of Niew Amsterdam* (New York: Byrd Press, 1955). This may be his son, also Tielman, born *c.* 1635 in Bremen.
91. UMJRL, STP 1/1 [unfol].
92. UMJRL, STP 1/1; TNA, CO 1/59, no. 49, f. 177.
93. TNA C11/421/9: November 7 and 13, 1718; Vere Langford Oliver, *The History of the Island of Antigua*, pp. 74, 242.
94. TNA, CO 152/7, no. 28.
95. Lefroy, *History of the Bermudas*, pp. 11–12.
96. TNA, CO 1/56, no. 53.
97. Behn, *Oroonoko*, pp. 109, 137, 182, 195.
98. Behn, *Oroonoko*, pp. 216–217.
99. William Byam, *An Exact Relation of the Most Execrable Attempts of John Allin* (London, 1665), pp. 5, 6.
100. TNA, CO 1/53, nos. 66, 79.
101. William Prynne, *A Fresh Discovery of Some Prodigious New Wandring-Blasing-Stars, & Firebrands, Stiling Themselves Nevv-Lights... VVhereunto Some Letters and Papers Lately Sent from the Sommer-Islands* (London, 1645), pp. 11–13.
102. J[ohn] A[llen], *Judicial Astrologers Totally Routed* ([London], 1659), p. 27. Among Norwood's defenders were William Leybourn, *The Compleat Surveyor* (London, 1653), and Baptist Sutton who purchased a copy of Leybourn that year and added notes to himself. Richard Norwood, *Trigonometrie. Or, The Doctrine of Triangles* (London, 1631); R[ichard] N[orwood], *Fortification or Architectvre Military* (London, 1639); Richard Norwood, *The Sea-Mans Practice* (London, 1655); *Mr. Richard Norwood's VVorks* (London: for Richard Mount "at the *Postern* on *Tower Hill*; where you may have all sorts of *Mathematical* and *Sea* Books," 1694); Edward Harris, "Bermuda's man of knots and degrees," *Heritage Matters* 2 (2008): 28–29. Norwood set up a school on Bermuda in 1637.
103. P. F. Campbell, "Aspects of Barbados land tenure, 1627–1663," *JBMHS* xxxvii.2 (1984): 112–158; Aubrey C. Land (ed.), *Bases of the Plantation Society* (New York: Harper & Row, 1969).
104. Larry Gragg, "Concerning Mr. Huncks": Barbados governors as "tough guys" in the early English empire," *JBMHS* xliii (1996–1997): 1–14.
105. TNA, CO 140/1, p. 236; NAJm, 1B/11/2/27B.
106. TNA, CO 1/66, no. 88; TNA, CO 1/27, no. 40; TNA, CO 140/3, no. 642.
107. Vincent Wing, *Geodaetes Practicus: Or, The Art of Surveying* (London, 1664).
108. NAS CS96/3097, December 31, 1718. By 1730 he had bought Hammond's Practical Surveyor; Harris, Description & Use of the Globes and Orrery; Love's Surveyor; and Surveyours Guide: NAS, CS96/3103 unfol.; George Atwell, *The Faithful Surveyor* (London, 1665).
109. NAS, GD43/933/1, f.b.

110. Warrants for land in South Carolina, Columbia Record Office, SC; Philip Lea, *A New Map of Carolina*, 1680s; Warren Ripley, *Charles Towne: the Birth of a City* (Charleston, 1970), p. 23.
111. BDA, RB3/1, p. 494 (1644): Thomas Middleton committing to the Provost Marshall.
112. John Hapcott (surveyor), JCB Library, Shelf Et647 1 Ms.v.
113. Diana Chudleigh, *Smith's Parish* (Hamilton: Bermuda National Trust, Bermuda's Architectural Heritage Series, 2005), pp. 26–45.
114. Gragg, *Englishmen Transplanted*, p. 180.
115. BDA, RB3/1, p. 106; Pius Malekandathil, "Winds of change and links of continuity: a study of the merchant groups of Kerala and the channels of their trade, 1000–1800," *Journal of the Economic and Social History of the Orient*, 50.2 (2007): 259–286. BDA RB3/48; RB3/1, p. 616; RB3/1, p. 854; RB3/1, p. 54.
116. BDA RB3/1, p. 40.
117. BDA RB3/1, pp. 40, 45–46.
118. Surrey HC, LM/2022; Sir Dalby Thomas, *An Historical Account of the Rise and Growth of the West-India Collonies* (London, 1690), p. 16.
119. *CJ*, iv, February 7, 1644(5); TNA, CO 1/21, no. 32; TNA, Shaftesbury Papers, Section IX., Bundle 48, no. 68; North Carolina Office of Archives and History, Albemarle County, letter no. 4, John Whitty, London, to Peter Carteret, Secretary for Albemarle County, November 2, 1665, ff. 9–10.
120. TNA, PRO 30/24/48/4, ff. 7–8^v.
121. TNA, CO 5/286, pp. 5, 6.
122. TNA, MPI/1/406.
123. Bristol RO, 8032(1); Susan Baldwin Bates and Harriott Cheves Leland (eds.), *Proprietary Records of South Carolina* (3 vols.) (Charleston, SC: History Press, 2007); SCDAH, Map Box 8–4; SCDAH, Certificates of Admeasurement for Charles Towne, 1678–1756.
124. TNA, CO 5/286.
125. BDA, RB 6/14, p. 359.
126. BDA, RB 3/1, pp. 14, 498; RB 3/7, p. 383; RB 3/5, pp. 474, 475, 639; RB6/14, p. 559.
127. BDA, St. John's burial register, January 5, 1692(3), p. 16; St. Michael's parish register, p. 263, October 12, 1681; St. Michael's parish register, p. 321, May 14, 1685; Gragg, *Quaker Community*, pp. 60, 134.
128. TNA, CO 323/2, no. 94; BL, IOR: E/3/3, ff. 32–34.
129. Richard Jobson, *The Golden Trade* (London, 1623), p. 28.
130. TNA, CO 1/44, no. 61.
131. TNA, Shaftesbury Papers, PRO30/24/48, endorsed bundle 48, no. 66.
132. TNA CO 137/9, no. 80. Emphasis added.
133. *Thurloe State Papers*, vol. v, pp. 146–158.
134. John Hapcott, "This plott representeth the forme": JCB, Shelf Et647 1 Ms.
135. JCB, Cabinet Gm667 Di Ms: at a scale of one inch to three miles, which is approximately 1:20,000.
136. The settlement of "Irishmen" in Barbados, referred not to an origin in Ireland, but to those transported by Thomas Irish: BDA, RB 3/1.
137. BL Sloane 3662, ff. 27–49. While indigenous and incoming peoples seemed to be living cheek-by-jowl, the reality of travel from one part of Surinam to another would be long and slow.

138. NA, DD.P6/1/22/20; Ripley, *Charles Towne*, p. 16.
139. Cary Carson, Norman F. Barka, William M. Kelso, Garry Wheeler Stone, and Dell Upton, "Impermanent architecture in the southern American colonies," *Winterthur Portfolio* 16.2–3 (1981): 135–196; Roger H. Leech, "Impermanent architecture in the English colonies of the eastern Caribbean: New contexts for innovation in the early Modern Atlantic World," *Perspectives in Vernacular Architecture* 10 (2005): 153–167; Jason D. Moser, Al Luckenbach, Sherri M. Marsh, and Donna Ware, "Architecture of Providence, Maryland," *Perspectives in Vernacular Architecture* 9 (2003): 197–214; John Michael Vlatch, "The Shotgun House: an African architectural legacy," in William R. Ferris, *Afro-American Folk Arts and Crafts* (Lean Marketing Press, 1986), pp. 275–294.
140. NAS, CS96/3102: "A Dwelling House being a Stone Pavilion of two Roomes one for a Hall below and a Bed Chamber above valued at £300/ Two Lodging Roomes Boarded & Shingled....150/ One ditto £50. A Madeira Wine Cellar £40...90."
141. Clifton Ellis and Rebecca Ginsburg, "Introduction," in Ellis and Ginsburg, *Cabin, Quarter, Plantation*, p. 3.
142. Gragg, *Englishmen Transplanted*, pp. 127–128.
143. DerbysRO, D239M/E20452.
144. B. W. Higman, *Jamaica Surveyed: Plantation Maps and Plans of the Eighteenth and Nineteenth Centuries* (Kingston: UWI Press, 1998), pp. 252–256.
145. Barbara Heath, "Space and place within plantation quarters in Virginia, 1700–1825," and Garrett Fesler, "Excavating the spaces and interpreting the places of enslaved Africans," in Ellis and Ginsburg, *Cabin, Quarter, Plantation*, pp. 156–76, 27–50.
146. [John Oldmixon], *The British Empire in America* (2 vols.) (London, 1708), vol. ii, p. 15.
147. CumbriaRO, Carlisle, D LONS/L4/2/2: mansion house, boiling house, curing house, still-house, 2 windmills, cattle mill, trash house, corn house, rum houses, stables, 40 cottages.
148. GA, D1610/p. 73.
149. GA, D1610, pp. 74, 71; NAS, CS96/3104, p. 2: November 11, 1731, "Began to lay our Negrohouses at the Morning Star"; W[illiam] D[ouglass], *Summary, Historical and Political, Of the first Planting, Progressive Improvements, and Present-State of the British Settlements in North-America* (2 vols.) (Boston, MA, 1747), vol. i, p. 118.
150. Jerome S. Handler, "Plantation slave settlements in Barbados, 1650s to 1834," in Alvin O. Thompson (ed.), *In the Shadow of the Plantation* (Kingston: Ian Randle, 2002), pp. 125–161.
151. Thomas N. Bisson, "Medieval lordship," *Speculum* 70.4 (1995): 743–759.
152. DevonRO, 1926B/T/F /1/12.
153. SurreyHC, LM/778/21/4 [copy].
154. The information in this paragraph comes from the conflation of information provided within NAS, CS96/3104. Moko or Moco, rendered "Moccow" by Cunyngham, was a diverse range of Northwest Bantu peoples, being shipped from ports on the lower Cross River. Igbo is one of the language groups of modern-day Nigeria; Mina is the collective name given to diverse groups shipped from Elmina Fort.
155. The 10-year-old boy had the same father, but a different mother.

156. Since her name is listed as both Moko and Mina, she may also have been the mother of a daughter, aged 4.
157. NAS, CS96/3104, p. 2. The sapodilla is an evergreen fruiting bush, *Manilkara zapota*. The Mammee apple, *Mammea americana*, of the family *Calophyllaceae*, is rendered in the ledger "Mamisapeta."
158. The grandfather was "Moccow Nero" or Carpenter Nero, and the grandmother "Ibo Rose." Their daughter was known as "Moccow Jeany." Nero's other three children were Pitchey and Jack, the sons of Nero and Rose, aged ten and six, and Nero's youngest child was Dinah, aged four.
159. Trevor Burnard, "Slave naming patterns: Onomastics and the taxonomy of race in eighteenth-century Jamaica," *Journal of Interdisciplinary History* 31.3 (2001): 325–346.
160. NAS, CS96/3104, p. 4.
161. NAS, CS96/3104, p. 61.
162. NAS, CS96/3104, pp. 4–7, 54–56, 60: figures compiled from inventories of December 25, 1731.
163. Philip D. Curtin, *The Atlantic Slave Trade: A Census* (Madison, WI: University of Wisconsin Press, 1969), pp. 154–155.
164. [Robertson], *Account of the Hurricane*, pp. 15–16; Matthew Mulcahy, *Hurricanes and Society in the British Greater Caribbean, 1624–1783* (Baltimore, MD: Johns Hopkins University Press, 2005).
165. UMJRL, STP 2/8: Stapleton's instructions to attorneys. The reference to "cashee" has proven difficult to trace: Stapleton's Irish birth may mean that it is akin to an Irish "cashel" (an enclosure by strong fence or wall). The same sense of internal and external security is evinced in an account of a joint black and white rising in New York in 1742: [Daniel Horsmanden?], *A Journal of the Proceedings In the Detection of the Conspiracy Formed by some White People, in Conjunction with Negro and Other Slaves, for Burning the City of New-York in America and Murdering the Inhabitants* (New York and London, 1747).
166. C. E. Orser, Jr., "The archaeology of the African Diaspora," *Annual Review of Anthropology* 27 (1998): 63–82, 66; Ross W. Jamieson, "Material culture and social death: African-American burial practices," *Historical Archaeology* 29.4 (1995): 39–58; Jerome S. Handler and Frederick W. Lange, *Plantation Slavery in Barbados: An Archaeological and Historical Investigation* (Cambridge, MA: Harvard University Press, 1978).
167. DerbysRO, D518M/F81; BDA, RB 6/12, p. 514; BDA, RB 6/2, p. 175.
168. Jerome S. Handler, "An African-type healer/diviner and his grave goods: a burial from a plantation slave cemetery in Barbados, West Indies," *International Journal of Historical Archaeology* 1.2 (1997): 91–130, 93; Orser, "Archaeology of African Diaspora," p. 67; J. Taylor, "Historic of his life and travels in America. Containing a full geographical description of the Island of Jamaica" (1688): Ms., National Library of Jamaica, Kingston. Catherine A. Reinhardt, Chapman University, California: "Remembering and Imagine Slavery: Postcolonial identities and the memorial landscape in the Eastern Caribbean," http://www1.chapman.edu/~reinhard/index_files/Page11419.htm (retrieved December 24, 2011).
169. Handler, "African type healer/diviner," pp. 112–116.
170. D. R. Watters, "Excavations at the Harney site slave cemetery, Montserrat, West Indies," *Annals of the Carnegie Museum* 56 (1987): 289–318; David R. Watters, "Historical archaeology in the British Caribbean," in Paul Farnsworth

(ed.), *Island Lives: Historical Archaeologies of the Caribbean* (Tuscaloosa: University of Alabama Press, 2001), pp. 82–102.

171. Handler and Lange, *Plantation Slavery*, pp. 158–168; Robert S. Corruccini, Jerome S. Handler, Robert J. Mutaw, and Frederick W. Lange, "Osteology of a slave burial population from Barbados, West Indies," *American Journal of Physical Anthropology* 59 (1982): 443–459; Keith P. Jacobi, Delia Collins Cook, Robert S. Corruccini, and Jerome S. Handler, "Congenital syphilis in the past: slaves at Newton Plantation, Barbados, West Indies," *American Journal of Physical Anthropology* 89 (1992): 145–158; Jerome S. Handler, "Determining African birth from skeletal remains: a note on tooth mutilation," *Historical Archaeology* 28.3 (1994): 113–119; Jerome S. Handler and Robert S. Corruccini, "Weaning among West Indian slaves: historical and bioanthropological evidence from Barbados," *William and Mary Quarterly*, 3rd series, 43.1 (1986): 111–117.

172. Michael L. Blakey, "The New York African Burial Ground Project: An examination of enslaved lives, a construction of ancestral ties," *Transforming Anthropology* 7.1 (1998); Joyce Hansen and Gary McGowan, *Breaking Ground Breaking Silence: The Story of New York's African Burial Ground* (New York: Henry Holt and Company, 1998); Christopher M. Stevenson, "Burial ground for Negroes, Richmond, Virginia: validation and assessment," June 25, 2008, Virginia Department for Historic Resources, http://www.dhr.virginia.gov/pdf_files/SlaveCemeteryReport.pdf (retrieved December 23, 2011).

173. BDA, Vestry minutes of St. John's, Barbados, pp. 47–48.

174. BDA, St. Michael's parish register, p. 270.

175. BDA, St. Michael's parish register, p. 245.

176. In many instances, the names suffer from probably having been mis-transcribed. St. Michael's parish register, pp. 165, 186, 205, 225: John Domew (bur. April 5, 1671), Sarah Japh (bur. November 11, 1673), John Gosnell (bur. March 29, 1676), Hagar (bur. September 23, 1678); John, the son of John and Hannah Dally (bur. December 4, 1679). BDA, RL 1/1, p. 204, St. Michael's, March 8, 1675(6); BDA, RL 1/1, p. 208, St. Michael's, November 8, 1676 ("free negroes"). Hannah, daughter of John and Hannah Dally ("negroes"), baptized April 3, 1681: BDA, RL 1/1, p. 255. Hannah would go on to marry a free black man, John Lambey, in 1710: BDA, RL 1/2, p. 84.

177. BDA, Burial register of St. John's, Barbados, p. 17; 26 [month illegible] 1700, Mary, wife of Major Thomas Rous, envaulted in St. Philip's.

178. BDA, parish register of St. Michael's, p. 8 (1649).

179. BDA, parish register of St. Michael's, p. 82.

180. BDA, RB 6/5, p. 505.

181. BDA, RB 6/12, p. 347.

182. SCLA, DR 37/2/Box 98/475.

183. BDA, RB6/16, p. 255.

184. As a study of "necrogeography" this account has a considerable way to travel, but it has not been undertaken for the seventeenth century and not for the West Indies, unlike the nineteenth century mid-west: see Richard V. Francaviglia, "The cemetery as an evolving cultural landscape" *Annals of the Association of American Geographers* 61.3 (1971): 501–509.

185. NAJm, wills, vol. 6, f. 54.

186. NAJm, wills, vol. 6, f. 25; DevonRO, 1926B/T/F/1/12.
187. Oliver, *Monumental Inscriptions*, p. 2.
188. Among the earliest with such additional character reference flourishes is that of Charles Atkinson, who had served as a secretary to Sir Thomas Lynch and Lord Vaughan as Governors of Jamaica, and who, just about to embark for England "was seized by an invidious and malignant feaver under a paroxisme." He died on November 20, 1678 and his memorial is in St. Catherine's, Spanish Town. It is blue marble, with the arms and crest of Atkinson of Newark, Nottinghamshire. Also in St. Catherine's, Colonel John Bourden was a councillor but also "a lover of justice a loving husband a faithful friend and a good master," born Coleraine 1633, died Jamaica August 18, 1697. Sarah Tarlow, *Bereavement and Commemoration: An Archaeology of Mortality* (Oxford: Wiley-Blackwell, 1999).
189. Left side of the chancel. Samuel Barwick Sen was commander of the forces of "his Native Country," and died on New Year's Day, 1732(3), aged 62, while his son, Samuel, died on June 4, 1741, aged 38; Oliver, *Monumental Inscriptions*, p. 135.
190. Gray marble memorial, south wall of St. James, Holetown, to Ann Woodbridge, died on October 3, 1739, aged 36; Oliver, *Monumental Inscriptions*, pp. 134–135, 137.
191. Vere Langford Oliver, *More Monumental Inscriptions: Tombstones of the British West Indies* (Borgo Press, 1993), pp. 99–100, 129.
192. Up to 1720, 131 names were listed, the earliest being Aaron de Mercado "Hebrew" (1660), Ester Gaon, "Hebrew" (1666), and Isaac L Rizio, "Hebrew" (1667): BDA, RL 1/86, pp. 968–70. A drawing of this can be found in Shilstone, *Monumental Inscriptions*, pp. xxvi, 81; Watson, "Sephardic Jews," pp. 37–58.
193. Shilstone, *Monumental Inscriptions*, p. 2; Watson, "Beyond the Bridge," p. 44.
194. William Copp, St. Thomas's, Barbados: BDA, RL 6/6, p. 518; BDA, RB 6/16, p. 163.
195. St. Michael's parish register: p. 247 (August 13, 1680); St. Michael's parish register, p. 268 (April 5, 1682); BDA, RL 6/8 p. 264.
196. BDA, St. John's burial register: October 20, 1667 and [?February] 11, 1668.
197. Oliver, *Monumental Inscriptions*, pp. 138, 144. BDA, RL 4/18, p. 106.
198. BDA, RL 6/12, p. 535.
199. TNA, CO 28/11, no. 18 (iv).
200. BLARS, HW/92/11.
201. TNA, PRO 30/24/48/4, ff. 7–8^v.
202. HALS, D/EPT 4104C.
203. NA, DD/SY/289+290.
204. TNA, CO 1/47, no. 96; *CJ x*, pp. 75–77; Parliamentary Archives, HL/PO/JO/10/3/185/47 and HL/PO/JO/10/1/453/672, January 24, 1693.
205. NA, DD/SY/288+290.
206. NA, DD/SY/292.
207. BDA, Levy book of St. Michael's parish; vestry minutes of the parish of St. John, 1649–1683. This is Highway 2A, "Spring Garden Highway."
208. BDA, RB 2/162; 2/258; BDA, RB 3/774; BDA, RB 6/11, p. 457.
209. John Ogilby, *Novissima et Acuratissima Barbados. Descriptio per Johannem Ogilvium. Cosmographum Regium*, London, 1672, hand-colored map, 14 x 12 ins.

210. E[dward] Littleton, *A Proposal for Maintaining and Repairing the Highways* (London, 1692), pp. 7–9.
211. St. Michael's parish registers, March 13, 1684, buried "Bernard Riddle dy'd in broad path" (p. 301); May 6, 1685, "a poor man y^t dyed in the broad path his name unknown" (p. 321).
212. "An Act for the High-ways," *The Laws of Jamaica* (London, 1683), pp. 22–25.
213. TNA, CO 140/1, no. 110; TNA, CO 154/4, pp. 1–19.
214. UMJRL, STP 1/1 [undocumented].
215. TCD MSS 736, pp. 183–184.
216. [Lanigan] Flannigan, *Antigua and the Antiguans* (London: Saunders and Otley, 1844), pp. 49–50; UMJRL, STP 1/1.
217. Sarah Barber, "Not worth one Groat: the status, gentility and credit of Lawrence and Sarah Crabb of Antigua," *Journal of Early American History* 1.1 (2011): 26–61.
218. Robert Baker, "A New and exact map of the Island of Antigua," (London: T. Bowles and John Bowles and Son, 1748); Samuel Copen, "A prospect of Bridgetown in Barbados," engraved by J. Kip, n.p., 1695; BDA, RB 6/43, p. 95; BDA, RB 6/1, p. 30.
219. "A discription of the Coleny of Surranam," 1667.
220. Bates and Leland, *Proprietary Records* iii, pt. 9, p. 38.
221. BDA, RB 6/40, p. 295.
222. BristolRO, 8032(1), 1699.
223. In Surinam we can putatively attribute the name "High Street," location of the only Anglican church, St. Brigid, renamed Hooge Straat which runs to the quayside market. In Charleston, this is King Street, formerly the "King's Highway."
224. *Cedrela Odorata*: "Gentleman lately arriv'd," *The history of Caledonia, or, The Scots Colony in Darien* (n.p., 1699), p. 46.
225. UMJRL, STP 1/1.
226. C[harles] M[orton], "The Life and Death of Nicholas Leverton," f. 3: manuscript draft, in fair hand ready for press, privately-held in the Leverton family.
227. TNA, CO 1/22, no. 47.
228. TNA, CO 1/46, no. 75.
229. Bertrand van Ruymbeke, *From New Babylon to Eden: The Huguenots and Their Migration to Colonial South Carolina* (Columbia: University of South Carolina Press, 2006), pp. 192–199.
230. TNA, CO 5/286, no. 20.
231. TNA, CO 5/290, p. 92.
232. TNA, CO 1/47, no. 75.
233. Debate still rages over the degree to which the Goose Creek Men were renegades, uncontrollable Barbadians, Anglicans, enslavers of indigenous peoples; a combination, all, or none: L. H. Roper, *Conceiving Carolina: Proprietors, Planters, and Plots, 1662–1729* (London: Palgrave Macmillan, 2004); Alan Gallay, *The Rise of the Indian Slave Trade in the American South, 1670–1717* (New Haven, CT: Yale University Press, 2003). Described as a "disturbing antiproprietary faction," van Ruymbeke has added to the literature that the Goose Creek Men were neither Barbadian nor Anglican: van Ruymbeke, *From Babylon to Eden*, pp. 33–34.
234. TNA, 30/24/48, pt. 3, no. 94, p. 310, they "came to a town of Negroes Spatious [and] great but all wooden buildings." There were also Spanish towns and Indian towns; TNA, CO 139/1, f. 21; TNA CO 140/1, pp. 91–92; TNA, CO 140/1, no. 34.

235. TNA, CO 140/1, nos. 34, 39.
236. TNA, CO 140/4, pp. 334–336.
237. TNA, CO 1/28, no. 69.
238. TNA, CO 8/1; TNA, CO 8/2.
239. TNA, CO 1/24, no. 8; CO 1/24, no. 25; TNA, CO 1/25, no. 29.
240. TNA, CO 1/25, no. 30; TNA, CO 5/287, pp. 150–159.
241. Bev Carey, *The Maroon Story: The Authentic and Original History of the Maroons in the History of Jamaica, 1480–1880* (Gordon Town, Jamaica: Agouti Press, 1997).
242. César de Rochefort, *The History of the Caribby-Islands, viz, Barbados, St Christophers, St Vincents, Martinico, Dominico, Barbouthos, Monserrat, Mevis, Antego, &c in all XXVIII in two books... renderd into English by John Davies* (n.p. 1666), p. 202; Pollitzer, *Gullah People*.
243. SHC, DD/WHh/1089, pt. 7, f. 102. Of the 107 slaves inventoried on the Bybrook estate in 1700, only two were noted runaways—Normandy had been absent for 12 months and not heard of: SHC, DD/WHh/1089, pt. 7, f. 116c.
244. TNA CO 1/30, no. 49; TNA, CO 1/3, nos. 3, 3i., ii.; TNA, CO 1/28, no. 32; Pawson and Buisseret, *Port Royal*, p. 41. Yallah or Yhallah was the name given to a river in Jamaica and therefore to Yallahs, a settlement on the southeast coast in the parish of St. Thomas. Yhallahs the pirate was also known as Captain Yellows and Jelles de Lescat.
245. LPL, FP xvii 99–100^v; *Historical Register* (1717), pp. 78–79, 80–81; *Weekly Journal or British Gazetteer,* January 12, 1717.
246. BLARS, L29/164, f. [3]; Michael Craton, *A History of the Bahamas* (Waterloo, ON: San Salvador Press, 3rd edn, 1986), pp. 72–111.
247. TNA, CO 23/13, nos. 56, 56 i; *Articles, depositions, &c. of the people of New Providence, in an assembly held at Nassau, October the 5th, 1701. against Elias. Haskett* (London, 1702); PBS, "The blurred racial lines of famous families," http://www.pbs.org/wgbh/pages/frontline/shows/secret/famous/elding.html (retrieved July 21, 2011).
248. TNA, CO 37/12, ff. 63–64^v, 65–68^v.
249. TNA, CO 37/11, f. 114^v.
250. Charles Johnson, *A General History of the Robberies and Murders of the Most Notorious Pyrates, and Also Their Policies, Discipline and Government* (London, 1724), p. 66.
251. Ibid., p. 67.
252. Ibid., pp. 67–71.
253. Ibid., pp. 71–72.
254. TNA, CO 412/30, no. 2, pp. 1–4.
255. William Dampier, *A New Voyage Round the World* (London, 1697), i, p. 10.
256. SHC, DD/WHh/1089, pts. 6, 7.
257. SHC, DD/X/PG.
258. SurreyHC, LM/COR/6/40.
259. "With these *Indians* [women in Darién] we made an exchange, or had a truck, as it is called, for Knives, Pins, Needles, or any other such like trifles": Basil Ringrose, *Bucaniers of America. The Second Volume* (London, 1685), p. 7; Cohen, "Amerindian Atlantic"; Amy Turner Bushnell, "Indigenous America and the limits of the Atlantic world," in Greene and Morgan, *Atlantic History: A Critical Appraisal*, pp. 191–222.

260. NAS, GD34/933/1, ff. e, g, h; Thomas, *Historical Account, op. cit.*
261. TNA CO 28/2, no. 102, 44, pp. 212–229.
262. Sir Robert Mountgomery, *A Discourse Concerning the design'd Establishment of a New Colony to the South of Carolina, in the Most delightful Country of the Universe* (London, 1717); TNA, PC 1/58/B2A, pt. 1.
263. Mountgomery, *Discourse*, pp. 10–12. Moll's map of the Americas made in 1720 shows Azilia separately marked as a buffer zone between French and Spanish, corresponding with modern-day Georgia: H[erman] Moll, *A New Map of the north Parts of America claimed by France*, 1720, JCB Map Collection, Cabinet C720 /2.
264. [George Berkeley], *A Proposal For the Better Supplying of Churches in Our Foreign Plantations* (London, 1724), p. 10.
265. George Berkeley, *The Works of George Berkeley* (London, 1784) (2 vols.), vol ii, p. 419: engraved folding plate "The City of Bermuda Metropolis of the Summer Islands"; Edward Harris, "Dean of The Berkeley Institute," *Heritage Matters* 3 (2010): 102–103.
266. TCD, MS 736, p. 90.
267. A[phra] Behn, *To the Most Illustrious Prince Christopher Duke of Albemarle, On His Voyage to His Government Of Jamaica. A Pindarick* (London, 1687); George Berkeley, "Verses on the prospect of planting arts and learning in America," in *Works*, vol. ii, pp. 443–444; Mountgomery, *Discourse*, p. 7.
268. UMJRL, STP 2/8 [c].
269. BDA, RB 6/11, p. 68.
270. James Dobie and John Shedden Dobie, *Cunninghame Topographized, by Timothy Pont, A.M., 1604–1608* (Glasgow, 1876); Ruth Duthie, "The planting plans of some seventeenth-century flower gardens," *Garden History* 18.2 (1990): 77–102.
271. NAS, CS96/3102, f. 6.
272. TNA, PROB 20/671.

2 Resource

1. Speed, *Prospect* (1646 edn), pp. 42, 55.
2. Mountgomery, *Discourse*, pp. 6, 12.
3. Ligon, *History*, frontispiece, p. 23; Stuart B. Schwartz, *Tropical Babylons: Sugar and the Making of the Atlantic World, 1450–1680* (University of North Carolina Press, 2011).
4. Dunn, *Sugar and Slaves*, pp. 188–189; Ligon, *History*, frontispiece and poem by Ligon's cousin, George Walsh, A.
5. Thomas, *Historical Account*, pp. 13–14.
6. Steven Pincus, *Protestantism and Patriotism: Ideologies and the Making of English Foreign Policy, 1650–1668* (Cambridge: Cambridge University Press, 1996).
7. [Samuel Lee], *Eleothriambos or the Triumph of Mercy in the Chariot of Praise* (London, 1677), pp. 40–41.
8. THE COMMONWEALTH OF UTOPIA: *Containing a Learned and Pleasant Discourse of the Best State of a Publike Weale, as It Is Found in the Government of the New Ile called Vtopia* (London, 1639): mentioning "Ile" only once in the title.
9. BACONIANA. *Or Certain Genuine Remains Of S^R. Francis Bacon, Baron of Verulam, and Viscount of St. Albans* (London, 1679), pp. 35–36.

10. *New Atlantis. A VVork unfinished*, Epistle to the Reader, W. Rawley (n.p, s.n. [London, 1658?]), p. 11; Bronwen Price (ed.), *Francis Bacon's New Atlantis: New Interdisciplinary Essays* (Manchester: Manchester University Press, 2002).
11. J. Spedding, R. L. Ellis, and D. D. Heath (eds.), *The Works of Francis Bacon* (14 vols.) (London, 1857–1874), vol. iii, p. 156; Francis Bacon, *Essays, Civil and Moral*, "Of Plantations" (first page).
12. Jeffrey Knapp, *An Empire Nowhere. England, America, and Literature from Utopia to The Tempest* (Berkeley, CA: UCP, 1992); Charles Frey, "*The Tempest* and the New World," *Shakespeare Quarterly* 30.1 (1979): 29–41; Thomas Bulger, "The utopic structure of *The Tempest*," *Utopian Studies* 5.1 (1994): 38–47; Meredith Anne Skura, "Discourse and the individual: the case of colonialism in *The Tempest*," *Shakespeare Quarterly* 40.1 (1989): 42–69; John Wylie, "New and old worlds: *The Tempest* and early colonial discourse," *Social & Cultural Geography* 1.1 (2000): 45–63.
13. "The Battle of the Summer Islands" (1645), in three cantos: G. Thorn Drury (ed.), *The Poems of Edmund Waller* (London, 1893), pp. 66–73; Timothy Raylor, "The early poetic career of Edmund Waller," *Huntington Library Quarterly* 69.2 (2006): 239–266.
14. Michael D. West, "Drayton's 'To the Virginia voyage': from heroic pastoral to mock-heroic," *Renaissance Quarterly* 24.4 (1971): 501–506; Rosalie L. Colie, "Marvell's "Bermudas" and the Puritan paradise," *Renaissance News* 10.2 (1957): 75–79.
15. Eileen Stamers-Smith, "Reflections of the Bermuda flora," *Garden History* 8.3 (1980): 115–127.
16. C. F. E. Hollis Hallett, *Butler's History of the Bermudas* (Bermuda Maritime Museum Press, 2007), pp. 220–221. See also Butler, from St. George, to Sir George Yardley, Virginia, December 2, 1621.
17. Lefroy, *History of the Bermudas*, pp. 10–11, 84–85 (BL Sloane MSS 750, the account of Nathaniel Butler).
18. George Berkeley, "A Proposal for the better supplying of Churches in our Foreign Plantations," in *The Works of George Berkeley* (2 vols.) (Dublin, 1784), pp. 11–13.
19. Ian Gregory Strachan, *Paradise and Plantation: Tourism and Culture in the Anglophone Caribbean* (University of Virginia Press, 2002), p. 34; Benjamin Bissell, *The American Indian in English Literature of the Eighteenth Century* (New Haven, CT: Yale University Press, 1925); JCB Map Collection, Cabinet Gm67 ThJ.
20. John Smith, *A Description of New England* (London, 1616), A3.
21. Philip Nichols, "Preacher," in *Sir Francis Drake Reuiued: Calling vpon This Dull or Effeminate Age, to followe His Noble Steps for Golde & Siluer* (London, 1626); Sir Francis Drake, Philip Nichols, and Francis Fletcher, "Preachers," in *Sir Francis Drake Revived. Who Is or May be a Pattern to stirre up all Heroicke and Active Spirits of These Times* (London, 1653); and still in 1683 "to divert that Spirit of Contention that is now arisen in every one almost against his Brother, and to excite, in the Spirits of Young People especially, an Æmulation of this Worthy Patriot in Advancing the Glory of their Country by Foreign Conquests": *The Voyages Of the Ever Renowned Sr. Francis Drake into the West Indies. Viz. His Great Adventures for Gold and Silver* (London, 1683), To the Reader, likely the words of the publisher, Thomas Malthus.

22. NA, DD/SY/289; Hakluyt, *Principal Navigations*, p. 265.
23. Ute Kuhlemann, "Between reproduction, invention and propaganda: Theodore de Bry's engravings after John White's watercolours," in Kim Sloan (ed.), *A New World: England's First View of America* (London: British Museum Press, 2007), pp. 78–92.
24. "THE pictures of sondry things collected and counterfeited according to the truth in the voyage made by Sr Walter Raleigh knight, for the discouery of La VIRGINEA" (1585): BM, P&D 1906,0509.1.1; Thomas Hariot, *A Briefe and True Report of the New Found Land of Virginia* (London, 1588: Frankfurt am Main, 1590); J[ames] Wooldrig [Wooldridge], "Indians of Virginia and North Carolina," c.1675, oil on linen, 752 x 1092 mm, Private Collection.
25. Hariot, *Briefe and True Report*, title page of London 1588 edn.
26. The Morgan Library & Museum, New York, MA 3900, the bequest of Clara S. Peck (1983): 199 images mostly of black chalk underdrawing, overlaid with pen, brown ink and watercolor, selectively glazed with gum, made c. 1586, bound in the late eighteenth century as *Histoire Naturelle des Indes* (binding: 300 x 210 mm; individual leaves: 293 x 197 mm).
27. Elsie Murray, "The "Noble Savage," *Scientific Monthly* 36.3 (1933): 250–257.
28. Alden T. Vaughan, "From white man to redskin: changing Anglo-American perceptions of the American Indian," *American Historical Review* 87.4 (1982): 917–53, 921–929.
29. BL Sloane 3662, ff. 37^v–42^v; Joyce Lorimer, *Sir Walter Raleigh's Discoverie of Guiana* (London: Hakluyt Society, 2006), p. 272.
30. TCD, MS 736, pp. 80–84; Bodl., Rawlinson MSS C vol. xciv; Vincent Harlow, *Colonising Expeditions to the West Indies and Guiana, 1623–1667* (Hakluyt Society, 2nd ser. vol. lvi, London, 1925), p. 28.
31. Ligon, *History*, pp. 29–30.
32. Behn, *Oroonoko*, pp. 3, 4–5, 6–7.
33. Behn, *Oroonoko*, pp. 8–9, 10.
34. Karen Ordahl Kupperman, *Settling with the Indians: the Meeting of English and Indian Cultures in America, 1580–1640* (London: Dent, 1980); Eadem., "English perceptions of treachery, 1583–1640: the case of the American savages," *Historical Journal* 20 (1977): 263–287; James Axtell, *The European and the Indian: Essays in the Ethnohistory of colonial north America* (Oxford: Oxford University Press, 1981); H. C. Porter, "Reflections on the ethnohistory of early colonial north America," *Journal of American Studies* 16.2 (1982): 243–254.
35. Behn, *Oroonoko*, p. 3.
36. BM, P&D 1906, 0509.2, and P&D 1906, 0509.1.13: "A chiefe Herowans wyfe of Pomeoc. and her daughter of the age of 8. or. 10. yeares," watercolor over black lead, touched with bodycolor, white (altered) and gold, 263 x 149 mms"; compare with Theodore de Bry engraving, "A chieff Lady of Pomeiooc," in Thomas Hariot, *A Breife and True Report* (Frankfurt am Main, 1590); Sloan, *New World*, pp. 62, 94, 122–123.
37. "An Acc^o of Indian trade sent to Carolina": TNA, PRO 30/24/48/13, f. 48, within the account of the costs of the ship *Carolina*.
38. Samuel Clarke, *A True and Faithful Account* (London, 1670), p. 16.
39. To go simpling was to gather these.

40. Poisonous weed was poison ivy, *Rhus toxicodendron*. Hallett, *Butler's History*, pp. 25–27.
41. Savile Reid, *The Birds of Bermuda* (Bermuda: Royal Gazette Office, 1883), p. 27: this is probably the Virginian partridge (*Ortyx Virginiana*).
42. Hallett, *Butler's History*, p. 29.
43. William Bullock, VIRGINIA *Impartially Examined* (London, Imprimatur, April 19, 1649), p. 8.
44. William Castell, *A Short Discoverie of the Coats and Continent of America* (London, 1644), p. 40, describing Guatemala; Richard Blome, *A Description of the Island of Jamaica* (London, 1672), p. 13.
45. TNA, CO 1/24, no. 8.
46. TNA, PRO 30/26/90, p. 44; TNA, PRO 30/26/90, pp. 15, 41.
47. J. K., *The Court and Country Cook* (London, 1702); Mary Eales, *Mrs Mary Eales's Receipts* (London, 1718); "A Gentleman Residing there", *The Groans of Jamaica* (London, 1714), p. 25.
48. TNA, CO 1/14, no. 35; TCD MS 736, pp. 80–84, 84–85,157–164, 158.
49. BDA, RB 3/1, p. 212; RB6/10, p. 181.
50. SurreyHC, LM/2022.
51. G. Terry Sharrer, "The indigo bonanza in South Carolina, 1740–90," *Technology and Culture* 12.3 (1971): 447–455.
52. TNA, CO 138/7, pp. 124, 125.
53. Davis H. Rembert Jr., "The indigo of commerce in colonial north America," *Economic Botany* 33.2 (1979): 128–134, 128.
54. BDA, RB 3/1, p. 56; SurreyHC, LM/2022.
55. William Bullock, *Virginia Impartially Examined* (London, 1649), pp. 30–33; Edward Williams, John Ferrar, and John Goddard, *Virginia, More Especially the South Part Thereof, Richly and Truly Valued* (London, 1650), p. 18.
56. UCL, MS ADD 70, [volume] f. 9^v; [volume] f. 35^v.
57. *A Brief Description of The Province of Carolina* (London, 1666), p. 4; H. B. Croom, *A Catalogue of Plants, Native or Naturalized, in the Vicinity of New Bern, North Carolina* (New York: G. P. Scott, 1837), p. 43.
58. T[homas] A[my] Gent., CAROLINA; *or a Description of the Present State of That Country, and The Natural Excellencies Thereof* (London, 1682), p. 16.
59. David G. Sweet, "Indigo in world history: production, distribution and consumption," http://davidgsweet.com/worldhistory/Indigo.pdf [retrieved June 18, 2012]; Elise Pinckney (ed.), *The Letterbook of Eliza Lucas Pinckney, 1739–1762* (Charleston: University of South Carolina Press, 1972); Sharrer, "Indigo bonanza," *op. cit.*; Ruth Stungo, "North American plants at the Chelsea Physic Garden: some new first records," *Garden History* 21.2 (1993): 247–249.
60. TNA, CO 154/1, pp. 79–87, 1670; UMJRL, STP 2/5.
61. TNA, CO 28/37, nos. 30, 31; CUL, Ch (H) Papers 37/1.
62. M. B. Hammond, "The Cotton Industry. An essay in American economic history: Part I. The cotton culture and the cotton trade," *Publications of the American Economic Association*, New Series, no. 1 (1897), pp. 3–382, 6.
63. Yields of around 177 pounds per acre for the years 1867–1900: Robert W. Fogel and Stanley L. Engerman, "Slave agriculture in the antebellum South," in Robert Whaples and Dianne C. Betts (eds.), *Historical Perspectives on the American Economy: Selected Readings* (Cambridge: Cambridge University Press, 1995), p. 235.
64. BDA, RB 3/1, pp. 109–110; BDA, RB 3/2, pp. 305–306, 307–308.
65. BDA, RB 3/1, p. 111; RB 3/1, p. 117.

66. A "flat bale" typical by the mid-eighteenth century, produced by a wooden screw press pushed to the limit, weighed 480 pounds with a footfall of nine square feet.
67. J. Edward Hutson (ed.), *The Voyage of Sir Henry Colt to the Islands of Barbados and St. Christopher, May–August 1631* (Barbados: Barbados National Trust, 2002); BDA, RB 3/1, p. 112.
68. BDA, RB 3/1, p. 116.
69. BDA, RB 3/1, pp. 13–14.
70. BDA, RB 3/1, pp. 121–122.
71. BDA, RB 3/1, p. 32.
72. BDA, RB 3/1, pp. 109–110.
73. *A Summarie and True Discourse of Sir Frances Drakes VVest Indian Voyage* (London, 1589), p. 20: reference to Dominica. *Discoverie of the Large, Rich, and Bevvtifvl Empire of Gviana* (London, 1596), p. 43.
74. *Orders and Constitvtions* (London, 1622), pp. 39, 43, 55–56.
75. *Orders and Constitvtions*, pp. 61–62.
76. William Golding, *Servants on Horse-Back* (n.p., 1648) pp. 5, 22–23.
77. Jonathan Israel, *Dutch Primacy in World Trade, 1585–1740* (Oxford: Oxford University Press, 1990), p. 66; Elizabeth Brooke Tolar, "Chain smoking: linking Virginia's and Barbados' commercial tobacco production," unpublished Masters' thesis, East Carolina University, 2010, p. 80.
78. C.T., *An Advice How to Plant Tobacco in England* (London, 1615), B; Marcy Norton, *Sacred Gifts, Profane Pleasures: A History of Tobacco and Chocolate in the Atlantic World* (Ithica, NY: Cornell University Press, 2008); TCD, MS 736, p. 158.
79. James A. Williamson, *The Caribbee Islands under the Proprietary Patents* (Oxford: Oxford University Press, 1926), pp. 9–10, 219; TNA, Chancery Proceedings Ch. I. C60/ no.38(i); *Winthrop Papers, Volume I, 1498–1628* vol. i (Massachusetts Historical Society, 1929), pp. 356–357.
80. Dunn, *Sugar and Slaves*, p. 50.
81. James Stewart, *A Counterblaste to Tobacco* (London, 1604), pp. B–B2; Everard Maynwaringe, *King James His Counterblast to Tobacco* (London, 1672).
82. Quoted in *The Touchstone or, Trial of Tobacco* (London, 1676), p. 30; [Anon], *The Armes of the Tobachonists* (broadsheet, London, 1630).
83. [Attributed to Blasius Multibibus, part of *A Solemne ioviall Disputation*], *The Smoking Age, or, The Man in the Mist* (Oenozphthopolis, i.e., London, 1617), p. 88.
84. Richard Hayes, *The Negociator's Magazine of Monies and Exchanges* (London, 1730), p. 157; B. E. Supple, "Currency and Commerce in the Early Seventeenth Century," *Economic History Review* (new series) 10.2 (1957): 239–255.
85. Paper credit was issued in South Carolina in 1702 for an expedition against San Augustín, in 1711 for an expedition against North Carolina, and 1715 for the Yamassee War: [Attributed to William Douglas], *A Discourse Concerning the Currencies of the British Plantations in America* (Boston, MA, 1740), p. 18.
86. Lou Jordan, "Somer Islands Hogge Money of 1616: the historical context," *The Colonial Newsletter* 123 (2003): 2465.
87. SCLA, DR 37/2/Box 98/487: A Jacobus was a gold coin of the reign of James I, worth 25s; a Guinea at this date was worth £1. A checkeen, cheffin, chquin, or Zechin was a coin of the Ottoman Empire: Solomon Lowe, *Arithmetic in two parts* (London, [1749]), p. 147.

88. Thomas, *Historical Account*, p. 9; SCLA, DR 37/2/Box 98/ 470.
89. [Douglas], *Discourse*, pp. 7–8.
90. A. Talbot Bethell, *The Early Settlers of the Bahamas* (Nassau, 3rd edn., 1937), pp. 88–89.
91. TCD, MS 736, pp. 87–94.
92. TCD, MS 736, pp. 95–96.
93. TCD, MS 736, p. 92.
94. BDA, RB 3/1–7 cover the years 1639–*c.* 1720; RB 3/48 is the index volume.
95. HALS DE/HL/12560.
96. Ligon, *History*, p. 85.
97. Ibid., p. 95.
98. SurreyHC, LM/2022 [b].
99. ULBL, ML v84/2.
100. BDA, St. John's parish vestry minutes, pp. 8, 58.
101. BDA, Levy Book of St. Michael, ff. 50, 52.
102. UMJRL, STP 2/8/1 [a].
103. C.T., *Advice*, A3; R. B[and], *London Tryacle, Being the Enemie to All Infectious Diseases* (London, 1612), p. 1.
104. Hannah Wolley, *The Queen-Like Closet* (London, 1670), p. 163: "Irish aquavitae" was aquavitae flavoured with aniseed, liquorice, dates, raisins, and sweetened with molasses.
105. Christopher Merret, *The Accomplisht Physician* (London, 1670), p. 78; Thomas Blount, *Nomo-Lexicon: A Law Dictionary* ([London], 1670), Yy; *An Act for the better ordering the selling of Wines by Retail*, 12 CII (1661).
106. *Act against Molosses*, Edinburgh, August 9, 1704.
107. HALS DE/HL/12560.
108. STP 2/8/1 [b].
109. NAJm, vol. 3, ff. 323–324, 1690: rum was valued at 1s 6d per gallon, wine at below 3d per gall.
110. TNA CO 1/18, no. 154; Ligon, *History*, p. 27.
111. TNA C110/175.
112. NAS, CS96/3102, n.p.
113. TCD, MS 736, p. 169.
114. SurreyHC, LM/2022.
115. BDA, RB 3/1, p. 126.
116. TNA, C110/175, no. 1.
117. Josiah Brown, *Reports of Cases, ... 1701, to ... 1779* (London, 1780), vol. iii, p. 285; TNA C110/175.
118. TNA C11/421/9.
119. Bryan Mawer, *Sugarbakers: From Sweat to Sweetness* (Welwyn Garden City: Anglo-German Family History Society, 2007), pp. 9, 27–28.
120. Patrick McGrath (ed.), *Merchants and Merchandise in Seventeenth-Century Bristol* (Bristol: Bristol Record Society Publications, 1955), vol. xix, pp. 57–58, 238.
121. BristolRO, AC/WO.16(6)a. I believe from other references that this is calculated in sterling. Aldworth Elbridge owned an $^{11}/_{16}$ share in The Spring, 960 acres (1723). The Elbridges were heavily encumbered, requiring partners and shareholders, but that would imply that production at its height was a mere pound of sugar per acre, which cannot be correct.
122. CKS, U908/T227/1: £1 *per cwt* considered in 1682 the price below which a ground could be abandoned for hop growing. CRO, Carlisle, D/LONS/W1/33.

123. TNA C110/175, no. 5.
124. LPL, FP ix, f. 76. The necessaries remained much the same: candles, soap, flour, cheese, butter, meat, and clothing. It is not clear whether the correspondent believes black cloth to have cost 14 pence or shillings a yard in England, which was sold for £7 10s 6d in Charles Town with a further £10 to make a suit. Holland linen was about 15s a yard, but in the English midlands around the same date, linen cloth was 22d per ell (45"), or wool jersey about 7d per yard: NA, DD/E/118/2.
125. TNA, C110/175.
126. TNA, CO 5/1184, p. 563; CO 194/2, nos. 44, 44i, 44ii; CO 137/9, no. 17.
127. UMJRL, STP 2/3. Rum was adopted as the Navy ration in 1687, and the ½ pint a day adopted in 1731.
128. *Acts of Assembly...Leeward Islands*, "Act for attainting...and for the better Government of Slaves," Antigua, December 9, 1723, pp. 206–17; Blome, *Description of the Island of Jamaica*, p. 90. In this case, the slaves of Jamaica were derided for spending Sundays in dancing, wrestling, or "truck[ing] away for basic clothing" rope which they had plaited from tree bark.
129. BDA, RB 3/1, p. 59.
130. Castell, *Short Discoverie*, p. 5.
131. CumbriaRO, Carlisle, D/LONS/L1/1/41/29.
132. CUL, Ch (H) Papers 37, 1–10: West Indies 1715–1719, Virginia 1715–1719; *The True State of England* (London, 1726), p. 115.
133. Edward Grimstone, *The Estates, Empires, & Principallities of The World* (London, 1615); Sir Francis Brewster, *Essays on Trade and Navigation* (London, 1695), p. 20.
134. BDA, RL 1/1, p. 103; BDA, RL 1/22, p. 24; BDA, RB 6/35, p. 482; CRO, Carlisle, D LONS/L4/1/69.
135. CUL, Ch (H) Papers 37, 1–10; Philip Miller, *The Gardener's Dictionary* (4 vols.) (9th edn., London, 1835), p. 421; Edward Strother, *Materia medica* (London, 1727), pp. 10–11, 79.
136. Eleanor Gibney, "*Lignum vitae*: Beauty, strength and the fallibility of medicine," *Newsletter of the St John Historical Society* (Virgin Islands), vol. ix.7 (2008): http://www.stjohnhistoricalsociety.org/Articles/LignumVitae.htm (retrieved May 11, 2012); Harold J. Cook, "Markets and cultures: medical specifics and the reconfiguration of the body in early modern Europe," *TRHS* 21 (2011): 123–145.
137. Adam Bowett, "The age of snakewood," *Furniture History*, xxxiv (1998): 212–225; JCB Library, "Discription of the Coleny of Surranan". L. B. Comvalius, *Surinamese Timber Species: Characteristics and Utilization* (Paramaribo, Suriname, 2010), suggests that "snakewood" refers not to the appearance of the veneer but to a Europeanization of the local name "*snek-udu*," of *Loxopterygium sagotii*; not the same snakewood as that of Guyana, which is *Brosimum guianense*. The consensus among workers of this now rare wood is that it is the very definition of hardwood.
138. F. Lewis Hinckley, *Directory of the Historic Cabinet Woods* (New York: Crown Publishers, 1960); SCLA, DR37/2/Box 98/499.
139. CUL, Ch (H) Papers 37/1 (1715) dry ginger and Jamaica pepper only, cotton wool; Ch (H) Papers 37/5 (1719) aniseed and green ginger.
140. CornwallRO, AR/10/619.

141. CornwallRO, DD/CY/1675, proved Prerogative Court of Canterbury, September 6, 1703.
142. DevonRO, 2065M-4/Z1; Mabel Quiller Couch, *Cornwall's Wonderland* (London and Toronto: J. M. Dent, n.d. [*c*. 1914]).
143. CornwallRO, AR10/403; AR/10/28, 1705; AR/10/408; CornwallRO, AR 12/61, 62; CornwallRO, CA/B47/43.
144. Cornwall RO, DD/T/1305 and 1312.
145. [Edward Littleton], *The Groans of the Plantations: or A True Account of Their Grievous and Extreme Sufferings by the Heavy Impositions upon Sugar* (London, 1689), p. 5.
146. Copen, "Prospect"; BDA, RB 6/43, p. 95; BDA, RB 6/1, p. 30.
147. TNA, CO 1/48, nos. 59, 59i.
148. TNA, CO 31/6, p. 13.
149. Copen, "Prospect"; SCLA, DR 37/2/Box 98/481.
150. SCLA, DR 37/2/Box 98/487, 1696.
151. UMJRL, STP 2/3.
152. This is described as a levy for Tatch houses. The word tatch or tache was that most frequently used by British producers of sugar and rum (and other commodities) for the containers in which they were produced and often shipped away from the West Indies. It derives from the old French, to mean plate of iron, but closer in meaning is *tacho*, used in Spanish America to mean "bucket" or specifically, as *tacho para acúzar*, a sugar pan, but it does not seem to have made its way into English language dictionaries. Nor was it the word used for the consignments of sugar that reached England, usually measured in hogsheads, or, if more general, "chests". M. Taylor and M. A. Getaz, "Sensors for crystallisation control in vacuum pans—a review of Fives Fletcher experience over the past 25 years," *International Sugar Journal* 112.1344 (2010): 678–685; Thomas Roughley, *The Jamaica Planter's Guide; or, A System for Planting and managing a Sugar Estate* (London: Longman, Hurst, Rees, Orme, and Brown, 1823), p. 360; Ligon, *History*, p. 40.
153. UMJRL, STP 2/3 (b), folio 8b.
154. The figure of 1½ d is arrived at by splitting the difference between the farm price for sugar in the 1660s and that in 1686 as noted in Nuala Zahedieh, *The Capital and the Colonies: London and the Atlantic Economy, 1660–1700* (Cambridge: Cambridge University Press, 2010), p. 176.
155. UMJRL, STP 2/3 (a), f. 8.
156. TNA, CO 1/9, nos. 61, 62, 63; Robert Brenner, *Merchants and Revolution: Commercial Change, Political Conflict and London's overseas Traders, 1550–1653* (Princeton: Princeton University Press, 2003), pp. 258–259.
157. Sir Benjamin Rudyerd, *A Speech Concerning A West Indie Association* (n.p. [London], 1641).
158. TNA, CO 1/14, no. 35; TCD MS 736, pp. 80–84, 84–85.
159. Brenner, *Merchants and Revolution*, p. 92; Williamson, *Proprietary Patents*, pp. 21–40; TNA, CO 1/9, no. 32.
160. Sarah Edwards Henshaw, *Our Family: A Little Account of It for My Descendants* (Oakland, CA: 1891), pp. 8, 11.
161. C. S. Firth and R. S. Rait (eds.), *Acts and Ordinances of the Interregnum, 1642–1660* (London, 1911), vol. ii, pp. 472, 669.
162. *CJ* i, p. 14.
163. TNA, SP 14/21.

164. Charles L. Bland, *A Vision of Unity: the Bland Family in England and America, 1555–1900* (Williamsville, NY: privately published, 1982).
165. Samuel Pepys, *Diary*, September 14, 1664; Neville Williams, "The tribulations of John Bland, merchant: London, Seville, Jamestown, Tangier, 1643–1680," *Virginia Magazine of History and Biography* 72.1 (1964): 19–41.
166. Possibly after Rowland Truelove, a London clothworker, who accumulated substantial lands in Virginia by transporting people there.
167. Williamson, *Proprietary Patents*, pp. 83–87.
168. HALS, DE/HL; TCD, MS 736, p. 77.
169. William B. Bidwell and Maija Jansson (eds.), *Proceedings in Parliament 1626* (vol. 1, House of Lords) (New Haven, CT: Yale University Press, 1991).
170. Edward Hyde, *The History of the Rebellion and Civil Wars in England* (6 vols.) (1888). £400,000 in 1640 would be worth £35 billion in 2005.
171. Gragg, "Concerning Mr. Huncks," *op. cit*; J. H. Bennett, "The English Caribbees in the period of the Civil war, 1642–1646," *WMQ*, 3rd series, vol. 24.3 (1967); Gary Puckrein, "Did Sir William Courteen really own Barbados?," *Huntington Library Quarterly* 44.2 (1981): 135–149.
172. *LJ* ix, pp. 49–54.
173. TNA, T 1/1, no. 54; *LJ* vol. vi, pp. 280, 563–564.
174. *LJ* vii, p. 578.
175. Firth and Rait, *Acts and Ordinances*, pp. 912–913.
176. HALS DE/HL/12557, [a]; 12613.
177. *LJ* ix, pp. 49–54; TCD, MS 736.
178. David J. Appleby, "'God forbid it should come to that': the feud between Colonel Molesworth and Major-General O'Brien in Portugal, 1663," *The Seventeenth Century* 26.2 (2011): 346–367.
179. HALS, DE/HL/12549.
180. HALS, DE/HL/12612.
181. John Raitby (ed.), *Statutes of the Realm* (London, 1819), vol. v, p. 291; HALS DE/HL/12602; Joseph Foster, *Alumni Oxonienses, 1500–1714* (London, 1891).
182. HALS, DE/HL/12553, [c]; TNA, CO 1/15, nos. 22 and 24.
183. HALS, DE/HL/12570.
184. HALS, DE/HL/12597; *Calendar of Treasury Papers*, vol. 1, pp. 1–15.
185. HALS, DE/HL/12611.
186. HALS, DE/HL/12553; 12568.
187. Basil Duke Henning, *The History of Parliament: The House of Commons, 1660–1690* (3 vols.) (London: Boydell and Brewer, 1983), pp. 466, 510.
188. HC, BLAC, Blaithwaite Box M13.
189. TNA, CO 1/19, no. 92, f. 110.
190. HALS, DE/HL, 12611 [b]; 12613.
191. Thomas Carew, *Hincillae Lacrymaw; or, An Epitome of the Life and Death of Sir William Courten and Sir Paul Pyndar* (London, 1681), p. 22.
192. TNA, T 1/1, no. 54.
193. TNA, CO 152/3, no. 16i; *Acts of Assembly Passed In the Island of Montserrat;…1688…1740* (London, 1740), pp. 1–4.
194. William A. Shaw (ed.), *Calendar of Treasury Books* (1676–1679), vol. V, pt.1 (London: HMSO, 1911), p. xv.
195. As claimed by Henry Guy: Disposition Book, vol. ii, p. 301, February 5, 1683(4).

196. TNA CO 1/44, no. 43; HALS, DE/HL, 12615; 12572; 12609 [d; 12612; 12613 [b].
197. TNA, CO 153/1, f. 27; Don Mitchell, "The second generation," Selected readings, "Anguilla from the Archives Series," The Anguilla Archaeological and Historical Society: http://aahsanguilla.com/Selected%20Readings/5.%20The%20Second%20Generation.pdf (retrieved, January 26, 2012); TNA, CO 1/27, no. 29; TNA, CO 1/27, nos. 30, 31; James S. Olsen and Robert Shadle (eds.), *Historical Dictionary of the British Empire* (Westport, CT: Greenwood Press, 1996), vol. i, p. 43; C. S. S. Higham, *History of the British Empire* (New York: Longmans, Green and Co., 1921), p. 54; Oliver, *Caribbeana*, vol. i, pp. 9–10.
198. TNA, CO 1/45, no. 78; CO 1/47, no. 45.
199. William Thomas Morgan, "The British West Indies during King William's War (1689–97)," *Journal of Modern History* 2.3 (1930): 378–409.
200. TNA, CO 153/4, pp. 325–338.
201. TNA, CO 153/5, pp. 6–8.
202. [Littleton], *Groans*, p. 2.
203. TNA, CO 71/ 2. nos. 1, 1 i, ii; Oldmixon, *History*, vol. ii, p. 52.
204. TNA, PRO 30/32/52.
205. UMJRL, STP 2/4; "Minute Book: July 1660," *Calendar of Treasury Books, Volume 1: 1660–1667* (London, 1904), p. 9; TNA CO 1/16, nos. 4, 5, and 6.
206. TNA, T 64/88.
207. TNA, CO 153/5, pp. 6–8; TNA, T 64/88, Apr., 1695; Douglas, *Discourse* p. 7.
208. The East India Company had more specific grades of servant, of which the most lowly was a Writer, employed to keep records, and the next level up was a Factor.
209. SHC, DD/X/PG.
210. BDA, RB 3/3, p. 532.
211. David Dobson, *Barbados and Scotland, Links 1627–1877* (Baltimore, MD: Genealogical Publishing Company, 2005), p. 112; TNA, CO 124/2.
212. BDA, RB 6/15, p. 247.
213. Russell R. Menard, *Sweet Negotiations: Sugar, Slavery and Plantation Agriculture in Early Barbados* (University of Virginia Press, 2006); NAS, GD34/843/1/20; GD34/843/2/2; GD34/843/5/17; GD34/920 (copy); GD34/921; GD34/922; GD34/923; GD34/924; CS7/569, ff. 287–9, 574; BDA, RB 3/3, p. 532.
214. HALS DE/HL/12578.
215. HALS, DE/HL/12560; 12561.
216. HALS, DE/HL/12591.
217. St. Michael's marriages, June 24, 1669: BDA, RL 1/1 p. 142; BDA, RB 6/8 p. 512; HALS, DE/HL/12561, 12580; John D. Runcie, "The Problem of Anglo-American Politics in Bellomont's New York," *WMQ*, 3rd series, 26.2 (1969): 191–217.
218. HALS, DE/HL/12596.
219. TNA, CO 152/3, no. 16, f. 73.
220. *The State of the Case*; [Littleton], *Groans*, p. 5.
221. BDA, RB 3/1, p. 754.
222. TNA, CO 1/20, no. 7.

223. TNA, CO 1/44, no. 45. Contemporaries used the word "cocket," the origin of which is obscure, as is the point at which "docket" became preferred. W. E. Minchinton, *The Naval Office Shipping Lists for Jamaica, 1683–1818* (Wakefield: Microform Academic Publishers, 1977).
224. UMJRL, STP 1/1 [undocumented minutes] [unfol.].
225. TNA, CO 1/3, no. 3.
226. TNA, CO 152/3, no. 16.
227. TNA, CO 1/62, no. 27.
228. TNA, CO 37/1, no. 6; Dobson, *Scottish Emigration*, pp. 60–61.
229. [Anon.], *The State of the Case of the Sugar Plantations in America* (London, 1695).
230. *An Answer to the Sugar Bakers or Sugar Refiners Paper* (London, 1695), p. 2
231. [Littleton], *Groans*, p. 10.
232. SHC, DD/WHh/1089, pt. 7, f. 115.
233. SHC, DD/WHh/1089, pt. 7, f. 109.
234. SHC, DD/WHh/1089, pt. 5, f. 9.
235. *Acts Of Assembly* (1690–1730) (London, 1734), p. 128.
236. Clarke, *True, and Faithful Account*, p. 81.
237. *State of the Case*.
238. *Answer to the Sugar Bakers*, p. 1; *Interest of the Nation*, p. 6.
239. [Littleton], *Groans*, pp. 3, 5–6; [Anon.], *The Linnen and Woollen Manufactory Discoursed with the Nature of Companies and Trade In General* (London, 1691).
240. [Anon.], *The Interest of the Nation as It Respects All the Sugar-Plantations Abroad, and Refining of Sugars at Home, Truly Stated* (London, 1691), p. 6; [Anon.], *The Irregular and Disorderly State of the Plantation-Trade Discuss'd* (n.p., [London?], [?1695]); DerbysRO, D239 M/E 17020–17021; TNA, CO 138/13, pp. 81–84.
241. [Littleton], *Groans*, pp. 5–6, 8, 11, 12, 16.
242. *State of the Case*; *Answer to the Sugar Bakers*, p. 1; [Littleton], *Groans* pp. 1, 2, 10.
243. *Interest of the Nation*, p. 6.
244. Mountgomery, *Discourse* p. 12.

3 Connection

1. "Elizabeth Daur: of Jane Long/ by a Negro": St. Philip baptism register, p. 48; Parish register St. Philip Barbados, March 11, 1687(8): p. 51; LPL, SPG General Correspondence, July 1707–1800, f. 67; Dunn, *Sugar and Slaves*, pp. 255–256; TNA, RG6/0499/f.365: General Register Office: Society of Friends' Registers, Notes and Certificates of Births, Marriages and Burials. The Monthly Meeting of Horsleydown provides no named evidence for Peter Perkins or Jane Perkins (neé Long), so they probably did not join the Quaker community, but were some of the anonymous London community recipients of charity, or Peter's body was discovered by the Quakers and thus buried within Park Burial Ground: Quaker Library, Euston, London, "The third Book of the Monthly Meeting...1690."
2. NAS, RH4/211; LPL SPG Papers, General Correspondence, July 1707–1800, ff. 64–76.
3. NAJm, Parish registers of St. Andrew, May 30, 1675, pp. 5, 20, 26.

4. "The form of solemnization of matrimony," *The Book of Common-Prayer* (edition consulted, Printed by Charles Bill, London, 1704), n.p.
5. Joseph Addison, *The Evidences of the Christian Religion* (London, 1730), p. 161; John Ayliffe, *Parergon Juris Canonici Anglicani* (London, 1726), p. 326.
6. Joseph Besse, *A Collection of the Sufferings of the People Called Quakers* (London, 1753), p. ii.
7. Richard Pinder, *The Spirit of Error, Found, and Discovered* (n.p., n.d. [1660?]); W[illiam] D[ewsbury], *This For Dear Friends In London, And them that are Aboard the Ship, in order to Transportation* (n.p., n.d. [?1665]).
8. William Brend, *A Seasonable Warning, and Wholesome Advice for Merchants, Owners and Masters of Ships, and That Are Occupied in the Great [sic] Waters* [n.p., dated December 17, 1664), broadsheet; Rev. Ch. 18 11–14.
9. Gragg, *Quaker Community*; TNA, CO 1/64, no. 12, ff. 24–24^v.
10. Gragg, *Quaker Community*, p. 154.
11. [?Robert Rich], *Hidden Things Brought to Light or the Discord of the Grand Quakers among Themselves* (n.p. [London], 1678), preface.
12. Robert Rich of Barbados, *Something in Answer to a Book...Called, The Hidden Things Brought to Light* (London, 1679); Robert Rich, *Mr. Robert Rich His Second Letters from Barbadoes* (London, 1679); Robert Rich, *An Epistle to the People Called Quakers* (London, 1680); Robert Rich, *Abstracts of Some Letters* (London, 1680); Nigel Smith, "Hidden things brought to light: enthusiasm and Quaker discourse," *Prose Studies* 17.3 (1994): 57–69.
13. *Hidden Things*, pp. 26–27.
14. TNA, CO 1/18, no. 65 [b]; TNA, CO 1/18, no. 65.i, April 30, 1664.
15. John Perrot, *To the Upright in Heart and Faithful People of God: Being an Epistle Witten in Barbado's* (London, 1662), written November 3, 1662, p. 10; J. P., *Glorious Glimmerings of the Life of Love, Unity, and Pure Joy* (London, 1663); John Perrot, *To All Simple, Honest-Intending, and Innocent People* (London, 1664); *The Vision of John Perrot* (London, 1672); [John Perrott], *Battering Rams against Rome* (London, 1661); J. P., *Immanuel the Salvation of Israel* (London, 1658); J. P., *Discoveries of the Day-Dawning to the Jewes* (London, 1661); [Rich], *Hidden Things*, p. 21; *Truth* Vindicated (London, 1665).
16. Besse, *Collections*, ii, p. 326.
17. TNA, CO 1/16, no. 106; BDA, RB 6/13, p. 237; BDA, RB 6/10, p. 147; BDA, RB 6/13, p. 115; Barry Reay, "Popular hostility towards Quakers in mid-seventeenth-century England," *Social History* 5.3 (1980): 387–407.
18. BDA, RB 6/10, p. 21; TNA, PROB 11/337; BDA, RB 6/8, p. 168.
19. DRO Jm, LOS 1&2/2.
20. TNA, CO 28/2, no. 22, [b]; Kristen Block, "Cultivating inner and outer plantations: profit, industry, and slavery in Early Quaker Migration to the New World," paper to Early American Economy and Society Markets and Morality Conference, 2008, http://www.librarycompany.org/Economics/2008Conference/pdfs/block10-08.pdf (retrieved 17.11.11); Besse, *Collection* ii, pp. 278–391.
21. Welch, *Slave Society*, pp. 119–120.
22. Besse, *Collection*, ii, pp. 352, 366; Margaret E. Hirst, *The Quakers in Peace and War: An Account of Their Peace Principles and Practice* (London: Swarthmore Press, 1923), p. 315. Stapleton complained that the arrival of the Quaker ship had turned 700 militiamen Quaker, who would not fight.

23. Besse, *Collection* ii, pp. 368–369.
24. Besse, *Collection* ii, p. 376; Edward Crisp, *A Compleat Description of the Province of Carolina* (London, 1711); Bishop Roberts and W. H. Toms, *The Ichnography of Charles-Town at High Water* (London, 1739). Besse's two-volume compendium was published in 1753, but *A Brief Account of the Sufferings of the Servants of the Lord Called Quakers: From Their First Arrival in the Island of Antegoa, under the Several Governours; from the Year 1660 to 1695* (London, 1706), endorsed "this book belongs to ye Meetting," is identical to that which appears in Besse: BLARS, PR/2/11/2/5.
25. Quaker Library, Euston, "The third Book of the Monthly Meeting of the People call'd Quakers at Horslydown, 1690," 1692 7th mo 7th.
26. BLARS, HW/85/1 [18thc copy]; BLARS, HW/85/2.
27. WSHC, 413/440.
28. *The Rules of Discipline of London Yearly Meeting* (London, 1834 edn.), pp. 95–96: "Friends, I take this my friend D. E. to be my wife, promising, through divine assistance, to be unto her a loving and faithful husband, until it shall please the Lord by death to separate us."
29. BLARS, HW/92/11.
30. NAJm, wills, vol. i, f. 183; NAJm, inventories, vol. i, f. 162; BDA, RB 6/43, p. 138.
31. BLARS, HW/85/10; BLARS, HW/85/8; Mabel Brailsford, *Quaker Women, 1650–1690* (London: Duckworth, 1915); BLARS, MW/85/51; *To the Yearly Meeting of Friends & Brethren in Philadelphia, America* (London, 1699); [Thomas Andrews], *A Modest Enquiry into the Weight of Theodore Eccleston's Reply* (London, 1709); Theodore Eccleston, *A Tender Farewel to My Loving Friends* (n.p., n.d. [London?, 1726?]).
32. TNA, RG6/497.
33. BDA, RB 6/16; BDA, RB 6/43, p. 378.
34. BDA, RB 6/6, p. 518.
35. TNA, CO 31/2; BDA, RB 6/43, p. 64; George Warne Labaw, *Preakness and the Preakness Reformed Church, Passaic County, New Jersey: a History 1695–1902* (Board of Publication of the Reformed Church of America, 1902), p. 7; James Steen, *History of Christ Church, Shrewsbury, New Jersey* ([New Jersey?], 1983), p. 14.
36. Henry F. Waters, *Genealogical Gleanings in England* (Boston: New England Historic and Genealogical Society, 1901), pp. 914–915.
37. *Philadelphia County Wills, 1682–1819* (Philadelphia: Historical Society of Pennsylvania, 1900), p. 314.
38. LancsRO, QSP 63/8.
39. LancsRO, QSP/263/19.
40. BDA, RB 3/2, p. 208.
41. LancsRO, DDF 1743; Caroline Fishwick (ed.), *A Calendar of Lancashire and Cheshire Exchequer Depositions by Commission, from 1558 to 1702* (Lancashire and Cheshire Record Society, 1885), pp. 5–6.
42. Middlesex Sessions Rolls, March-December 1660, May 5, 12 Charles II.
43. James C. Brandow, *Genealogies of Barbados Families* (Baltimore, MD: Genealogical Publishing Company, 1983), pp. 370, 340–341; BDA, RB3/5 pp. 333, 336, 641; J. R. Woodhead, *The Rulers of London 1660–1689* (London: London and Middlesex Archaeological Society, 1966). Oliver, *Monumental Inscriptions*, p. 30; DRO, D5557/2/120/2.

44. DRO, D5557/2/111/2; BDA, RL 1/1, p. 165.
45. DRO, D5557/2/111/1; BDA RL 1/1, p. 171.
46. BDA, RL1/1, p. 218.
47. DRO, D5557/2/120/1.
48. DRO, D5557/2/120/2; WSRO, GOODWOOD/E601–E630.
49. *Orders and Constitvtions* (London, 1622), p. 77.
50. DRO,D5557/2/120/5;D5557/2/120/6;D5557/2/120/7;D5557/2/120/8; D5557/2/126.
51. BDA, RB 6/11, p. 185.
52. John Atkins, *A Voyage to Guinea, Brasil, and the West-Indies* (London, 1735), preface, p. iii.
53. Amanda E. Herbert, *Female Alliances: Gender, Identity, and Friendship in Early-Modern Britain* (New Haven, CT: Yale University Press, 2014).
54. Trevor Burnard, *Mastery, Tyranny, and Desire: Thomas Thistlewood and His Slaves in the Anglo-Jamaican World* (Chapel Hill: University of North Carolina Press, 2004), p. 210; Douglas Hall, *In Miserable Slavery: Thomas Thistlewood in Jamaica, 1750–86* (Kingston: UWI Press, 1989); Saidiya Hartman, "Venus in Two Acts," *Small Axe,* vol. 12.2 (2008), pp. 1–14; Sarah E. Yeh, "'A sink of all filthiness': gender, family, and identity in the British Atlantic, 1688–1763," *The Historian* 68.1 (2006): 66–88.
55. Behn, *Oroonoko,* pp. 24–25.
56. Ibid., p. 27.
57. Ibid., pp. 105–106.
58. Ibid., pp. 27–28, 29–30.
59. Ligon, *History,* p. 47.
60. TNA, CO 5/1261, no. 126. See also TNA CO 5/1261, no.73; and TNA, CO 5/1289, pp. 409–425.
61. LPL, FP xv, ff. 216–16^v, 249–250^v.
62. Willem Bosman, *A New and Accurate Description of the Coast of Guinea* (London, 1705), pp. 193, 197.
63. LPL, FP ix, ff. 1, 92–93^v.
64. He did not explain why: one suggestion is that although the man increases the chances of fathering a large number of children, the number of children per woman is reduced.
65. Robert Robertson, *A Detection of the State and Situation of the Present Sugar Planters* (London, 1732), pp. 42–44; Richard B. Sheridan, "Africa and the Caribbean in the Atlantic slave trade," *American Historical Review* 77.1 (1972): 15–35. This would, however, make more sense if the small number of women formed polyandrous partnerships with many men.
66. Cecilia A. Green, "'A civil inconvenience'? The vexed question of slave marriage in the British West Indies," *Law and History Review* 25.1 (2007): 1–59; Franklin W. Knight (ed.), *General History of the Caribbean:* vol.iii "The Slave Societies of the Caribbean" (London: UNESCO Publishing/Macmillan, 1997).
67. NAS, CS96/3102; CS96/3103; CS96/3104; CS96/3105.
68. Lucinda, born March 15, 1728(9), and Sarah, born March 8, 1731(2): NAS, CS96/3102, pp. 1, 4.
69. It is impossible to state any of these things with confidence, as the records are not only biased on the basis of the reasons for which they were compiled, but are far from accurate and often confuse or conflate names. The ages of any

slaves born before Cunyngham started to keep his detailed records are formulaic estimates, unchanging from one year's list to the next. Not everyone is given full family listings and cross-referencing allows for mistakes to creep in.

70. NAS, CS96/3102, f. 12b.
71. UMJRL, STP Box 2, 2/8.
72. NAS, CS96/3104, p. 68; CS96/3102, n.p.
73. Burnard, "Slave naming patterns" *op.cit.* The term "plantation" is reserved for definitions of land/place, eliding connections between people and connections between people and land. "Plantation Society" implies one must be a determinant of the other.
74. Only one of Arnold's children was alive in 1739. It may have been the case that the couple had no living children at the time Cunyngham made this list, but since they were illegitimate, it is unlikely he would include them. TNA, PROB 18/60/22: the case described as "Cunyngham versus Cunygham," is Elizabeth Arnold versus Mary Gainer. The legitimate marriage to Bonneton is described as "a former venture."
75. Oldmixon, *British Empire in America,* pp. 231–232.
76. TNA, PROB 20/671: the will of Robert Cunyngham, made on October 27, 1743. He died on November 13, 1743 and the will was brought in May 14, 1744. Lanahan and Robinson appear in this list of St. Kitts household, but are not named in Cunyngham's last will (there were at least three drafts but only the final one survives), whereas Hay was listed in the will but not in the household in 1734.
77. TNA, PROB 18/60/22.
78. *A Letter to the Right Reverend the Lord Bishop of London...In which Is Inserted, A Short Essay Concerning the Conversion of the Negro=Slaves in our Sugar-Colonies* (written June 1727) (London, 1730), pp. 8–9; [Daniel Defoe], *The Family Instructor* (London, 1720), p. 262.
79. Robert Burton [attributed to Nathaniel Crouch], *The English Empire in America* ([Dublin], 1729, 7th edn), p. 130.
80. *Letter to the...Bishop of London,* p. 27.
81. Ibid., p. 21.
82. [Daniel Defoe], *The Family Instructor in Three Parts* (London, 1715, 2nd edn), p. 267.
83. [Daniel Defoe], *The Family Instructor. In Two Parts. Vol. II* (London, 1720, 2nd edn), pp. 197. There was no mention of slaves in the three-part instructor published in Glasgow in 1717.
84. Royal Institution of Cornwall, Truro, HU/14/16, February 6, 20 Jas I/57 Jas VI; Alison Grant, *Atlantic Adventure: John Delbridge of Barnstaple, 1564–1639* (published by the author, 1996); *Eadem.,* "Bermuda adventurer: John Delbridge of Barnstaple, 1564–1639," *Bermuda Journal of Archaeology and Maritime History* 3 (1991): 1–18.
85. SHC, D\P\gst/2/1/3.
86. DRO, D5557/2/120/3, 4, 5.
87. SHC, DD\FS 2/2/4.
88. TNA, PRO 30/26/90, pp. 46–47.
89. GA, D2659/2 [photocopy, original at Dyrham Park]; BDA, RB 6/1, p. 146; RB 6/15, p. 403; RB 6/11, p. 253; RB 6/11, p. 272; RB 6/11, p. 374; RB 6/6, p. 329.

90. Robert Gibbes was sheriff of South Carolina in 1684 and governor in 1710, despite using bribery to achieve the office. He died in South Carolina on June 24, 1715.
91. Naomi Tadmor, "The concept of the household-family in eighteenth-century England," *Past and Present* 151 (1996): 111–140.
92. BL, Add. MSS 18,683, ff. 1–12^v: ff. 6–7, f. 6^v, ff. 8^v–9^v.
93. BDA, RB 3/1, p. 707; RB 3/1, p. 224; RB 6/14, p. 479.
94. SHC, DD/WHh/1090, pt. 2/1; J. H. Lawrence Archer, *Monumental Inscriptions of the British West Indies* (London: Chatto and Windus, 1875), pp. 38, 49.
95. TNA, CO 1/22, no. 35; TNA, CO 389/5, pp. 154–156; TNA, CO 1/35, nos. 63, 63i-iv; TNA, CO 1/36, no. 5; TNA, CO 1/34, no. 6; Lennox Honychurch, "The Kalinago fight for Oüaladli and Oüahómoni: a clash of cultures over possession of Antigua and Barbuda," http://www.cavehill.uwi.edu/BNCCde/antigua/conference/papers/honychurch.html (retrieved June 25, 2013].
96. NAJm wills, vol. 6, f. 63; NAJm inventories, vol. iii, f. 326.
97. GA, D2659.
98. Lothrop Withington, "Virginia gleanings in England" in *The Virginia Magazine of History and Biography*, reprinted as *Virginia Gleanings in England* (Baltimore, MD: Genealogical Publishing, 1980), p. 13; BDA, RB 6/13, p. 339; BDA, RL 1/1, p. 398; BDA, RL 1/22, p. 21; BDA, RB 5/522 and 523.
99. DRO, D5557/2/120/3.
100. TNA, CO 28/11, no. 18(iv).
101. BDA, RB 6/5, p. 505.
102. TNA, C110/175.
103. TNA, C110/175; Barber, "Not worth one Groat," pp. 46–48.
104. *A Collection of Voyages and Travels* (4 vols.) (London, 1704); Toby L. Ditz, "Shipwrecked; or, masculinity imperiled: mercantile representations of failure and the gendered self in eighteenth-century Philadelphia," *Journal of American History* 81.1 (1994): 51–80.
105. James Byres, *A Letter to a Friend at Edinburgh from Rotterdam; Giving an account of the Scots affairs in Darien* (n.p., 1702), p. 6.
106. Ibid., pp. 17, 20.
107. Ibid., pp. 51–52, 56, 69–70.
108. Byres, *Letter*, p. 99; John Prebble, *The Darien Disaster* (London: Secker and Warburg, 1968), p. 245.
109. R. M. K. [Roderick Mackenzie], *A Full and Exact Account of the Proceedings of the Court of Directors and Council-General of the Company of Scotland Trading to African and the Indies* (n.p., 1706), pp. 17–18, 32; Watt, *Price of Scotland*, pp. 34–35.
110. House of Commons, *The Report of Mr. Paterson's Petition, July the 10th, 1713* (n.p., n.d. [London, 1713]), n.p; *Report on Mr. Paterson's Petition Presented to the Honourable House of Commons by Sir James Campbell, Die Jovis 14 Aprilis, 1715*, p. 7.
111. Walter Harris, "Anti Dariensi," *A New Darien Artifice Laid Open* (London, 1701), p. 3; Idem., *A Defence of the Scots Abdicating Darien* (1700), Epistle dedicatory.
112. DevonRO, 4652 M-O/Z/18.

113. "An Act for giving like Remedy upon Promissory Notes, as is now used upon Bills of Exchange" (London, 1705).
114. LMA, DL/C/239, ff. 31–31v; Natasha Glaisyer, "Merchants at the Royal Exchange, 1660–1720," in Ann Saunders (ed.), *The Royal Exchange* (London Topographical Society, publication no. 152, 1997), pp. 198–205.
115. If this is Captain Joseph Wild, he may not have been so fortunate two years later, when one of his mariners, William Flood, was murdered onboard ship, but the inquest, after seven hours' deliberation, agreed a verdict of death from fever, and Wild and his associates claimed the jury had been cowed by the intimidating presence of Sir Henry Morgan: TNA, CO 1/52, nos. 95, 95i, and ii.
116. TNA, PRO 30/26/90, pp. 53, 55.
117. DevonRO, 4652/M-O/Z/18.
118. See the survival of printed shipping orders and handwritten bills of exchange among the Helyar MSS (SHC, DD/WHh), but the Helyars were unusual in the volume of papers which they kept and which survive, and the extent to which they used both bills of exchange and printed shipping orders. The Bank of England issued printed bills of exchange for the first time in 1717.
119. BDA, RB 3/1, pp. 300, 342, 428, 756–757.
120. TNA, PRO 30/26/90, p. 53; Ian Atherton, "The itch grown a disease: manuscript transmission of news in the seventeenth century," *Prose Studies: History, Theory, Criticism* 21.2 (1998): 39–65. There were bill-brokers, exchange-brokers, stock-brokers, and so on, all of which were derided for their lack of honesty.
121. *Mercurius Politicus* (London, September 10–17, 1657), issue 381; *True Protestant Mercury or Occurrences Forein and Domestick* (London), October 21, 1682, issue 186.
122. *London Post with Intelligence Foreign and Domestick* (London), September 15–18, 1699, issue 45.
123. TNA, CO 1/18, no. 65 [b].
124. *Loyal Protestant and True Domestick Intelligence* (London), August 26, 1682, issue 199; Michael Harris, "Exchanging information: print and business at the Royal Exchange in the late seventeenth century," in Saunders (ed.), *Royal Exchange*, pp. 188–197.
125. *An Elegy on the Death of Thomas Merry, Esq; of St. Ann's Lane, who died on St. Bartholomew's day, 1682* (broadsheet), endorsed "A tory thing a Jeer on him [and] ye Whigs 29 Aug. 1682."
126. *Post Boy and Historical Account* (London), August 8–10, 1695, issue 40.
127. TNA CO 1/53, no. 32, f. 113.
128. A. O. Exquemelin, *The History of the Bucaniers of America* (London, 1704, 3rd edn), p. 48.
129. [Anon], *The Broken Merchants Complaint* ([London], 1683); [Anon], *Ape-Gentle-vvoman, or the Character of an Exchange-Wench* (London, 1673).
130. Nicholas Leverton, Surinam, to [Charles Morton], May 13, 1662, "Transcribed by me the 21 of March 8^2/$_3$": in private hands.
131. Meaning those in England: in Surinam his congregation was concerned he used neither the Book of Common Prayer nor the sign of the cross at baptism.
132. BDA, RB 6/9, p. 467; BDA, RL 1/1, p. 211; BDA, RB 4/11, p. 158.
133. LMA, ACC/0249/1496; *CJ* x, p. 742; *LJ* 15, p. 145.

134. TNA, C110/175—underlining in the original; Barber, "Not worth one Groat", *op. cit.*
135. UCL, ADD MS 70, [loose] f. 16.
136. UCL ADD MS 70, [loose] f. 4, [loose] f. 18, f. 57, f. 80^v, ff. 104–105.
137. UCL ADD MS 70, [loose] f. 4.
138. Frank M. Coleman, *Hobbes and America: Exploring the Constitutional Foundations* (Toronto/Buffalo: University of Toronto Press, 1977), p. 66; Thomas Hobbes, *Philosophical Rudiments Concerning Government and Society* (translation by Hobbes of "De Cive: or the Citizen"), in Bernard Gert (ed.), *Man and Citizen: Thomas Hobbes* (Harvester/Humanities Press, 1972), p. 111.
139. Richard Ashcraft, "Ideology and class in Hobbes' political theory," *Political Theory* 6.1 (1978): 27–62; David Burchill, "The disciplined citizen: Thomas Hobbes, neostoicism and the critique of classical citizenship," *Australian Journal of Politics and History* 45.4 (1999): 506–524; Craig Muldrew, "Interpreting the market: the ethics of credit and community relations in early-modern England," *Social History* 18.2 (1993): 163–183.
140. Lillington, "Condition of the Island," [a].
141. CornwallRO, DD/CN/3478.
142. TNA C110/175: "no.5."
143. DRO, D5557/2/120/1.
144. ULBC, ML, vol. 84/ 4, 8, 10.
145. *A Collection of the State Papers of John Thurloe* (London, 1742), vol. 3, pp. 614–631.
146. BristolRO, AC/WO/9/58, February 10, 1726(7).
147. Sir Hans Sloane, *A Voyage to the Islands Madera, Barbados, Nieves, S. Christophers and Jamaica* (London, 1707, 2 vols.), vol. i, p. 46; Sarah Barber, "Who owns knowledge? Heritage, intellectual property and access in and to the history of Antigua and Barbuda," *Archival Science* 12.1 (2012): 1–17.
148. TNA, C110/175, no. 2; Barber, "Not worth one Groat," pp. 38–39; TNA, CO 152/2, no. 44, f. 114.
149. NAJm, wills, vol. vi, f. 25.
150. Presumably Diego.
151. NAJm, wills, vol. xi, f. 53.
152. Devon RO, 1926 B/T/F 1/1/2.
153. BL, Add MSS 31,181, ff. 71–72.
154. BDA, Vestry minutes St. John's, Barbados, pp. 6–9, 17.
155. BDA, Vestry minutes St. John's, pp. 10, 21–22.
156. BDA, RB 3/5, pp. 901, 953; BDA, St. John's vestry minutes, pp. 1–13.
157. BDA, RB 6/8, p. 39; BDA, RB 6/8, p. 47; BDA, Vestry minutes St John's, p. 61.
158. BDA, Vestry minutes St. John's, p. 63.
159. LPL, xv, f. 192.
160. His brother was Rev. Mr. Timothy Hallett, vicar of St. Michael the Archangel, Lyme Regis, between 1663 and 1729, minister there during the upbringing of Thomas Coram: DHC, PE/LR: RE1/1, p. 33; H. F. B. Compston, *Thomas Coram: Churchman, Empire Builder and Philanthropist* (London: SPCK, 1918), pp. 21–22.
161. NAJm, wills, vol. i, f. 183.
162. SHC, LM/778/21/4.

163. Karen Ordahl Kupperman, *Providence Island, 1630–1641: The Other Puritan Colony* (Cambridge: Cambridge University Press, 1993), pp. 3–5.
164. Bodl. Oxf., MS. Eng.hist/c.477, ff. 263–264ᵛ; MS.Eng.hist./c.477/ff. 147–148.
165. Abraham Jackson, SORROVVES LENITIVE (London, 1614); Richard Stock, *The Churches Lamentation for the Losse of the Godly* (London, 1614). Prince Henry had taken an active interest in the development of American colonies, and was responsible for despatching Sir Thomas Dale to Virginia, where the Laws Divine Moral and Martial attempted to bring practical and puritan morality to the struggling Jamestown settlement.
166. Edmund Calamy, *An Abridgment of Mr. Baxter's History of His Life and Times* (London, 1702); John Walker, *An Attempt towards Recovering an Account of the Numbers and Sufferings of the Clergy of the Church of England* (London, 1714).
167. John Josslyn, *An Account of Two Voyages to New-England* (London, 1674), p. 277. It is my belief that John Oxenbridge was the brother of Clement Oxenbridge MP, republican controller of the prize, active in naval affairs under the Protectorate, who survived the Restoration and went on the set up a postal office.
168. BL Sloane 758.
169. *Broken Merchants Complaint*, p. 9.
170. Alexander Garden, *Some Crude Enthusiastick Notions* (London, 1740); Alexander Garden, *The Doctrine of Justification According to the Scriptures, and the Articles, and Homilies of the Church of England, Explained and Vindicated* (Charles Town, 1742).
171. HALS, DE/HL/12601.
172. SurreyHC, QS2/6/1717/Eas/65.
173. TNA, CO 140/1, pp. 263–264.
174. TNA, CO 140/1, pp. 278–282, 291.
175. TNA, CO 28/2, no. 22.
176. Gragg, *Quaker Community*, pp. 152–153. This second oath removed John Holder from the Assembly place in St Phillip's.
177. TNA, CO 1/65, nos. 38, 38i–xiv.
178. TNA, CO 137/2, no. 61, f. 121; Richardson Wright, *Revels in Jamaica* (New York: Dodd Mead & Co., 1937), pp. 12–13.
179. TNA, CO 137/2, f. 123.
180. TNA, PRO 30/24/48/64.
181. TNA, CO 5/288, p. 34.
182. [Daniel Defoe], *Party-Tyranny or, An Occasional Bill in Miniature; As now Practised in CAROLINA*, (London, 1705) in Salley, *Narratives*, p. 239; John Ash, "The present state of affairs in Carolina," within *The Case Of Protestant Dissenters in Carolina* (London, 1706), p. 30.
183. BDA, RB 6/9, p. 42.
184. Stapleton was governor of Nevis between 1672 and 1685. Stapleton papers are extant at Bangor University (Stapleton-Cotton MSS, GB 0222 STAP), and John Rylands Library, University of Manchester (John Rylands Library, STP). J. R. V. Johnston, *The Stapleton Sugar Plantations in the Leeward Islands* (Manchester: MUP, 1965). He started his plantation empire in Montserrat (Waterwork plantation, St. Peter's), followed by Cayon Quarter, St. Christopher's. He had an interest with his brother, Redmond, in two

plantations in Antigua, called Carleton, and he lived on a plantation in the parish of St. John Figtree, Nevis.
185. Bodl.Oxf., MS Carte 40, ff. 321–321^v.
186. CumbriaRO, Carlisle, D/LONS/L1/1/41/29, [b].
187. LPL, FP xix, ff. 22–23^v; LPL, FP xix, ff. 24–24^v.
188. "Staw," to mean of position, degree, or rank.
189. TNA, CO 1/66, no. 112 (f. 278); Robert Hermann Schomburgk, *The History of Barbados* (London, 1847), pp. 295–306; TNA, CO 1/42, no. 143; Peter Thompson, "Henry Drax's instructions of the management of a seventeenth-century Barbadian sugar plantation," *WMQ*, 3rd series, 66.3 (2009): 565–604.
190. Psalms 20.1–2; [Andrew Dickson White], *Farewell Sermons of some of the Most Eminent of the Nonconformist Ministers* (London, 1812): Thomas Jaccomb on Ps.73.34, p. 141.
191. "[A]s if we could not be safe under the conduct of his Majesty [William III]": [Anon], *An Answer to Mr. Toland's Reasons for Addressing His Majesty to Invite into England Their Highnesses the Electress Dowager, and the Electoral Prince of Hanover* (London, 1702), p. 5; [John Anderson], The Countrey-Man's Letter To The Curat ([?Edinburgh], 1711), p. 36: "*Knox*, as having been the most Eminent of all our Reformers, by whom our Reformation was mainly advanc'd, and under whose Conduct it was carri'd on, and therefore Deserving to lead the Van"; [Anon], *Address To The People of England: Shewing The Unworthiness of their Behaviour to King George* (London, 1715), p. 10: "about five Years ago, when Queen ANNE was turning out this very Ministry, under whose Conduct she had reigned so gloriously."
192. John Hallett, for example, was framed here as a reliable supporter of Established principles, but was a personal thorn in the side of Governors Kendall and Dutton: Susan Dwyer Amussen, *Caribbean Exchanges: Slavery and the Transformation of English Society, 1640–1700* (Chapel Hill: University of North Carolina Press, 2007), pp. 145–150.
193. TNA, CO 1/42, nos. 143, 144; Richard S. Dunn, "The Barbados census of 1680: profile of the richest colony in English America," *WMQ*, 3rd series, 26.1 (1969): 3–30.
194. TNA, CO 1/56, no. 155.
195. Oldmixon, *British Empire* ii, pp. 74–75.
196. TNA, CO 28/9, no.18 (b); TNA CO 28/7, no. 35; TNA, CO 28/7, nos. 35, 35.i; UN, MeC 1/2/43 [a]; Oldmixon, *British Empire* ii p. 74; CO 29/9, pp. 7–47. Granville seems to have been confused about the real first names of several councillors, including Lillington. George Ramsay is untraceable, other than being the name of the Councillor excluded by both Granville and Oldmixon's later account, but this is most likely Gilbert Ramsay, a Scottish Episcopalian minister serving in Barbados. There were a number of Ramsays on Barbados, and a David Ramsay is also indicted with Cryer.
197. *London Gazette* issue 4277, November 6, 1706; Oldmixon, *British Empire*, ii, p. 75.
198. TNA, PRO/30/26/90.
199. Oldmixon, *British Empire*, ii, pp. 73–74.
200. TNA, CO 28/12, nos. 26–26ix; TNA, CO 28/11, nos. 18–18^v.
201. TNA, CO 388/76, no. 57.

202. TNA, CO 28/10, no. 37; Barber, "Let him be an Englishman"; TNA, PRO 30/26/90.
203. TNA, CO 28/43, no. 37; TNA, CO 28/12, no. 34.
204. UN, MeC 1/2/43: G[eorge] Lillington, Barbados, to Chief Justice Parker, August 3, 1710.
205. HALS, D/EP/F.143.
206. The disputed island Treasurership and an excise bill.
207. HALS, D/EP/F143.
208. A. B., *An Answer to the Arguments in the Lord Bishop of Oxford's Speech on the Impeachment of Dr. Henry Sacheverell* (London, 1710), p. 6.
209. John Poyer, *The History of Barbados* (London: Frank Cass, 1971), pp. 201–204; TNA, PRO 30/26/90, ff. 46, 66, 67.
210. Jonathan Swift, *The Journal to Stella* (edited by George A. Aitken), letter 62, March 1713.
211. William Cleland, *The Present State of the Sugar Plantations Considered* (London, 1713), p. 14.
212. TNA, CO 28/4, nos. 47, 47i, 47ii.
213. LPL, FP xix, ff. 54–55^v.
214. BDA, RB 6/40, p. 291; RB 6/43, p. 384; RB 6/41, p. 352; RB 6/11, p. 98.
215. William Copp married Elizabeth, daughter of James Ayshford: they had a surviving daughter Mary. George and Margaret were married before 1690.
216. Oldmixon, *British Empire in America*, ii, pp. 69–70, 70–71.
217. HALS, D/EP/F.143.
218. Lillington, "Condition of the Island," [a]; TNA, PRO 30/26/90, p. 20.
219. BDA, RB 6/5, p. 505.
220. TNA, CO 28/15, nos. 54, 54i–lix, ii (e); Simon David Smith, *Slavery, Family, and Gentry Capitalism in the British Atlantic: The World of the Lascelles, 1648–1834* (Cambridge: Cambridge University Press, 2006), pp. 63–65.
221. WYAS, SpSt/10/2/5.
222. TNA, PRO 30/26/90, unfol.
223. TNA, PRO 30/26/90, pp. 54–55, 46–47, 48; TNA, PRO 30/26/90, p. 40.
224. TNA, PRO 30/26/90, p. 65.
225. J. D. Davies, "The Navy, Parliament and political crisis in the reign of Charles II," *Historical Journal* 36.2 (1993): 271–288, 271; Stephen Saunders Webb, "Army and empire: English garrison government in Britain and America, 1569–1763," *WMQ*, 3rd series, 34.1 (1977): 1–31, 24.
226. TNA CO 1/53, no. 32, f. 113.

4 Body

1. TNA, CO 152/8, no.9 [unfol.].
2. TNA, CO 152/8, no.43i, f.472.
3. TNA, CO 152/42, no.29; CO152/6 no.63.
4. Helen Hill Miller, *Governor Parke of Virginia: "The Greatest Hector in Town"* (Chapel Hill, NC: Algonquin Books, 1989), pp. 189–190.
5. TNA, CO 152/9, no. 18; Vincent Harlow, *Christopher Codrington* (Oxford: Clarendon, 1928), pp. 188–195.

6. TNA, CO 7/1, no. 19; TNA, CO 152/8, no. 43i, f.478; Oliver, *History*, p. 2. Jacob M. Price, *Perry of London: A Family and a Firm on the Seaborne Frontier, 1615–1753* (Cambridge, MA: Harvard University Press, 1992).
7. Oliver, *History of Antigua*, pp. 20–22; Henry A. M. Smith, "Georgetown: The Original Plan and the Earliest Settlers," *The South Carolina Historical and Genealogical Magazine* 9.2 (1908): pp. 85–101.
8. Oliver, *History* p. 23; TNA, CO 152/2.
9. TNA, CO 152/8, no.43i, f.478.
10. TNA, CO 152/8, no.41, ff. 422–423^v, f.422^v.
11. Anon, *A Letter to Mr. George French* (London, 1718), p. 4.
12. [Anon], *Some Instances of the Oppression and Male Administration of Col. PARKE* (?London, ?1713), pp. 1–2; TNA, CO 152/42, no.105 [1713].
13. TNA, CO 152/8, no.43i, unfol.
14. Natalie Zacek, *Settler Society in the English Leeward Islands* (Cambridge: Cambridge University Press, 2010), pp. 192–194: Eadem, "Sex, Sexuality, and Social Control in the Eighteenth-Century Leeward Islands," in Merril D. Smith, *Sex and Sexuality in Early America* (New York: New York University Press, 1998), Chapter 8.
15. *Some Instances*, p. 3.
16. George French, *An Answer to a Scurrilous Libel* (London, 1719), pp. 47–48; TNA, CO 7/1, no. 19.
17. Thomas Fuller, *The Holy State* (Cambridge, 1642), p. 397, for the difference between ravishment (rape) and defilement (which implies consent).
18. TNA, CO 152/7, no. 44; TNA, CO 153/10, pp. 148–150.
19. *Some Instances*, p. 4.
20. The will of Daniel Parke, dated at St John's, January 29, 1709(10); proved May 1711; TNA, CO 152/8, no.43i, f.478; Oliver, *History*, pp. 203–204, 206.
21. Dunbar *v* Custis: *Acts of the Privy Council*, vol. iv, pp. 288–289; BL, Add MSS 36217; George Adrian Washburne, *Imperial Control of the Administration of Justice in the Thirteen American Colonies, 1684–1776* (Studies in History, Economics and Public Law, vol. 105.2 [New York: Columbia University Press, 1923]), pp. 139–140; Marion Tinling (ed.), *Correspondence of the Three William Byrds of Westover, Virginia, 1684–1706* (Charlottesville: University of Virginia Press, 1977), i, pp. 351–352.
22. [Anon], *Letter to…French*, pp. 3, 6. The reference to "swelling" the length of a pamphlet was repeated in *Some Instances*.
23. TNA, CO 152/42, no.18; George French, *The History Of Col. Parke's Administration* (London, 1717), p. 8; [Ned Ward], *The Secret History Of The Calves-Head Club, Compleat: Or, The Republican Unmask'd* (London, 1705).
24. TNA, CO 152/8, nos.9, 9i.-xix, no.45, f.538^v; TNA, CO 153/10, pp. 288–300; Flannigan, *Antigua*, p. 73; *Some Instances*, p. 3; TNA, CO 152/42, no.25iii; [Anon], *Truth brought to Light; Or, Murder will out* (London, 1713), p. 1.
25. French, *History*, note at bottom of page B2; *Letter to…French*, pp. 5, 6.
26. TNA, CO 7/1, no. 19; French, *An Answer*, p. 25; French, *History*, pp. 180–182.
27. French, History, pp. 12–13, 90–94.

28. *Some Instances*, p. 1; TNA, CO 152/7, nos.45, 45.i; TNA, CO 152/8, nos.43, 43i–xxvi.
29. TNA, CO 152/42, nos. 59, 55, 21, 22, 23; TNA, CO 152/42, nos. 44, 47–52; BDA, RB6/2, p. 66.
30. *Some Instances*, p. 2; Natalie Zacek, "A Death in the Morning: The Murder of Daniel Parke," in Robert Olwell and Alan Tully (eds.), *Cultures and Identities in Colonial British America* (Baltimore, MD: Johns Hopkins University Press, 2006), pp. 223–243.
31. *Truth brought to Light*, p. 3.
32. TNA, CO 152/42, no. 54i.
33. *Some Instances*, p. 4.
34. TNA, CO 152/42, nos. 59, 55, 21, 22, 23; Flannigan, *Antigua*, p. 77.
35. French, *History*, preface.
36. TNA, CO 5/865, no. 65. John Felton was the assassin of the Duke of Buckingham, Johan de Witt was the radical republican leader of the United Provinces of the Netherlands, lynched by a mob, who subsequently are supposed to have eaten parts of his body. It was certainly dismembered. Attributed to Jan de Baen: *The Corpses of the Brothers De Witt, on the Groene Zoodje at the Lange Vijverberg in The Hague, 20 August 1672*, oil on canvas, 69.5 × 56 cms., c.1672–1702, Rijksmuseum, Amsterdam.
37. Byam, *Exact Relation*, p. 4.
38. *A NARRATIVE of AFFAIRS Lately received from His Majesties Island of Jamaica* (London, 1683), pp. 4–5.
39. William Gordon, *A Sermon Preach'd at the Funeral of the Honourable Colonel Christopher Codrington* (London, 1710), p. 8.
40. Hans Baron, "Secularization of Wisdom and Political Humanism in the Renaissance," *Journal of the History of Ideas* 21.1 (1960): 131–150; Elizabeth Briant, "From Vita Contemplativa to Vita Activa : Modern Instrumentalization of Theory and the Problem of Measure," *International Journal of Philosophical Studies* 9.1 (2001): 19–40.
41. TNA, PRO 30/26/90, p. 20; TNA, CO 152/8, no. 43i, f. 472.
42. He was appointed Lieutenant-Governor of Jamaica in 1687: he died aged 35.
43. TNA, CO152/6, nos. 5, 6; TNA CO152/6 no.6.
44. SCLA, DR 37/2/Box 98/475.
45. TNA, CO 153/4, pp. 416–418.
46. ROLLR, DG7 Box 4982, ff. 2–10, f.6^v.
47. TNA, Domestic Corresp. Jac. I., vol.clvi, no. 1, pp. 56–57.
48. TNA, SP14/90, no.24.
49. C[harles] M[orton], "The Life and Death of Mr Nicholas Leuerton," 1670: MS in private hands.
50. Henry Adis, *A Letter Sent from Syrranam* (London, 1664), p. 6.
51. TNA, CO 1/17, no.80.
52. Sloane, *Voyage*, vol. i, p. vi.
53. Blome, *Description*, pp. 21–26; TNA, CO 1/24, no.8.
54. "The grievances instanced, proved and perticularized," October 1622, printed in Vernon A. Ives, *The Rich Papers: Letters from Bermuda, 1615–1646* (Toronto: University of Toronto Press, 1984), pp. 237–239.
55. LPL, FP xvii f.48^v, 49; LPL, FP xix f.50.
56. TNA, CO 155/2, pp. 142–143.

57. TNA, CO 28/2, no. 109.
58. TNA, CO 1/31, no. 62.
59. HALS, DE/HL/, 12552: "Mr Molls [Mole's] accompt," 1628.
60. TNA, CO 155/2, pp. 142–143.
61. TNA, CO 1/15, no. 31.
62. TNA, SP 25/77, p. 949.
63. UMJRL, STP 2/3 (public accounts for Montserrat, 1672–1674): salt-beef was delivered in barrels at 500 pounds sugar per barrel.
64. Mutton 400 pounds per barrel: "To Jno Hudgson for a Barrel of herrings for ye massons—250 (lbs sugar)."
65. Act no. 48: "An Act appointing the Prices of Meat, and regulating Markets," *An Abridgment Of The Acts of Assembly Passed in the Island of Jamaica, From 1681, to 1737, inclusive* (London, 1743), p. 22.
66. LPL, FP xvii, 9–10.
67. CumbriaRO, Carlisle, D/LONS/L1/41/29a [b].
68. UMJRL, STP 1/1 [undocumented minutes].
69. Sa[muel] Clarke, *A Geographicall Description of All the Countries in the Known VVorld* (London, 1657), p. 181.
70. "N. N. Gent," *America: Or An Exact Description of the West-Indies* (London, 1655), pp. 127–129.
71. Sloane, *Voyage* i, p. xxv. The Cotton Leaf-worm (*Alabama argillacea*) is the larvae of a moth of the *Noctuidae* family, endemic in south and central America, ravaging cotton crops. TCD, MS 736, pp. 80–82: cassava was brought as a provision crop from Guiana to Barbados in 1626. Britons were aware of its poisonous properties and how to prepare it from an early stage: it was a lesson imparted by Sir Richard Hawkins, *The Observations of Sir Richard Havvkins...in 1593* (London, 1622), p. 61.
72. John Atkins, *A Voyage To Guinea, Brasil, and the West-Indies*, 2nd edn (London, 1737), p. 43.
73. John Josselyn, *An Account of Two Voyages to New-England* (London, 1674), pp. 210–211.
74. Samuel Clarke, *A True, and Faithful Account* (London, 1670), pp. 65–66.
75. UMJRL, STP 2/8/1 [b].
76. "Philotheos Physiologus" [Thomas Tryon], *Friendly Advice to the Gentlemen-Planters of the East and West Indies* (n.p., 1684), pp. 133–134.
77. Larry Gragg, "The Pious and the Profane: The Religious Life of Early Barbados Planters," *Historian*, 62.2 (2000): 265–284.
78. UMJRL, STP 2/3, f.11.
79. ULBC, ML v.84/10; TNA, CO 152/8, no. 9vii, f.75.
80. E[lisha] Coles, *An English Dictionary* (London, 1677), n.p. A "canting" word for London, however, was "Rum-vile."
81. Clarke, *Account*, pp. 60, 63–64.
82. TCD, MSS 736, pp. 183–184; BL, Sloane MS 3926, in C. H. Firth (ed.), *The Narrative of General Venables* (London: Camden Society, 2nd ser., 1900), pp. 144–169, 147.
83. Clarke, *Account*, pp. 66–67; ULBC, ML box 67/53, n.d.
84. NAJm, inventories vol. 3, ff. 323–324; NAJm, wills, vol. 3 f.127; BL, Maps K.Top.123.50.
85. LPL, FP xix, ff. 40–41^v.
86. UCL, ADD MS 70, ff. 104–105.

87. UCL, ADD MS 70, [loose] f.4.
88. Clarke, *Account*, p. 67.
89. UMJRL, STP 2/5 [unfol.].
90. Cara Anzilotti, "Autonomy and the Female Planter in Colonial South Carolina," *Journal of Southern History* lxiii.2 (1997): pp. 239–268, p. 239.
91. E[dmund] H[ickeringill], *Jamaica viewed* (London, 1661), pp. 7–8; Hans Sloane, *A Voyage to the Islands Madera, Barbados, Nieves, S. Christophers and Jamaica* (2 vols) (London, 1707) vol. i, p. clii.
92. Surrey HC, LM/2022.
93. Richard Stafford of Bermuda to the Royal Society: *Philosophical Transactions* iii (1668): p. 794.
94. UMJRL, STP 8/1 [c]; W[illiam] Lewis, *The New Dispensatory* (London: 6th ed., n.d., [1799?]), pp. 219–220.
95. CRO, Carlisle, D/LONS/L1/1/41/29a; Thomas Trapham, *A Discourse on the State of Health in the Island of Jamaica* (London, 1679), Chapter 10.
96. DRO, D5557/2/111/2.
97. There seemed to be the prospect of a "good stomach" in Carolina: TNA, PRO 30/24/48/77.
98. Blome, *Description*, p. 26.
99. Gragg, *Englishmen Transplanted*, p. 66.
100. BDA, RL 1/28, p. 1.
101. TNA, CO 1/40, nos. 98, 98 i, ii.
102. BDA, St John's vestry minutes; LPL, FP xvi/1, April 6, 1731.
103. C[harles] M[orton], "Life and Death of Mr Nicholas Leverton," ff. 16^v–17; Robert Davies (ed.), *The Life of Marmaduke Rawdon of York* (London: Camden Society, 1863).
104. TNA, PROB. 18/60/22.
105. John Savage, "'Black Magic' and White Terror: Slave Poisoning and Colonial Society in Early 19th Century Martinique," *Journal of Social History* 40.3 (2007): pp. 635–662, makes a convincing case for the deliberative agency of slaves in using poison as an act of resistance, but for a French colony in the 1820s.
106. TNA, CO 154/4, pp. 641–644.
107. Frederick Dalcho, *An Historical Account of the Protestant Episcopal Church in South-Carolina* (Charleston, SC: Thayer, 1820), p. 22.
108. NA, DD/SY/292. A calendure was heat stroke or fever brought on by excessive heat. There were Yellow Fever epidemics in Charles Town in 1699, 1706, 1711, 1717, 1718, and 1719, before a huge outbreak in 1730.
109. John Duffy, *Epidemics in Colonial America* (Baton Rouge: Louisiana State University Press, 1953), p. 75.
110. Gilbert Guttery, appointed in 1712: the post was abolished in 1721.
111. TNA, CO 28/4 nos. 45 and 46.
112. Duffy, *Epidemics*; and George Rosen, Review of Duffy in *American Journal of Public Health* 44 (1954): 269–270, 269. Economically significant diseases were listed as malaria, dysentery, and those affecting respiration, which is confusing, since diphtheria, itself a form of respiratory disease, was included along with smallpox and yellow fever as a sudden and terrifying attacker. Whitrow's comment (Devon RO 4652M-O/Z/18) was that "each of the Gentlemen abovementioned were pretty healthy in the Evening but never lived to see the next Sun. [and] were in their Graves before it's setting"; UCL, ADD MS 70, [loose] f.2^r, f.61^v.

113. Margaret Simons Middleton, *Henrietta Johnston* (Columbia: University of South Carolina Press, 1966), p. 27; Dalcho, *Episcopal Church*, p. 37.
114. DevonRO, 4652M-O/Z/18.
115. NAS, GD34/933/1; TNA, CO 1/22, no. 47.
116. Daniel Defoe, *The Life and Strange Surprizing Adventures of Robinson Crusoe* (London, 1719), p. 101.
117. NAS, CS96/3014, p. 1.
118. Thomas Trapham, *A DISCOURSE on the State of Health in the ISLAND of JAMAICA* (London, 1679), pp. 68–69.
119. Major John Scott, "A Discription of Guyana," 1669: BL 3662, ff. 37^v-42^v.
120. William Byam, Governor of Antigua, to William Lord Willoughby, Governor of Barbados, ?1670: TNA, CO 1/25, no. 28*.
121. Devon RO, 4652M-O/Z/18: [Benjamin Whitrow], Charles Town to [Joseph Helby, London], September 8, 1712 [copy letter]. Two weeks later there were still signs of flux, though he did not think he would die, and was now taking medicine for it.
122. Bartholomew Gracedieu and Gilbert Heathcote, Agents for Jamaica, to Council of Trade and Plantations: TNA, CO 137/4, pp. 136–188.
123. Memorial to Henry Berkeley, who had been the son of the said Maurice, born in St. Christopher's, January 1734, in the church of St. George's, Basseterre, St. Kitts; Vere Langford Oliver, *Monumental Inscriptions of the British West Indies* (Dorchester: Friary Press, 1927), pp. 132–133; I have been unable to trace the first name of Miss Tobin, but she was presumably a member of the family later recorded as holding Stony Grove estate in the southwest parish of St John Figtree, east of Charlestown. The Tobins opposed Abolition.
124. TNA, CO 1/28 no. 12: Deputy Governor Christopher Codrington, Barbados, to [Sec. Lord Arlington], February 7, 1672; Edward Cranfield and Marcus Brandt, Surinam, to Sec. Sir Joseph Williamson, July 11, 1675: TNA, CO 1/34, no. 113.
125. TNA, CO 5/289, no. 22: Edward Randolph, Carolina, to Council of Trade and Plantations, March 16, 1699; Sir Robert Mountgomery, *A Discourse Concerning the Design'd Establishment of a New Colony to the South of Carolina* (London, 1717).
126. TNA, CO 152/2, nos.51, 51i.
127. Kenneth Kiple, *The Caribbean Slave: A Biological History* (Cambridge: Cambridge University Press, 2002).
128. Trevor Burnard and Kenneth Morgan, "The Dynamics of the Slave Market and Slave Purchasing Patterns in Jamaica, 1655–1788," *WMQ*, 3rd series, 58.1 (2001): 205–228.
129. Susan E. Klepp, "Seasoning and Society: Racial Differences in Mortality in Eighteenth-Century Philadelphia," *WMQ*, 3rd series, 51.3 (1994), pp. 473–506.
130. "An Act to prevent the landing or keeping of negroes infected with small-pox in any of the three towns of St. Catherine, Port Royal, and Kingston," May 5, 1732 (*Journals of the Assembly of Jamaica* iii: 85–90); Richard B. Sheridan, *Doctors and Slaves: A Medical and Demographic History of Slavery in the British West Indies, 1680–1834* (Cambridge: Cambridge University Press, 1985), pp. 131–134.
131. [Robert Robertson], *A Speech by Mr John Talbot Compo-bell, a Free Christian—Negro* (London, 1736), p. 13.

132. [Littleton], *Groans of the Plantations*, p. 6.
133. It is very difficult to find studies of slavery separate from studies of the Slave Trade, most work concentrates on the eighteenth century, and the second half at that, and there is more work available on Spanish, Dutch, and French attitudes toward Africans, slaves, and slavery than on British: Shula Marks, "Khoisan Resistance to the Dutch in the Seventeenth and Eighteenth Centuries," *Journal of African History* 13.1 (1972): 55–80; Arthur L. Stinchcombe, "Freedom and Oppression of Slaves in the Eighteenth-Century Caribbean," *American Sociological Review* 59.6 (1994): 911–929; Linda A. Newson and Susie Minchin, "Diets, Food Supplies and the African Slave Trade in Early Seventeenth-Century Spanish America," *The Americas* 63.4 (2007): 517–550; Sue Peabody, "A Nation Born to Slavery": Missionaries and Racial Discourse in Seventeenth-Century French Antilles," *Journal of Social History* 38.1 (2004): pp. 113–126.
134. George Abbot, *A Briefe Description of the Whole World*, 5th edn (London, 1664), pp. 176–177. Abbot wrote his history in 1599 and it was reprinted several times, first appearing under his name in 1634.
135. For the former—in which a sinful act in the midst of piety would "look like a Negro in the midst of glorious beauties, as a dash of Hell in the Landshape of Heaven"—see Richard Allestree, *Forty Sermons whereof Twenty one are now first Publish'd* (London and Oxford, 1684). The black skins of Aphra Behn's heroes, Oroonoko and Imoinda, were rhapsodized, though as we have seen, Oroonoko's other features were atypically white, their beauty heightened by being sheathed in black skin.
136. UMJRL, STP 1/1 [undocumented minutes], 1680–1681: the culprits bringing them onto Antigua were Otto Eden and Peter Hall.
137. Reports of scalping in the seventeenth century come from Virginia, Pennsylvania, and Albany. I do not wish to enter here the controversy over who learned of scalping from whom: James Axtell, *The European and the Indian: Essays in the Ethnohistory of colonial North America* (Oxford: Oxford University Press, 1982); Henry J. Young, "Note on Scalp Bounties in Pennsylvania," *Pennsylvania History* 24.3 (1957): pp. 207–218.
138. See correspondence: [?1702] Peter Dyer to the Earl of Nottingham on the advantage of an attack on Cuba (TNA, CO 318/3, nos. 2, 2i); July 11, 1705: TNA, CO 137/7, no. 8; October 4, 1705, Secretary Hedges to Governor Handasyd of Jamaica: TNA, CO 324/30, pp. 43, 44. The decision taken by the Board of Trade and Plantations was that should the Spanish not abide by the truce and rules of engagement, the same treatment would be meted out to Spanish prisoners held by the English.
139. Peter Dyer, to the Lords of Trade and Plantations, September 1, 1705, *Journal of the Board of Trade*: TNA, CO. 318/3. no. 24, ff. 50–51.
140. Thomas Trapham, *Discourse* p. 111.
141. TNA, CO 5/1409, pp. 579–588; TNA, CO 31/6, pp. 264–275.
142. TNA, CO 1/25, no. 1. Woolding refers to securing something, such as a mast, by wrapping it with a rope, and thus a rope, particularly knotted, and held across the eyes, tightened by twisting on a stick, would have this effect.
143. Binning, *Case of Conscience* p. 43: "Ring-leaders of wickednesse, Refractory and Incorrigible persons should have been made examples to others, and this would have prevented much mischief."

144. Diana Paton, "Punishment, Crime, and the Bodies of Slaves in Eighteenth-Century Jamaica," *Journal of Social History* 34.4 (2001): 923–954: see pages 926–932; David Barry Gaspar, "With a Rod of Iron: Barbados Slave Laws as a Model for Jamaica, South Carolina, and Antigua, 1661–1697," in Darlene Clark Hine and Jacqueline McLeod (eds.), *Boundaries: Comparative History of Black People in Diaspora* (Bloomington: Indiana University Press, 1999), pp. 343–366.
145. No. 21, "An Act for the good governing of Servants, and ordering the Rights between Masters and Servants," September 27, 1661, p. 25 and no. 329, "An Act for the Governing of Negroes," August 8, 1688, p. 156, in William Rawlin, *The Laws of Barbados, Collected In One Volume* (London, 1699).
146. TCD, MS 736, pp. 99–103.
147. TCD MS 736, pp. 103–104.
148. TCD, MS 736, p. 105.
149. TCD, MS 736, pp. 105–106; Nicholas Darnell Davis, *The Cavaliers & Roundheads of Barbados, 1650–1652* (Demerara: Argosy Press, 1882), p. 60.
150. TNA, PRO 30/24/48/66.
151. David F. Marley, *Pirates of the Americas Volume 1: 1650–1685* (Santa Barbara, CA: ABC-Clio, 2010), pp. 638–639; TNA, CO 152/37, no. 69.
152. TNA CO 28/37, no. 16, ff. 112–114^v; TNA, CO 323/2, no. 124; TNA, CO 153/4.
153. TNA, CO 28/17, ff. 266–269^v.
154. TNA PC1/58/B2A, Pt1.
155. UMJRL, STP 2/3 f.13: the fine was 200 pounds sugar.
156. Behn, *Oroonoko*, pp. 237–239; William Byam, *An Exact Relation of the Most Execrable Attempts of John Allin* (London, 1665), pp. 4, 8–9, 11.
157. BDA, RB4/23, p. 254; TNA, CO 155/2, p. 535.
158. Words put into the mouth of the manumitted slave character, John Talbot Compo-bell, it is assumed by Rev. Robert Robertson, who although from Nevis composed an impersonation narrative about Jamaica: [Robertson], *A Speech*, p. 48. Attributed to Rev. Robert Robertson, "The Speech of Caribus in Answer to Moses Bon Saam" in *Prompter* 18 (January 1735): 91–93; *The Speech of Mr John Talbot Compo-bell, a Free Christian-Negro to His Countrymen in the Mountains of Jamaica* (London, 1736).
159. *Bermuda Historical Quarterly* 1.1 (1944), p. 6.
160. UMJRL, STP 2/3, f. 1.
161. TNA, CO 1/58, no. 43.
162. TNA CO 155/1, p. 333.
163. Sloane, *Voyage*, vol.i, p. lvii; Richard B. Sheridan, *Doctors and Slaves: A Medical and Demographic History of Slavery in the British West Indies, 1680–1834* (Cambridge: Cambridge University Press, 1985), p. 190.
164. Behn, *Oroonoko*, pp. 237–239.
165. James Field, "A Letter from the Reverend Mr. James Field, Rector of St. Johns in Antegoa, concerning Two Cases of Wounds in the Stomach, to Mr. John Douglas, Surgeon, F.R.S.," *Philosophical Transactions* 32 (1722–1723): 78–79, 79.
166. TNA, CO 137/8, nos. 39, 39i; TNA, CO 138/12, pp. 397–399.
167. NAS, CS96/3102.
168. NAS, CS96/3014, p. 4, p. 11; NAS, CS96/3102: April 27, 1735, cost 4s 4d.; NAS, CS96/3104, p. 55.

169. "N.Dead 18 [July 1734] My Negroman Sterat died being scalded in the Lees of the Stills ten Day's ago": NAS, CS96/3102. A smith called Anthony Forester invented a device to utilize transferable heat from one cauldron to another, rather than consuming coal: Oxf.Bodl., MS Eng.Hist./c.478/f.305, Many more examples of injuries come from the late eighteenth century: Sheridan, *Doctors and Slaves*, pp. 189–190; James Grainger, *An Essay on the More Common West-India Diseases* (Edinburgh, 1802).

170. "Although my skin be black, within my veins / Runs bloud as red, and Royal as the best": Aphra Behn, *Abdelazer, or, The Moor's Revenge a Tragedy* (London, 1677), Act 1, scene i, p. 5; Behn, *Oroonoko*, pp. 20–21, 23, 24, [my emphasis].

171. Sarah Barber, *A Revolutionary Rogue: Henry Marten and the English Republic* (Stroud: Sutton, 2000), pp. 136–140.

172. [Robertson], *John Talbot Compo-bell*, p. 38.

173. Mr Lister, "An Extract of a Letter of Mr. Listers, Containing Some Observations Made at the Barbado's," *Philosophical Transactions* 10 (1675): 399–400, 400.

174. William Byrd, "An Account of a Negro-Boy That is Dappel'd in Several Places of His Body with White Spots," *Philosophical Transactions* 19 (1695): 781–782. Byrd observed the boy, aged eleven, in Virginia: Maude I Woodfin, "William Byrd and the Royal Society," *Virginia Magazine of History and Biography* 40 (1932): 23–34 and 111–123; George L. Sioussat, "The 'Philosophical Transactions' of the Royal Society in the Libraries of William Byrd of Westover, Benjamin Franklin, and the American Philosophical Society," *Proceedings of the American Philosophical Society* 93.2 (1949): pp. 99–113.

175. "X.A.," "An Account of a Faetus, Voided by the Ulcerated navil of a Negro in Nevis, by Mr. James Brodie; Communicated by Dr. Preston," *Philosophical Transactions* 19 (1695–1697): 580–581; James Brodie was a captain, surgeon to Hamilton's regiment in the Leeward Islands, well supported by the officers.

176. DevonRO, 4652M-O/Z/18.

177. Behn, *Oroonoko*, pp. 5–7.

178. "The manner of their attire and painting them selues when they goe to their generall huntings, or at theire solemn feasts," "A chiefe Herowans wyfe of Pomeoc," "One of the wyues of Wyngyno," "Of Florida": Sloan, *A New World*, pp. 120–121, 122–123, 126–127, 130–131, 134–135, 136–137.

179. Hariot, *Briefe and True Report*, appendix; Sloan, *A New World*, pp. 152–161; [Robert Beverley], *The History and Present State of Virginia* (London, 1705), iii, pp. 5–12.

180. The word "tattoo" ("tatow") came into the English language in the late eighteenth century, from James Cook's voyages to Polynesia.

181. Lionel Wafer, *A New Voyage And Description of the Isthmus of America*, 2nd edn (London, 1704), pp. 26, 32.

182. Ibid., pp. 110–111.

183. Roger L'Estrange, *The Confession and Execution of the Prisoners at Tyburn on Wednesday the 5th of this Instant July, 1676* (London, 1676), p. 2.

184. TNA, CO 1/46, no. 133, 133i; TNA, CO 1/50, no. 100, f. 99.

185. CKS, Q/SRg/m.8d Maidstone, 1598; Q/SRg/m.4 Canterbury 1597/8.

186. Lefroy, *Memorials*, ii, p. 388; 602; TNA, CO 1/59, no. 39.

187. TNA, CO 140/3, pp. 212–217.
188. NorthumbriaRO, QSI/1, f106r (514) 17 Oct., 8 Jas. I (1610); CCALSS, ZS/BT/2, 1655–1723.
189. TNA, CO 152/3, nos.3, 3i–xxi; TNA, CO 152/1, no. 4, 4i.
190. NAS, CS96/3103, unfol.; Judith Banister (ed.), *English Silver Hallmarks* (Slough: W. Foulsham, 1970), p. 92. Ambrose Heal, *The London Goldsmiths, 1200–1800* (Cambridge: Cambridge University Press, 1935), p. 133.
191. NAS, CS96/3103, p. 6: September 16, 1730, "Sundry Acco^{ts} to Mr John Craig & Co/ Plant at Cayon in S. Christophers for a Negro silver mark 16s."
192. NAS, GD34/933/1.
193. TNA, CO 1/67, no. 95.
194. UCL, ADD MS 70, [loose] f. 2.
195. UCL, ADD MS 70, ff. 22v-23.
196. TNA, C110/175.
197. LPL, SPG General Correspondence, ff. 75, 76.
198. UCL, ADD MS 70, f. 27; TNA, CO 1/42, f. 194.
199. UCL, ADD MS 70, f. 29^v.
200. "A familiar Description of the Mosqueto Kingdom," in *Collection of Voyages and Travels*, vi, p. 288.
201. A rare survival of a Monmouth cap can be found in Nelson Museum & Local History Centre, Monmouth, Item reference GTJ01788.
202. "Twenty Ordinary hatts for men cannot worke in the Sun without them": SHC, DD/WHh/1090 pt.2/1; BDA, RB 3/1, p. 803.
203. William Bullock, *Virginia Impartially Examined* (London, 1649), p. 36.
204. Surrey HC, LM/2022.
205. HALS, DE/HL/12552, no. 3 (unfol).
206. TNA, CO 124/2, pp. 321–322; TNA, CO 124/2, p. 324.
207. NAS, CS96/3014, ff. 1^v, 9.
208. NAAB, Roe Box 187: Antigua, 26 March 1684(5).
209. Ligon, *History*, showing runaways wearing only loincloths; Henry Whistler, "Journal of the West India Expedition," in C. H. Firth (ed.), *The Narrative of General Venables* (London: Longmans, 1900), p. 146; Alexander Gunkel and Jerome S. Handler, "A Swiss Medical Doctor's Description of Barbados in 1661: The Account of Felix Christian Spoeri," *JBMHS* 31 (1969): 3–13, 7; Jean-Baptiste du Tertre, *L'Histoire générale des Antilles habitées par les Français* (4 vols) (Paris, 1667–1671), depicted slaves in cotton shorts when working with sugar. Jennifer L. Morgan, *Laboring Women: Reproduction and Gender in New World Slavery* (Philadelphia: Pennsylvania University Press, 2004.
210. JCB, Cabinet Blathwayt 30, "Monserrat Insula Entire and in 4 parts herein Inclosed," the map of Montserrat from the "Blathwayt Atlas" (1673); Pulsipher, "Assessing the usefulness."
211. Infected by "chego's, Sloane was treated by a woman "who had been a Queen in her own Country." The chigger was removed with a pin, the wound sterilized with hot tobacco ash: Sloane, *Voyage*, vol. i, p. cxxiv.
212. [Robertson], *John Talbot Compo-bell*, p. 67.
213. R. B., *The English Empire in America*, 5th edn (London, 1711), p. 136.
214. NAS, CS96/3096/1, ff. 5,9^a.
215. TNA, PROB 18/60/22, f.b.

216. TNA, CO 138/6, pp. 39–41.
217. TNA, C110/175.
218. TNA, CO 152/8, no. 15viii.
219. NAAB, ROE box 187.
220. Sloane, *Voyage*, vol. i, pp. cliii, cxxviii.
221. Trapham, DISCOURSE, pp. 113, 114–115, 120–121; M. T. Ashworth, "Tercentenary of the First English Book on Tropical Medicine, by Thomas Trapham of Jamaica," *British Medical Journal* (1979): 475–477.
222. Trapham, DISCOURSE, pp. 111–112. Guinea worms, *Dracunculus medinensis*, are parasitic nematodes transmitted to humans (primarily in Africa) via infected water.
223. "An Attempt to Prove the Antiquity of the Venereal Disease, Long Before the Discovery of the West-Indies; in a Letter from Mr. William Beckett, Surgeon, to Dr. James Douglass, M.D. and R.Soc.Soc. and By Him Communicated to the Royal Society," *Philosophical Transactions* 30 (1717–1719): 839–847.
224. Trapham, DISCOURSE, pp. 125–126.
225. L. S., *Profulaction: Or Some Considerations of a Notable Experiment To Root out the French Pox from the English Nation* (London, 1673), pp. 82–86; Kevin P. Siena, "Pollution, Promiscuity, and the Pox: English Venereology and the Early Modern Medical Discourse on Social and Sexual Danger," *Journal of the History of Sexuality* 8.4 (1998): 553–574.
226. UCL, ADD MS f. 27; John Ward Dean, *Memoir of Rev. Michael Wrigglesworth, Author of The Day of Doom* (Albany, NY: Joel Munsell, 1871), pp. 76–77: James Thatcher, *American Medical Biography* (2 vols) (Boston, MA: Richardson & Lord and Cottons & Barnard, 1828), i p. 293; Andrew Wear, *Knowledge and Practice in English Medicine, 1550–1680* (Cambridge: Cambridge University Press, 2000), p. 436.
227. [Thomas Trapham], *Some Observations Made upon the Bermudas Berries:… shewing Their Admirable Virtues in Curing The Green-Sickness* (London, 1694), p. 6.
228. Trapham, DISCOURSE, p. 112
229. TNA, CO 1/30, no. 55.
230. *Laws of Jamaica, 1683*, preface d2–d3; Trapham, DISCOURSE, p. 69.
231. Sloane, *Voyage*, vol. i, p. cxlvii.
232. ROLLR, DG7 Box 4982, f. 4^v.
233. Herbert S. Klein and Stanley L. Engerman, "Fertility Differentials between Slaves in the United States and the British West Indies: A Note on Lactation Practices and Their Possible Implications," *WMQ*, 3rd series, 35.2 (1978): 357–374.
234. *Bermuda Historical Quarterly* 1.2 (1944), p. 47.
235. NAS, CS96/3102, ff. 1, 6.
236. NAS, CS96/3096/1 "Genealogie of the Earl of Glenairns Family."
237. TNA, PROB 18/60/22: These were also silver, further conflating Cunyngham's materiality, construction of status and brand.
238. Sloane, *Voyage*, vol. i.
239. Londa Schiebinger, "Feminist History of Colonial Science," *Hypatia* 19.1 (2004): 233–254; *Eadem*, "Exotic Abortifacients: The Global Politics of Plants in the 18th Century," *Endeavour* 24.3 (2000): 117–121; *Eadem*, *Plants and Empire: Colonial Bioprospecting in the Atlantic World* (Cambridge, MA: Harvard University Press, 2004).

240. Robert Braxton Bird, "18th Century Transformations of the Jamaican Plantocracy: Edward Long and Bryan Edwards," unpublished Masters' thesis, Florida State University, 2007, p. 17.
241. TNA, PROB 18/60/22.
242. Sloane, *Voyage*, i, p. cxlviii.
243. DRO, D5557/2/120/8; Sloane, *A Voyage*, vol. i, p. cxxxi.
244. BL Sloane 2302; Jerome S. Handler and Robert S. Corruccini, "Weaning among West Indian Slaves: Historical and Bioanthropological Evidence from Barbados," *WMQ*, 3rd ser. 43.1 (1986): 111–117.
245. This was not the case further north: TNA, CO 5/1263, no. 6.
246. Bushel and Bond, *Narrative of the Late Dreadful Fire*, p. 2; TNA, CO 1/30, no. 55; *A Country Dialogue between William and James* (n.p., 1692); *The Dreadful Voice of Fire, Begun at Edinburgh, 3rd February 1700* (n.p., 1700).
247. Anthony Horneck, *The Great Law of Consideration* (London, 1677), Epistle Dedicatory, pp. v–vi, 227–228.
248. [Dr.] John Wilkins [Dean of Ripon, FRS], *An Essay towards a Real Character, and a Philosophical Language* (London, 1668), n.p., "Advertisement to the Reader."
249. UCL, ADD MS 70, ff. 27–27ᵛ.
250. TNA, CO 1/65, nos. 50, 50 i–xx; CO 29/4, pp. 7–17.
251. Trapham, *Discourse*, p. 50; *The Laws of Jamaica* (London, 1683), preface d2–d3.
252. UMJRL, STP 2/8 [c]: I have been unable to decipher "Maligeto."
253. Hugh Binning, *An Usefull Case of Conscience* (Edinburgh? [certainly Scotland], s.n., 1693), p. 43.
254. Hugh Binning, *The Sinners Sanctuary* (Edinburgh, 1670), pp. 149–150.

5 Will

1. Abbreviated to Eleuthera. W. Hubert Miller, "The Colonization of the Bahamas, 1647–1670," *WMQ* 3rd ser., 2.1 (1945): 33–46.
2. Articles and Orders, made and agreed upon the 9th Day of July, 1647... By the Company of Adventurers for the Plantation of the Islands of Eleutheria, formerly called Buhama in America (n.p., [1647]), broadsheet; The Winthrop Papers: Collections of the Massachusetts Historical Society, 5th ser. 1 (1871), pp. 340–343.
3. Michael Craton, *A History of the Bahamas* (Waterloo, ON: San Salvador Press, 3rd edn, 1986), pp. 54–61.
4. TNA, PRO 30/24/48/49, f. 125. "Lethargy dropsy" may have been a cholera form of gastroenteritis; TNA, PRO 30/24/48/66.
5. TNA, PRO 30/24/48, no. 66; Authorized Bible: Matt. 7: 20 and 22.
6. L. H. Roper, *Conceiving Carolina: Proprietors, Planters, and Plots, 1662–1729* (London: Macmillan, 2004), pp. 41–45.
7. [Thomas Hodges], *Plantation Justice, Shewing the Constitution of Their Courts and What Sort of Judges They Have in Them* (London, 1701), pp. 3, 10.
8. Isaiah Berlin, *Two Concepts of Liberty* (Oxford: Clarendon Press, 1958); Jonathan Lear, *Radical Hope: Ethics in the Face of Cultural Devastation* (New Haven, CT: Harvard University Press, 2008); Jimmy Casas Kalusen, "Room Enough: America, Natural Liberty, and Consent in Locke's *Second Treatise*," *Journal of Politics* 69.3 (2007): 760–769.

9. Sir Anthony Fitzherbert, *The newe boke of Iustices of the peas* (1538), f. 127b; Sir Edward Coke, *The first Part of the Institutes of the Lawes of England*, part II. x. §170; David Armitage, "John Locke, Carolina and the *Two Treatises of Government*," *Political Theory* 32.5 (2004): 602–627.

10. Demission of the Crown by Mary, Queen of Scots, Convention of Edinburgh, July 25, 1567: 1567/7/25/1; and Parliament of Edinburgh, December 6, 1567; NAS, CS96/3096/1.

11. Fitzherbert, *Husbandry*, p. 73.

12. Byam, *Exact Relation*, p. 4.

13. Christopher Tomlins, "The Legal Cartography of Colonization, the Legal Polyphony of Settlement: English Intrusions on the American Mainland in the Seventeenth Century," *Law and Social Inquiry* 26.2 (2001): 315–372.

14. Sarah Barber, "Power in the English Caribbean: The Proprietorship of Lord Willoughby of Parham," in L. H. Roper and B. Van Ruymbeke (eds.), *Constructing Early Modern Empires: Proprietary Ventures in the Atlantic World, 1500–1750* (Leiden: Brill, 2004), pp. 189–212; TCD, MS 736 pp. 40–41.

15. Robert Filmer, *Patriarcha: Or The Natural Power of Kings* (London, 1680): scholars debate whether it was written in the 1630s or 1640s.

16. James Daly, *Sir Robert Filmer and English political Thought* (Toronto/Buffalo/London: University of Toronto Press, 1979); R. W. K. Hinton, "Husbands, Fathers and Conquerors," *Political Studies* 15.3 (1967): 291–300.

17. Filmer, *Patriarcha*, Chapter 1: "The First Kings were Fathers of Families," I/4 (1680 edn, p. 12).

18. Genesis 9:20. The focus here is on Noah the husbandman, and not on the representations and long line of misinterpretations of the misnamed "curse of Ham," the three sons of Noah representing European, Semitic, and Hamitic peoples, or that this was the pretext for slavery or racism: Benjamin Braude, "The Sons of Noah and the Construction of Ethnic and Geographical Identities in the Medieval and Early-Modern Periods," *WMQ*, 3rd ser., 54.1 (1997): pp. 103–142.

19. [Robert Robertson], *The Speech of Mr John Talbot Compo-bell, a Free Christian-Negro to His Countrymen in the Mountains of Jamaica* (London, 1736) purports to demonstrate the beneficent effect of Christianity on black people in the colonies, in comparison with the brutal violence and unrest practiced by maroon communities under the leadership of another "Free Negro," Moses Bon Sàam. Robertson constructed a debate between two black men about what Isaiah Berlin would later call "positive" (self-restraint) and "negative" (absence of restraint) liberty.

20. Sir Robert Filmer, *Patriarcha and Other Writings* (edited by Johann Sommerville, Cambridge Texts in the History of Political Thought [Cambridge: Cambridge University Press, 1991]), *Patriarcha*, p. 14; *Observations concerning the Originall of Government*, p. 187.

21. Rev. Mr. William Smith, *A Natural History of Nevis* (Cambridge, 1745), Letter iii, pp. 79–80, 84. Debating whether Scripture, Hobbes, Pufendorf, or Machiavelli expressed the greatest casuistry.

22. Smith, *Natural History*, pp. 83–84.

23. Ibid., p. 80.

24. TCD, MS 736; Charles Rogers, "Notes in the History of Sir Jerome Alexander, Second Justice of the Court of Common Pleas, and Founder of

the Alexander Library, Trinity College," *TRHS* 1 (1872): 220–240 and 2 (1873): 94–116.
25. TCD, MS 736, pp. 36–40.
26. TCD, MS 736 pp. 80–81.
27. John Cordy Jeaffreson, *A Young Squire of the Seventeenth Century* (2 vols.) (London: Hurst & Blackett, 1878), i, pp. 4–5.
28. TCD, MS 736, p. 109.
29. TCD, MS 736, pp. 112–114, p. 114: Jer.22:13–14: "Woe unto him that buildeth his house by unrighteousness, and his chambers by wrong; that useth his neighbour's service without wages, and giveth him not for his work; / That saith, I will build me a wide house and large chambers, and cutteth him out windows; and it is cieled with cedar, and painted with vermillion."
30. TCD, MS 736, p. 115.
31. TCD, MS 736, pp. 117–118.
32. TCD, MS 736, pp. 5–11; TCD MS 736, pp. 14–28.
33. BL, Sloane 159(5), ff. 20–21; TNA, CO 1/20, no. 155; TNA, CO 1/19, no. 92, f. 109^v.
34. TNA, CO 1/14, nos. 18, 19, 20.
35. This Sir Robert Harley was a fellow royalist conspirator in Barbados, the brother of Sir Edward Harley and uncle to the future first Earl of Oxford of the same name. It is claimed that Harley was established at the plantation in Surinam called St. John's Hill, which is where, in *Oroonoko*, Aphra Behn claimed she lived: Harrison Gray Platt Jr., "Astrea and Celadon: An Untouched Portrait of Aphra Behn," *PMLA* 49.2 (1934): 544–559.
36. NA, DD. P6/1/22/20.
37. David Dobson, *Directory of Scots Banished to the American Plantations, 1650–1775* (Baltimore, MD: Genealogical Publishing, 1983); Smith, *Natural History*, pp. 77–79.
38. BL, Add. MSS 18,683, f. 6^v.
39. [John Locke], *Two Treatises of Government* (London, 1690).
40. Locke, *Two Treatises*, pp. 336–337; Herman Lebovics, "The Uses of America in Locke's Second Treatise of Government," *JHI* 47.4 (1986): pp. 567–581; Barbara Arneil, "Trade, Plantations, and Property: John Locke and the Economic Defense of Colonialism," *JHI* 55.4 (1994): pp. 591–609; Jimmy Casas Klausen, "Room Enough: America, Natural Liberty, and Consent in Locke's *Second Treatise*," *Journal of Politics* 69.3 (2007): 760–769.
41. "The Fundamental Constitutions of Carolina," nos. i and ii, from John Locke, *The Works of John Locke in Nine Volumes* (London: Rivington, 1824) 12th edn, vol. 9. This section makes no comment either way as to whether Locke was responsible for the words or the sentiments behind the Constitutions.
42. William Bennett Munro, *The Seigniorial System in Canada: A Study in French Colonial Policy* (Cambridge, MA: Harvard University Press, 1906); Munro, *The Seigneurs of Old Canada: A Chronicle of New-World Feudalism* (Glasgow, 1920); Roper, *Conceiving Carolina*, pp. 29–49, p. 31.
43. BristolRO, 8032(1).
44. Mountgomery, *Discourse*, p. 2.
45. Mountgomery, *Discourse*, pp. 1, 3–4; TNA, PC 1/58/B2A Pt.1.
46. H[erman] Moll, *A New Map of the North Parts of America Claimed by France* (London: John King, 1720); Donald W. Large, "The Land Law of Scotland—A

Comparison with American and English concepts," *Environmental Law* 17.1 (1986–1987): 1–42.
47. D. J. A. Clines, "The Image of God in Man," *Tyndale Bulletin* 19 (1968): 53–103.
48. Genesis: 1.30–31, 2.5, 2.8, 2.20–23.
49. Michael McGiffert, "From Moses to Adam: The Making of the Covenant of Works," *Sixteenth Century Journal* 19.2 (1998): 131–155; J. B. Ames, "Law and Morals," *Harvard Law Review* (1908); Adam Gifford Jr., "The Evolution of the Social Contract," *Constitutional Political Economy* 13 (2002): 361–379; *Idem.*, "Being and Time: On the Nature of the Evolution of Institutions," *Journal of Bioeconomics* 1 (1999): 127–149.
50. McGiffert, "Moses to Adam," pp. 138–140.
51. G. E. Aylmer, "The Meaning and Definition of 'property' in Seventeenth-Century England," *Past and Present* 86 (1980): 87–97.
52. Abraham's son, Isaac, had two sons. Esau was a hunter, and Jacob was a shepherd. Therefore the people of Israel had dominion over the smaller "wild" animals which were hunted, and the larger livestock which constituted moveable property, but lived on the land: Gen:28.13.
53. John Boys, *An Exposition of the Dominical Epistles and Gospels Used in Our English Liturgie* (London, 1610), pp. 81–82.
54. TNA, CO 31/1, p. 656.
55. Roger Coke, *Treatises of the Nature of Man* (London, 1685), "The Design," E.
56. Roger Coke, *A Detection of the Court and State of England* (2 vols) (London, 1694); *Idem.*, *A Discourse Of Trade* (London, 1670); *Idem.*, *England's Improvements* (London, 1675); *Justice Vindicated from the False Fucus put upon it by Thomas White Gent. Mr Thomas Hobbs, And Hugo Grotius. As Also Elements Of Power and Subjection* (London, 1660); *Idem.*, *Reflections upon the East-Indy and Royal African Companies* (London, 1695).
57. Claire Priest, "Creating an American Property Law: Alienability and Its Limits in American History," *Harvard Law Review* 120.2 (2006): 385–458.
58. Lois Green Carr and Lorena S. Walsh, "The Planter's Wife: The Experience of White Women in seventeenth-Century Maryland," *WMQ* 34.4 (1977): 542–571.
59. TNA, CO 152/42, no. 105, f. 214[v].
60. TNA, PROB 18/60/22.
61. Cara Anzilotti, *In the Affairs of the World: Women, Patriarchy, and Power in Colonial South Carolina* (Westport, CT: Greenwood Press, 2002).
62. TNA, PRO 30/24/48/32, ff. 37–38[v]; TNA, PRO 30/24/48, no. 21(2), f. 41.
63. Anzilotti, "Autonomy and the Female Planter," pp. 244–245; Edward McCrady, *An Historic Church, the Westminster Abbey of South Carolina : A Sketch of St. Philip's Church, Charleston, S.C* (Charleston, SC: Walker, Evans and Cogswll, 1901), p. 10; Nancy C. Wooten, "Beautiful Faces without Names," *Times and Democrat*, SC, March 3, 2007.
64. Bates and Leland, *Proprietary Records*, iii, p. 132; *The Surveyor's Notebook for Charles Town, 1732–1752* (Columbia: SC Department of Archives and History).
65. Linda Sturtz, "Review of *In the Affairs of the World: Women, Patriarchy, and Power in Colonial South Carolina*," *Journal of American History* 90.3 (2003): 995–996.

66. Terri L. Snyder, "Review: Ordinary People," *WMQ*, 3rd. series, 60.1 (2003): 225–229; Anzilotti, *Affairs of the World*, pp. 58–60; [Mary Astell], *An Essay in Defence of the Female Sex* (London, 1696), p. 22; TNA, CO 1/53, no. 102.
67. Robert D. Mitchell, "American Origins and Regional Institutions: The Seventeenth-Century Chesapeake," *Annals of the Association of American Geographers* 73.3 (1983): 404–420; Philippe Rosenberg, "Thomas Tryon and the Seventeenth-Century Dimensions of Antislavery," *WMQ*, 3rd ser., 61.4 (2004): 609–642.
68. Susan Staves, "Chattel Property Rules and the Construction of Englishness, 1660–1800," *Law and History Review* 12.1 (1994): 123–153; John Brewer and Susan Staves (eds.), *Early Modern Conceptions of Property* (London: Routledge, 1995).
69. In the seventeenth-century torrid zone, the four could be (1) merchant ships; (2) army versus militia defense; (3) sugar and the 4½ percent levy, or the monopoly within the slave trade of the Royal African Company; (4) women, servants, slaves, and/or livestock as chattel.
70. William Walter Hening, *Statutes at Large* (Richmond, VA, 1812) vol. 1, pp. 128–129; *The Tragical Relation of the Virginia Assembly, 1624*, in Lyon Gardiner Tyler, *Narratives of Early Virginia, 1606–1625* (New York: Charles Scribner's Sons, 1907), pp. 421–426.
71. Oliver, *History of…Antigua*, vol. iii, pp. 30–32; TNA, CO 1/57, nos. 109, 110.
72. Bullock, VIRGINIA *Impartially Examined*, p. 66.
73. Oliver, *Island of Antigua*, p. 30.
74. BLARS, R6/21 1/40, p. 6.
75. BLARS, R6/21 1/40, p. 3; LMA, Parish registers of St. Mary Woolnoth.
76. Sir Josiah Child, *A Discourse about Trade* ([London], 1690), pp. 169–172; David Souden, "'Rogues, Whores and Vagabonds'? Indentured Servant Emigrants to North America, and the Case of Mid-Seventeenth-Century Bristol," *Social History* 3.1 (1978): 23–41; John Wareing, "Preventative and Punitive Regulation in Seventeenth-Century Social Policy: Conflicts of Interest and the Failure to Make 'Stealing and Transporting Children, and Other Persons' a Felony, 1645–73," *Social History* 27.3 (2002): 288–308.
77. [Marcellus Rivers and Oxenbridge Foyle], *Englands Slavery, Or Barbados Merchandize* (London, "Printed in the Eleventh year of *Englands* Liberty. 1659."), p. 5.
78. BDA, Transcript of Acts of Barbados 1682–1698, pp. 86–92.
79. BDA, Transcript Acts, 1682–1698, pp. 191–93; BDA, RB 6/6, pp. 125–126.
80. BL, Lansdowne MSS vol. 256, f. 265: Aubrey Gwynne (ed.), "Documents Relating to the Irish in the West Indies," *Analecta Hibernica* 4 (1932): 157–158; Jill Sheppard, *The "Redlegs" of Barbados* (New York: kto press, 1977); TNA, CO 1/21, no. 170; Hilary McD. Beckles, "A 'Riotous and Unruly Lot': Irish Indentured Servants and Freemen in the English West Indies, 1644–1713," *WMQ*, 3rd ser., 47.4 (1990): 503–522.
81. Gwynne, "Irish in the West Indies," p. 159.
82. Beckles, "Riotous and Unruly Lot," pp. 512–516.
83. Gwynne, "Irish in the West Indies," pp. 236–238; Beckles, "Riotous and Unruly Lot," pp. 516–517.

84. BDA, RB 6/15, p. 142.
85. Richard Tuck, "Power and Authority in Seventeenth-Century England," *Historical Journal* 17.1 (1974): 43–61.
86. Ligon, *History*, p. 44.
87. *Of the Island of BARBADOS. Made and Enacted since the Reducement of the same, unto the Authority of the Common-wealth of England* (London, [1652]), pp. 111–116.
88. UCL, ADD MS 70, ff. 123v–124, f. 123^v.
89. [Hodges], *Present state of Justice* p. 3.
90. Richard Hall, *Acts, Passed in the Island of Barbados. From 1643 to 1762, Inclusive* (London, 1764): "An Act for the good governing of Servants, and ordaining the Rights between Masters and Servants," September 27, 1661, pp. 35–42, preamble, p. 35.
91. "Act for the good governing of Servants," clause xx, in Hall, *Acts*, p. 41. Emphasis added.
92. DevonRO, QS 128/ Topsham 126/ 7, 8, 9, 11, 12; QS/128/57/4.
93. *The Algier Slaves Releasement: or the Unchangeable Boat-wain* (broadsheet, London, n.d. [1685]); *The Batchelor's Triumph: Or, The Single-Man's Happiness* (London, 1675), broadsheet.
94. *Apprentices no Slaves: An Answer to a Namelesse Pamphlet lately published as an Act, Declaring hat Habit Apprentices are to Wear* (London, 1662), p. 6.
95. Job Hartop, *The Rare Trauailes of Iob Hortop* (London, 1591); Anon, *Light Shining in BUCKINGHAMSHIRE, or, A Discovery of the Main Ground; Originall Cause of All the Slavery in the World* (n.p., 1648); Anon, *A Declaration of the Commoners of England, to His Excellency the Lord General Cromwel: Concerning the Crown, Government, Liberty, and Priviledges of the People; and the Setting of the Land Free from all Taxes, Slavery, and Oppressions* (London, 1652); Anon, *Law Unknown, OR, Judgement Unjust* (n.p., 1662); Richard Ames, *Chuse Which You Will, Liberty or Slavery... the Danger of Being Again Subjected to a POPISH PRINCE* (London, 1692); Anon, *A DIALOGUE betwixt Whig and Tory, alias Williamite and Jacobite... and all those who prefer English Liberty, and Protestant Religion, to French Slavery and Popery* (n.p., 1693); Anon, *England's Deliverance from Popery and Slavery* (London, 1695); Anon, *The People of Scotland's Groans and Lamentable Complaints* (n.p., n.d., [1700]).
96. Job Hartop, *The Rare Trauailes of Iob Hortop* (2nd expanded ed., for William Wright, London, 1591), 24pp, C3^v; Daniel J. Vitkus (ed.), *Piracy, Slavery, and Redemption: Barbary Captivity Narratives from Early Modern England* (New York: Columbia University Press, 2001); Anna Suranyi, *The Genius of the English Nation: Travel Writing and National Identity in Early Modern England* (Newark, NJ: University of Delaware Press, 2008).
97. Anon, *Considerations upon the Trade to Guinea* (London, 1708), pp. 29–30; Anon, *Some Short Remarks,... Considerations upon the Trade to Guinea* (n.p., 1709), p. 1.
98. Shaunnagh Dorsett, "'Since Time Immemorial': A Story of Common Law Jurisdiction, Native Title and the Case of Tanistry," *Melbourne University Law Review* 26 (2002): 32–59.
99. Burnard, "Slave Naming Patterns," pp. 328, 330–331; Jerome S. Handler and JoAnn Jacoby, "Slave Names and Naming in Barbados, 1650–1830," *WMQ* liii (1996): 692–697.

100. *Of the Island of* BARBADOS., p. 44.
101. Ibid., pp. 81–83.
102. SHC, DD\CM 3; Frederick Brown and Raymond Gorges, *The Story of a Family... Being a History of the Family of Gorges* (Boston, MA, 1944); NAJm, wills vol. iii, f. 127; *The Continuation of the Laws of Jamaica... Being the Second Volume* (London, 1698), p. 65.
103. Rawlin, *Laws of Barbados*, pp. 58, 68, 72–73.
104. Ibid., p. 115.
105. Daniel Horsmanden, *A* JOURNAL *of the* PROCEEDINGS *in the Detection of the* CONSPIRACY (New York, 1744).
106. Locke, *Two Treatises*, ii, p. 32.
107. Dunn, *Sugar and Slaves*, pp. 238–241; Hilary Beckles, *General History of the Caribbean*, vol. iii (London: UNESCO/Macmillan, 1997), p. 201. It is phenomenally difficult to find any text of the "Barbados Slave Code" of 1661: Act 94 of *An abridgement of the laws in force and use in Her Majesty's plantations; (viz.) of Virginia, Jamaica, Barbadoes, Maryland, New-England, New-York* (London, 1704) gives only one Act, and does not specify a date. The previous codification of Barbados laws was that made by Searle in the 1650s: *Of the Island of* BARBADOS.
108. "An act for the better ordering and governing of Negroes," September 27, 1661, TNA, CO 30/2, pp. 16–26; Anthony McFarlane, *The British in the Americas, 1480–1815* (London: Longman, 1994), p. 135; Rawlin, *Laws of Barbados*: Act no. 329, August 8, 1688, pp. 156–164; Christopher Tomlins, *Freedom Bound: Law, Labor, and Civic Identity in Colonizing English America, 1580–1865* (Cambridge: Cambridge University Press, 2010), pp. 442–451; Edward B. Rugemer, "The Development of Master and Race in the Comprehensive Slave Codes of the Greater Caribbean during the Seventeenth Century," *WMQ* 70.3 (2013): 429–458.
109. Rawlin, *Laws of Barbados*, preamble, p. 156.
110. [Robertson], *John Talbot Compo-bell*, pp. 48–49.
111. Ibid., p. 51.
112. Robert South, *Twelve Sermons Preached upon Several Occasions* (London, 1694); Idem., "Sermon II: Of the Love of Christ to his Disciples," (John xv.15): *Sermons preached upon several Occasions* (London, 1737), vol. ii, pp. 45–80, pp. 53–54: with "(or Slave)" added after each reference to "Servant" by Robert Robertson, *The Speech*, p. 51.
113. Morgan Godwyn, *Trade Preferr'd before Religion, and Christ Made to Give Place to Mammon* (London, 1685).
114. Thomas Tryon, *The Negro's Complaint of Their Hard Servitude* (London, 1684): the message watered by making the master a French Catholic; *Idem., A Discourse in Way of a Dialogue, between an Ethiopean or Negro-Slave and a Christian, That Was His Master in America* (London, 1684), published together as *Friendly Advice*; Idem., *Tryon's Letters* (London, 1700), pp. 199–200; Rosenberg, "Thomas Tryon," p. 627.
115. [Robertson], *John Talbot Compo-bell*, pp. 16, 36. On the latter page is listed the mercantilist economist, Charles d'Avenant, particularly in *An Essay upon the Ways and Means of Supplying the War* (London, 1695), and [Walter Moyle], *The Second Part of an Argument, Shewing, that a Standing Army Is inconsistent with A Free Government* (London, 1697).
116. [Robertson] *The Speech*, pp. 30–31.

117. *Abridgement of the laws*, p. 33.
118. Rosenberg, "Tryon and Antislavery," p. 613; Timothy Morton, "Plantation in Wrath," in Timothy Morton and Nigel Smith (eds.), *Radicalism in British literary Culture, 1650–1830: From Revolution to Revolution* (Cambridge: Cambridge University Press, 2002), pp. 70–88.
119. Besse, *A Collection of the Sufferings*, ii, p. 308. Emphasis added.
120. Cleland, *State of Sugar*, p. 4.
121. Berkeley, "A Proposal," *Works*, pp. 422–423.
122. A. J. Williams-Myers, "Slavery, Rebellion, and Revolution in the Americas: A Historiographical Scenario on the Theses of Genovese and Others," *Journal of Black Studies* 26.4 (1996): 381–400, 388; Eugene D. Genovese, *From Rebellion to Revolution: Afro-American Slave revolts in the Making of the Wider World* (Baton Rouge: Louisiana State University Press, 1979).
123. Mervyn C. Alleyne, "Continuity versus Creativity in Afro-American Language and Culture," in Salikoko S. Mufwene (ed.), *Africanisms in Afro-American Language Varieties* (Athens: University of Georgia Press, 1993), pp. 167–181.
124. Norman Klein, "The Two Asantes: Competing Interpretations of 'Slavery' in Akan-Asante Culture and Society," *Institute of African Studies Research Review* 12.1 (1980): 37–50.
125. TNA, CO 152/4, no. 73ii.
126. TNA, CO 152/4, no. 73.
127. LPL, MS 1123/2 item 167; Bodl.Rawlinson MSS C 983, ff. 157–158.
128. Harlow, *Codrington*, pp. 121–122.
129. Gordon, *Sermon*, Epistle dedicatory.
130. TNA, CO 158/8, no. 43a.
131. Harlow, *Codrington*, pp. 122–124; App. A, p. 218.
132. Alfred Caldecott, *The Church in the West Indies* (London: Frank Cass, 1898), p. 65; Ligon, *History*, p. 50.
133. Richard Baxter, *A Christian Directory* (London, 1673); George Fox, *Gospel Family-Order…the Ordering of Families, Both of Whites, Blacks and Indians* ([London], 1676); Morgan Godwyn, *Negro's and Indians Advocate*; Tryon, *Friendly Advcie* [sic].
134. [Robertson], *John Talbot Compo-bell*, pp. 15–17; Robert Sanderson, *XXXIV Sermons* (2 vols.) (London, 1671), ii, pp. 93–105; George Berkeley, *A Sermon Preached before the Incorporated Society for the Propagation of the Gospel in Foreign Parts* (London, 1732), pp. 19, 20.
135. Carter G. Woodson, "The Beginnings of the Miscegenation of the Whites and Blacks," *Journal of Negro History* iii.4 (1918): 335–353; Virginia Bernhard, "Bermuda and Virginia in the Seventeenth Century: A Comparative View," *Journal of Social History* 19.1 (1985); Steve Martinot, "The Racialized Construction of Class in the United States," *Social Justice* 27.1 (79) (2000): 49–60.
136. Godwyn, *Negro's & Indians Advocate*, pp. 22–23.
137. LPL, FP xv, ff. 216–216ᵛ.
138. BDA, RB 6/9, p. 210; RB 6/3, p. 12. Isabella, Margery, and John were the probable children of Ann and William Lesley.
139. LPL, FP xix, f. 104.
140. LPL, FP xix, f. 26; FP xix ff. 60–61.
141. LPL, FP xvii, ff. 93–95.
142. TNA, CO 1/53, no. 66; TNA, CO 1/53, no. 79.

143. TNA, CO 1/47, no. 99.
144. Salley, *Narratives* pp. 216, 217.
145. Thomas Bray, *Apostolick Charity*, (London, 1698).
146. LPL, FP xv, ff. 216–216ᵛ.
147. TNA, CO 1/10, no. 36.
148. LPL, FP xvii ff. 171–172; Oliver, *Caribbeana* vol. iii,, p. 343.
149. [Robertson], *John Talbot Compo-bell*, p. 33; LPL, FP xix, f. 26.
150. LPL, FP xv, ff. 259–259ᵛ; "A Breife Narrative of the Trade and Present Condition of the Company of Royall Adventurers of England trading into Africa," TNA, CO 1/19, no. 5, ff. 7–8ᵛ, f. 7.
151. LPL, FP xv, ff. 249–250ᵛ.
152. Vincent Alsop, *A Reply to the Reverend Dean of St. Pauls's Reflections on the Rector of Sutton, &c.* (London, 1681), p. 127.
153. Dunn gives the figure of 34 mulattoes and Negroes baptized, married, or buried in St. Michael's, Bridgetown between 1670 and 1687: Dunn, *Sugar and Slaves*, p. 255.
154. BDA, RL 1/1, parish register of St. Michael's, p. 280: "Hannah a negro woman of Capᵗ Wallyes gone for Carolina." William Walley had a plantation at Goose Creek and married Yeamans's widow, Margaret. It most likely refers to him, as he is listed in Barbados in 1677, sending muscovado to Andrew Percivall in Carolina: "Abstract of the records of the Register of the Province, 1675–1696," p. 165, September 14, 1677.
155. St. Philip's, Barbados parish register: BDA, p. 65, April 3, 1698: "William; Edward; Henry, Margaret, Hannah and Elizabeth, Children of a free Mulatto Woman named Rose; baptized 28 February 1697"; April 24, 1698, "Jane Daur: of Rose a free mulatto Woman."
156. The "surname," Cornsoe, does not appear anywhere in the records of Barbados except for a freed slave, John: Dunn, *Sugar and Slaves*, p. 255; St. Michael's parish register, pp. 320, 327; "Mingo A Negro Slave," St. Philip's baptisms, p. 69, January 14, 1701(2); St. Philip's baptisms, p. 80, 9 (September) 1711, "Charles Akinboy a negro Slave"; Trevor Burnard, "Slave Naming Patterns: Onomastics and the Taxonomy of Race in Eighteenth-Century Jamaica," *Journal of Interdisciplinary History* 31.3 (2001): 325–346.
157. [Morgan Godwyn], *The Revival: Or Directions for a Sculpture* (London, 1682), broadsheet.
158. TNA, CO 1/37, no. 22.
159. LPL, FP xv, ff. 266–267.
160. BDA, RL 1/29, pp. 21, 24.
161. When the Monmouth rebels transported to Barbados died on the island, they were noted as such at burial: 10 Jan., 1687, Bernard Bryan; 11 Feb., 1688, William Saunders living with Mr. Thomas Estwick. Many Catholics were buried in the Anglican churchyard, marked "RC."
162. TNA, CO 1/37.
163. TNA, CO 1/35, pp. 328–332.
164. TNA, CO 1/11, no. 25.
165. TNA, CO 31/1, p. 16.
166. Notts.RO, DD/P/6/1/22/21: Commission of appointment by Francis Lord Willoughby of Parham, General and Governor of Barbados and the Caribbee Islands to Sir Robert Harley, June 18, 1663. The seal is intact and in good condition.

167. UCL, ADD MS 70, f. 92ᵛ; TNA, CO 1/57, no. 144; TNA, CO 1/57, no. 144; CO 5/723, pp. 94–96; TNA, CO 1/57, no. 93; TNA, CO 5/904, pp. 227–228; TNA, CO 1/57, no. 125.
168. TNA, CO 137/2, nos. 5, 70ᵛ.
169. TNA, CO 31/5, pp. 273–274, no. 177; CO 137/3, no. 91.
170. TNA, CO 137/5, no. 18.
171. [Cleland], *Present State*, pp. 4, 8.
172. Robert Sandford, *A Relation of a Voyage on the Coast of the Province of Carolina* (1666): Salley, p. 91.
173. Richard Baxter, *A Christian Directory* (London, 1673), p. 807.
174. TNA, CO 29/2, pp. 1–14.
175. TNA, CO 153/4, pp. 103–104.
176. [Robertson], *John Talbot Compo-bell*, p. 42, probably refers to the rising at Sutton's Estate, Marshall Pen, to the north of Mandeville, but Robertson seems to be confused as to whether this was a rebellion by Coromanti or by Creole maroons; Carey, *Maroon Story*, pp. 146–147.
177. [Robertson], *John Talbot Compo-bell*, p. 70.
178. TNA, CO 124/1, pp. 138–142.
179. BL, Sloane 758, unfol: "yᵉ negroes over-breeds us."
180. [Robertson], *John Talbot Compo-bell*, pp. 2, 3. References to the "civil war" in Kongo, between Kongo and Angola, date the account of his enslavement to between *c.* 1670 and *c.* 1710: a Lord Mayor of London involved in the Slave Trade might further narrow it to before 1690. There is no evidence that any Bishop of London visited the West Indies but likely refers to Henry Compton.
181. TNA, CO 1/53, no. 102, ff. 264–265ᵛ.
182. SHC, DD/WHh/1089pt.6/43 and 62.
183. SHC, DD/WHh/1090pt2/1.
184. Carey, *Maroon Story*, pp. 148–152.
185. TNA, CO 140/4, pp. 125–127, 136–140; CO 5/1135, pp. 8–9.
186. TNA, CO 140/4, pp. 185–191; Carey, *Maroon Story*, p. 152.
187. The original has "rooted" rather than "routed": TNA, CO 155/1, f. 61ᵛ.
188. TNA, CO 155/1 f. 62ᵛ.
189. Oliver, *History of Antigua*, p. 172.
190. TNA, CO 155/1 f. 62,62ᵛ.
191. TNA, CO 155/1, f. 63.
192. TNA, CO 155/1, f. 64.
193. TNA, CO 140/6, pp. 119–121.
194. TNA, CO 155/1, ff. 97–99, ff. 97ᵛ–98, 99–101ᵛ.
195. TNA, CO 155/1, ff. 171–173.
196. TNA, CO 31/2, pp. 388, 390.
197. TNA, CO 1/21, no. 170; Beckles, "Riotous and Unruly Lot," p. 511.
198. TNA, CO 37/25, no. 1.
199. TNA, CO 124/1, pp. 12–18; E. O. Winzerling, *The Beginning of British Honduras, 1506–1765* (New York: North River Press, 1946), pp. 32–38.
200. Kupperman, *Providence Island*, pp. 241–242.
201. TNA, Shaftesbury Papers, PRO 30/24/48, endorsed bundle 48, no. 66.
202. Steele, *The Tatler*, no. 69, September 17, 1709, pp. 181–184.
203. TNA, CO 1/15, no. 91.
204. TNA, PRO 30/24/48/4.

205. TNA, CO 1/15, no. 95.
206. TNA, CO 155/1, no. 62, f. 164; Henry Adis, *A Letter sent from Syrranam*; Anon, *A Brief Description of the Province of Carolina on the Coasts of Floreda* (London, 1666); TNA, SP 25/76, pp. 304–306, p. 305.
207. Anon, *The Case Of Protestant Dissenters in Carolina* (London, 1706).
208. TNA, CO 1/19, no. 92, f. 109^v.
209. C[harles] W[oodmason], *Journal of C.W. Clerk, Itinerant Minister in South Carolina, 1766, 1767, 1768*, in Richard J Hooker (ed.), *The Carolina Backcountry on the Eve of the Revolution* (Chapel Hill: University North Carolina Press, 1973), pp. 60–61.
210. TNA CO 1/19, no. 92, ff. 209–210^v, f. 209.
211. CumbriaRO, Carlisle, D/LONS/Li/41/1/29b; TNA, CO 1/64 no. 17.
212. BL, Eg.3662; Charles Gehring and Jacob Schiltkamp (eds.), *Curaçao Papers, 1640–1665* (New York: New Netherland Research Center and the New Netherland Institute, 2011), pp. 125–126, 187–189; Robert Sanford, *Surinam Justice* (London, 1662); William Byam, "Exact Narrative": Oxf. Bodl.Lib. Rawlinson MSS A 175; Byam, *Exact Relation*; JCB Library, Cabinet Gm667 Di Ms.
213. NA, DD/4P/41/23.
214. Woodmason, *Journal*, pp. 60–61.
215. Sanford, *Surinam Justice*, pp. 9,11, 22, 23; TNA, CO 1/16, no. 102; TNA, CO 152/42, no. 43, f. 114^v; Barber, "Power in the English Caribbean," pp. 207–210.
216. TNA, CO 28/2, no. 22.
217. TNA, CO 1/64, no. 3, ff. 4–8^v, f. 6^v.
218. TNA, CO 1/53 no. 32.
219. TNA, CO 1/17, nos. 30 and 30 i–v.
220. Harlow, *Codrington*, pp. 46–47, App. B, pp. 221–225; "In Natalem Sereniss: Principis Walliae," in *Strenae Natalitiae Academiae Oxoniensis in Celsissimum Principem* (Oxford: 1688).
221. TNA, CO 152/2, nos. 44, 45.
222. Frank M. Coleman, *Hobbes and America: Exploring the Constitutional Foundations* (Toronto/Buffalo: University of Toronto Press, 1977), p. 66; Thomas Hobbes, *Philosophical Rudiments concerning Government and Society* (translation by Hobbes of "De Cive: Or the Citizen"), in Bernard Gert (ed.), *Man and Citizen: Thomas Hobbes* (Harvester/Humanities Press, 1972), pp. 87–386.
223. Barbara Arneil, "Women as Wives, Servants and Slaves: Rethinking the Public/Private Division," *Canadian Journal of Political Science* 34.1 (2001): 29–54.
224. Matthew W. Binney, "Milton, Locke and the Early Modern Framework of Cosmopolitan Right," *Modern Language Review* 105.1 (2010): pp. 31–52; Mary Nyquist, "Slavery, Resistance, and Nation in Milton and Locke," in David Loewenstein and Paul Stevens (eds.), *Early Modern Nationalism and Milton's England* (Toronto: University of Toronto Press, 2008), pp. 356–400.

Conclusion: Design

1. John Ogilby, *America: Being The Latest, and Most Accurate Description of the New World* (London, 1671), p. 36.

2. Karen Ordahl Kupperman, "Errand to the Indies: Puritan Colonization from Providence Island through the Western Design," *WMQ*, 3rd ser. 45.1 (1988): 70–99; David Armitage, "The Cromwellian Protectorate and the Languages of Empire," *Historical Journal* 35.3 (1992): 531–555; "Narrative, by General Venables," in *Interesting Tracts, Relating to the Island of Jamaica* (St. Iago de la Vega, 1800), p. 6; TNA, SP 25/76, pp. 304–306, p. 305.
3. HC, BLAC, M35b.
4. HC, BLAC, M44a (b).
5. LPL, FP xv, ff. 216–216^v.
6. HC, BLAC, M44a (a).
7. HC, BLAC, M44a (c); S.D. Smith, *Slavery, Family and Genry Capitalism in the British Atlantic: The World of the Lascelles, 1648–1834* (Cambridge: Cambridge University Press, 2006), p. 68.
8. Archibald Ballantyne, *Lord Carteret: A Political Biography, 1690–1763* (London: Richard Bentley, 1887), pp. 84–85; HC, BLAC, M44a (b); TNA, CO 28/44, f. 46.
9. HC, BLAC, M44a (a); TNA, CO 28/17, ff. 301, 302^v–304^v, 305^v–307^v.
10. Council of Virginia, *A Trve Declaration of the Estate of the Colonie in Virginia* (London, 1610), frontispiece.
11. TCD, MS 736, p. 90.
12. SHC, DD/WHh/1090, pt. 3, no. 43.
13. Natasha Glaisyer, "Networking: Trade and Exchange in the Eighteenth-Century British Empire," *Historical Journal* 47.2 (2004): 451–476; John Brewer, *The Sinews of Power: War, Money, and the English State, 1688–1783* (Cambridge, MA: Harvard University Press, 1988); Patrick K. O'Brien, "The Political-Economy of British Taxation, 1660–1815," *Economic History Review*, 2nd ser. xli.1 (1988): 1–32.
14. Jeannette D. Black, *The Blathwayt Atlas* (Providence, RI: Brown University Press, 1975), vol.ii, p. 3; *A New Map of the North Parts of America Claimed by France*, based on surveys by Nathaniel Blackmore, Richard Berisford, and Thomas Nairn in Carolina, and rendered by Herman Moll in 1720: JCB Cabinet C720/2; John Mitchell, *The Present State of Great Britain and North America* (London, 1767), p. 194.
15. Jack P. Greene, *Imperatives, Behaviors, and Identities: Essays in Early American Cultural History* (Charlottesville: University of Virginia Press, 1992), pp. 38–39.
16. *The Representation and Memorial of the Council of the Island of Jamaica* (London, 1716), p. 24.
17. TNA, CO 137/14; Frank Cundall, "The Press and Printers of Jamaica Prior to 1820," *Proceedings of the American Antiquarian Society*, new ser., 26 (1916): pp. 290–412; Massachusetts Historical Society, Francis Russell Hart collection, Box 1 Folder 19.
18. Cundall, "Press and Printers," pp. 290–291; William Waller Hening, *Statutes at Large* vol. ii (New York, 1823), p. 511.
19. Kenneth Morgan, "Bristol West India Merchants in the Eighteenth Century," *TRHS*, 6th ser., 3 (1993): pp. 185–208.

Bibliographical Essay

Grand Narratives: Empire and Independence

In the nineteenth century and into the twentieth, scholars maintained there was a reason the small people had disappeared from the record. They were concerned with creating grand narratives to explain their political present: on one side of the Atlantic, the British Empire at its zenith, and on the other, the independence of character that enabled 13 states to break away. The imperial narrative traced structure, systems, centralization, order, and profit, and determined the cataloging of the "State Papers," reposed in the Public Record Office (now The National Archives), and codified in the *Calendar of State Papers; Colonial Series, America and West Indies*, edited by W. N. Sainsbury, J. W. Fortescue, and others (London: 1860–1994) (45 vols.). The advent of digitization makes the life of the historian easier, but the *Calendars* are excellent examples of the tyranny of indexers. Some attempt to isolate those records that addressed the period before the imperial codification became systemic were made by C. S. S. Higham, *The Colonial Entry Books: A Brief Guide to the Colonial Records in the Public Record Office before 1696* (London: Macmillan, 1921) and Winfred T. Root, best known as an historian of Pennsylvania's relationship with Britain, who looked at the early management of "The Lords of Trade and Plantations, 1675–1696": *American Historical Review* 23.1 (1917): 20–41. According to Richard R. Johnson (*William and Mary Quarterly* 43.4 (1986): 519–541), Charles McLean Andrews invented American colonial history—*Guide to the Materials for American History to 1783, in the Public Record Office of Great Britain* (Carnegie Institution, 1912) and the four volumes of *The Colonial Period of American History* (New Haven, CT: Yale University Press, 1934–1937)—and was the driving force behind the flagship periodical in which this retrospective appears. However, equally important was Herbert L. Osgood, *The American Colonies in the Seventeenth Century* (New York: Columbia University Press, 1904–1907) (3 vols.).

The "independence narrative" sought to draw the Caribbean into the orbit of the (Anglophone) Americas, rather than England's empire. The American Revolution became a build up of libertarian fervor sparked by the 1763 Treaty of Paris that ended the Europeans' Seven Years' War, or the French and Indian War in North America. It came to a head with the Declaration of Independence in 1776, and was consolidated by another Treaty of Paris and the American Constitutional Convention. It became imperative, therefore, to explore the roots of independence in an earlier period, an approach pioneered by Jack Greene and Bernard Bailyn. From the former came Jack P. Greene (ed.), *Settlements to Society, 1584–1763* (New York: McGraw Hill, 1966); *Great Britain and the American Colonies, 1606–1763* (Documentary History of the United States) (Harper & Row, 1970); *Pursuits of Happiness: The Social Development of Early Modern British Colonies and the Formation of American Culture* (Chapel Hill and London: University of North Carolina Press, 1988). Bernard Bailyn's contributions included *The New England Merchants in the Seventeenth Century* (Cambridge, MA: Harvard University Press, 1955); *The Ideological Origins of the American Revolution* (Cambridge, MA: Harvard University Press, 1967); *Voyagers to the West: A Passage in the Peopling of America on the Eve of the Revolution* (New York: Knopf, 1986). Both Bailyn and Greene sought to explore the Anglophone Americas as a whole, but in their search for that fiery righteous and individualistic character that drove American Independence, it was more easily found in New England and Chesapeake. The Caribbean was left behind.

The Localist Narrative

The most obvious answer was that puritanism did not thrive in a godless Caribbean created for commodity, trade, and profit, which continued to tie it inextricably to the mother country. North America was now independent States: the Caribbean remained colonial and dependent. Nevertheless, this meant that soldiers, governors, clergy, civil servants continued to travel to and settle in the Caribbean, and developed a love for and interest in preserving its history. The most famous of the antiquarian historians was Vere Langford Oliver, whose various papers appeared in a quarterly, multivolume collection, published in London between 1910 and 1920: *Caribbeana*. In the late nineteenth century, West Indian records' offices were established, and in a massive exercise that managed to be vandalism and preservation at the same time, copied out parish registers, plat books, patents, and inventories, and destroyed the fragile originals. While many of the documents relating to the Caribbean empire went "home" with the colonizers, a new generation of local people and expatriate settlers could now spend extensive time in the archives. Among the most notable are Henry Fraser, Warren Alleyne, Jill Sheppard, and Ronald Hughes, with an emphasis on Barbados and reminders of the interconnectedness of the region and its North and South American frontiers.

The Sugar and Slavery Narrative

Barbados combined uninterrupted English possession with the earliest expansion into intensive sugar cultivation, and because there seemed to be an obvious seventeenth-century historian of the "sugar turn" in Richard Ligon, Barbados became modern historians' model of colonial development against which there was a tendency to measure elsewhere and find it wanting. Barbados was the original "sugar island" and in giving it importance within global politico-economic systems historians charted the switch to commodity monoculture that was, in order to remain profitable, capital, land and labor intensive. Richard B. Sheridan published *Development of the Plantations to 1750* in 1970 (Barbados: Caribbean Universities Press) and then *Sugar and Slavery: An Economic History of the British West Indies, 1623–1775* (Kingston, Jamaica: Canoe Press, 1974), while in 1972 emerged the work that established Richard Dunn as the starting point for any study of early English colonialism in the West Indies: Richard S. Dunn, *Sugar and Slaves: The Rise of the Planter Class in the English West Indies, 1624–1713* (Chapel Hill: University of North Carolina Press, 1972). Dunn was based at the University of Pennsylvania, which became a centre for the study of American/African/European interactions: Gary B. Nash produced a forward for the 2000 reissue of *Sugar and Slaves*, and a festschrift in Dunn's honor: Nicholas Canny, Joe Illick, and Gary B. Nash (eds.), *Empire, Society, and Labor: Essays in Honor of Richard S. Dunn* (College Park, PA, 1997, supplement no. 64 of *Pennsylvania History*).

The theme of labor systems, particularly focusing on Barbados, was continued by Sir Hilary Beckles—Hilary McD. Beckles, *White Servitude and Black Slavery in Barbados, 1627–1715* (Knoxville: University of Tennessee Press, 1989); *Natural Rebels: A Social History of Enslaved Black Women in Barbados* (Brunswick, NJ: Rutgers University Press, 1989); *A History of Barbados: From Amerindian Settlement to Nation-State* (Cambridge: Cambridge University Press, 1990). Also influential was Gary A. Puckrein, *Little England: Plantation Society and Anglo-Barbadian Politics, 1627–1700* (New York: New York University Press, 1987). These specific Caribbean studies of the plantation system formed contributions to a wider debate about the structural, cultural, and historical differences between American development north of Virginia and that to the south. Aubrey Land's edited collection, *Bases of the Plantation Society* (New York: Harper & Row, 1969) and the work of Philip D. Curtin—*The Atlantic Slave Trade: A Census* (Madison: University of Wisconsin Press, 1969); *The Rise and Fall of the Plantation Complex: Essays in Atlantic History* (Cambridge: Cambridge University Press, 1990)—are noteworthy here. However, the *Oxford English Dictionary* dates the earliest use of the term "plantocracy" to describe the system's white elite to 1840, and among "plantation" compounds, "Plantation Society" is not listed. An academic journal was set up in 1979, edited and published in New Orleans, titled *Plantation Society in the Americas*, "An interdisciplinary journal of tropical and subtropical history and culture," but it is dangerous to project back into the seventeenth-century terms that came into use because a post-emancipation era needed to describe that from which society had been liberated.

The New Fluidity

There have been several scholars whose detailed reconstructions, often of localized space, have nuanced what has gone before and expanded it into new fields. Larry Gragg has made two important interventions in reshaping our view of Barbados, not to mention numerous articles: *Englishmen Transplanted: The English Colonization of Barbados, 1627–1660* (Oxford: Oxford University Press, 2003); and *The Quaker Community on Barbados: Challenging the Planter Class* (Columbia/London: University of Missouri Press, 2009). Karen Ordahl Kupperman, *Providence Island, 1630–1641: The Other Puritan Colony* (Cambridge: Cambridge University Press, 1993) is a masterpiece of the place-specific study. For the Leeward Islands there has been Howard A. Fergus, *Montserrat: History of a Caribbean Colony* (London: Macmillan, 1994); Brian Dyde, *A History of Antigua: The unsuspecting Isle* (London: Macmillan, 2000); David Barry Gaspar, *Bondmen and Rebels: A Study of Master-Slave Relations in Antigua* (Baltimore, MD: Johns Hopkins University Press, 1985); culminating in Natalie A. Zacek, *Settler Society in the English Leeward Islands, 1670–1776* (Cambridge: Cambridge University Press, 2010). Michael Craton has written widely on the region, including his study of Bahamas, and *Searching for the Invisible Man: Slaves and Plantation Life in Jamaica* (Cambridge, MA: Harvard University Press, 1978). Trevor Burnard, while specializing in eighteenth-century Jamaica, has thrown considerable light on that island's colonial history: *Mastery, Tyranny, and Desire: Thomas Thistlewood and His Slaves in the Anglo-Jamaican World* (Chapel Hill: University of North Carolina Press, 1993). As far as the mainland colonies are concerned, scholars are indebted to Joyce Lorimer for her studies for the Hakluyt Society: *English and Irish Settlement on the River Amazon, 1550–1646* (London: 1990) and *Sir Walter Ralegh's* Discoverie of Guiana (London: Ashgate, 2006); and a revival of interest in positioning the Carolinas within the wider torrid zone region is due to L. H. Roper, *Conceiving Carolina: Proprietors, Planters, and Plots, 1662–1729* (London: Macmillan, 2004).

Many of these scholars have been influenced by, and have themselves, generated an interest in searching wider and harder for the means to recover otherwise subjugated histories. The social and biomedical sciences—with recent advances in genetics—have led the way in this respect. The work of anthropologist Jerome S. Handler has broken new frontiers of research in recovering the black body and slave society—<http://jeromehandler.org/>—and archaeologists who can materialize history from land and seabed are constantly recovering new material data that adjusts and readjusts our view of the region's history. On the back of John Pocock's plea for a new British history, which could transcend parochial national history and rehabilitate imperial history without becoming too Whiggish—J. G. A. Pocock, "British History: A Plea for a New Subject," *Journal of Modern History* 47 (1975): 601–624, and again in *The Discovery of Islands: Essays in British History* (Cambridge: Cambridge University Press, 2005)—historians were faced with the dilemmas of how to write a history of and what to call the collection of islands at the northeastern edge of the Atlantic Ocean, and then as the peoples of these islands transported themselves, and then Africans, west, the complexities were multiplied, seemingly ad infinitum.

Atlantic Narratives

As if to illustrate skeptics' misgivings that this was old-fashioned imperial history in a politically correct disguise, referring to the British and Irish islands as the "Atlantic Archipelago" or "the entirety of these islands" highlighted the existence of other island archipelagos in the Atlantic and reinforced a Eurocentric gaze. There was a new interest in the contributions of Scotland—Allan I. Macinnes, *Union and Empire: The Making of the United Kingdom in 1707* (Cambridge: Cambridge University Press, 2007); T. M. Devine, *Scotland's Empire: The Origins of the Global Diaspora* (London: Penguin, 2012)—and a revival in studies of the Irish contribution to the Americas to renationalize the work begun by Kenneth R. Andrews, Nicholas P. Canny, P. E. H. Hair, and David B. Quinn, *The Westward Enterprise: English Activities in Ireland, the Atlantic, and America, 1480–1650* (Liverpool University Press, 1978). A new wave of grand(er) narratives now posited the Atlantic as the chief agent: David Armitage and Michael J. Braddick (eds.), *The British Atlantic World, 1500–1800* (London: Palgrave Macmillan, 2002). Bernard Bailyn's seminar series shaped scholarship in this field and was encapsulated in *Atlantic History: Concept and Contours* (Cambridge, MA: Harvard University Press, 2005). Jack P. Greene and Philip D. Morgan edited *Atlantic History: A Critical Appraisal* (Oxford: Oxford University Press, 2009). Nicholas Canny and Philip Morgan edited *The Oxford Handbook of the Atlantic World: 1450–1850* (Oxford: Oxford University Press, 2011), and Philip Curtin's *Rise and Fall of the Plantation Complex* also paid tribute to the Atlantic factor. Alison Games has made important interventions—"Atlantic History: Definitions, Challenges, and Opportunities," *American Historical Review* 111.3 (2006): 741–757, and edited with Adam Rothman, *Major Problems in Atlantic History: Documents and Essays* (Stamford, CT: Cengage Learning, 2007)—as has Carla Gardina Pestana (*The English Atlantic in the Age of Revolution* [Cambridge, MA: Harvard University Press, 2004]). Evidence of a renewed focus on the early period of British intervention and a more sociocultural approach is provided by the studies of Susan Dwyer Amussen, *Caribbean Exchanges: Slavery and the Transformation of English Society, 1640–1700* (Chapel Hill: University of North Carolina Press, 2007), Kirsten Block, *Ordinary Lives in the Early Caribbean: Religion, Colonial Competition, and the Politics of Profit* (Athens: University of Georgia Press, 2012), Jenny Shaw, *Everyday Life in the Early English Caribbean: Irish, Africans, and the Construction of Difference* (Athens: University of Georgia Press, 2013). The four-volume critical edition—Carla Gardina Pestana and Sharon V. Salinger (eds.), *The Early English Caribbean, 1570–1700* (London: Pickering and Chatto, 2014)—will make available to a wider audience the major printed primary sources, which, together with the manuscript emphasis of this book, will seal the importance of this particular place, time, and the diverse people who contested it.

Historians have opened Pandora's Box in their search for ever wider and more nuanced contextualization. These studies remain Anglophone, about

Anglophone hegemony and within a delineated time. Many of the authors outlined here, including this one, are part of moves to contextualize colonialism in a more global and at least European whole. But to those whose question to me is "how does your Caribbean compare with...?" my answer is "there has to be some limits."

Index

Adis, Henry, 101, 124, 188
Africa(ns), 5, 10, 25, 26, 29–31, 91, 96, 127, 133, 134–5, 141, 145, 147, 149, 157, 170–5, 180, 181, 196
  Asante, 175
  Awy, 92
  Bambara, 30, 92
  Coromanti, 90, 91, 157, 175, 176, 184
  Creole, 6, 30, 31, 91, 92, 119, 140, 177, 178, 182, 185
  Igbo, 29, 30, 92, 204, 205
  Kongo, 6, 30, 92, 140, 250
  Mandinka, 26, 30
  maroon, 37, 40, 175, 176, 183, 184, 186
  Mina, 29, 91, 92, 205
  Moko, 29, 92, 204, 205
  Papel, 30
Albemarle, Dukes of. *See* Monck
Allin, John, 22, 122, 138, 189
allspice. *See* Jamaica pepper
Anderson, Rev. John, 114
Anglican Church. *See* Church of England
Antigua, 6, 10, 12, 14, 16, 17, 19, 21, 23, 28, 30–1, 36, 38, 40, 61, 63, 74, 78, 86, 97, 102, 103, 104, 111, 119, 120, 123, 124, 133, 135, 143, 144, 145, 146–7, 165, 176, 182, 184, 185
  Falmouth, 17, 18, 36
  Parham Town, 21, 36, 65, 78
  St. John's (parish), 18, 19, 21, 36, 78
  St. Philip's (parish), 17
Anzilotti, Cara, 164
Arnold, Elizabeth, 92, 93, 95, 131, 146, 149, 150, 164, 224
Ashley-Cooper, Anthony, first Earl of Shaftesbury, Lord Proprietor of Carolina, 25, 26, 101, 109, 112, 156

Ashton, Henry, Governor of Antigua, 1640–1652, 15, 23, 41, 123, 133
Atkins, Jonathan, Governor of Barbados, 1674–1680, 76, 77, 89, 111, 112, 179, 181
Atkinson, Catherine, 119–20, 121

Bacon, Sir Francis, 14, 25, 47, 158, 161, 187, 194
Bahamas, 12, 13, 39, 58, 98, 130, 155
  Eleutheria (also Eluthera, originally Segatoo), 125, 155
  Providence (New), 86
baptism, 6, 33, 60, 83, 124, 178, 180–1, 182
Barbados. *Barbados is referenced on nearly every page, and therefore only specific place references to the island are listed in the index*
  Bridgetown, 17, 18, 32, 33, 35, 41, 60, 65, 73, 83, 85, 86, 106, 130, 132, 137, 151, 180, 183, 190, 195
  Carlisle Bay, 11, 66
  Fontabelle, 20–1, 64
  Holetown, 17, 24, 33, 73
  Indian Bridge (*see* Bridgetown)
  Mile and a Quarter, 24, 35
  Oistin's Town, 17
  Speightstown, 11, 17, 35
  St. Andrew's (parish), 62, 131
  St. James's (parish), 9, 33, 104
  St. John's (parish), 17, 19, 26, 32, 34, 59, 89, 105, 106, 172, 178
  St. Michael's (parish), 17, 20, 32, 33, 36, 60, 83, 106, 180
  St. Philip's (parish), 29, 53, 83, 86, 89, 131, 180
  St. Thomas's, 32, 87, 115, 193
Barbuda, 10, 104, 177
Barwick, Samuel, 33, 95

Baxter, Richard, 177, 182
Beeston, Sir William, Governor of Jamaica, 1693–1702, 182
Behn, Aphra, 22, 50, 90–1, 122, 140, 141, 174, 176
Berkeley, Bishop George, 42, 44, 48, 126, 175, 177
Bermuda, 10, 11, 14, 15, 17, 18, 20, 22, 24, 39, 40, 42, 45, 47–8, 51, 52, 56, 57, 58, 63, 70, 78, 83, 84, 86, 89, 94, 106, 107, 110–11, 124, 125–6, 130, 131, 138, 139, 142, 148, 150, 155, 175, 186, 188, 189, 190, 194
   St. George's, 17, 18, 22
Berringer, Colonel Benjamin, 19, 111, 131
Berringer-Yeamans, Margaret, 111, 131, 249
Blathwayt, William, 95, 145, 184
Blome, Richard, 1, 2–3, 130
Borraston, Joseph, 184–5
Boseman, William, 77
breasts, 139, 145, 149, 150
Brenner, Robert, 67
Bridge, (Sir) Tobias, 75, 110, 116
brokers, 67, 83, 100, 143
Burnard, Trevor, 90, 256
burial, 17, 28, 31–4, 44, 83, 86, 87, 115, 135, 181
Butler, Nathaniel, Governor of Bermuda, 1619–1622, 20, 24, 51, 52, 97, 107, 183
Byam, William, 13, 27, 36, 133
Byres, James, 98

cacao. *See* chocolate
Carlisle, Earl of. *See* Hay, James
Carolina, 1, 12, 13, 23, 25, 34, 35, 37, 45, 50, 54, 58, 63, 87, 94, 95, 99, 100–1, 107, 109, 112, 129, 131, 132–3, 134, 137, 141, 145, 155–6, 157, 159, 160–2, 164, 180, 186, 188, 189
   Albemarle, 25, 34, 187
   Azilia, 42, 43, 45, 81, 161, 168
   Berkeley County, 110
   Cape Fear, 95
   Charles Town (Charleston), 13, 18, 24, 25, 36, 39, 40, 63, 86, 131, 132, 216
   Colleton County, 110
   Fundamental Constitutions of, 160–1, 189
   Goose Creek, 36, 37, 208
   Outer Banks, 39, 40
   Roanoke ("Virginia"), 1, 20, 48, 49, 54, 142
ceremonial, 20, 49, 91, 176, 178–9, 181–3, 185, 190
Chester, Edward, 120
children, 29, 30, 32, 44, 83, 85, 86, 88, 89, 91, 92, 93, 94, 95, 96–8, 105, 106, 116, 120, 121, 124, 127, 131, 133, 140, 141, 145, 147, 148, 149, 157, 165–6, 169, 172, 178, 180, 182, 183, 189
   child-birth, 96, 148–9, 169
   pregnancy, 138, 141, 169
   wet-nurses, 150
chocolate, 52, 62, 64, 65, 87
Christianity, 29, 31, 37, 41–2, 83, 84, 91, 106, 129, 156, 157, 160, 174–80, 196
   Baptists, 85, 89, 181, 188
   covenant theology, 106, 107, 162–3
   enthusiasm, 107, 187
   Huguenots, 169
   Presbyterians, 24, 85, 179
   Quakers (*see* separate heading)
   Society for the Propagation of the Gospel, 104, 105–6, 131, 133, 177, 179
Church of England, 16, 22, 32, 33, 34, 48, 83, 86, 94, 102, 105, 106, 109, 124, 166, 178–9, 180, 188, 193
churches, 16, 17, 19, 20, 24, 26, 27, 32, 33, 34, 35, 42, 83, 111, 157, 164, 178, 179, 181
Clarendon, Earl of. *See* Hyde, Edward
Clarke, Samuel, 51, 126, 129
Cleland, William, 114, 115, 116
clothing, 58, 143, 144–6
   cloth, 55, 56, 63, 143–4, 146
   hats, 105, 144, 146–7
   and indenture, 125, 144–5
   lace, 105, 144, 146–7
   livery, 121, 145–6, 196
   Monmouth cap, 144–5, 239
   nakedness, 49, 56, 90, 137, 142, 145, 146, 147, 157
   shirts, 62, 105, 144, 145
   suits, 51, 144, 145, 146
   tailors, 144, 146

Codrington, Colonel Sir Christopher, Governor of the Leeward Islands and Barbados, 10, 12, 14, 28, 30, 54, 65, 75, 80, 104, 106, 120, 123, 131, 134, 143, 176–7, 190
coin, 57–8, 115, 142
  pieces of eight, 58, 76, 101
Coke, Sir Edward, 156, 163
Coke, Roger, 163
Colleton, Sir John, 34, 161
Colleton, Sir Peter, 111, 112
Colleton, Thomas, 111, 112
Colt, Sir Henry, 55
Coming, John, 164
companies, 16, 17, 109, 143, 172
  Adventures for Bermuda, 15, 20, 22, 56, 57, 106, 149
  Darien (Company of Scotland or Scottish Darien Company), 98
  Grocers, 60
  Providence Island, 20, 67, 106
  Royal African Company, 60, 80, 171, 177, 195
  Virginia, 68, 167
  West India, 67
Coney, Richard, Governor of Bermuda, 22, 142
Consett, Elizabeth, 105, 131
Consett, William, 105
Consett's, 105–6, 131, 177
Cook, Bernard, 138, 139
Cook, Sarah, 139
Copen, Samuel, 17, 36, 66
corn, 13, 124, 140
cotton, 24, 53, 54, 57, 58, 62, 63, 65, 66, 76, 77, 79, 80, 214, 233
Courteen, Sir William, 36, 58, 67, 72, 74, 158
courtship, 90, 91, 114, 144
Crab Island (Vieques, Virgin Islands, Puerto Rico), 182, 185
Crabb, Lawrence, 10, 36, 61, 62, 63, 65, 98, 102, 104, 144
Crabb, Sarah, 19, 97, 102, 103
credit, 66, 71, 98, 102, 103, 116, 177
  paper, 57, 112, 115, 194
creditors, 10, 69, 74, 76, 104, 106, 152
  Earl of Carlisle's, 70–3, 74, 75, 77, 107
Crowe, Mitford, Governor of Barbados, 1707–1710, 21, 112, 113, 114

Cruikshank, Rev. James, 128
Cryer, Commissary Rev. Benjamin, 19, 59, 113, 114
Cunyngham, Robert, 14, 29–30, 44, 61, 91–3, 95, 131, 140, 143, 145–6, 149, 157, 160, 164, 186, 195
customs (economic). *See* duties

Darién, 12, 35, 39, 98, 100, 114, 142, 209
Deane, Captain Henry, 116
debt, 10, 15, 40, 55, 69, 70, 72, 73, 76, 80, 95, 99, 101, 102, 106, 112, 115, 128, 129, 152, 172, 194
  suit for (*see* Court of Chancery)
Defoe, Daniel, 93, 94, 107, 110
disease, 32, 33, 97, 123, 124, 130, 132, 134, 234, 235
  venereal, 64, 120, 135, 147–8, 206
Dominica, 56, 134, 157, 182
Drake, Sir Francis, 1, 48, 56, 211
Drax, Henry, 111, 112
Drax, Sir James, 46, 59, 60, 171, 172
drinks, 46, 51, 52, 60, 145, 152, 176
  alcohol, 93, 101, 123, 128, 129, 130, 137, 147, 150, 152, 177, 181, 190, 194
  brandy, 52, 66, 124, 128
  citron water, 52, 113
  mobby, 128, 167
  punch, 128, 146
  rum, 31, 59, 60–1, 63, 64, 79, 80, 125, 128, 129, 135, 176, 183
  wine, 34, 52, 60, 103, 128, 152, 181
Drummond, Thomas, 98
Du Saussay, 120
duties, 53, 58, 64, 71, 74, 78, 194
  anchorage, 69
  caskage, 79
  Four and a Half (*see* taxes)
  freight, 56, 79
  wharfage, 65, 68, 104
Dutton, Sir Richard: Governor of Barbados, 1683–1685, 19, 20, 22, 65, 112, 163, 178–9

Elbridge, Aldworth, 62, 215
elections, 86, 104, 108–11, 113, 190
Exchange, The Royal, 99, 100, 101, 165

family, 7, 25, 29, 30, 34, 35, 48, 50, 62, 83, 88–9, 91–7, 102, 104, 107, 111, 120, 121, 125, 127, 130, 145, 146, 157, 159, 160, 164, 165, 166, 174, 177, 184, 186, 195
Farmer, Samuel, 188–9
Faucett, Rev. James, 83
feudalism, 28, 81, 156–7, 161–2, 164, 177, 181, 189
  aristocracy, 53, 69, 72, 81, 157, 159, 189
  manor, 6, 61, 161, 194
  Palatine, 157, 161
  title, 15, 155, 161, 189
Field, Rev. James, 124, 140
Filmer, Sir Robert, 157, 159–60
food, 7, 11, 49, 68, 124–6, 144
  African, 126–7
  cassava, 6, 27, 31, 49–50, 53, 126, 127, 128, 233
  corn, 36, 51, 53, 124, 140, 204
  "Indian provisions," 6, 27, 126, 194
  potatoes, 7, 24, 44, 51, 53, 64, 126, 128, 167
Four and a Half. *See* tax
Foyle, Oxenbridge, 166–7
Franch, Lucia, 120
Freeman, Humphrey, 108
French, George, 120, 121
Friends, Society of. *See* Quakers
friendship, 7, 33, 48, 68, 89, 90, 93, 95, 97, 98, 99, 101–3, 104, 106, 107, 109, 114, 115, 116, 152, 159, 165, 176, 190, 195
Fullwood, Rev. Samuel, 193, 194

Gage, Thomas, 1
Gamble, George, 175–6
gardens, 6, 14, 28, 29, 42–3, 44, 45, 47, 48, 49, 54, 92, 162, 194–5
Gibbes, Alice, 95, 96
ginger, 53, 64, 65
Godwyn, Morgan, 173, 177
Gordon, Rev. William, 122, 123, 177
Granville, Sir Bevill, Governor of Barbados, 1703–1706, 21, 52–3, 57, 95, 99, 112–13, 114, 115, 116–17, 119, 123, 194
Grey, Ralph, Governor of Barbados, 1697–1701, 112, 114, 115

Guianas, 5, 6, 13, 36, 38, 48, 50, 53, 56, 67, 106, 133, 135, 159
  Corentyne River (Suriname), 49
  Surinam(e), 10, 13, 22, 27, 36, 64, 72, 73, 78, 90, 101, 102, 104, 106, 122, 124, 129, 131, 134, 138, 140, 150, 159, 174, 176, 181, 188, 189
  Tourarica, 27, 36
  Waini River (Guyana), 49
  Wild Coast, 133
  Willoughby fort, 11, 22, 36

Hallett, John, 29, 32
Hamilton, Archibald, Governor of Jamaica, 1711–1716, 179
Hamilton, Walter, Governor of the Leeward Islands, 1710–1711, 1715–1721, 111, 114, 121
Handler, Jerome, 31, 256
Hariot, Thomas, 49, 142
Harleston, Affra, 164
Harley, Sir Robert, 27, 159, 181, 243
Harrison, Thomas, 106
Havercamp, Godfrey, 67, 68, 69, 71
Hawley, Henry, Governor of Barbados, 1630–1640, 69, 76, 102, 125, 137
Hay, Archibald, of Haystoun, 76
Hay, James, first earl of Carlisle, Lord Proprietor of the Caribbees or Carliola, 5, 23, 58, 67, 68–9, 137, 145, 157, 158
  patent as, 5, 69, 70, 73, 137, 158, 159
Hay, James, second earl of Carlisle, Lord Proprietor of the Caribbees, 23, 70, 71, 76, 133, 143, 159
Hay, earls of Kinnoull, 70, 72
health, 9, 48, 49, 52, 103, 123, 126, 130, 147, 148
  public, 132
  seasoning, 80, 133–4
Helyar, Cary, 96
Helyar, William, 78–9
Henshaw, Anne, 72
Henshaw, Benjamin, 67, 68
Henshaw, Thomas, 72, 107
Hewetson, Captain Thomas, 97, 138
Hilliard, Colonel William, 171–2, 181
Hilton, Rowland, 29, 106
Hobbes, Thomas, 103, 151, 188, 190–1
Hodges, Thomas, 156, 169

Holt, Rev Arthur, 179, 180, 181, 182
Hortop, Job, 170
household, 30, 31, 92, 93, 94, 95, 126, 157, 172, 174, 177, 186, 189, 191
Hunter, General Robert, 187
Husbands, Sir Samuel, 35, 48, 53
Hutcheson, Archibald, Attorney-General of the Leeward Islands, 95
Hyde, Sir Edward, Earl of Clarendon, 69, 71, 159

illness, 96, 130, 133, 147, 150
  ague, 123, 132, 133, 178
  belly-ache, 130
  clorosis, 148
  dropsy, 133
  fever, 32, 83, 89, 112, 130–1, 132, 133, 134
  flux, 132, 133, 134, 138
  pox (*see* disease, venereal)
  worms, 51, 147
  yaws, 133
  Yellow fever, 132
indigenes, 1, 5, 6, 10, 12, 13, 14, 26, 27, 28, 36–7, 41, 44, 49–51, 52, 56, 63, 96, 124, 126, 127, 129, 135, 144, 157, 158, 170, 172, 177, 182, 191, 196
  Algonquian, 49
  Arawak, 5, 49, 83, 197, 199
  cannibalism, 5, 182
  Cherokee, 6, 37, 157, 159
  Kalinago, 5, 6, 13, 14, 36, 37, 67, 72, 75, 90, 96, 135, 141–2, 157, 182
  Kuna, 6, 142
  Miskitu, 144
  Pomeiooc, 49, 212
  Secoton, 49
  Tuscacora, 182
  Warao, 49
indigo, 53–4, 55, 62, 64, 66
injury, 129, 140
Ivy, Colonel Thomas, 109

Jamaica, 1, 2–3, 5, 12, 13, 15, 18, 23, 26, 28, 35, 37, 38, 39, 44, 52, 53, 54, 57, 58, 60, 62, 64, 78, 79, 83, 84, 85, 86, 87, 90, 96, 98, 99, 100, 101, 105, 108, 117, 122, 123, 124, 125, 128, 130, 134, 136, 139, 140, 142, 144, 146, 148, 150, 151, 152, 157, 172, 176, 181, 182–3, 184, 188, 190, 193, 195
  Clarendon (parish), 108, 109, 184
  Kingston, 187
  Port Morant, 85, 95
  Port Royal, 18, 33, 60, 128, 146, 150, 182
  Spanish Town (St. Iago de la Vega), 17, 18, 108, 182
  St. Andrew's (parish), 83
  St. Ann's (parish), 184
  St. Catherine's (parish), 108, 179
  St. Thomas in the East (parish), 28
  St. Thomas in the Vale (parish), 78, 184
  Yallahs, 62, 106, 209
Jamaica pepper (allspice), 52, 53, 62, 64, 65, 139
Jeaffreson, Christopher, 102, 103, 129, 133, 143, 144, 148, 152, 168
Jeaffreson, John, 14, 158, 194
Jeaffreson, Samuel, 14
Jewish communities, 17, 27, 33–4, 60, 178, 181, 189
  synagogues, 17
Johnson, Sir Nathaniel, 15
Johnston, Rev. Gideon, 132–3
Jones, John, 88–9, 96

Kendall, James, Governor of Barbados 1690–1694, 86, 108, 112, 190
Keynell, Colonel Christopher, Governor of Antigua, 1652–1660, 14

Lanier, Clement, 121
law, 13, 15, 22, 23, 40, 41, 47, 50, 73, 76, 114, 115, 136, 137, 158, 160, 161, 162, 163, 164, 166, 167, 171, 173, 183, 186, 191, 196
  Chancery, Court of, 70, 98–9
  of nature, 61, 151, 163, 174, 188
Le Jau, Rev. Francis, 132
Legay, Peter, 89, 96
Lesley, Rev. William, 178
Leverton, Nicholas, 101, 102, 106, 124, 131, 188, 226
Ley, James, first Earl of Marlborough, 67

264 INDEX

Ley, James, third Earl of Marlborough, 72, 158
Ligon, Richard, 45–6, 49, 59, 91, 168, 177, 254
Lillington, George, 32, 97, 103, 112–15, 117
Littleton, Edward, 35, 75, 134, 195
Locke, John, 9, 156, 157, 159–60, 172, 189
Long, Jane, 83–4, 96, 180, 195, 220
Lowther, Christopher, 64
Lowther, family of, 28, 110
Lowther, Robert, Governor of Barbados, 1711–1720, 112, 138
Lynch, Sir Thomas, Governor of Jamaica (three terms), 1, 39, 96, 122, 178, 190

Mackenzie, Roderick, 98
maize. *See* corn
maps, 2–3, 4, 9, 17, 21, 23, 28, 43, 45, 145
  "Blathwayt" (of Montserrat), 145
  Blome, Richard (T. Bowen), 1, 2–3
  Hapcott, John, 24, 203
  Lea, Philip, 17
  Moll, Herman, 1, 4, 43
  Moxon, Joseph, 9
  Norwood, Richard, 15, 20, 23
  Ogilby, John, 193
  Rogers, Mordecai, 23
  survey, 13, 16, 17, 20, 22–4, 25, 26, 28, 45, 56, 59, 187, 193
marriage, 7, 83, 84, 86–7, 89, 90, 91, 93, 94–5, 96, 102, 107, 110, 111, 113, 115, 121, 124, 131, 172
Marshall, Rev. Samuel, 132
Martin, Major Samuel, 176
Marvell, Andrew, 47, 107, 189
Matthew, Sir William, Governor of the Leeward Islands, 1704, 123
May, Rev. William, 187–8
medicine, 53, 64, 97, 177
  antimony, 148
  balm, 143, 153
  bleeding, 134
  "Peruvian bark," 64
  purgatives, 130, 134, 148
Merrifield, Ralph, 67
Modyford, Sir Thomas, 2, 37, 85, 96
molasses, 60, 61, 64, 79, 80

Mole, George, 67, 68, 69, 125
Molesworth, Hender, Governor of Jamaica 1684–1687, 1688–1689, 104–5, 184
Monck, Christopher, Earl of Albemarle, Governor of Jamaica, 1687–1688, 44, 123, 151, 189
monkeys, 14, 41, 52, 147
Montgomery, Sir Robert, 42, 43, 44, 45, 80, 157, 161, 195
Montserrat, 11, 12, 21, 31, 54, 66, 67, 69, 125, 129, 138, 139, 145, 165, 182, 185
  Kinsale, 11
  Plymouth, 11, 21
  St. George's (parish), 94
More, Sir Poynings, 24–5, 53, 59, 61
Morgan, Sir Henry, Lieutenant-Governor of Jamaica, three terms, 6, 40, 101, 117, 190
Morton, Charles, puritan divine, 106, 107

Nevis, 11, 12, 14, 24, 31, 39, 67, 86, 91, 110, 134, 139, 144, 153, 157, 176, 185
  Charlestown, 18, 132, 195
  St. George Gingerland (parish), 83
news, 40, 99–101, 119, 123, 131, 176, 184, 195
  press, 99, 100, 113, 181, 195
Newton, Samuel, 31, 111
Nimrod, 157, 158, 162
Norwood, Andrew, surveyor, 17
Norwood, Richard, surveyor, 15, 20, 23

Oldmixon, John, 28, 29
Osborne, Roger, Governor of Montserrat, 21
Owen, William, 109, 186
Oxenbridge, John, 101, 106, 107, 189, 228
Oxenford, John, customs' official, 64

parishes, 16–17, 19, 32, 33, 34, 35, 59, 60, 63, 88, 105, 106, 108, 164, 169, 191
  churchwardens, 16, 59, 105, 114
  overseers, 56, 59, 105
  relief, 59, 105, 106
  vestry, 16, 17, 19, 32, 35, 59, 105, 111, 137

Parke, Daniel, Governor of the Leeward Islands, 1706–1710, 10, 21, 119–22, 123, 157, 160, 163, 177, 190
parrots, 49, 52
party (political faction), 7, 22, 108, 107, 113, 115, 158, 167, 170, 182
  country, 115, 121
  Establishment, 112, 114, 188, 189
  Jacobite, 111, 117, 138, 151, 189, 190
  puritan, 22, 47, 67, 106, 117, 150
  republican, 38, 57, 109, 114, 120, 157, 188, 189
  royalist, 45, 47, 71, 114, 166, 187, 188
  Tory, 114, 117, 189, 190
  Whig, 101, 112, 114, 117, 189, 190
Paterson, William, 1, 98
Peniston, William, 142
Pennsylvania, 88, 190
Perkins, Peter, 6, 83–4, 90, 96, 180, 195, 220
Perry, Edward, 119–20
Perry, John, 120
pineapples, 46, 53, 64, 128
plantation society, 15, 41, 78, 90, 195, 255, 256
Plaxton, George, 194
poison, 51, 102, 126, 127, 131–2, 140, 148, 170
  ivy, 51
  Manchineel, 126
  as metaphor, 98, 121, 127, 128
Pole, Mary, 88, 89, 96, 103, 150
Pollington, Alexander, 165–6
Popple, Alured, 159
Povey, Thomas, 68
Powell, Captain Henry, 53, 56, 67, 72, 137, 158
Powell, Captain John, 49, 53, 67, 72, 137
Powrey, William, agent of the Earls of Carlisle, 76
Powrey, William, agent of Carlisle's creditors, 77
Providence (island), 2, 12, 14, 20, 35, 106, 107, 135, 145, 183, 186, 188
punishment, 84, 129, 136–7, 138, 139–40, 149, 164, 168, 171, 173, 177, 184, 187
  amputation, 38, 185
  branding, 7, 142–3, 146, 153, 164, 167, 170, 177, 196
  burning, 136, 139, 183, 185
  death, 84, 139, 166, 183–4
  dismemberment, 136, 138, 139, 140
  gagging, 137
  pillory, 137, 138, 167
  slave codes, 136, 173
  stigmatising, 137, 142
  stocks, 32, 84, 120
  transportation, 5, 10, 12, 40, 41, 84, 140, 142, 148, 167
  whipping, 84, 120, 121, 136–40, 142, 152, 171, 181, 183

Quakers, 26, 32, 34, 44, 83, 84–8, 89, 100, 106, 107, 108, 111, 115, 166, 175, 179, 181, 190
  Alexander, Jane, 87, 106
  Alexander, Nicholas, 106
  Barrow, Robert, 34, 87
  Copp, William, 87, 89, 115, 230
  Eccleston, Theodore, 86, 87, 88
  Fox, George, 85, 86
  Penn, William, 86
  Perrott, John, 85, 86, 96
  Pilgrim, Thomas, 85, 89, 96
  Rous, John, 84, 86
Quintyne, Mary. *See* Pole, Mary
Quintyne, Thomas, 89, 94, 96, 97

Raleigh, Sir Walter, 1, 48, 56
rape. *See* violence
Rawlin, William, 58, 136, 172
Rener, Ambitt, 131
Richier, Isaac, Governor of Bermuda, 1691–1693, 11, 78, 110, 126, 130, 189
Rivers, Marcellus, 166
Robertson, Rev. Robert, 30, 91, 134, 141, 174, 180, 188
  as John Talbot Compo-bell, 141, 174, 188, 237, 250
Robinson, Sir Robert, Governor of Bermuda, 1687–1690, 78, 138
Russell, Colonel Randal, Governor of Nevis, 1672–1676, 14, 110
Russell, Francis, Governor of Barbados, 1694–1696, 20, 32, 58, 64–5, 66, 123, 182
Russell, Valentine, judge in Antigua, 21

Sanford, Robert, 10, 182, 189
Sayle, William, Governor of Bermuda, 1643–1644, Bahamas 1646–1657, Carolina 1670–1671, 10, 155
Scrivener, William, 109
Searle, Daniel, Governor of Barbados, 1652–1660, 167, 168
sects, 22, 23, 37, 85, 100, 101, 142, 181, 189
Sheridan, Richard, 91, 134
Sherrard, Rev. Hope, 186
skin, 7, 49, 63, 126, 127, 129, 133, 135, 143, 145, 147, 148, 152, 172
  color, 49, 53, 135, 141, 170, 171, 176, 177, 236
  painting, 141, 142
  piercing, 141
  tattooing, 141–2
Sloane, Sir Hans, 127, 139, 147, 148, 149, 150
Smith, Captain John, 20, 48
Smith, Robert, 184, 190
Smith, Rev. William, 157
Society for the Promotion of the Gospel in Foreign Parts, 104, 105, 131, 133, 177, 179
Society of Friends. *See* Quakers
Spooner, John, Attorney General of St Christopher's, 20, 140
St. Christopher's (later St Kitts), 14, 19, 21, 30, 33, 38, 54, 61, 67, 68, 69, 70, 76, 93, 96, 102, 114, 116, 131, 133, 137, 143, 144, 148, 149, 157, 158, 178
  Basseterre, 26, 29, 195
  Bloody Point, 14
  Cayon, 14, 29, 44, 140, 146
  Pelham River, 14, 199
St. Croix (Santa Cruz), 67, 72
St. Lucia, 37, 56, 126, 135, 182
St. Vincent, 10, 37, 56, 126, 135, 182
Stanfast, Colonel John, 20, 111
Stapleton, Sir William, Governor-General of the Leeward Islands, 1672–1685, 12, 31, 36, 39, 60, 75, 76, 77, 78, 92, 110, 116, 127, 129, 145, 146, 153, 228–9
Staves, Susan, 164–5
Stede, Sir Edwin, Governor of Barbados, 1685–1690, 60, 76, 111, 112, 152, 173

Studd, Abraham, 167
sugar, 6, 7, 11, 19, 24, 27, 31, 38, 46–7, 53, 54, 59–62, 64, 65, 66, 73, 74, 77, 78–9, 80, 81, 101, 104, 105, 110, 114, 125, 139, 140, 166, 173, 185, 217
  baked, 64, 79
  candying, 46, 53
  cane, 29, 46, 53, 59, 61, 78, 79, 128, 145, 183
  muscovado, 59, 79
  plant (buildings/equipment for the production of), 19, 20, 28, 46, 60, 66, 79, 172, 217
  refined, 6, 59, 64, 65, 79
Sullivan, Catherine, 120, 121
Surinam(e). *See* Guianas

Tabor, Rev. Richard, 179
taxes, 15, 16, 40, 41, 45, 46, 56, 58, 62, 68, 69, 73, 74, 75, 76, 78, 80, 108, 194, 195
  customs, 41, 46, 59, 64, 69, 70, 71, 76, 77, 195
  customs' agents, 40, 74, 75, 77, 119, 194
  customs' houses, 21, 78, 120
  farmers, 73, 74, 76
  fines, 12, 56, 66, 78, 88, 109, 138, 139
  Four and a Half, the, 73–8, 195
  levies, 35, 56, 60, 66, 69, 71, 73, 74, 76, 78, 108, 138, 194
  poll tax, 58, 69
Thornhill, Sir Timothy, 20, 75
tobacco, 7, 31, 47, 51, 53, 54, 55–7, 58, 60, 63, 64, 65, 67, 69, 76, 78, 79, 80, 81
Tobago, 12, 37, 106, 124, 135, 138
Towers, John, 109
Trade and Plantation, Board of (also Committee of, Council of and Lords of), 46, 61, 77, 113, 135, 156, 176
Trapham, Thomas, 147, 148, 152
Trefry, John, overseer of Willoughby's estates in Surinam, 90, 91
Trinidad, 37, 49, 56, 57
Tryon, Thomas, 9, 127, 128, 152, 153, 196
Tucker, Daniel, Governor of Bermuda, 1616–1619, 15, 17, 22, 47

Turks and Caicos, 39
turtles, 20, 51, 103, 124

utopia, 47, 195
  Eden, 45, 162, 195
  Land of Cockayne, 51
  More, Sir Thomas, 47
  The Tempest (William Shakespeare), 47, 50

Venables, General Robert, 193
vessels, 17, 25, 36, 40, 62, 84, 104, 132
  canoes, 13, 56, 139
  periagos, 36, 37, 49
  The Bristol, 123
  The Carlile, 67, 68, 125
  The Meteor, 167
  The Orange Blossom, 14
  The Truelove, 68
  The William and John, 10, 67
violence, 120, 122, 127, 129, 135, 175, 182–3, 186, 196
  rape, 120, 135, 163, 173, 178, 182, 183
  uprising, 38, 113, 122, 129, 139, 150, 167, 168, 174, 176, 181, 182, 183, 184–5, 186, 190
Vleck, Tielman van, 21, 125

Waad, Samuel, 21
Wafer, Lionel, 142
Waller, Edmund, 47, 48
Warner, Sir Thomas, 14, 96, 125
West, Joseph, Governor of Carolina, three separate terms, 137, 155
Whaley, William, 96, 184
Whistler, Henry, 128, 152

White, John, 49, 141
Whitrow, Benjamin, 99, 100, 134, 141
Wilkie, Thomas, 179, 180
Willoughby, Francis, fifth Lord Willoughby of Parham, 13, 22, 37, 59, 70, 71, 72, 73, 74, 75, 101, 102, 122, 157, 159, 160, 181, 188, 189
Willoughby, Henry, 131
Willoughby, William, sixth Lord Willoughby of Parham, 13, 22, 37, 59, 70, 71, 72, 73, 74, 75, 101, 102, 122, 157, 159, 160, 181, 188, 189
Windsor, Thomas Lord, Governor of Jamaica 1662, 178
Wither, George, 48, 57
Wolverston, Charles, Governor of Barbados, 1628–1629, 69, 158
wood, 5, 25, 59, 62
  building, 17, 19, 24, 27, 29, 65
  cabinet, 62, 64
  fustic, 59, 64
  ironwood, 18
  lignum vitae, 18, 64
  palmetto, 17, 18, 64, 143
  woodland, 9, 13, 27, 32, 35, 38, 53, 56
Woodward, Thomas, 34, 187
Worsley, Henry, Governor of Barbados, 1722–1727, 179, 194, 195

Yeamans, John, Lieutenant-Governor of Antigua, 111, 131
Yeamans, Sir John, Governor of Carolina, 1672–1674, 19, 111, 131, 155, 157

CPSIA information can be obtained
at www.ICGtesting.com
Printed in the USA
LVHW101028150620
658048LV00007BA/1033